D1792351

Mashiach:

Who? What? Why? How? Where? and When?

Mashiach:

Who? What? Why? How? Where? and When?

by
Chaim Kramer

Published by
BRESLOV RESEARCH INSTITUTE
Jerusalem/New York

Copyright © Breslov Research Institute 1994
ISBN 0-930213-54-8

No part of this publication may be translated,
reproduced, stored in any retrieval system or transmitted,
in any form or by any means,
electronic, mechanical, photocopying, recording or otherwise,
without prior permission in writing from the publishers.

First Edition

For further information:
Breslov Research Institute
POB 5370
Jerusalem, Israel

or:

Breslov Research Institute
POB 587
Monsey, NY 10952-0587

e-mail: info@breslov.org
INTERNET: http//www.breslov.org

Printed in Israel

in loving memory
of our dear parents

Rabbi Zvi Aryeh Benzion
and
Zipporah Rosenfeld

who pioneered the English translations of
the teachings of

Rebbe Nachman of Breslov

and who devoted their lives to the
dissemination of those teachings;
who inspired an awe of God
and a love for *Eretz Yisrael*
in those who knew them.

by their children

Rosenfeld, Kramer and **Maimon families**

Guide to the Book

This book explains what we can expect of Mashiach — and what we should expect of ourselves if we wish to share in the ideals Mashiach represents.

The book is divided into seven parts, with two appendices:

1. Prologue: How life will be when Mashiach comes.

2. Who is Mashiach? As the world leader, what type of person will he be? What leadership qualities will he possess?

3. What is Mashiach's mission? What must he do to bring the world to perfection?

4. Why hasn't Mashiach come yet?

5. How will Mashiach bring the world to perfection? How will he be able to accomplish this "mission impossible?"

6. Where will the action take place when Mashiach arrives? This section explores the key concepts of Exile and Exodus, Jew and Non-Jew, the Holy Land and Jerusalem, and the eternal joy to be revealed in the messianic era.

7. When is Mashiach coming? How can we make it happen?

Appendix A: The full text of Rebbe Nachman's story of the "Master of Prayer," which is one of the major foundations of the book.

Appendix B: Charts and diagrams elucidating basic kabbalistic concepts appearing in the book. Gematria chart giving numerical values of the letters of the Hebrew alphabet.

*

This book is based on material drawn from the Bible, Talmud, Midrash and Kabbalah and their commentaries, and on the teachings of Rebbe Nachman of Breslov (1772-1810) and his major disciple, Reb Noson (1780-1844). Because of the enormous volume of material about Mashiach, it has been necessary to be selective.

The messianic ideal includes a variety of components: revelation of the unity of God on all levels, good health, immense wealth, universal peace and the rectification of all humanity, even the worst sinners. Various aspects of the messianic mosaic are discussed in detail in the earlier sections of the book. Inevitably there is some overlap and repetition at certain points, because each aspect is ultimately bound up with all the others. Part VI shows how all the parts of the mosaic fit together into one whole.

A number of kabbalistic concepts are crucial to the understanding of how Mashiach will be able to rectify the world. While these concepts appear in various places throughout the book, they are discussed in detail in Part V. This book is not intended as a kabbalah primer, but those unfamiliar with kabbalistic concepts will find everything necessary to understand our discussions. Additional explanatory charts and diagrams are provided in Appendix B.

Table of Contents

Mashiach: Prologue

1. Imagine! 3
   - Mashiach, a windfall and a scorpion 5
2. "For on that Day..." 8
   - The past... 9
   - ...the present... 10
   - ...and the Future 11
   - The messianic era 12

Mashiach: Who?

3. Mashiach 17
   - The Soul of Mashiach 18
   - Adam, David, Mashiach 21
   - Leadership 22
   - The anointed one 23
4. Who is Mashiach? 25
   - Two Mashiachs? 26
   - Moshe, the Mashiach?! 28
   - King David 31
   - So, who is Mashiach? 33
   - From darkness, light! 34

Mashiach: What?

5. What is Mashiach? 39
   - Mashiach's weapons 40
   - Prayer: the main weapon 41
   - But if everything is so good...? 44
   - Prayer and the Holy Temple 46
6. Building the Third Temple 48
   - The Sanctuary 49
   - Daat — the Holy Temple 51
   - The Sacrifices 53
   - Man-made or built by Heaven? 55
   - The Ingathering of the Exiles 56
7. "And he will breathe the fear of God" 59
   - What is the "Fear of God?" 60
   - The mitzvot 62
   - The Voice of Rebuke — building Jerusalem . . 64
   - Purity and morality 68
   - In review 72
8. Truth endures 73
   - ...flock together 74
   - "He will judge righteously..." 75

	The good, the bad and the ugly	78
	Reward and punishment	79
	The true leader	80
	"Chad Gadya — One Kid"	82
9.	Mashiach: the Era of Miracles	85
	"Gold and silver gods"	87
	Divine Providence	90
	Daat and faith	92
10.	The Wondrous Advisor	94
	Free will	94
	Free will in messianic times	95
	The Eternal Torah	99
	The Written Law and the Oral Law	100
	The "New" Torah	101
	The "New Testament"	104
11.	My very own Mashiach!	107
	The messianic ideal	108
	Mashiach and the tzaddikim	111
	Torah and prayer	112
	"V'naharu eilav... all the nations will flow to it"	114

Mashiach: Why?

12.	Why hasn't Mashiach come yet?	119
	The 974 generations	121
13.	The Master of Prayer	123
	The Land of Wealth	124
	The Holy Assembly	125
	The chronicles	127
14.	The Holy Assembly	133
	The storm wind	134
	Seeking honor	135
	Murder, Incorporated	137
	"Be fruitful and multiply"	140
	"To eat, or not to eat...?"	142
	"To speak or not to speak...is that a question?"	144
	"Let's party..."	147
	The People of the Book	149
	Wealth	151
	The prayer group	152
15.	Judaism today: A fashionable look at the Emperor's New Clothes	154
	The Emperor's New Clothes	155
	"Honorable indeed"	159
	What a waste!	161
	Marriage: a family "institution"	163
	The anorexic heavyweight!	165
	Freedom from speech!	167
	"That's entertainment!"	169

Higher? education	172
Money makes the world go 'round	177
The main goal: prayer	180
Prayer: the feminist movement	182
16. So why hasn't Mashiach come yet?	185

Mashiach: How?

17. Creation	191
The origins of Creation	192
The Vacated Space	195
The Paradox of the Vacated Space	196
The Light of the Infinite	199
18. The Sefirot	201
The Ten Sefirot and Man	206
Atik: the place of Mashiach	208
19. The Fall of Man	210
"In a Godly image"	211
The holy sparks	213
20. The Rectification	214
Reincarnation	214
Reincarnation and exile	216
The power of repentance	219
Daat	220
Descent for the sake of ascent	221
The Generation of the Exodus	223
Mordekhai, Haman and Purim	225

Mashiach: Where?

21. The search is on!	231
22. The Exile	233
A state of mind	233
The physical exile	236
Ayeh? Where is God?	240
23. Jew and Non-Jew	243
The sparks and the dross	243
Esav and Yishmael	245
"He has swallowed..."	249
The good, the bad and the ugly	252
24. The Ingathering of the Exiles	255
The rectification of Judgment	255
The Godly image	258
Torah and the Godly image	261
Amalek	263
25. The Holy Land	268
The Biblical borders	269
Future borders	270

Why a Holy Land?	274
Returning to the Land	277
26. Jerusalem and the Holy Temple	280
Jerusalem	281
The Holy Temple	283
Charity	285
27. Getting it together	290
The Torah of Atik	292
28. Joy: the World of Freedom	296
Patience	298
Azamra!	299
Joy and Thanksgiving	301
29. In review	305

Mashiach: When?

30. When is Mashiach coming?	309
The birth pangs of Mashiach	311
I believe...	312
"Wait for him..."	313
31. Elijah the Prophet	315
To make peace...	317
Never on a Friday...	319
32. Mashiach, a windfall and a scorpion	321
Mashiach, a windfall and a scorpion	323
33. Today!	327
Appendix A: The Master of Prayer	329
Appendix B: Charts and Diagrams	365

הוקדש לעילוי נשמת הילד

יהודה יוסף אליהו חיים
בן ר' **נחמן ומרים פוטרמן** ז"ל

נפ' **כ"ח אייר** תשנ"ה
ת.נ.צ.ב.ה.

in memory of
Yehudah Yosef Eliyahu Chaim

Many thanks to all those
who screened this work,
"covering my inadequacies"
and making this book possible:
A.S., S.L.M., M.M., A.G., H.B., C.R.

and above all to
G.K.
who deserves a redemption
more than can be expressed

           C.K.

Part I

Mashiach:

Prologue

1

Imagine!

Imagine living in a world above time and space: a world with transportation but without traffic jams. Imagine not having to wait on line in the supermarket — even in the express lane! Everyone comes and goes as they please (of course they pay for their goods — money will be no problem).

Imagine a sumptuous home-cooked meal that should take hours to prepare. All you need to do is wish for it and it's yours, instantaneously. Imagine plucking ready-to-wear clothing right off a tree, just your size and style.

Imagine wishing to communicate with a relative or friend who is far away. There's no need to lift a telephone to make the connection. You can just *go there* and *see them* — faster than you can push the buttons on your touch-tone phone. And imagine total recall: never fumbling for the right word or phrase, or stumbling over an assumed fact stored away in memory.

Imagine never worrying about the next mortgage or tuition payment, or about affording your next vacation. You'll have incredible wealth, never lacking anything your heart desires. And so will everyone you know — for poverty will no longer exist.

Imagine a world with the ideal environment: no air pollution, no holes in the ozone layer, no acid rain, no rain forest destruction and no nuclear or chemical waste to worry about. The temperature is just right: not too hot and not too cold. No hurricanes or tornadoes or sandstorms, no icy rains or sleet. There will be plentiful rainfall, but never on anyone's picnic or parade. Animals will also be secure. No poaching of elephants or rhinoceros for their tusks, no wanton destruction of minks or ermine.

Imagine people luxuriating in the warmth of the sun, without fear of sunburn — or of skin cancer. A world without illness or suffering: no cancer, no heart disease, no AIDS; no bronchitis, tuberculosis, typhus, malaria or even the flu or the common cold. Everybody goes busily about their daily lives without incurring even a scratch or stubbing a toe.

Imagine a world without jealousies and without hatred; without arrogance or anger; without the pursuit of power to intimidate or dominate others. Instead, it will be a world in which people will love and respect one another — simply for what they are — without any ulterior motives.

Sound utopian? It certainly does and definitely does not seem even remotely feasible in our age. But then, prior to 1800, *nobody* thought that many of the comforts of today's world would *ever* exist. A forty-mile trip was, if one was lucky, an all-day affair in a horse-drawn buggy over dirt roads. Today, many people commute that distance in less than an hour without a second thought. Communication between cities used to take weeks, but today you can telephone or fax halfway around the globe in less than a minute.

Suits and dresses, pants, skirts and shirts are available by the thousands straight off the rack, but two centuries ago people were fortunate if they found enough ready-made yarn to knit a pair socks. And all foods were "raw materials," with every dinner having to be made from scratch — not some *cordon bleu* microwave dinner available from your local supermarket.

The world's technology has advanced at an incredible pace since the Industrial Revolution. In its early years, inventions were introduced every few years. In today's world, technology jumps forward by gigantic leaps at an increasingly dizzying pace. Progress seems to scream out to everyone: "Move forward! Move! Move! Move!" But the questions stand out: "Why?" "For what purpose?" and "To what end?"

*

Mashiach, a windfall and a scorpion

> "Three [things] come unexpectedly [to a person]: Mashiach, a windfall and a scorpion."
>
> Sanhedrin 97a

God created Adam, the First Man, with the intention that a human being in corporeal form be able to live a spiritual life. Adam and Eve were placed in the Garden of Eden, a spiritually rich and rewarding environment, to facilitate this goal. But on their very first day of life, they transgressed. Man was severely punished — banished from Paradise — and penalized with the need to struggle in order to sustain himself in a material world. He must now work very hard (Genesis 3:19), "By the sweat of his brow," to find spirituality.

But the question remains, if man was penalized with the need to pursue the material, how can he ever attain spirituality? And even more baffling, what of those who succumb to their physical lusts and temptations, causing man and mankind to plunge deeper into materialism? If, on their very first day of life, Adam and Eve were unable to maintain a spiritual existence, is there a chance for anybody to ever ascend from that abyss into which mankind has fallen? Has it ever happened? And, if so, is it possible that *all* of mankind could ever make that ascent?

Before God created the world, He knew of man's fallibility — after all, it was He Who created the evil inclination. He knew that man would be lax in his pursuit of the spiritual. But God created the world to reveal His goodness (*Etz Chaim, Shaar HaKlalim* 1) and His plan is that everyone should benefit from His goodness — even the unworthy. Thus, everyone (well, almost everyone; see below Part VI) can, through some means, find rectification for his deeds and attain a level of perfection.

*

But who in his right mind would even think that this is possible? As the world plummets to new depths of corruption and immorality, of perversity and depravity, one wonders how any rectification could ever take place — let alone one in which the *entire* world reaches a stage of perfection! But then again, not all that long ago, nobody believed man would ever fly. We have reached a perplexing stage in history. Contemporary man has lived through a century of some of the most despicable and bestial behaviors ever exhibited by the human race — against humans, animals and the environment. And yet man has a better chance of living today than ever before. Life expectancy has risen, health care is infinitely better, the global standard of living rises each year and man has been blessed with wonderful inventions that have benefitted countless lives.

We are beset by a profound paradox as we approach the 21st century. At the very same time that the technology of modern communication forces everyone into contact with everyone else, those small crevices that divide all the various levels of our society are widening into yawning fissures. The loftier the heights man reaches through his intellect — as evidenced in his scientific and technological breakthroughs — the greater the depravity that is revealed in his soul.

The explanations that are offered for this are all abstract, like the very concept of Mashiach. But therein lies a profound commentary on contemporary life.

We constantly find ourselves with "windfalls" — with even more breakthroughs in technology yet to come. Concurrently, we also find ourselves beset by life's "scorpions." The only answer that connects these two opposites is that we are in the "End of Days," with the arrival of the Mashiach imminent. Therefore, the unexpected always happens.

Global stability no longer exists, but in a sense the world seems a safer place to live, with a moratorium on the proliferation of nuclear weapons, and war in general in the process of being checked. The environment is deteriorating, yet man is living longer. The great financial institutions upon which western civilization has relied are crumbling, yet the standard of living steadily rises, with more people able to enjoy the windfalls of life. In short, as the 20th century draws to a close, there is no longer any tangible explanation for the way the world continues.

Yet it does continue, and any day now Mashiach will arrive and set things right. In fact, his presence is *already* here and can be easily felt by everyone, if we but choose to feel it. The purpose of this work is to introduce the reader to the kind of life we will live when Mashiach comes; how to experience it in a microcosmic manner in the present; and ways in which we can hasten its advent. By exploring day-to-day life, we will be able to see how Mashiach is so much a part of it already.

*

And then, "The wolf will live with the lamb and the leopard will lie down with the goat; the calf and the lion will dwell together... the cow will graze with the bear and their young will forage side by side; and the lion, like cattle, will eat straw. The child will play with the cobra... for the world will be filled with the knowledge of God..." (Isaiah 11:6-9).

* * *

2

"For on that Day..."

In order to see how much Mashiach is a part of our daily lives, we must first analyze the concept of Mashiach and why it is necessary. Furthermore, we have to contrast life as it once was, as it is now, and as it will be in the Days of Mashiach, especially as is seen by our Prophets and Sages. Their portrait, however, is not a clear one to us, as it seems to contain contradictory opinions. *RaMBaM* (Rabbi Moshe ben Maimon or Maimonides; 1135-1204) writes that the differing prophecies should be accepted as allegories until Mashiach himself comes. We will then see them unfolding before our eyes and understand their intent retroactively (*Yad HaChazakah, Hilkhot Melakhim* 12:1; see also *Likutey Moharan* I, 186). In view of this, we will present the material as a mosaic. As the book progresses, we will be able to see the transition from the past to the future as the messianic concepts begin to fit into place.

*

God revealed Himself to Abraham in the Covenant of the Halves (*Brit bein HaBetarim*; Genesis 15). He informed Abraham of the exile of his descendants to a foreign land (i.e. Egypt). At the same time, He also revealed to him all the four exiles that his descendants would endure and their ultimate salvation (*Bereishit Rabbah* 44:19). Thus, even before the first exile, all the other exiles as well as the final redemption, were made known.

When Moshe Rabeinu (Moses) sang his Song of Salvation at the Red Sea, he spoke of the destruction of the two Temples, the exile of the Jews and their return to the Holy Land. "You shall bring them and plant them on the mountain of Your heritage; the place of Your habitation which You, God, have made; the Temple, God, which Your hands have established. God will reign forever" (Exodus 15:17-18). Our Sages teach (cf. Rashi, loc. cit.), that the three parts of this quotation allude to the three Temples. Two have been built and destroyed, for they were built by man. The Third Temple, which will be built by God's Hands, will remain forever. Then, having revealed His sovereignty to all, "God will reign forever." Thus, the current exile was foretold nearly 1400 years before its advent.

Furthermore, prior to the destruction of the First Temple, many of the Prophets (Isaiah, Amos, Michah, etc.) envisaged its destruction, its reconstruction and the Roman exile that followed it. And, at the same time, they described in glowing detail the ingathering of the exiles from the diaspora to the Holy Land, the rebuilding of the Third Temple and the future glory of the Jews. Jeremiah and Ezekiel, witnesses to the destruction of the Temple and the barbaric cruelty of Nebuchadnezzar during the deportation of the Jews to Babylon, prophesied magnificent endings to the saga of the exile.

Thus, thousands of years ago, our Prophets and Sages revealed certain patterns of history. Reviewing just a few episodes in Jewish history will enable us to better focus on what is unfolding before our own eyes and what is awaiting us in the future.

*

The past...

The Prophets foresaw a devastating ruination of the Holy Land along with a seemingly endless exile of the Jewish Nation. Throughout history, as soon as the Jews settled into a country with "apparent" acceptance, the ugly specter of antisemitism arose. Spain had its Golden Era, followed by the cruel Inquisition. Medieval Europe found France, Germany and England accepting the Jews and then expelling them, after many bloodbaths (the Crusades, etc.). When the expulsion orders were rescinded, the Jews were allowed to settle only in restricted ghettos. In Eastern Europe, the Jews were at first welcomed for their business acumen, only to become the victims of blood libels and the Chmelnitzky massacres. In the Mediterranean and Arab countries, the Jews found somewhat more "tolerant" hosts. They were granted several "rights," but these were always subject to severe restrictions combined with relentless taxation. Thus, security was never the norm in their community life. And more recently, Jews who had become members of the elite in Germany and in socialist Russia were victims of the Holocaust and Communist repressions. In North America, the progression of rising antisemitism continues, as it will until the Mashiach comes.

*

...the present...

> *"I will make them and their surroundings a blessing... the trees shall bear fruit and the earth shall yield crops..."*
>
> Ezekiel 34:26-27

But the Prophets also foresaw an end to this exile. When Mashiach comes he will gather in the exiles from all over the world and the Jews will flock to their homeland in droves. The Talmud teaches (Ketuvot 111b) that the Holy Land is true to its masters, the Jews. When they are in the Land, it bears fruit. When they are not, it is barren. When speaking of the ruins of the Holy Land, Ezekiel states that the return of the Jews will bring about the resurrection of the Land, causing the Land to bear fruits and to grow grass for the pasture of animals (see Ezekiel Chapters 34-36). We, today, behold this resurrection. Since the end of the nineteenth century when the Jews began their large-scale return, the produce has constantly grown bigger, sweeter and better. And, as apparent from Ezekiel's prophecies, all this is to begin to take place prior to the coming of the Mashiach.

*

> *"In place of copper, I will bring gold; in place of iron, I will bring silver..."*
>
> Isaiah 60:17

As for the exile itself, we are currently witness to the gradual return of a dispersed nation to its rightful land. Isaiah speaks of the return from

Assyria and Egypt. Obadiah speaks of the return from France and Spain, while others speak of the return from the four corners of the globe. And the return will be in direct contrast to the expulsion: throughout the long exiles, the nations plundered Jewish wealth. Country after country, kingdom after kingdom, taxed the Jews incessantly. Beyond this, the rulers would unleash the peasants to further rob and plunder Jewish possessions. But, when Mashiach comes, all that was stolen will be returned — with interest. Thus the Prophet states, "In place of copper, I will bring gold; in place of iron, I will bring silver..." And we see today that both individuals and governments are contributing money for the rebuilding of the Holy Land, even though Mashiach's presence has not yet been revealed!

Isaiah (2:4) speaks of "beating swords into plowshares." Recent world events have seen armament industries beginning to utilize their manufacturing might for the production of what will be needed in the era of peace. In fact, for the first time in history, armies are involved in feeding the hungry! We can see that the beginnings of the messianic days are already upon us.

*

...and the Future

The world will operate on a system of visual reality of God. Whereas today people view everyday life as being under the jurisdiction of the forces of nature, in the future people will openly see the Hand of God guiding us through His Divine Providence. Miracles — occurrences above space and time — will become the norm. The Prophet Michah (7:15) states, "As during the Exodus from Egypt, God will perform wonders." The *Zohar* (I, 261b) teaches that the miracles performed in Egypt were from the forty-ninth Gate of Understanding, the highest level anyone can perceive while in this world. But those of the messianic era will emanate from the Fiftieth Gate, the highest of levels. In that age of miracles, God will be revealed for all to see. "He will not hide, and your eyes shall see your Master" (Isaiah 30:20). This means that even though man is corporeal, he will see the spiritual. And his very corporeality will be transformed!

Everyone will have untold wealth; no-one will have any feelings of jealousy or envy. Gold and silver, diamonds, emeralds, rubies, sapphires and all the money people wish for will be at their fingertips (or in their checking account). (For what purpose will be discussed below Part VI). Need a 60-carat diamond, D color, flawless, for your wife's birthday? Just ask the angel and he'll cut it to size for you from his "underwater" inventory (see Bava Batra 75a). And all this will occur at a time when everyone ceases to pursue wealth.

All food will taste incredibly delicious. Mountains will literally drip honey and other sweet fluids (Joel 4:18; Amos 9:13). Water will also have the taste of sweet drinks. Fresh loaves of bread will grow directly on trees (which is the basis for the blessing, "Who brings forth *bread* from the earth)" (Shabbat 30b). And yet, it will be a time when man will be satisfied with dry bread and a measure of water (see Isaiah 30:20) — for all the wonderful tastes in the world will be included in this bread. It will be similar to eating manna.

Clothing of fine silk and other materials will grow ready-to-wear on the trees (Shabbat 30b). Just seek out a "38 long" or "size 10" tree and you'll find what you're looking for. Your house will have the finest marble floors, walls and whatever else your interior decorating requires — with plenty of closet space for your wardrobe. And no seasonal changes will be necessary, as the weather will be adjusted for "year round comfort."

All the above contradicts the laws of nature and defies the imagination. Yet, today we are living in this "age of enlightenment." If we but open our minds we can see how some of the aforementioned are becoming reality. We don't even have to stretch our imagination — the messianic mosaic becomes a giant magnet, drawing all its fragments together for us.

*

The messianic era

Our Sages use several terms when speaking about the future. What is quite apparent from the various commentaries is that each of these refers to a different time. They are:

Ikv'ta d'Mashicha ("the Footsteps of Mashiach"), sometimes known as **Chevlei Mashiach** ("the birthpangs of Mashiach"), which refers to the time of great suffering which must be endured prior to Mashiach's coming (see below, Chapter 30).

Yemot HaMashiach ("the Days of Mashiach" or "Messianic Era") refers to the period when Mashiach is becoming revealed in the world.

Techiyat HaMeitim ("the Resurrection"), **Olam HaBa** (the "World to Come") and **l'Atid LaVo** ("the Forthcoming Future"), all refer to the different stages of the Future and will occur some time after Mashiach's arrival and revelation.

For the purposes of this book we are combining the two concepts of *Ikv'ta d'Mashicha* and *Yemot HaMashiach* into one expression, "The Days of Mashiach." The reason for this is that we are in an era that encompasses both ideas, as will become obvious as the book unfolds. Furthermore, we will be speaking in the main of two periods: the Days of Mashiach and the Future. As explained at the beginning of this chapter, it is impossible for us to know *now*, exactly how each era of the messianic experience will manifest itself. Furthermore, several of the messianic concepts and their explanations might seem contradictory. To help guide us through this maze, our discussions will be based upon the premise that we are already in the Days of Mashiach and can assume a presence of Mashiach in the world — if we truly want him. In this sense, the Days of Mashiach are days as we know them, run according to the laws of nature. And, when we speak about the Future, we will then be referring to the era of miraculous living, when God's Divine Providence will be revealed to all.

*

According to the Prophets and Sages, there is a definite day set forth in God's plan for the coming of the Mashiach, which will signify an end to suffering and poverty, hatred, jealousy and war. This day, however, has never been revealed to anyone — and it remains God's closely guarded secret. The reason for this is that the day of salvation can either be brought forward or delayed, according to man's deeds. But, it cannot extend beyond the end of the sixth millennium (the year 6,000) (see Sanhedrin 97a). At the time of this writing in the year 5755 (1995), there are less than two hundred fifty years remaining at most. Thus, we are already in the final Days of Mashiach.

Hatred, envy, rage, arrogance and all other evil characteristics will be removed from the world. The wolf will remain a wolf and the sheep a sheep; but the wolf's predatory instinct of killing for survival will become a thing of the past. So too will man be freed from his primal, baser characteristics — avarice, gluttony and immorality. With this new-found freedom from all material lust, man will have the ability to seek true intellect, the knowledge of the Infinite God. Each day will bring forth newer wonders, greater intellect and newer, greater revelations of the Infinite One, God. And each day, man will revel in the glory of God and serve Him — "for the world will be full of the knowledge of God..." (Isaiah 11:6-9).

* * *

Part II

Mashiach:

Who?

This section describes the attributes of leadership as exemplified by Jewish leaders of the past. It forms the basis of what characteristics we must look for in the ultimate leader of all mankind — the Mashiach.

3

Mashiach

The question, "Who is Mashiach," has brought in its wake a plethora of answers. Mankind, when suffering, tends to seek alleviation for its pain. But for several millennia, men have conceived fictional answers, which more often than not have aggravated their suffering. Our Sages teach that the Talmudic giant, Rabbi Akiva, mistakenly accepted Bar Koziva (Bar Kokhva) as a messiah (*Yerushalmi, Taanit* 4:8; see also below, Chapter 32, concerning similar occurrences throughout Jewish history). A century prior to Rabbi Akiva, false messianism spawned a new religion. During the periods of the Gaonim and Rishonim (7th-12th centuries), several false messiahs arose. The Rambam wrote his famous *Iggeret Teiman* ("The Letter to Yemen") warning against false messianism. Reeling heavily from the Chmelnitzky massacres, Shabbatai Zvi's efforts to be proclaimed Mashiach tore the entire Jewish Nation asunder (circa 1660s). More recently, several types of "messia*nisms*" have arisen: capital*ism*, social*ism*, egalitaria*nism*, Zio*nism*, anti-Zio*nism* and so on. Each "ism" has a noble purpose rooted in a theme of Mashiach: a wealthy world, an egalitarian world, a return to Zion and a world where belief in God is the only way of life. All of these ideas base themselves on one aspect of the utopia that will exist during messianic times.

But, being human inventions, man-made solutions are dangerously misleading and only serve to obscure the question of "Who is Mashiach" even more. Mashiach cannot be a *chasid*, because the *mitnagdim* would never accept him. But then, would the *chassidim* accept a "*litvak*?" Will the Mashiach be of Sefardic or Ashkenazic lineage? Would a reconstructionist Mashiach be palatable to orthodox Jews or can reform and conservative Jewry accept an orthodox Mashiach? Will secularists accept religion as *the* answer? And what of the gentile nations, especially those with very strong antisemitic leanings? Who will Mashiach be for them?

Furthermore, Mashiach is described as, "Poor, riding on a donkey" (Zekhariah 9:9). One would think that someone of Mashiach's status, the leader of all mankind, would parade down the street in a Rolls Royce or an open Cadillac stretch-limousine. Can you imagine the reception of a world leader driving a Valiant or a Fiat — much less a donkey?!

So, "Who is Mashiach?" What kind of person would even think of undertaking the job of resolving all the differences within the Jewish People itself — let alone for all mankind?

But Mashiach was created and prepared for his mission prior to the Creation of the world (Pesachim 54a). He cannot be chosen by man, for he was designated for his mission by God. As we will see below when discussing the Creation and the subsequent "Fall of Man" (Part V), Mashiach's soul is rooted in the loftiest of levels, the level of Keter (*Atik*) (see Appendix B, chart of the Sefirot and the divine personae). This is absolutely necessary, for Mashiach must be able to transcend anything and everything in the world — even and especially all evil that was ever perpetrated — to rectify and perfect all mankind. Thus, Mashiach must be someone extremely unique and very awesome.

Let us now explore what our Sages teach regarding who Mashiach should be.

*

The Soul of Mashiach

The ARI writes: Mashiach will be born from man and woman as any other human being. He will be very righteous, and perform many meritorious deeds, thereby constantly elevating himself. His efforts will ultimately bring him to a very exalted level, at which point he will be able to receive his *Yechidah*, the Unique Soul that was prepared for him prior to Creation. He will then realize who he is and what his mission will be. He will be endowed by Heaven with the power to fulfill his task (Arba Meot Shekel Kesef, p.241; see also Zohar II, 7b-8b, Matok Midvash, ibid.; Zohar HaRakia, Shemot p.56b). In this sense, he will be similar to Moshe, our first redeemer.

Moshe Rabeinu was also born of a man and a woman and lived a life of righteousness. By the time he turned eighty, he had risen to such an exalted level that he merited the revelation at the burning bush (Exodus 3-4). At the bush, he received a much loftier soul, one capable of transcending all the diversities of the Jewish Nation. He was therefore able to descend into Egypt and redeem the Jews (Shaar HaPesukim, Shemot, p.129). Mashiach will likewise be born into an ordinary family and suffer the pangs of growing up as does everyone else. Rebbe Nachman once remarked, "Mashiach's parents won't be so *ay, ay, ay* (i.e. such great people)...!" (Siach Sarfei Kodesh I-83).

In explaining why this is so, the ARI teaches that there are certain souls which stem from very high levels, such as those of Abraham, King David and the Mashiach. When these souls are ready to descend to this world, there is great opposition from the *kelipot* (forces of evil). They argue that "Since these soul are so great, not only will they not succumb to evil, but they will bring others to recognize and serve God!" God's own Attribute of Judgment is "forced" to concede, for such souls can overcome the forces of evil, negate free will, and bring about an open revelation of Godliness. How then can these great souls descend?

God uses a ruse to trick the forces of evil. He consents to the transmigration of these souls through unsophisticated — even wicked — people. Upon seeing that these great souls are very near the realm of evil, the *kelipot* agree to the soul's descent, thinking that they will prevail over it and cause it to sin (see Shaar HaGilgulim #38).

Following this short introduction, we can now begin to trace the transmigration of Mashiach's soul since we know that Mashiach is a descendant of King David.

*

When Sodom was overturned, Lot escaped to the hills with his two daughters. Entering a cave, they found wine. Upon witnessing the total destruction of Sodom and the surrounding area, Lot's eldest daughter believed that only they had been spared, while the rest of the world was destroyed. She made her father drunk and cohabitated with him. From their union a son, Moab, was born (Genesis 19).

Nearly one hundred seventy years later, Judah, one of the twelve sons of Jacob, was on his way to shear his flock when he was seduced by Tamar, his widowed daughter-in-law. She had dressed up as a harlot in order to disguise her true identity and conceive a child from Judah. Judah was wholly righteous, however, and such subterfuge would have got Tamar nowhere had not an angel literally coerced him into her tent against his will. As a result of their union, Tamar bore twin boys, the elder of whom was named Peretz, the forebear of King David (Genesis 38; Ruth 4:18-22; see *Bereishit Rabbah* 85:8).

Thus, the soul of King David, the ancestor of the Mashiach, could only descend into the world through a series of questionable relationships. The first of these was that of Lot and his daughter. The second was that of Judah and his daughter-in-law, whom he mistakenly took for a harlot.

Some three hundred fifty years later, Ruth was born to the Moabite nation. She married Machlon, a scion of the Tribe of Judah, when he was in the land of Moab. After Machlon died, Ruth, together with her mother-in-law, Naomi, returned to Beth Lechem (Bethlehem) where Ruth, now a Jewess, married Boaz, a descendant of Peretz and the leading judge in the land at the time. Their son, Oved, was Yishai's (Jesse's) father and King David's grandfather (Ruth 1-4).

But Ruth's marriage wasn't readily accepted by everyone. Torah law forbids a Moabite from marrying into the Jewish community (Deuteronomy 23:4). The Talmud details a dispute over whether the injunction applies only to males, or also to female converts. At the time of Ruth's conversion, the general consensus ruled in favor of the females. Thus, Oved, Yishai and Yishai's elder children were accepted as proper Jews. But, prior to King David's birth, the ruling was applied to female Moabite converts. Thus, upon his birth, King David was shunned and treated as an outcast, unable to join his father's family and the Jewish community. This is the meaning of (Psalms 69:9), "I was a stranger to my brothers; an alien to my mother's children" (see Midrashim, loc.cit.). It wasn't until he was twenty-eight years old and faced Goliath the Philistine, that the dispute arose again. Due to Samuel, the leading Sage and Prophet at the time, the ruling was decided, once and for all, to permit the conversion of female Moabites. Only then was King David, who ultimately became the paradigm of Jewish rulership, finally accepted into the community (see Yevamot 76b-77a).

But even so David's life was never easy. He had to flee the relentless pursuits of his father-in-law, King Saul, who sought to kill him. After David was proclaimed King of Israel he faced many wars, internal opposition from his own army staff and even a household insurrection. The Books of Samuel and Chronicles detail the suffering that King David endured throughout his entire lifetime.

This was the way God *had* to bring forth the soul of King David, the paradigm of Jewish *Malkhut* (Royalty), to this earth. From amidst such dubious and persecuted beginnings, from such intense sufferings, there arose a leader of uncompromising honesty and enduring humility.

King David studied Torah continuously in order to be better equipped to judge his people. He constantly beseeched God for proper guidance in all his endeavors. If war was called for, he stood in the forefront, leading his people with unswerving self-sacrifice. He was a leader imbued with absolute dedication to the people whom he served; a leader who paved the path to peace, who laid the foundations for a Holy Temple, so that generations to come could experience spirituality in their midst and thereby come to recognize God.

*

Adam, David, Mashiach

When Adam, the First Man, prophetically beheld the soul of King David, he was shown that it had no life — that it was destined to be stillborn. Created to live for a thousand years, Adam gave King David a gift of seventy years from his life (Zohar I, 55a). In fact, the name ADaM is an acrostic for Adam, David and Mashiach. This alludes to the fact that King David's life is inextricably bound up with Adam's, as well as with that of his descendant, Mashiach.

As the First Man, Adam was to elevate the world to a state of perfection. And he would have done this had he not partaken of the Tree of Knowledge of Good and Evil (this is elaborated upon below; see Part V, "The Fall of Man"). By not exercising restraint, Adam erred, casting all of mankind into a life of materialism. The ARI teaches that King David was the embodiment of Adam's soul since it was Adam's life that sustained him. Bathsheba was a reincarnation of Eve. Thus, Bathsheba was destined for King David from the time of Creation. But King David also erred, marrying Bathsheba prematurely (see Sanhedrin 107a). As a result, King David did not reach the required state of perfection, and he could not, at that time, rectify the world. The task is now left for the Mashiach (see also Rashi, Genesis 15:11). (Restraint and patience are messianic characteristics which are discussed at length in Parts III-IV).

Like King David in his time, Mashiach too must suffer the embarrassments and abuse heaped upon the Jews. More so in fact, as he is their ultimate leader. In addition, he suffers all the vindictiveness and derision of our persecutors over the several millennia of our exile. The Psalmist prayed (Psalms 89:51-52), "Remember, God, the disgrace of Your servants... the insults of many nations... They have insulted You, they have insulted Your Mashiach." Still, Mashiach is of true nobility. He is one who places the needs of *all* his subjects — indeed the entire world — before his own. Therefore, despite the abuse he has suffered and endured, he will rise above it all, and his leadership will demonstrate the path of honesty and integrity for all mankind to follow. Mashiach will attain the highest perfection. Then, through the truth and faith that he will reveal, the Holy Temple will be rebuilt, and God, in His glory, will be revealed for all mankind to behold. For it is only through true leadership that Malkhut, the Kingship of God, can be manifest.

*

Leadership

King David is the personification of Malkhut, Jewish kingship and leadership. Thus, trying to understand or emulate him will give us an idea of who Mashiach should be.

The story of King David's life reads as a never-ending saga of a pursued individual. Whatever he did, he faced relentless opposition. Despite his familial rejection, his solitary stand against the giant Goliath, his being chased like a criminal by King Saul, countless wars, mutiny in his household, etc., he was always available for his subjects. His life was one of total self-sacrifice, to God and to his people.

We do not find King David looking for the approval of his people. He never canvassed the nation to see what was "politically correct" or which popular issues could sway the vote. He wasn't interested in popularity polls. And he never sold his nation for personal or dubious gains. He accepted full responsibility for his actions. His commitment to truth was total and he never sought self-aggrandizement for his deeds. This is in stark contrast to contemporary "leadership" — political, financial, religious and so on — who always watch the polls before announcing their positions (and change them as often as necessary).

When seeking a true leader, we must seek one whom we are able to follow. A leader leads his people, he does not follow their desires. This is not to deny that the people may have good intentions. But it does not necessarily follow that the average person's outlook on life is such that his choice of direction is acceptable to all humanity. Thus, Mashiach must possess true leadership qualities (discussed below in Chapter 4 and in Part III) such as those displayed by King David.

*

The anointed one

> *"Upon [the Mashiach] will descend a spirit of God; a spirit of wisdom and understanding, a spirit of advice and strength, a spirit of knowledge and fear of God. And he shall breathe the fear of God: he will not judge by what he sees nor by what he hears. He will judge righteously..."*
>
> Isaiah 11:2-4

MaShiaCh is so called because he will be specially anointed, as the verse states (Psalms 45:8), "You loved righteousness and despised wickedness; therefore God will anoint you (M'ShoChakha) with the oil of joy." Fine oils and perfumes attract people. Like fine oil, Mashiach will have the power to draw the whole world to his teachings (see *Likutey Halakhot, Birkat HaReiach* 3:8; *ibid.* 4:5). In fact, Mashiach is so fully bound up with the concept of fine aroma that his sense of smell is extremely acute. The Talmud thus teaches (*Sanhedrin* 93b), "Mashiach will be able to judge by his sense of smell."

This idea can be carried further. "The world was chaos and confusion, with darkness upon the depths; but the spirit of God hovered over the waters" (Genesis 1:2). "The spirit of God" — this refers to the Mashiach (*Bereishit Rabbah* 2:4; *Zohar* I, 240a). The Midrash teaches that the chaos, confusion, darkness and the depths, etc. refer to sufferings of this world. What sustains a person through all his suffering? Hope for a better future; light at the end of a long tunnel. And if a person, overwhelmed by his suffering, faints and must be revived, smelling salts are used.

God created this world with all the chaos "necessary" to direct us away from spirituality. However, He also created and placed in our midst the means for survival and hope — Mashiach. The "spirit of Mashiach" is the ray of hope to which we can cling, the sweet smelling fragrance of joy and expectation that everything will turn out for the best (see *Likutey Halakhot, Birkat HaReiach* 4:21).

How closely Mashiach is related to the "sense of smell" and its deeper meanings will be discussed below (Part III). We have attempted here to introduce the idea of the Mashiach as being present in our generation — indeed in all generations. The fact that God placed the spirit of Mashiach into our lives from the very beginning of Creation has important relevance to our understanding of the concept of "Who is Mashiach" and how we can relate to him on a personal level. Now that we have had a glimpse of the nature of Mashiach, we can analyze the various teachings of our Sages regarding who Mashiach is. Although some of these teachings might sound contrary and paradoxical, they are all parts of the great drama of Mashiach.

* * *

4

Who is Mashiach?

> *"The staff will not depart from Judah, nor the scepter from his descendants (lit. from between his feet), until the coming of Shiloh to whom all nations will submit."*
>
> Genesis 49:10

The Patriarch Jacob, when blessing his children before he passed away, blessed Judah with the quality of royalty and leadership. From his tribe would come forth King David and eventually Shiloh, who is the Mashiach (Onkelos; Rashi, ad.loc.). Furthermore, Mashiach is known as *ben David* — the son of King David. This is seen clearly from the Talmud (Sanhedrin 96b-99a) which devotes several pages to describing the generation of Mashiach's arrival. Throughout, it refers to "the son of David." This is readily understood, for God promised King David that the Kingdom of Israel will forever be under the leadership of his descendants (2 Samuel 7:16).

The Prophet Zekhariah (Zekhariah 12) depicts a fierce battle over the city of Jerusalem prior to Mashiach's reign. At the gates of the city, the battle will claim the life of the "Mashiach." The Talmud teaches (Sukkah 52a), "The family of King David, who will be within the city, will survive and eulogize the fallen Mashiach, who is the Mashiach *ben Yosef* — the son of Joseph." On the one hand, we see there are two Mashiachs, one of whom will die. On the other hand, we have a tradition that, because of Isaac's self-sacrifice at the time of the *Akeidah* ("The Binding of Isaac"), Mashiach ben Yosef will be spared (Tikkuney Zohar p.139b; see also ibid. 146b).

Questions arise. Is Mashiach *ben Yosef* or *ben David*? Obviously, there are two "Mashiachs." Will "he" or "they" live or die? And we generally speak about Mashiach in the singular, as one person. The contradictions seem glaring. But, since each of the two is called Mashiach, each one must have a different function which he alone can and must fulfill. In the same vein, the "life and death" of Mashiach also implies different stages of the revelation of the Mashiach.

*

Two Mashiachs?

The Mashiach whom we all await, the one who will be king over all Israel and return us all to the service of God, is from the Davidic dynasty. His function is to remove the barriers that we have placed between ourselves, and to draw us all together under the dominion of God. As such, this Mashiach will emit the sweet fragrance of the fear of God and will bring everyone to recognize Him.

Mashiach is present in every generation. He must be, for he can be summoned at a moment's notice (Sanhedrin 98a). Thus, his "spirit" has always been with us, from the very beginning of time. Yet, if the generation isn't worthy, and Mashiach does not redeem us, then who is — or was — the Mashiach of that generation?

This is where Mashiach ben Yosef enters the picture. The character of Mashiach ben Yosef is embodied in the tzaddikim of each generation (see Likutey Halakhot, Hodaah 6:20). For every tzaddik who establishes a house of prayer or study in order to direct people to serve God is engaged in the building of the Holy Temple — the work of the Mashiach (Likutey Halakhot, Minchah 7:67; cf. Megilah 29a).

We have seen that King David is the paradigm of Malkhut, Jewish leadership. Joseph, on the other hand, is considered the paradigm of the tzaddik, the truly righteous man. Our Sages teach that the title "tzaddik" applies specifically to one who maintains a strict moral code regarding sexual behavior (Zohar I, 59b). Potifar was a high-ranking officer in the Egyptian government and bought Joseph as a slave. Potifar's wife set her eyes upon him and harassed him for a full year. Joseph resisted every advance, and was subsequently imprisoned for rejecting immorality. For this, Joseph merited the title "tzaddik."

So it is with every righteous person who attains a high level of purity. That person embodies the idea of the tzaddik who is worthy of being the Mashiach. The Talmud thus asks: Who is Mashiach? What is Mashiach's name? What will he be called?

> Rabbi Shiloh's school taught that Mashiach's name is Shiloh. Rabbi Yanai's school taught that his name is Yinon. Rabbi Chaninah's school said Mashiach's name is Chaninah, while Menachem ben Chezkiyah's school said that Mashiach's name is Menachem. Some called him, 'the leper from the house of Rabbi Judah the Prince,' due to the suffering he endures for the entire nation. Rav Nachman said, 'If Mashiach is among the living, I am he.' Rav said, 'If Mashiach is among the living, he is like Rabbi Judah the Prince' (Sanhedrin 98b).

Each tzaddik reflects the awesome power of the Mashiach. As such, each of the aforementioned rabbis was known as being an aspect of the Mashiach and, had the generation been worthy, could have effected the redemption. Interestingly, the four proper names used: Menachem, Shiloh, Yinon and Chaninah form the acrostic MaShiYaCh. For the tzaddikim in each generation do their best to bring about the redemption.

If a generation is found worthy, Mashiach could come instantaneously. But if the generation is unworthy, how, or even why, should Mashiach come? Therefore, the tzaddikim in each generation seek to bring people back to God, to live a moral and righteous life. They are constantly doing battle with the forces of evil, while revealing faith and spirituality in the midst of a materialistic world.

Yerushalayim (Jerusalem) conceptually stands for the "awe of God," for the word *YeRuShaLayiM* is a combination of two words, *YiRah*, "awe" and *ShaLeM*, "perfect" — "perfect awe." The tzaddikim are constantly waging war to instill in us the awe of God. As such, "Jerusalem," the scene of the final battle prior to Mashiach's victory, can be interpreted as the "arena of battle" where the tzaddikim battle the enemies — the surrounding cultures of atheism and materialism that besiege "Jerusalem," our fear of God. The losses are heavy and, despite their massive efforts to reveal Godliness, the tzaddikim die amidst their struggle. When the battle is finally won, then Mashiach ben David will appear. Jerusalem (fear of God) and the Holy Temple will then be built.

The ARI explains that, although Mashiach ben Yosef is slated to be killed by the wicked, this will not happen. The fact that the exile continues unabated means that Mashiach ben Yosef is given the chance to be reincarnated in every generation, to challenge the wicked by bringing people back to God. Though he must die each time, he is not actually killed in battle. Rather, he is taken by God and spared death at the hands of the wicked. Indeed, Mashiach's "death" is really an allegory for his unsuccessful battle against evil. This is why he must return each time to pick up where he left off, until wickedness is finally overcome.

This description of Mashiach ben Yosef and his "death" provides an important link in our understanding of the concept of the "two Mashiachs." But there is more to the matter of "Who is Mashiach" awaiting us.

*

Moshe, the Mashiach?!

> *"That which was, will be... for there is nothing new under the sun."*
>
> Ecclesiastes 1:9

We find that the souls of certain tzaddikim were prepared long before their birth to fulfill a special mission in life. In the Creation account, the verse states (Genesis 2:7), "God created *HaAdam* (the Man)." The Midrash comments (Bereishit Rabbah 14:6), '*the* Man,' refers to Abraham. Then why wasn't Abraham the first man? This was intentional, so that if Adam, the First Man, should sin, Abraham would come and rectify his mistake. The Midrash also teaches that Moshe was destined to be a redeemer. Jeremiah was told (Jeremiah 1:5), "Before you were formed in the womb you were destined to be a prophet." Mordekhai (of Purim fame) was prepared for his mission to save the Jews from Haman's decree, and so on (Bereishit

Rabbah 30:8). The Talmud speaks about several other tzaddikim who were prepared in advance for their missions: Rabbi Judah the Prince, Shmuel, Rav Ashi, etc. (Bava Metzia 86a). Mashiach was also prepared for his mission — to rectify the entire world — long before it was even created (Pesachim 54a).

We find many teachings that indicate that Moshe is the Mashiach. "Moshe led his flock to the desert..." (Exodus 3:1). When God spoke to Moshe, He said, "The desert is a sign for you. You will lead your flock to the desert, and leave them there. In the Future — i.e. in the Days of Mashiach — *you* will redeem them from the desert" (Shemot Rabbah 2:4).

The *Tikkuney Zohar* states clearly, "*Mah she'hayah hu she'yihiyeh*" ("That which was is what will be"; Ecclesiastes 1:9). The acrostic of *Mah She'hayah Hu* is MoSheH. That is, the same redeemer who took us out of Egypt, formed us into a nation and gave us the Torah, will be our redeemer in the Future. He will take us out of our exile, establish us as a united nation and reveal the Torah to us in a much deeper way (Tikkuney Zohar #69, p.111b; see also Zohar II, 120a). (More about the deeper mysteries of the Torah is presented below, Chapter 10.)

Furthermore, Jacob blessed Judah, saying that "The staff shall not depart from Judah...until the coming of Shiloh...." (Genesis 49:10). As mentioned, Shiloh is Mashiach. It should not be surprising therefore to learn that the numerical value of SHILoH (שילה) is equivalent to that of MoSheH (משה), 345. The *Zohar* thus teaches explicitly that Moshe *is* the Mashiach (Zohar I, 25b).

Moshe is also the paradigm of true leadership, perhaps in an even deeper sense than King David. Moshe demonstrated total self-sacrifice. When the Jews made the golden calf, God wanted to destroy them on account of their idolatry. Moshe said to God (Exodus 32:32), "If You do not forgive *them*, then You will have to destroy *me* as well!" In addition, he was a leader for *every single* person. As awesome a figure as he was, able to remain in Heaven without food and drink for forty consecutive days on three successive occasions, he nevertheless made himself available to every person who sought his counsel (see Rashi, Numbers 27:16-18).

He even tried to reach out to the Mixed Multitude, to bring them under the yoke of God, advising and directing them on the proper path for each person to follow acccording to his own ability. This is true leadership, worthy of the Mashiach.

*

But what does all this mean? How can there be a Mashiach ben Yosef, a Mashiach ben David *and* Moshe who is considered the Mashiach himself? The *Zohar*'s teaching (I, 25b) based on the verse about Shiloh, actually provides the answer.

"The staff shall not depart from Judah" — this is Mashiach ben David.

"Nor the scepter from between his feet" — this is Mashiach ben Yosef.

"Until the coming of Shiloh" — this is Moshe.

Actually, the two Mashiachs will each represent a separate idea with a specific mission, as will Moshe. Kabbalistically, the world is based on a "three-column" system: right, left and center. (This will be discussed at length below in Part V; see also Appendix B). For the moment, we shall portray these three columns as Chesed (Lovingkindness) on the right, Gevurah (Judgment) on the left, and Tiferet (Beauty) in the middle. The idea of these "three" is that both Chesed and Gevurah are absolute necessities in life. One always wishes to move forward in life (represented by Chesed) but restraint (i.e. Judgment) is necessary. Restraint is a crucial component in life, but can inhibit one's growth. Thus, a conflict arises. One should strive for the perfect balance between the two: Tiferet. This is true beauty — when one sees a perfect merging and balance between two opposites.

The "three columns" are also represented by the three Patriarchs: Abraham, Isaac and Jacob. Abraham was known for his acts of kindness. Isaac represents judgment, for he was ready to make the ultimate sacrifice to God — his own life. Jacob blended the qualities of both his forebears, and thereby was able to father the Jewish Nation and initiate the inception of Mashiach. This is because he harnessed his forebears' dissimilar qualities. It is therefore taught (*Likutey Moharan* II, 83), "Mashiach is inclusive [of all the characteristics] of the Patriarchs."

Mashiach ben Yosef represents the "left column" of Judgment. His reign is therefore marked by battle, in order to vanquish the Jews' enemies. Mashiach ben David's reign will be a peaceful one. As such, he represents the "right column," where Chesed is revealed. But it is Moshe — only Moshe — who is able to combine the two concepts together in a perfect blend. Moshe is the innermost personification of Tiferet (cf. *Etz Chaim* 32:1; *Zohar* II, 120a). Moshe thus personifies both the qualities of the Patriarchs (the beginnings of the Jewish Nation) and those of the Redeemers of Israel (the Mashiachs).

Moshe is the Mashiach whose contribution will be the spread of the knowledge of Godliness, through the Torah that he already revealed — and through that broader knowledge of Torah which he will reveal in the Future. He will be accompanied by the two Mashiachs who will inspire humanity with the divine attributes of Chesed and Gevurah to bring the world to perfection.

This leaves us with one more paradox to analyze: It is taught that King David himself will be the Mashiach (*Zohar* I, 82b).

*

King David

In the Kabbalah, we find that all the higher Sefirot align in order to bring *shefa,* spiritual energy or bounty, to Malkhut, the lowest sefirah (see below, Chapter 18; see also Appendix B). All spiritual energy must be channeled into Malkhut which in turn transmits it to the lower worlds. King David was also able to receive this energy and transmit it to his kingdom. For this reason, he is considered the paradigm of Jewish leadership, for he negated himself totally for the benefit of his subjects.

The idea of leadership is to project competence and strength — not mastery — amongst one's followers. This was King David's uniqueness. He was at once a fiery leader who would charge forth in battle, and a humble man who would stand meekly before his rabbis and his subjects (see *Berakhot* 3b-4a). As the personification of Malkhut, King David will be the one to lead the Jews as a nation in the Future.

In fact, King David is "the poor one, riding on a donkey." That is, King David always felt himself a poor, defenseless person, pouring out his troubled heart to God, seeking guidance and help for himself and his subjects. Thus, "poor" actually refers to humility, a major trait of both King David and the Mashiach (*Likutey Halakhot, Minchah* 7:41).

But isn't this becoming too complicated? Isn't Mashiach an individual? Yet, we already have two Mashiachs and Moshe. Is there room for another leader?

*

Based on the prophet Ezekiel's Vision of the Chariot and Throne (Ezekiel 1), the Midrash describes God's Throne of Glory as having "four legs," with four angelic creatures attached to each leg to "carry" it (*Pirkey Rebbi Eliezer* 4). Kabbalistically, these four legs correspond to the four sefirot of Chesed, Gevurah, Tiferet and Malkhut, which play a major role in revealing Godliness in the world. We have seen that the first three correspond to Moshe and the two Mashiachs. King David corresponds to the fourth "leg," to Malkhut (*Zohar* II, 107a). It is through these four attributes that Godliness can be "carried and conveyed" to this world. For God's Holy Name, the Tetragrammaton, consists of four letters, *YHVH*. The four concepts of Mashiach correspond to the revelation of the four attributes of Godliness that emanate from these four letters.

As we have seen, the two Mashiachs — ben David and ben Yosef — will use justice and righteousness respectively to battle and overcome evil, in order to bring everyone to recognize God. Moshe personifies the Torah. He was the one who was able to bring it forth into the world. But what is King David's quality?

MaShiaCH is etymologically related to the word *MaSiaCH*, which means "to speak" or "to cause to speak." Throughout his life, King David put all his strength into speech — singing and praying to God. No matter what happened, his first recourse was prayer. "A psalm of David: I will sing of love and justice; to You, O God, I will sing" (Psalms 101:1). What did David mean? The Talmud teaches (*Berakhot* 60b), "David said: Whether You show me love (kindness) or justice (suffering), I will sing to You!" King

David thus personifies prayer and song to God. Prayer to God in itself denotes a recognition of God as Sovereign of the universe. As this is the goal of the Mashiach, this quality of King David is what will be revealed in the Future. The verse thus states (Isaiah 56:7), "For My house will be a house of prayer for all the nations."

Many of the prophets also describe the Future as an era of prayer and song to God. "Sing to God a new song for He has wrought wonders..." (Psalms 98:1). "And you will sing praises of the Lord" (Joel 2:26). "...Sing with gladness for Jacob, call out on the hilltops of the nations, announce, praise and say, 'God, save Your nation, the remnant of Israel.' I will gather them..." (Jeremiah 31:7). Since King David exemplifies the highest level of speech (*masiach*), namely, prayer, he is also known as the Mashiach. (The "Song of the Future," which is alluded to here, will be discussed below, Part III.).

*

So, who is Mashiach?

Thus far, we have seen that Mashiach is Moshe, King David, Mashiach ben Yosef and Mashiach ben David. But who is he really? From all that we have seen about the identity of Mashiach, whenever Mashiach is mentioned throughout Torah literature, he is *always* spoken of as a single person, one individual who will conquer the world and bring us all to recognize and serve God. Then who — or what — is Mashiach?

The answer to "Who?" is something we will only know when he comes. At the present time, we have absolutely no idea of who he is or will be. The answer to "What?" is that the Mashiach ben David and Mashiach ben Yosef personify the *ideals* with which Mashiach will conquer the world — justice and righteousness. Moshe Rabeinu and King David personify the *qualities* that Mashiach will reveal in the world — Torah and prayer (see *Likutey Halakhot, Rosh Chodesh* 5:2).

Going back to the question of "Who?" again, it is clear that Mashiach is an extremely complex character. From the few teachings mentioned in this chapter — and they will be developed later on — let us now tentatively piece together a composite picture of who Mashiach will be:

1) Mashiach will be a human being, born of man and woman.

2) Mashiach is a very righteous person and is present in every generation.

3) Mashiach will embody the highest standard of morality.

4) Mashiach will be the king of the entire world, accepted by both Jew and gentile alike. His power will stem from his awesome level of fear of God that will radiate a "sweet fragrance" to draw the people to him.

5) As chief arbiter of justice, Mashiach will have an acute "sense of smell" — to ascertain truth and falsehood.

6) Mashiach will have a very keen ability to advise each and every person how to rectify and improve his/her life, each according to his/her individual abilities.

7) Mashiach will disseminate faith in God. At the same time, he will battle the forces of evil and destroy idolatry, thereby introducing throughout the world a spiritual way of life.

8) Mashiach will spread the knowledge of Torah on a much deeper level than can be grasped today.

9) Mashiach will reveal Chesed. Everyone will enjoy good health and abundant wealth.

10) Mashiach will reveal the awesome power of song and prayer and will spread their use as *the* means of communication with God.

*

From darkness, light!

We have introduced here several major concepts regarding Mashiach. But perhaps the most important one is "we have absolutely no idea who he is." Too often, we form an idea and maintain it, thinking that we are on the right track So, we might think we know "who" or "what" Mashiach is — or should be. Yes, we have proof to support our way of thinking. But is it the truth? The absolute truth?

This is especially true in our era, when Mashiach is so very near. The fervor of messianism fills the air — and rightfully so — for as we have seen, Mashiach is present in each generation. People of all walks of life and all persuasions *think* that they have the answer. Still, people hear what they want to hear, see what they want to see. Yet, if Rabbi Akiva and many leading tzaddikim throughout the ages could err about "Who is Mashiach?" — what chance do we really have of not making a similar mistake? (see above, Chapter 3).

Then who are we to look for? We must first and foremost accept our limitations. In this way, we can open our minds and willingly look about for *all* possibilities. This does not mean, God forbid, that we ought to foolishly accept something false as a messianic alternative. But at least we do have guidelines (several of which are listed above) through which to protect ourselves from error.

One of the most interesting legends about Mashiach is that he was born on Tishah b'Av, the day of the destruction of the Holy Temple and the beginning of the exile (*Eikhah Rabbah* 1:51). In fact, Mashiach could not have been born before the destruction, for of what use is a redeemer when everything seems right? However, on the very day of the destruction, at the moment when everything seemed lost, the ray of hope that redemption is nigh was already revealed.

Rabbi Menachem Mendel of Kotzk used to say, "I could never accept a God that I understand!" God doesn't have to fit into any of our "pictures" of Him. He is so far beyond our comprehension that it's impossible even to try to imagine what He is thinking or doing! Even the greatness of the tzaddikim we've heard and read about stand far beyond our ability to gauge (see *Likutey Moharan* II, 52). How much more so is this true of Mashiach.

Many times in life we cling to a certain belief, hoping that we can build and rebuild our lives around the things with which we are most familiar. After all, familiarity is what we rely upon to form our opinions. But who is to say that this is the way our lives really should be? Is there nothing more? Have we truly explored *all* the possibilities available to us? We could be staring Mashiach straight in the eye and it might never occur to us that it is he!

Sometimes we require a total overhaul of our way of thinking to be able to see what we *really* should be doing, where we *really* should be heading. This can only be accomplished when faced with a total "destruction" of our "self-made temples" — i.e. a willingness to accept that former assumptions might have been in error. We can then open our minds and hearts to examine a completely new approach in life in order to fully recognize God and serve Him properly.

Mashiach was prepared even before the Creation to set us on the right spiritual path that will bring each of us closer to God. By incorporating into our consciousness the concepts of Mashiach detailed above, we are ready to experience the lifestyle we will all be living then.

We can search for faith. We can search for spirituality. We can search for truth, righteousness and good deeds. And we can pray that we merit to see our intended goal — the Mashiach.

* * *

Part III

Mashiach:

What?

This section deals with the ideals that will prevail in the messianic era, and with the powers of the Mashiach, as described by the prophets. Since the prophecies are veiled, we will attempt to elucidate the ideas found in them in contemporary terms applicable to modern man.

5

What is Mashiach?

Or rather, what is the *mission* of Mashiach? What must Mashiach do in order to be the Mashiach? What must he accomplish to complete his mission? The Rambam (Maimonides) writes:

> If a king [i.e. leader] arises from the Davidic dynasty who is immersed in Torah and involved with mitzvot like David his ancestor — in accord with the Written and Oral Torah — and he leads the Jewish Nation to comply with the Torah and strengthen their observance of its laws, and fights God's battles... We may *assume* he is the Mashiach. If he does this successfully, and then builds the Holy Temple on its original site, and gathers all the dispersed Jews, then we may be *certain* that he is Mashiach. He will then perfect the entire world and bring all men to serve God in unity. It has thus been prophesied (Zefaniah 3:9), "I will then imbue all people with a pure tongue, that they may call in the Name of God, and all serve Him in one manner" (*Yad HaChazakah, Melakhim* 11:4).

Thus, in a nutshell, Mashiach's "mission impossible" is to "conquer" the entire world and place all of us under God's dominion. He must bring the entire world to recognize God and return to Him. His mission becomes a reality when he succeeds in building the Holy Temple and gathering the entire Jewish People to the Holy Land.

It's not as simple as it sounds — and it doesn't sound simple to begin with! The world population today is nearing six billion people and growing faster every day. How can one person undertake such a mission? In this and the following chapters, we will explore some of the qualities that the

Mashiach will need to fulfill this "mission impossible." We will also discuss these qualities as they are applicable to our daily lives.

*

Mashiach's weapons

In order to wage battle and win a war, an army must be armed with the proper weapons. Until the 20th century, most conflicts consisted of hand-to-hand combat along with heavy cannon. Then came armored tanks and submarines, followed by fighter jets. By the 1990s, high-tech weaponry became the favorite of "armchair generals," for simply by pushing a few buttons they can reach targets thousands of miles away in a matter of minutes. Rebbe Nachman once commented on man's penchant for advanced armories: "It is not to man's credit to invent weapons that can destroy thousands of lives in an instant. Is there a greater foolishness than this?!" (*Tzaddik* #546). Yet, Mashiach has to wage war and conquer the entire planet — which requires weapons. If Mashiach is so brilliant that he won't resort to the foolishness of war, what will these weapons be?

When discussing "Who is Mashiach," some examples of true leadership given were Moshe Rabeinu and King David. By focusing on their accomplishments, we may be able to identify several parallel or complementary qualities that Mashiach must possess. Let us review some of the qualities of Moshe and David, so that we may better understand the mission of Mashiach, and how Mashiach will be able to implement that mission.

— Humility and awe of God are synonymous (cf. *Avodah Zarah* 20b). Mashiach's power will be revealed through his great fear of God and utter humility. The same attributes are found in Moshe and King David.

— Mashiach will promulgate faith in God and battle idolatry. Moshe visited the Jews in Egypt who were downtrodden and subdued, broken by their bondage. Yet, when he revealed himself as their redeemer, they believed in him and turned to God. King David similarly instilled faith in his subjects, as is seen in the Books of Samuel, Chronicles and Kings.

What is Mashiach? / 41

- Moshe received the Torah from God and brought it down to a level at which each individual could relate to it. Whenever the Jews sinned, Moshe prayed to God on their behalf. The Talmud contains many references to King David's Torah scholarship and his ability to relate to each individual. In addition, his Book of Psalms consists of heartfelt prayers that apply to every single person. (However, as individuals, Moshe is seen as the paradigm of Torah while King David is the paradigm of prayer.) Mashiach will disseminate the knowledge of Torah in global proportions, and will reveal the awesome power of prayer. He will make known the use of prayer as *the* means of communication with God.
- Moshe was the first redeemer of the Jews. King David was the first to establish them in their land by vanquishing their enemies and heralding an era of peace. Mashiach will restore the Jewish People to the Holy Land and herald an era of world peace.
- Moshe built the Sanctuary. King David built the foundations for the Holy Temple and saw to the funding of its erection. Mashiach will build the Third Temple.

*

Thus we see that Mashiach has quite a few weapons in his arsenal: Torah, prayer and good deeds, humility and righteousness. It is with these weapons that Mashiach will battle — and win. In fact, Rebbe Nachman said (Siach Sarfei Kodesh I-67), "Mashiach will conquer the entire world without firing a single shot!"

*

Prayer: the main weapon

Prayer and praise to God will be the staple of life in the Days of Mashiach, as is evident in the books of the Prophets (several verses will be quoted below during our discussions). Mashiach's mission is to conquer the entire world and direct his subjects to the service of God. Since the main service of God is prayer (cf. Taanit 2a), Mashiach must develop every person's sense of prayer, in order to fully bring forth its power.

The word for prayer in Hebrew is *Tefilah*. That our primary connection to God is through prayer is seen in this word. *TeFiLah* is etymologically related to the word *naFTuLey*, which means to join (Rashi, Genesis 30:8). Prayer, then, is *the* gate through which a person must enter in order to attach himself to Godliness. Therefore, the more one engages in prayer, the closer one can draw to God (Likutey Moharan II, 84).

*

"The breath of our nostrils, the Mashiach of God."

Lamentations 4:20

Our Sages teach that Mashiach's soul originates in an extremely lofty level. Its root is in Atik, Keter, and its life-force is drawn from the "nose of Arikh Anpin," the highest divine persona of Atzilut (Zohar II, 177a; see Appendix B). The nose has two apertures, one on the right and one on the left. These two apertures allude to the two Mashiachs (Likutey Moharan I, 16). This is why the concept of Mashiach is so closely associated with "the nose" — and hence his acute sense of smell. This is also why Mashiach will "*breathe* the fear of God," since his soul is rooted in the place of breathing, the nose. And this "nose," the source of life of the Mashiach, alludes to prayer. Rebbe Nachman thus taught:

> Mashiach's main weapon is prayer. Prayer is the "aspect" of *ChoTeM* (the nose). Isaiah thus said (Isaiah 48:9), "For My Name's sake I will defer My anger. For the sake of My praise [i.e. prayer] — *eChTaM lakh* — I will restrain for you."
>
> Through the "nose," Mashiach obtains his essential vitality. All the wars he will wage and all the conquests he will make shall emanate from there [i.e. "the nose" — prayer], as in (Isaiah 11:3), "He shall breathe the fear of God" (*Likutey Moharan* I, 2:2; see also below, pp.61-62).

Thus, prayer is represented by the nose. And the nose is breathing, life itself.

As seen from the Book of Psalms, King David built his kingdom with the power of prayer. Whatever he sought — physical or financial needs, victory over his enemies or, most importantly, devotion to God — he poured out his heart in praise and in prayer. This is why his kingdom ascended; for prayer is Malkhut (Kingship). Developing prayer as he did, the Jewish kingdom flourished. Conversely, the weakening of prayer heralded the descent of the Jewish kingdom. Today, in the current exile, the Kingdom of God has very little standing. This is because prayer is neglected, as our Sages teach, "Prayer stands at the very heights of the universe, but is very neglected" (Berakhot 6b, Rashi, s.v. devarim; see below, Part IV). When prayer is elevated to its rightful position, the kingdom of Mashiach, the Malkhut of God, will be revealed (Likutey Halakhot, Rosh Chodesh 5:2).

In addition, Mashiach is described as "poor, riding a donkey" (see Chapters 3-4), which alludes to his humility. Nowhere is humility more evident than when a person turns to God. By praying, a person acknowledges his own inadequacies; to implement his intentions, he accepts that he must defer to and depend upon a Power greater than himself — God. Thus, prayer symbolizes humility, an important trait of the Mashiach (see Likutey Halakhot, Minchah 7:40). This is why prayer is so essential to Mashiach's character.

Because prayer is bound up conceptually with Mashiach, and Mashiach can come at any moment, prayer — as a messianic manifestation — should be a major factor in our daily lives. Indeed it is, for each person has a "little bit of Mashiach in him" (Likutey Moharan I, 78). We are thus commanded to pray thrice daily, aside from additional prayers (e.g. Psalms, *Tikkun Chatzot* ["The Midnight Lament"]) that many recite. Thus, involving oneself in prayer to the point where one can actually feel one's heart pouring out before God is a messianic experience which one can taste even now!

*

To summarize the above concepts: first of all, there is "the nose," which is related to prayer and the Mashiach. Thus, the very essence of Mashiach is prayer. Each person utilizes some tool or "weapon" to which he has a close affinity in accomplishing his goals. Mashiach's main weapon, with which he will conquer the world, will be prayer.

The nose is the organ of breathing, which a person must do constantly in order to maintain life. The greater the physical effort one expends in one's work, the more difficult the breathing becomes — and the more one becomes conscious of one's breathing efforts. This concept also applies to every person's prayers. In order to create a connection with God, each person must pray. Prayer then becomes his source of life. Without prayer, he only exists, but does not *live* a full life (see Likutey Moharan I, 9:1). And, just as breathing sustains each person, whether one is conscious of it or not, so too, Mashiach, the world's ultimate rectification, has sustained the world from its inception, whether we are conscious of it or not (see above, Chapter 3).

Thus, the greater the effort a person puts into his daily prayers, the more a person practices solitary service of God, the more a person experiences God. (This practice is called *hitbodedut*, Rebbe Nachman's suggested path of offering one's private, secluded prayer in one's own words; see Outpouring of the Soul). And, since experiencing God is the goal of the messianic era, the more a person prays, the closer he comes to the messianic experience — to the idea of Mashiach.

*

But if everything is so good...?

After Mashiach comes, there will be only good health and abundant wealth. All one's material possessions will be beneficial. No-one will experience aches or pain, or suffer the pangs of hunger and want (see Ezekiel 36:29; Isaiah 51:19-23). This sounds very delightful. And it will be. But then, the question arises, "Why will prayer be of such importance then, if I'll have everything I need?"

As we know it today, prayer may seem to some a rite that was established centuries and millennia ago, without any relevance to contemporary life. This, however, is very far from the truth. If we examine the structure of the prayers, we see that there are several basic elements: praise and thanks to God, and requests. And each of these elements itself includes several components.

Praise to God can mean several things. It means simply to praise God for Who He is, the Creator of all, acknowledging His exaltedness (as one would praise a great king). It also means that we glorify God as the Benefactor of all, thereby showing our appreciation for all that we have.

When we think of the myriad good moments of our lives, we take heed of the countless "little kindnesses" that we have seen, and these "little bits" add up to many, many reasons to be thankful to God.

Requests too are many-faceted. There are supplications for health and wealth, prayers for children, living quarters, parent-child relationships, school and education, vacation time, and so on. And there are spiritual requests: for Torah knowledge and understanding, to be able to perform mitzvot and acts of kindness, to give charity and to feel that special closeness to God.

Thus, prayer has many aspects which can apply at any time or place. But although in this world there are reasons to make requests for physical needs, in the Days of Mashiach these reasons will no longer exist. What will our prayers be then? The answer can be found in the Midrash (Vayikra Rabbah 9:7):

> In the Future, all sacrifices will be voided, save for the Thanksgiving offering. All prayers will be unnecessary except for those praising God. For it is written (Jeremiah 33:10-11), "In the Future will be heard... the sound of joy... the voice that says, 'Praise God'... when they bring the Thanksgiving offering in the House of God...."

Thus, the sound of joy and happiness, the desire and delight of all mankind, will be found in thanksgiving and praise of God. But this too begs an explanation and can be clarified by the following:

> The main joy and delight of the World to Come is in the [offering of] thanks and praise to God's Great and Holy Name and in the recognition of God. For through this, one comes closer to God. The more a person knows of God and recognizes Him, the closer he can come to God. This is the meaning of (Isaiah 11:9), "For the earth will be filled with the knowledge of God..." (*Likutey Moharan* II, 2:1).

If a person feels gratitude towards someone, the gratitude is manifested in his thanks. The deeper the gratitude, the greater the thanks. The same is true of one's awareness of nobility or royalty. The deeper the recognition, the greater the awe and praise one will offer.

In the future, man will lack nothing. Fear and suffering will be a thing of the past, for which man will be ever grateful to God. Lacking nothing, mankind will seek only spiritual knowledge. Therefore, even one's requests will be a kind of praise of God — because the greater one's perception of Godliness, the more one will want to praise and laud God and His glory. For a person will begin *at each moment* to attain ever greater levels of God-awareness. Since God is infinite, the totality of God-awareness that can be attained is endless. Therefore, with each new perception, appreciation of God and His greatness will grow. This will bring a person to pray spontaneously and willingly to God.

This is the idea of prayer that is so bound up with Mashiach. Since Mashiach will herald the era of total God-awareness, he will also herald the dawning of an age where prayer is the basic component of a person's day. This prayer will be offered in a house of prayer — God's House — the Holy Temple.

*

Prayer and the Holy Temple

It is Mashiach's job to build the Holy Temple. But, it is not only *his* job. Each of us has a responsibility to work towards building the Temple, and even if we are not capable of doing the job, we are never exempt from *trying* (cf. Avot 2:16). For in truth, we are the ones who err and sin, and therefore we are the ones who need exoneration. If we were all perfect, we wouldn't need a Mashiach. The Talmud thus teaches that the leader's position and his level of importance depend on the level of his people (see Berakhot 32a).

We need the Mashiach — yet he needs us too. Each person's inner "spark of Mashiach" is waiting to be ignited. With our prayers we are contributing to Mashiach's "armory" to conquer the world and bring it to recognize God's dominion. We are contributing directly to the coming of Mashiach — to good health, financial security, world peace and heightened awareness of God.

And, interestingly, the more we pray, the greater our effort, the more Mashiach will be able to repay us for our efforts. For (Hagai 2:9), "The glory of the latter house (i.e. the Third Temple) will be greater than that of the former..." The first two Temples were houses of prayer for the Jews only, while the Third Temple will be a house of prayer for all nations. For then, through our prayers, God's glory will be revealed to everyone, not only to those who engaged in prayer to Him. This will result in an even greater glorification of God, which in turn will result in an even greater revelation of Godliness, so that our awareness of God will become even more heightened! (see *Likutey Moharan* I, 10:2-3).

When we view the building of the Holy Temple as one of Mashiach's obligations, we see that each person, through his prayers, has a portion in that Holy Temple that Mashiach will build. The level of messianic perception that a person will experience will be directly proportionate to the quantity and the quality of the "building blocks" he or she provided through his or her prayers. In a less revealed way, the effort one puts into prayer now also brings a person closer to God, even prior to the coming of the Mashiach. And ultimately, when the time is ripe and Mashiach is revealed, all the efforts one has placed in one's prayers will be revealed through the Holy Temple — which Mashiach will build from all the prayers of mankind. Figuratively speaking, each stone will have its own "plaque," "*donated by...*" through the efforts of each person's prayers.

* * *

6

Building the Third Temple

One can draw close to God through prayer. But how close? Will it be a lasting relationship or just that of an acquaintance? One measure of the closeness of a friendship is the accessibility of the friend's dwelling. God wants His house to be built so that all mankind can "visit" Him and have access to Him. His dwelling is the Holy Temple. One who feels close to God will be sure to "visit" Him continually. This is why God's House, i.e. the Holy Temple, will be called "A house of prayer for all the nations" (Isaiah 56:7) — so that all may make that connection with Him.

In this chapter we will discuss the relevance of the Holy Temple and the significance of the sacrifices. Also discussed is how everyone has his own individual Holy Temple — conceptually his intellect. Since the Temple represents the focal point of service to God, a place where all peoples will gather to serve Him, we will also present a discussion about the Ingathering of the Exiles (which will be elaborated upon in Part VI).

*

The first dwelling place of God was the Sanctuary in the desert built by Moshe (Exodus 39-40). The second was the Holy Temple in Jerusalem. Though built by King Solomon, the foundation work and the funding were provided by King David. Thus, the work to make a dwelling place for God was already begun by the [aspect of] Mashiach. Since Mashiach exemplifies prayer, we must examine how prayer fits in with the other messianic concepts, such as the Holy Temple.

One of the fundamental aspects of Mashiach's mission is to build the

Holy Temple. One simple reason is that the Temple will be the ultimate gathering place for people to relate directly to God. On a deeper level, it is the prayers themselves that are the building blocks of the Holy Temple. It is the Jewish People's yearning and praying throughout the ages to see the Holy Temple rebuilt that will reveal Mashiach to us.

*

The Sanctuary

"And Moshe raised up the Sanctuary."

Exodus 40:18

When the Jews made the golden calf, Moshe prayed for forgiveness. God's reply was to command Moshe to build the Sanctuary (see Rashi, Exodus 31:18). Thus, the Sanctuary was a result of Moshe's prayers. But it wasn't only Moshe who prayed. The Jews also repented for their sin. Therefore, it was the combined prayers of Moshe and the Jews that actually built the Sanctuary (see Likutey Halakhot, Nachlot 4:8).

The Sanctuary consisted of many items. It had furniture and other objects: the Ark of the Covenant, the Cherubim, the Menorah, the Table, the Incense Altar, etc. These items had several accessories: poles, forks, spoons, oil, the showbread, spices for the incense offering, and so on. There were clasps, boards, bars, pillars, pegs and sockets and several types of animal-skin coverings. The Sanctuary was built by all of Israel. Some contributed precious jewels, gold, silver or copper. Some contributed wood, other building materials, oil, etc. Others donated their services as craftsmen, weavers, etc. But everyone was somehow involved.

Thus it was that several people donated their resources or their efforts to one beam, carving and forming it until it was ready for use in the Sanctuary. Others may have contributed to a pillar, others to a peg or a spoon, still others to the Ark, and so on. This is why the Torah details the work of each item twice, the first time with the commandment to build, the second time as it was built. This shows us the importance of each and every person's contribution. It also suggests that, if it were not a joint effort, it could not have been built. The Sanctuary in Hebrew is called miShKaN, from the root word ShaKheN, meaning neighbor (see Likutey Halakhot, Arvit 4:34). This is because one person could not have done everything. It had to be a communal effort.

Still, no-one was able to *erect* the Mishkan, the Sanctuary. As much as they tried, they could not assemble the Sanctuary. Only Moshe was able to assemble it, which he did single-handedly! And thus the Torah details the effort Moshe made in building it (Exodus 39:33-40:33). "The Mishkan was brought to Moshe...." detailing each item brought to him. Then, in the next chapter, the Torah describes Moshe assembling the Sanctuary and bringing the sacrifices.

*

And the obvious question is, "Why?" Why, in spite of all the expense, hard work and effort, were the Jews unable to erect the Sanctuary? They had made a golden calf and repented. As proof that their repentance was accepted, God commanded them to build a Sanctuary that "He may dwell amongst them." Yet, when they finished their work related to building that Sanctuary, the components lay scattered about, unable to serve any purpose, until Moshe assembled the Sanctuary. Why?

The reason goes far back in history:

Adam was the embodiment of all the souls of humanity. As the First Man, he was able to have a perfect relationship with God. Therefore, all his descendants, each "a part of Adam's soul," are a part of that greater whole — the perfect relationship with God. Thus, every person, anyone who has ever lived, has a purpose in his life. And each person must try his best to fulfill his mission, which is to develop his own relationship with God. But Adam sinned, plunging mankind into imperfection. He repented, but was not able to rectify his error on his own. For this purpose, Abraham and other future tzaddikim had to add their merit to that of Adam's repentance (see above, Chapter 3; below, Parts V-VI).

When the Jews accepted the Torah at Sinai, they attained a state of perfection (Shabbat 146a). They were able to experience an open revelation of Godliness. However, when they made the golden calf they shattered this perfection. They needed Moshe, a tzaddik, someone who was unblemished, to rectify their sin.

The purpose of the Jews' efforts in building the Sanctuary was to restore their "shattered vessel" to a state of perfection. When the Sanctuary was built, God was to reveal Himself through His Divine Presence. But something was lacking for the Mishkan to be completed. All the pieces were there, but they could not be put together. The pieces had to be brought to Moshe (an unblemished tzaddik), to put every piece in its proper place. Only then was the Sanctuary able to be assembled. This is because only Moshe (conceptually the Mashiach; as above, Part II) knows the proper location for each piece and is capable of putting everything in its rightful place.

It is for this reason that one's prayers should be offered to God by binding oneself to the tzaddikim of the generation. Since the tzaddikim represent Moshe-Mashiach (see Chapter 4), they are the ones who know how to direct our prayers towards their proper objective. This is alluded to in our Sages' statement (Berakhot 28b), "Everyone should pray towards the Holy Temple." That is, everyone should pray with the intent of building the Holy Temple with his prayers. Since neither the Sanctuary nor the Holy Temple can be built by common men — it must be built by the great tzaddikim — one's prayers should be directed through the tzaddikim (Likutey Moharan I, 2:6). (This does not mean to pray to the tzaddikim, God forbid, for that is idolatry. It does mean to pray in accordance with the guidance of the tzaddikim.) Then one's prayers, one manifestation of Mashiach, have a chance of reaching their mark.

*

Daat — the Holy Temple

> "Whoever has Daat, knowledge, it is as if the Holy Temple was built in his days."
>
> Berakhot 33a

It is Mashiach's responsibility to build the Holy Temple, which is constructed by the prayers of mankind. However, the Temple will be used not only for prayer but also for sacrifices upon the altar. This is a major purpose of the Holy Temple. So, we may ask, is the building of the Third Temple, for which we long so much, intended just to accommodate the offering of some sacrifices? There must be more to this than meets the eye. What, in fact, *is* the Temple, and what do the sacrifices represent?

The messianic era will herald the dawning of an age of great intellectual progress, of knowledge of God. The technological advances of recent years are very great revelations of knowledge, but they lack endurance. Their built-in obsolescence indicates that there must be something beyond them, that there *is* a knowledge greater than all the advances which can be made by researchers and scientists. And there is: spirituality; Godliness.

We have seen (above, Chapter 4) that the world was established on a system of three columns. This is manifest in the three Patriarchs and in the three attributes of Chesed, Gevurah and Tiferet. When examining the array of the highest sefirot, the *Mochin* ("intellect powers"), we see that they are also arranged in three columns: Keter (Crown) in the middle, Chokhmah (Wisdom) on the right, and Binah (Understanding) on the left (see Appendix B).

In the Kabbalah, Keter is seen as ineffable because of its loftiness, and is often not referred to openly — which in itself is an aspect of Mashiach, who is beyond description. Instead of Keter, we have the quasi-sefirah Daat (Knowledge). When referring to the Mochin, the Kabbalah thus generally mentions the three sefirot, Chokhmah, Binah and Daat (see Appendix B). Daat, the external manifestation of Keter, is thus a manifestation of the Mashiach.

As noted, the three Mochin are also arrayed in three columns: right, left and center. Chokhmah is on the "right side" and parallels the wisdom that one possesses, i.e. what the person has studied and knows. Binah is on the "left" and corresponds to the use of that wisdom in building one's life. Daat is the final application of one's learning — a complete building that is functional. Daat is the "center column" — the blend of the wisdom that one has acquired with the ability to use it logically, in order to arrive at responsible and rewarding conclusions.

When analyzing our Sages' statement about Daat being synonymous with the Holy Temple, we can better understand what the building of the Holy Temple means on several levels. The first is the physical structure. It will contain an altar upon which to offer the various sacrifices. But this Holy Temple will also represent the building of one's *mind* — to a level of Daat and purity. This will be a level at which one is capable of receiving spiritual influx and developing an expanded awareness of God. But, developing this awareness does not come easily. Sacrifices must be made.

*

The Sacrifices

> *"For on that day...a fountain shall flow from the House of God..."*
> Joel 4:18

What does it mean to offer a sacrifice in the Holy Temple, and what is its relevance to us? In Hebrew, a sacrifice is called *korban*. Its purpose is to be an offering to God — whether a thanksgiving offering or a sin or burnt offering. The ARI explains that a human being is the highest form of life. When he sins, he loses his human advantage and descends to the level of an animal. Therefore, in his repentance, he brings an animal for a sacrifice, indicating that he wishes to "sacrifice" his base, animalistic tendencies and return to his former level, that of a human being. The sinner comes to the House of God and offers his animal upon the altar. By taking a lower form of life and offering it to God, one elevates the lowest levels to the highest levels. Conversely, he is drawing God, as it were, from His lofty residence, and revealing His presence even on the lowest levels. This binds all the worlds together — the lowly material world with the spiritual universes — bringing forth a revelation of Godliness that was hitherto unrecognized (see Pri Etz Chaim, Shaar HaTefilah 5; see also Appendix B on the levels of the universes).

We can now take this further. The word *KoRBan* (קרבן) stems from the word *KaReV* (קרב) — to draw near. (The b and v are represented by the same letter in Hebrew: ב, *bet, vet*.) Thus, a sacrifice which a person makes for the sake of God is the act which draws him near to God. When bringing a sacrifice, neither the *kohen* (priest) nor the animal are allowed to have a blemish (Leviticus 21:18, 22:20). Therefore, the act of bringing a sacrifice indicates that, in serving God, a person should strive to attain perfection. The verse which speaks about the thanksgiving offering (Leviticus 7:11) calls it *zevach hashlamim* ("peace offering"). *ShaLeM* means complete or perfect, as well as *ShaLoM*, peace. Thus, bringing the thanksgiving offering is akin to drawing near to God by attaining perfection. For the *korban* brings all the worlds to their perfection. This in turn brings peace, the peace that will reign in the Days of Mashiach (*Likutey Moharan* I, 14:8). Another reason that this brings peace is because each person is a microcosm of the universe. Since prayer brings the worlds together, prayer will bring each person — each world — together.

The reason why the Temple is the necessary location for the sacrifices which draw a person near to God is that the Holy Temple corresponds to Daat, knowledge of God. This knowledge, which will be revealed to all in the Future, is the "fountain of wisdom" which will continuously flow from the Holy Temple, i.e. the expanded intellect. The Prophet Joel foresaw an era in which this knowledge will be available for all, for then people will have risen above their animalistic instincts, which bar the way to their understanding of the Divine.

We see then that a person's mind is the Holy Temple. Or, at least, it could be. By controlling one's baser instincts and seeing to it that the intellect — not the emotions — is in charge, he is sacrificing "an animal" in his own Holy Temple. This person, even today, merits a revelation of Godliness similar to the revelation of Godliness that will be available in the Days of the Mashiach.

(Several other concepts of the Holy Temple and perfection, and how they are tied together with the concept of awe of God, another aspect of the Mashiach, will be discussed in the following chapters.)

*

Man-made or built by Heaven?

Rambam writes that Mashiach will build the Holy Temple (*Yad HaChazakah, Melakhim* 11:4). Rashi maintains that the Third Temple will be built by God Himself (Rashi, Exodus 15:17; Rashi is supported by the *Tikkuney Zohar* #8, p.24a). How can these differing views be resolved?

In certain ways, the answer depends upon the differing opinions in the Talmud (*Berakhot* 34b) regarding life in Mashiach's time. Will it be miraculous? Or will it be an extension of life as we know it now — but without hatred and jealousies, without illness and poverty?

Numerous sources that speak about the Days of Mashiach indicate that both views are valid. That is, when Mashiach is fully revealed to all and is accepted as the king of the world, then everything in life will be miraculous. However, we are currently in the concluding centuries of the sixth millennium. The transition from our daily lives to the actual revelation and reign of Mashiach will therefore progress as life does now — albeit with continual advances in the standard of living — in areas of health, comfort, aging and so on.

As we have seen, the concept of Mashiach is that of Daat, greater knowledge and awareness of God. In this sense, we can already see the rebuilding of the Temple through Mashiach. In our current age, with its all consuming materialism, there is a very noticeable arousal of spirituality. The paradoxes of life are demanding answers to questions that people never would have thought of asking before. Thus, Daat *is* being built. Every person's individual Holy Temple is slowly — and surely — being put together, to become a natural dwelling place for spirituality.

> "**Moshkheini acharekha narutzah** — *Draw me to You, then we will run."*
>
> Songs 1:4

The consonants of the word *MiShKaN*, Sanctuary, are the same as *MoShKheiNi*, which means "draw me." A person's deep, inner desire is to be drawn to spirituality, to God (*Likutey Halakhot, Eiruvei Techumin* 5:20; see below, Chapter 20). But he needs the tools with which to develop this desire to its fullest potential. Prayer is that tool. As we have seen, prayer,

Mashiach and the Holy Temple are conceptually one. Through prayer, one feels *moshkheini*, the draw of spirituality. That is, one feels one's own individual "Holy Temple" being built. *MiShKaN* also resembles the word *SheKhiNah*, i.e. God's Divine Presence. Building one's mind to receive God's Divine Presence is building the Sanctuary or Temple.

Therefore, when we ask if the Temple will be man-made or built by Heaven, we find that both opinions are correct. According to Rambam, since Mashiach's power — the power of prayer — is already prevalent in the world, each person is currently building his individual Holy Temple. Rashi's opinion will be borne out when all mankind is ready for Mashiach. Then the building of the Holy Temple will be done by God Himself — a building that will never be destroyed again.

*

The Ingathering of the Exiles

"God builds Jerusalem; He ingathers the scattered of Israel."
Psalms 147:2

Complementing the building of the Holy Temple, Mashiach must also gather the exiled Jewish Nation to the Holy Land. It therefore seems that this important mission must be bound up with the Holy Temple. And it is — very much so.

Exile is not only a physical condition. It is also a state of mind. The verse states (Isaiah 5:13; see *Sanhedrin* 92a), "My nation has gone into exile because it has no knowledge." By partaking of the Tree of Knowledge, Adam fell from his level of true knowledge. His intellect — and that of all mankind, his descendants — now contains a mixture of good and evil. This fall from true knowledge caused Adam's exile from the Garden of Eden. And so it is today. Mankind's descent from the pursuit of true knowledge, of spirituality, is the primary reason for all exiles.

Today, exile is manifest in all aspects of life. For example, people travel far and wide looking for business opportunities. People travel all over looking for a bargain. People migrate, thinking that perhaps there's a better life awaiting them somewhere else.... These are all forms of exile.

Exile also does not necessarily mean a physical uprooting from one's homeland. Exile means an uprooting from one's accustomed environment, where the exiled person finds himself "forced" to adapt to new surroundings. Jewish culture, mandated by God at Sinai, is a self-contained culture that encompasses the life and lifestyle of a person from cradle to grave. Unfortunately, the scattering of the Jewish Nation around the globe has brought it into contact with so many varying cultures that one may find it difficult to discern what is really Jewish and what is not. Nearly two thousand years of dispersion — Europe, the Mediterranean basin, the Middle East, the Far East, Australia and the Western Hemisphere — have introduced varying lifestyles into our nation's way of life, with each sub-group raising the banner of authentic Judaism. Thus, the exile is not as much a physical dispersion as it is a state of mind — an exile from Godliness which allows for the absorption of gentile cultures to appear as part of an "authentic" Jewish idea. This results in Jews pursuing a new-found way of life as if it were true Judaism (see Likutey Moharan I, 36:1).

This is the main suffering of the exile and the main decline of true knowledge. The Revelation at Sinai led to the conquest of the Holy Land, where the Holy Temple was built. This was God's House where He revealed Himself through His Divine Presence. The exile was caused by a decline in the search for spirituality. Jews became less committed and began searching the surrounding cultures for direction. This ultimately led to idolatry and the destruction of the Holy Temple. Thus, the exile was already taking place, even though the Jews were in their land and had a Temple of their own. Conversely, the end of the exile and the rebuilding of the Holy Temple will take place only when the Jews begin to search again for spirituality. How this will work is discussed below at length (Part VI).

We have seen that exile stems from a lack of Daat while the messianic concept is that of the building of Daat. The more intense one's search for spirituality, the greater is one's contribution to the revelation of Daat in the world. Since every person's search is for the common goal — Daat

— the search leads to the building of the Holy Temple, the manifestation of Daat. When a person seriously and earnestly strives towards his goal, then he will make great sacrifices to attain that goal. Therefore, the search for spirituality is in itself the force that will draw the entire Jewish People to their homeland, the Holy Land, where the Temple is being erected.

Interestingly, the Talmud teaches (Pesachim 87b), "God exiled the Jews only so that converts may join their ranks." This ties in nicely with our discussion. Though the Jews regressed in their spiritual endeavors, in the Days of Mashiach they will renew their search for spirituality. As they begin to search for the true Daat, this will cause a general surge in the search for spirituality that will inspire even their non-Jewish neighbors.

*

And then the prophecy will be fulfilled (Isaiah 2:2-3), "In the End of Days the mountain of God's House shall be established over all the other mountains and exalted above the hills; and all the nations shall come streaming to it. Nations will come and say, 'Come, let us go up to the Mountain of God, to the House of the God of Jacob; He will teach us His ways and we will walk in His paths.' For out of Zion shall go forth Torah and the Word of God from Jerusalem."

* * *

7

"And he will breathe the fear of God"

> *"Upon him [the Mashiach] will descend a spirit of God; a spirit of wisdom and understanding, a spirit of advice and strength, a spirit of knowledge and fear of God. And he will breathe the fear of God: he will not judge by what he sees or by what he hears. He will judge the poor righteously and the meek with equity. He will smite the wicked with the rod of his mouth, and with the spirit of his lips he will slay evildoers..."*
>
> Isaiah 11:2-4

As discussed above, Mashiach's main weapon will be prayer. With prayer he will vanquish his enemies and build a Holy Temple, a place where holiness and spirituality will reside so that everyone can experience God. But what is he fighting for? And against? Who are his enemies? Doesn't vanquishing enemies bring animosity? If so, how will he be willingly accepted as the leader of the people he conquers? For the answer, we must further study the idea of Mashiach as the aspect of "the nose" (see Chapter 5).

In this chapter, we will discuss the idea of Mashiach's breath with the fear of God and how his fear will influence people to draw near to God. His very being will exude a feeling of love and awe of God. Since serving God is accomplished by performing the mitzvot, Mashiach will be empowered to instill into mankind the desire to fulfill the mitzvot. We will also discuss Mashiach's unique power of the "nose" which will enable him to rebuke people in a positive matter, without having to impose his will upon them. And, since the nose corresponds to purity, as it is accustomed to savoring sweet smells and rejecting foul odors, through his acute sense of smell Mashiach will be able to introduce a morally pure way of life.

*

Mashiach will "breathe the fear of God," since his soul is rooted in the place of breathing, the nose. Through the "nose," Mashiach obtains all his essential vitality. Conversely, anger is also expressed by the nose, as in (Numbers 25:4), "His nose flared with anger." Thus, the deeds of Mashiach along with his prayers will restrain God's anger at its source — the nose. For that anger stems from a person's evil deeds. Prayer, i.e. repentance, supplication and the resulting recognition of God can help convert that anger into kindness and mercy.

Thus, "the nose" implies great kindness (i.e. Mashiach), and it also implies anger, which results in suffering. Mashiach's duty is to reveal God's greatness which will manifest itself in kindness, good health and blessings. This denotes a total negation of sin and wrongdoing. "When evil is done away with, there will also be no more anger" (Sifri 13:18). It is for this reason that Mashiach will "breathe the fear of God." For he will elevate the idea of fear from the fear of punishment to an exalted level of awe.

*

What is the "Fear of God?"

"Fear! — this is the gateway to Heaven!"
Zohar I, 7b; Likutey Moharan I, 14:12

Two basic qualities are involved in serving God: love and fear. Love is the positive characteristic that draws a person to his beloved. One who has love of God will be zealous when worshiping God. Fear, on the other hand, carries a negative connotation — as when one is afraid of punishment. Worshiping God out of fear for one's well-being could hardly be done with a full heart.

Luckily, this is not the fear of God that will be prevalent in the Days of Mashiach. That fear will be the awe and respect that is befitting true royalty and leadership. The awe of God that will be widespread then will automatically lead people away from evil and towards God. This will eliminate sin and lead to ever greater revelations of kindness.

Today, we live in a world where many fears exist. There is fear of poverty, ill-health, criminals, fear of the authorities, of running a red light, a bounced check and so on. Each of these fears is rooted in Gevurah, Judgment and Punishment; whether it be a fear of punishment itself or any other type of suffering which a person may deserve as a consequence of his deeds.

Mashiach will be a judge — the ultimate judge — and will rid the world of suffering. Fear will then be elevated to the awe of God, i.e. respect for God for What He is.

The crucial importance of such respect is expounded in the Talmud.

> "One who studies Torah without awe of Heaven is compared to one who has been given the keys to the inner storehouse, but not the keys to the outer gate. How can this person enter?" (Shabbat 31a).

Torah, God's Divine Knowledge through which we can come to know Him and grow close to Him, is sealed off from us if we lack awe and reverence for God. Torah learned without reverence becomes an academic and sterile subject which many people can master but never truly benefit from. Worse, without reverence, the Torah becomes a potion of death (Yoma 72b) — for the person then utilizes the divine to abandon God. This can be compared to a commoner using royal furnishings (e.g. government property) for personal use.

The *Zohar* therefore calls true awe "the gateway to Heaven." Awe is the awareness that God is near us and before us at all times. When one internalizes this idea, one begins to understand everything in life in terms of its divine implications. Instead of "a commoner making use of royal property," we begin linking everything mundane to the Divine. We become aware of, and attached to, God, constantly. This principle applies at all times during a person's life, so that one need not await the Days of Mashiach to feel and experience Godliness. All a person needs to do is to arouse his own sense of perception of God. Then he can experience this heightened awareness — just as we will in messianic times (but on a higher level).

Mashiach will "breathe the awe of God." Using prayer as his main "weapon," Mashiach will develop the concept of "the nose" to its fullest. Being the breath of our nostrils, he will help us direct our very life-force to search for God, all the while abandoning sin and drawing ourselves towards His mitzvot. In Mashiach's time, each person will be filled with "breath" that contains awe of God for, with each breath we draw in, we will attain a greater awareness of God, hence a growth of that awe. And this awe will permeate all levels of Creation, so that everyone will have the chance to return to God. Then great kindness — and love — will reign.

*

The mitzvot

Gevurah is the divine attribute associated with Judgment, which denotes restriction. In Kabbalistic terminology, restrictions and constrictions are known as *tzimtzumim*. Fear stems from Gevurah. A person might be afraid to "step out of line" for fear of retribution. As we have seen, however, there is a higher level of fear, that of revering and respecting God because of His awesomeness. One who has internalized this kind of awe will also never willingly "cross the line." But what is this "line?" It is the mitzvot of the Torah, the boundaries God set within which we should live our lives.

God is known as the *Ein Sof*, The Infinite One. The concept of infinity defies imagination, for no matter how great the human mind, it is finite. As such, one cannot even begin to perceive infinity. How then could a person ever hope to grasp any concept of God? He is far, far beyond man's intellect! But it was precisely for this reason that God gave us the Torah with its mitzvot.

The Torah is an extension of God's intellect, the "blueprint" He drew up to enable us to walk through life. The Torah contains 613 mitzvot. Each mitzvah is a conduit through which we can bind ourselves to God and come to know Him. Torah and mitzvot are constrictions through

"And he will breathe the fear of God" / 63

which the Infinite Light of God *can* be channeled down to us, finite human beings, in order to partake of spirituality (Likutey Moharan I, 30:3).

To live in accord with the dictates of the Torah is to accept the restrictions placed upon our lives by God. The Torah, as we see it now, constricts the light of Godliness. This enables us to focus upon Godliness and absorb it. At the same time, Torah has an opposite effect, for it opens up for us the Light of the Infinite One by providing the means through which to seek God. When Mashiach comes, everyone will serve God and live according to His dictates. The Torah will then "remove its cloak," some of the constrictions of Godliness, as a higher level of Torah is revealed — the *Torah of Atik* (explained below, Chapter 10). The Torah of Atik is the same Torah that we have today, but it will transcend its present constrictions. We will then be able to *perceive* more openly the Godliness that lies within Torah (Likutey Moharan I, 33:4).

Remembering that Mashiach corresponds to the nose, we can understand that his "breathing" will have a very positive effect upon mankind. The verse, "And he will breathe the fear of God," in Hebrew is, *"Vaharicho b'Yirat HaShem."* Our Sages teach that *B'YiRAT* (fear) (ביראת) is the *gematria* (numerical equivalent; see Appendix B) of 613 (תרי"ג). Thus, the breath that Mashiach will breathe will emanate from the Torah and its 613 mitzvot (Tikkuney Zohar, Introduction p.5b). This is (Genesis 1:2) "The spirit of God [that] hovered over the waters." The spirit is Mashiach and the waters are the Torah. Mashiach's spirit is embedded in the Torah and he will draw his breath, the awe of God, from it. With this spirit, he will be able to "breathe into others," filling them with a feeling of awe and respect for God (see Likutey Moharan I, 8:2).

*

One might think that there are too many mitzvot to fulfill, or perhaps that these mitzvot are too restrictive. But one should bear in mind that the mitzvot are God's commandments and are eternal, as is God Himself. Therefore, they must have purpose and definition even in today's world. Furthermore, everyone lives with restrictions. Civilization dictates its restrictions, high society has its own guidelines, capitalists, communists, democracies and dictatorships alike mandate their boundaries, even as do the criminal world and the animal kingdom.

Each person, no matter where, lives with restrictions. But none of the rules imposed by man upon his fellow has ever endured. "Civilization" is neither stable nor enduring — its foundations are established on sands that shift according to the whims of its leaders and power players who are in the position to impose their will upon others. Each nation keeps changing its "rulebook" to keep up with its "ideal" way of life. History, however, has shown us how all civilizations eventually crumbled. Whereas human restrictions are vulnerable to human sentiments, accepting the mitzvot of the Torah as divine restrictions make them more palatable and easier to observe.

By virtue of his ability to perform mitzvot, every person is able to advance the revelation of Godliness, even in today's world. Each mitzvah performed is an additional revelation of the Light of the Infinite One. (That is, each mitzvah is a constriction of God's Light and, having been performed, now radiates that spiritual light in this material world.) Every act of kindness or charity, each Shabbat observed or prayer offered, and likewise every mitzvah, has the power to arouse the awe of Heaven that Mashiach will eventually make widespread.

*

The Voice of Rebuke — building Jerusalem

We have seen how Mashiach represents Daat, and that the increase of this Daat will be a primary factor in bringing about the Ingathering of the Exiles. This too is an aspect of the nose, for Mashiach will exude "sweet-smelling fragrances" to attract his following. How will this work?

The soul is compared to "the nose." When speaking about what blessing to recite on sweet-smelling spices, our Sages teach (Berakhot 43b), "From where do we learn that we must recite a blessing on spices? The verse states (Psalms 150:6), 'Let every *neshamah*, every soul that breathes, bless God.' When does the *neshamah* (soul), rather than the body, benefit? With sweet fragrances." Another verse states (Genesis 2:7), "He breathed into his nostrils the breath of life (*nishmat chaim*)." The soul originally entered the material body through the nose. The nose and the soul are parallel concepts.

A person who covers himself with sweet fragrances smells attractive. Conversely, a person who fouls his body emits a rancid odor. The same is true of the soul. A person who performs good deeds radiates a sweet aroma. But one who commits sins pollutes his soul, causing a stench. Mashiach's job is to bring everyone back to God, even the worst sinner. In Rebbe Nachman's teachings, we find this concept of "soul-fragrances" connected with bringing others back to God. This entire discourse is found in *Likutey Moharan* II, 8. The following is taken from there:

> Rebuke is a very great mitzvah. But one who gives rebuke must be careful not to arouse a "bad smell." If something that is decaying is left untouched, it might not emit a foul odor. Once moved, however, it begins to give off a stink. Similarly, one who offers rebuke but doesn't know how to give it properly, can cause a "foul stench" to be given off from a person who has sinned. Then, not only won't the person be aroused to God, but the rebuke might drive him further away, for improper rebuke can weaken the soul and diminish its strength.
>
> When the Jews made the golden calf, Moshe rebuked them, but his rebuke was given in such a manner that it aroused in them a savory smell (*Shabbat* 88b). Because of this, they were able to repent and afterwards build the Sanctuary. Proper rebuke thus strengthens the soul by instilling awe of God in a person (a function of the nose, as above). Conversely, improper rebuke, or rebuke given by an unworthy person, weakens a person's soul even more and drives him further away. The rectification for one who has sinned and weakened his soul is the "Voice of Rebuke." This Voice is akin to (Isaiah 58:1), "Raise your voice *k'shophar*, like the shofar...."

Rebbe Nachman continues his discourse, connecting the Voice of Rebuke to the sense of smell and its ability to arouse a person to recognize God in a favorable manner.

> There is a garden where fragrant smells and fear of God bloom. For (Genesis 2:10), "The river flows from Eden and waters the Garden..." "River" represents the Voice of Rebuke as in (Psalms 93:3), "The rivers have lifted

their voice." This "Voice" which waters the garden (the sweet smells) stems from Eden, the source of the "Song of the Future" (Tikkuney Zohar #21, p.51b).

This Song is a "fourfold song," which God will use to arouse and awaken everyone when He renews the world in the Future. The "Voice of Rebuke" — K'ShoPhaR — is the acrostic of *Pashut, Kaful, Shilush, Ribu'a* (single, double, triple, fourfold). With this "Voice" the garden is watered and the sweet-smelling fragrances of the souls will be strengthened. Great kindness will then be revealed, as in (Proverbs 28:23), "He who rebukes another will afterwards find favor."

We see then that the Voice of Rebuke is rooted in Eden, which corresponds to Keter, the source of Mashiach's vitality (see Tikkuney Zohar 55, p.88a). At the level of Keter only kindness exists. Thus the rebuke given will reveal that kindness, causing people to draw near to Mashiach. Rebbe Nachman explains the idea of the "fourfold song" and the "Ten Types of Song." By way of introduction, the Book of Psalms is composed of Ten Types of Song which include every type of song in the world (Pesachim 117a). These Ten Types of Song correspond to the Ten Sefirot (Tikkuney Zohar #13), thus encompassing — and transcending — everything in Creation. This is why song strikes deeply into a person's soul, for it extends from Keter down to each person, on whichever level he may be. Thus, the Voice of Rebuke will draw people near to God through the power of song and joy. (Below, in Part VI, Chapter 28, the concept of song (the Ten Types, etc.) and joy will be discussed in greater detail.)

The fourfold Song of the Future contains all the Ten Types of Song and will be played on a 72-stringed instrument (Tikkuney Zohar #21, p.51b). The reason for this is that the "Fourfold Song" is rooted in the Tetragrammaton — Yod-Heh-Vav-Heh — God's Name of Four Letters. When writing this Holy Name Yod, Yod-Heh, Yod-Heh-Vav, Yod-Heh-Vav-Heh, returning back to the first letter each time to obtain a single, double, triple and fourfold Name, we obtain a total of 10 letters corresponding to the Ten Types of Song. Furthermore, adding the numerical equivalent of the sum of the letters yields a numerical value of 72 (see Appendix B). Seventy-two is the gematria of Chesed (חסד) and it is written (Psalms 89:3), "The world is built through Chesed." Thus, when one who knows how to give rebuke does so, he communicates this rebuke as the Song of the Future, arousing a sweet fragrance, revealing great kindness and strengthening the souls.

Mashiach will possess this "Voice of Rebuke" because MaShIaCh is like MaSIaCh, "one who speaks." Since Mashiach is bound together with all souls through his acute sense of smell (i.e. "the nose"), he will be able to rebuke everyone properly, to arouse awe within them and draw them closer to God. His voice will be the flowing "River" from Eden, from which emanate aromatic fragrances (i.e. *shemen MIShChah*; see above, Chapter 3), so that everyone will be drawn to the "savory smell" of Mashiach.

*

In an era wherein mankind has been victimized by the media, it is difficult to find a "Voice of Rebuke" that can be heard, let alone one that will be listened to. From early childhood, rebuke has become a tool to belittle another (deserving or otherwise). The media glorify abuse and slander, using it in any manner possible — news releases, investigative reporting or even entertainment (?!) — to promote their own objectives (generally the bottom line). Respect for others, rooted in the fear of God, is browbeaten. Thus, a voice of reason cannot easily make an impression on people who feel that only paths of folly are ultimately rewarding. Witness the anti-drug and anti-alcohol campaigns in which logic rarely makes a dent. But if one takes a careful look at society — despite the pressures to legalize drugs — one can see a serious and growing grass-roots movement to eradicate substance abuse. So too, given its propensity for survival, mankind is resurrecting its former ideals of respect for others and beginning to seek justice for victims, while searching for meaning and self-respect. (These attributes will be elaborated upon below, in Part IV).

It is this attribute of Mashiach, the power to reach out to everyone and make each person feel self-respect, that will gather in the exiles and subsequently build the Holy Temple. For just as the Holy Temple is built through prayer, it is also built by good deeds (*Likutey Halakhot, Hashkamat HaBoker* 1:4).

Mashiach will thus reach out to everyone — to each on his or her level — to arouse in them whatever good they possess. People will learn to concentrate on and develop their own individual good points, gradually improving themselves, their lot and their lives as a whole. This includes seeking the good points in others and relating to them, while overlooking their negative traits. The "good points" become the building blocks of the Holy Temple and cement friendships and relationships. Mashiach will then have the necessary "building blocks and cement" with which to erect the Holy Temple.

*

This helps clarify the concept of the building of Jerusalem, which takes place gradually as the exiles are gathered into the Holy Land. Our Sages teach that (Kiddushin 32b), "Fear is in the heart." One who accepts upon himself fear of God "builds" his heart by attuning it to Godliness. This person is on the road to perfection for (Zohar II, 79a; see Likutey Moharan I, 14:8), "Where there is fear [of God], one finds perfection." As mentioned, Jerusalem, YeRuShaLayiM, is YiRah ShaLeM, perfect or complete fear (Chapter 4). Thus, as one attains fear of God, one *is* actively engaged in the building of Jerusalem! Generally speaking, the verse teaches that (Psalms 147:2), "God builds Jerusalem; He ingathers the scattered of Israel." In an individual sense, by building his own Jerusalem — by implanting fear of God in his heart — each person causes the Voice of Rebuke to spread out and gather in the exiles (see Berakhot 49a).

*

Purity and morality

One other aspect of "the nose" that is used to define Mashiach is purity. More specifically, this refers to sexual purity. And one who is pure can detect purity in others. Mashiach's sense of smell is so acute that he will immediately be able to identify who has guarded the covenant — the Covenant of Abraham — and who hasn't. It is in this area, it seems, that Mashiach's most difficult battle will take place — as appears quite obvious from today's world.

Joseph was the paradigm of the *tzaddik*. He was a servant in

Potifar's house, and for a full year Potifar's wife tried to seduce him. Joseph withstood the test and was crowned with the title tzaddik, which denotes sexual purity. Mashiach is therefore associated with the name of "Mashiach ben Yosef," because of his high level of morality. However, our Sages teach that Mashiach ben Yosef will be killed in battle, which indicates the severity of the battle for morality in immoral surroundings — for the casualties are many. (Mashiach's "death" is discussed above, Chapter 4). Therefore, before he attained the great levels of knowledge which enabled him to rule over Egypt, Joseph was tested for his sexual purity. When he passed his test the Torah gave witness (Genesis 41:39), "There is none as perceptive and wise" (Likutey Moharan I, 36:2). Joseph's purity brought him to Daat — and so it can be with everyone.

> Moshe is the Daat of Torah (Etz Chaim 32:1). He merited Daat for he received the Torah and transmitted it to the entire world. Furthermore, Moshe himself corresponds to the Torah — for MoSheH RaBeINU (משה רבינו) is the numerical equivalent of 613, corresponding to the mitzvot of the Torah. For Moshe to receive the Torah, he had to maintain the highest level of purity. Bilaam, his adversary and archenemy, who tried to destroy the Jews, was so impure that he had bestial relations with his donkey (see Likutey Moharan I, 36:1-2, 4).

We see that the higher a person's level of purity, the greater the perception of Torah and Godliness he can attain. Conversely, the lower he descends, the more he distances himself from spiritual wisdom. He becomes trapped in his own exile and alienated from those around him. He experiences acute depression because immorality stems from depression and leads a person deeper into depression (see Likutey Moharan I, 36:4).

On the other hand, one who tries to maintain purity can depart from exile and merit revelations of Godliness. This person is one who is joyous — he maintains a positive frame of mind and seeks Godliness no matter where he is. He does not allow the exile to overwhelm him and therefore merits true freedom. For with joy and positive thinking, one merits to depart from the exile (see Likutey Moharan II, 10).

*

One reason for the necessity of sexual purity is that Mashiach's main weapon is prayer (Chapter 5). Our Sages compare prayer to arrows which must be directed to their target. These "arrows" require a bow from which they must be aimed, and this "bow" is the *brit*, the sexual organ. One who keeps himself sexually pure merits dynamic power and is in control of his prayers, making them more potent (see Likutey Moharan II, 83).

Brit in Hebrew means "Covenant," for the Covenant that God made with Abraham was circumcision, alluding to sexual purity. God also made a covenant with Noah after the deluge — the rainbow. This was a sign of God's promise not to destroy humanity, even if it descends to the depravity of the Generation of the Flood (which engaged in homosexuality and bestiality). The rainbow in Hebrew is *keshet*, which also translates as bow. Thus, the Covenant of the Flood, "the bow," corresponds to the Covenant of Abraham, i.e. sexual purity. When one attains purity, one can control one's "arrows" — one's prayers — and thereby direct one's prayers to their proper place.

Prayer and purity correspond to "the nose," the concept of breathing — clean, fresh air. They represent the ability to find direction in life and to aim for proper goals. Since Mashiach represents an exalted level of prayer, his purity must be on the highest of levels. Conversely, one who is immoral evidences a lack of self-control. He loses the ability to distinguish between right and wrong. He loses all control over the direction of his life (cf. Likutey Moharan I, 31:4). Every course taken by such a person is then beset with barriers and snares that eventually lead him into deeper pits of physicality. "For one who blemishes the Brit falls into the pursuit of materialism" (Likutey Moharan I, 23:3).

*

Exile consists of descending from spirituality into depravity, whether that be immorality, avarice, arrogance, anger or some other evil lust or characteristic (see also above, Chapter 6). But the most "all-encompassing evil" is that of sexual immorality. This constitutes Mashiach's main battle, for the Days of Mashiach are destined to bring new exalted revelations of Torah and Godliness. Therefore, in order for us to be able to receive these revelations, we must suffer the pains of severe tests of morality. When we emerge successfully, then we can merit Daat, the Torah of the Future, the Torah of Atik, which will reveal all the mysteries of the world.

Since Mashiach represents great intellect, sexual purity also applies to this intellect. The verse states (Genesis 4:1) "And Adam *knew* his wife..." referring to their conjugal relationship. As opposed to illicit and forbidden relationships, cohabitation in a lawful marriage is pure and holy. It implies peace and cooperation between opposites, conceptually Chokhmah and Binah, which produce Daat. It reveals the love each has for the partner and raises the couple's mutual respect. Furthermore, it brings forth greater knowledge in the world — for each birth brings another child, a new mind and intellect which is capable of recognizing God (see *Likutey Halakhot, Pidyon Peter Chamor* 3:2).

Mashiach is represented by "the nose," our source of life and breath. With a Mashiach, there is hope that family life and purity can be reestablished. As long as we breathe the breath of hope — the breath of prayer and reliance upon God — there is hope that Mashiach will come and fully purify our lives. The verse thus states (Lamentations 4:20), "The breath of our nostrils [is] the Mashiach of God." If our breath yearns for purity, then it draws from the Mashiach of God, who is *the* power of purity and morality.

*

And, though the battle for sexual purity is extremely formidable, it is not a lost battle; not by a long shot. The Baal Shem Tov once told a parable illustrating the difficulties the Jews will encounter in the End of Days:

> The battle of the Days of Mashiach is compared to two well-matched men fighting each other for their lives. When one sees that the other is getting the upper hand, he strengthens himself a little extra. This gives him the strength to overcome his adversary. But then, the adversary does the same and draws a little more strength from his inner resources. Then the first man does the same — until the better man wins. So too, as the Evil One sees that his end is near — because Mashiach will eradicate evil — he draws upon his inner resources.

We are presently witnessing an overwhelming force of evil trying to engulf the entire planet. But good is enduring while evil is not. Therefore, the time will come when the power of evil will yield completely to that of good.

Mashiach will eventually purify the sexually depraved so that even the adulterers, child abusers and other — even worse — evildoers, will be reformed. The "smokescreen" that society hides behind will be removed and each person will sense the stench of evil and flee from it — towards Mashiach's sweet-smelling fragrance. Then purity will reign.

*

In review

In this chapter we have seen that Mashiach's breath power is directly related to the awe and reverence for God, which includes the fulfilling of mitzvot. The mitzvot, as we have seen, are constrictions through which a physical human being can begin to perceive spirituality. The more mitzvot a person performs, the greater his ability to perceive the Divine. The same is true of morality, for without it one lacks a "functioning nose" with which to discern purity. Having fear of God, accepting the yoke of Heaven, performing the mitzvot and adhering to the Torah's code of moral behavior, all these allow a person to ascend the ladder of spirituality and to experience the messianic era in his own life.

Furthermore, Mashiach's power to draw people to him is due to the "nose," the sweet-smelling odor he will exude. This savory smell will be evident in his Voice of Rebuke, his ability to relate to each person on his own level in a favorable manner. This will be accomplished by guiding each person to develop himself to his own full potential, through kind words of encouragement, not reproach. The Voice of Rebuke will reveal joy in the world through the Ten Types of Song, which correspond to the Tetragrammaton, God Himself!

* * *

8

Truth endures

We have seen thus far how Mashiach will draw people to him: he will reveal the awesome power of prayer which leads to peace, and will build the Holy Temple which represents great Daat (Intellect). He will promulgate the fear of God, elevating love, awe and respect, so that they once again become dominant characteristics in our world. And he will disseminate family purity. These qualities will bring people together, heralding an era of peace and harmony.

Yet another of Mashiach's functions will be to establish true justice. He will reveal an absolute truth, clarifying all the "gray" areas so that people will recognize — and accept — what is the *real* truth. His ability to reveal this truth comes from his source, Atik, for this is the level of absolute truth (see *Likutey Halakhot, Dayanim* 3:26).

In this chapter, we will discuss the concept of Mashiach's administering justice by revealing absolute truth. When one can clearly see the truth, one is not deterred by rationalizations and other obstacles, and will voluntarily draw close to God. Also discussed is how one merits reward and punishment.

*

Mashiach's expertise in revealing truth will stem from his "peace process" — his ability to draw all types of people to himself. People will want to be close to him and bask in his light, smelling his sweet fragrance. The only way this can happen is if people are at peace, without heaping verbal abuse upon one another. And when there is peace, genuine dialogue will become commonplace. In today's world, dialogue can be summed up in the following manner:

What is a monologue? "When one person speaks and others listen."

What is a dialogue? "When two people speak and nobody listens!"

But the word Mashiach is similar to the word *MaSiaCh*, "one who speaks." Believe it or not, in the Days of Mashiach, people will open up and speak about what is *really* on their minds. And, most surprising of all, the manner in which they will give others a "peace" of their mind, will actually lead to friendship!

*

...flock together

> *"In the Days of Mashiach, the truth will be* ne'ederet, *absent."*
> Isaiah 59:15
>
> *"Ne'EDeRet. This is like EDeR, a flock. In the period of the Footsteps of the Mashiach, the truth will be divided into "flocks" with each one claiming to have the exclusive truth."*
> Sanhedrin 97a
>
> Drawing everyone to God — that all may "join shoulders" to serve Him in unison — takes place in every generation. According to [the level of] the peace between people, they willingly investigate and examine truth and speak openly to one another. Reaching a level of truth, i.e. an awareness of God, they discard their idolatries and draw themselves to Truth (i.e. God)
> (*Likutey Moharan* I, 27:1).

Mashiach's assignments are many and diverse. But through it all, his mission has one major objective — to bring everyone to the service of God. Even given the extraordinary tools that he will have, this is still a formidable task, for each person is different and views truth differently from his fellows. The task becomes even more formidable when one considers the diverse elements of humanity. Among the non-Jewish philosophies, several billion people practice numerous disparate religions, or no religion at all. And among the Jews themselves, there are many different groups — each claiming a monopoly on the truth of how God is to be "served or accommodated." This is the Talmud's lament, that truth is divided among many groups, with everyone laying claim to the truth. How can Mashiach get us all on the right track?

Therefore, Mashiach's first task is to introduce the art of dialogue. He will draw people together with their friends and neighbors, near and far. Then, with true sincerity, they can openly discuss "the truth" — each from his own vantage point. But what if a person's "truth" is based on falsehood, or is simply misguided? What if it is idolatrous? Should everyone "accept" the other's view? Surely this is impossible — as well as forbidden! Then, of what use is dialogue?

The Talmud teaches (Sotah 9b), "Words of truth are recognized." If people are at peace, they don't try to ram their theories down others' throats. They *speak* honestly and openly with each other. Since they have mutual respect for one another, each is willing to accept the other person for who he is and what his beliefs are. By opening and maintaining a dialogue, people will begin to converse, truth will be spoken — and recognized. Then, "I will imbue all peoples will a pure tongue; that they may call in the Name of God and all serve Him in one manner" (Zefaniah 3:9). In fact, the "clear tongue," i.e. true speech, will *itself* signal the nations and call them all to serve God! (Likutey Moharan I, 62:4; ibid. 66:3).

It is thus taught (The Aleph-Bet Book Truth A:8), "From the air breathed by the liar, the evil inclination is created. When Mashiach comes, there will no longer be falsehood, therefore there will no longer be any evil inclination." For (Zekhariah 13:2), "On that day I will cut out the false prophets and the spirit of impurity will I cause to pass from the land."

*

"He will judge righteously..."

It isn't enough, however, simply to seek the truth. Being human, we are all still very susceptible to falling victim to "near truths" and half-truths. As chief arbiter of justice, Mashiach will have an acute "sense of smell" to ascertain real truth and falsehood. His power will help guide each person on the proper path to seek truth.

To better understand this, we refer to Rashi's commentary on the Breastplate of the High Priest which was worn while he performed his service in the Holy Temple (Exodus 28:15). The Breastplate is called "*Choshen HaMishpat* — the Judgment Breastplate" as it was to effect forgiveness to the Jews for judicial errors. The word judgment connotes the three stages of a judiciary process: 1) the claims; 2) the court's decision; 3) meting out the punishment due. But Rashi also translates *Choshen Mishpat* as a *Decision* Breastplate, since it always "chooses the right (i.e. truthful) decision."

Truth is a very special quality. Absolute truth is even more remarkable — and extremely rare. For, in the main, truth stands alone, unaided. One steeped in such truth does not need the "assistance" of others. One who, on the other hand, craves respect or power, recognition or material possessions, is a "needy person" — one who "needs" others. This person is not truthful in his intentions, for everything he does is for the benefit of himself — with the (willing or unwilling) participation of others. His thoughts cannot be pure.

> There are those who pray and put efforts into their prayers, but are quite conscious of others who are watching them. Their effort becomes thwarted and can lead to devotion solely to impress others. And even if one begins one's prayers with good intentions, those [peripheral] thoughts recur. The person may try to pray with a feeling of truth; nevertheless, he is not very "truthful," for he requires the help of others to supplement his devotions.
>
> The same is true in all areas of life. Some people desire honor and respect. Everything they do will reflect this need for respect. Others will use flattery for financial gain, for positions of power, and so on. These people are not truthful. They are "needy people" — for everything they do requires the assistance of others (*Likutey Moharan* I, 66:3).

One of Mashiach's great strengths is that he is "poor" and will come "riding a donkey," i.e. he will possess extreme humility. He will submit himself totally to God and His Will. As such, he will not seek anybody's approval or politically correct solutions. He will be the paradigm of true prayer, one who prays to God solely for God's honor. He will also judge and use his powers solely for the sake of God. He will not be a "needy person." On the contrary, his example will demonstrate the beauty of living a life of independent truth — being honest with oneself at all times.

*

As previously mentioned, another of Mashiach's functions will be to administer justice. As king, he must lead wisely and mediate between his subjects, so that his decisions will bring people together under the banner of the One God. And yet, there are wicked people in the world. How are they to be dealt with? Are they to be rewarded with eternal life and repentance, regardless of their deeds? What system of justice will Mashiach employ?

We must therefore define wickedness and differentiate between wickedness and transgression — between evil and wrongdoing. The Talmud defines sin in three categories: error, intentional sin and rebellious sin. Error is the easiest to rectify, for a person's intent was good though the deed turned out wrong (but see *Likutey Moharan* I, 19:9; ibid. 30:6). Intentional sins are those that a person committed out of lust. He felt *compelled* to follow the dictates of his heart and succumbed. However, had he been able to distract his evil inclination, he might not have committed the sin. These two categories of sinners are wrong, but are closer to rectification than the third category.

Rebels, those who deliberately try to defy God, have no justification. Such people seek no gain from their deeds. They require no self-gratification or self-aggrandizement. It is such people who try their best to remove any vestige of Godliness from the world. Since they tried so very hard to remove Godliness, they have distanced themselves totally from any aspect of the messianic delights which reveal Godliness.

*

The good, the bad and the ugly

> *He will not judge by what he sees, or by what he hears. He will judge the poor righteously... with the spirit of his lips he will slay evildoers..."*
>
> Isaiah 11:3-4

It is Mashiach's task to judge everyone and place each person in his rightful place, in order for everyone to attain his rightful level of spirituality, according to his deeds and efforts. Those who searched for a spiritual life but erred along the way, together with those who succumbed to enticement, will be judged in a righteous manner.

"He will not judge by what he sees or hears..." for if he did, then a person's deeds would demand justice and harsh punishment. Rather, "He will judge the poor righteously" — those who are impoverished without good deeds. Mashiach's acute sense of smell will detect the "soul of the matter" (smell is associated with the soul; as above, Chapter 7) — a person's deepest inner feelings and unwillingness to sin, though he succumbed. This person will eventually be cleansed and exonerated, through Mashiach's prayers and efforts as judge on his behalf. But what about the rebel?

> The essence of everything in this world can be seen in its "face." Just as a man is instantly recognizable by his face, so too everything in existence can be recognized by its "face." This can be understood in business, where we first look to see what is on the "surface" of the deal — is the merchandise good, the price reasonable, etc. Only afterwards, if the product looks good, do we start to read the fine print. In this sense, the "face" relates to truth, for we can rarely "dress up" the true value of an item. This is why, when a merchant is honest and the merchandise he is selling is priced accordingly, he has an "enlightened face." His face discloses his inner truth (*Likutey Halakhot, Giluach* 4:2).

Mashiach's truth is on his "face," which will be openly revealed to all. Those who have sought to destroy spirituality have always given reasons supporting their views. "It's not egalitarian..." "It's not humanistic..." "It's not pluralistic..." etc. But in fact, their intent was to deny truth, to deny God. But, "Words of truth are recognizable!" These people scream out, "It's the truth!" The word "truth" is always on their tongues — as they impose their views upon others (see *Likutey Halakhot, Shabbat* 7:64). But, having distanced themselves from God to the point of denial, these people are no longer able to partake of truth, of Godliness. Thus, they must be destroyed. How? By the revelation of truth — the very truth that they denied.

Their destruction comes about by the revelation of truth. People will engage in dialogue, eventually "stumbling" over the truth. As truth is recognized and revealed, those who have denied it will see the folly of their ways. Mashiach needs only to reveal the truth, that God exists. He does not need to strike anyone or mete out physical punishment. The revelation of truth itself is all the punishment the wicked require. They had sought power and glory in a world where Power and Glory — of God — already exist. They will thus bear witness to their own downfall. This is the meaning of, "With the spirit of his lips will he slay the wicked." For with nothing more than the revelation of truth, all the idolatries and falsehoods, all the fabricated ideologies and dishonesties, will simply disintegrate (see *Likutey Moharan* I, 66:3).

Thus we may conclude that Mashiach will rectify the sins of those who sinned in less severe ways, by showing them how to repent; he will rectify the sins of rebels by *bringing* even them to repentance, when they are faced with the absolute truth.

*

Reward and punishment

This is an interesting point, for there are many allusions in the Prophets and Talmudic literature to the punishment of the wicked prior to the Days of Mashiach. Yet, we also find many teachings in the Talmud, the *Zohar* and the ARI which refer to the rectification and exoneration of *all* humanity: not only the Jews but of the Mixed Multitude and the non-Jews as well; and not only of those who erred, but also of rebellious sinners. (This point will be elaborated upon below in Parts V-VI, where we will discuss how Mashiach will rectify mankind even after its fall into total depravity.)

Man will be rewarded (or punished) according to his deeds and efforts. The greater a person's efforts to attain spirituality, the greater his reward and his capacity to perceive more exalted levels of Godliness. One who has placed minimum effort into serving God will also be rectified, but his capacity to grow spiritually in the future will be limited by his minimal effort. Evildoers too will be rectified, but with nothing to show for all their years and efforts. At first, their punishment consists of continuous humiliation over their evil deeds (see Likutey Moharan I, 10:9). Afterwards they too will be rectified. But their rewards can be compared to the difference between just barely making it through the month, making it through the month comfortably, or having several hundred million dollars behind you, besides your monthly income (cf. Likutey Halakhot, Eiruvei Techumin 5:39). To understand this a little better, one must realize that God's meting out judgment against the wicked is not meant solely to punish them for their wrongdoings. God's "punishment" is *the* means of cleansing a person of his blemishes (Likutey Halakhot, Ribit 5:12). Consider the following:

Jeremiah was the Prophet during the destruction of the First Temple. He was shown the composite parts of the Jewish Nation in exile, the good and the evil. "God showed me two DUDA'ey (baskets) of figs...one contained very good figs...the other contained figs so terrible that they could not be eaten" (Jeremiah 24:1-2). Those Jews who were good were very good, but those who despoiled themselves and their characters were "inedible." But another verse states (Songs 7:14), "The DUDA'im (mandrakes) give off a savory smell." And our Sages explain (Shir HaShirim Rabbah 7:14), "This teaches that both the good and bad 'figs' will eventually be exonerated and exude a savory smell." This is the power of Mashiach, who exudes a sweet fragrance of rectification, which will eventually bring everyone — even those who rebel against God — to accept the truth and to earn their ultimate reward (see Likutey Halakhot, Eiruvei Techumin 5:38).

*

The true leader

Because truth has become so polarized in our times, nobody is willing to give credence to the possibility that "*I*" might be in error. It is for this reason, more than any other, that Mashiach will have such a difficult time. Moshe was a true leader, yet he was under criticism and attack several times by those who "knew better." Korach, the spies, Zimri, even his own sister Miriam, all approached Moshe with ideas and suggestions on how to "improve" the religion, the lot of the people, and so on. So strife reared its ugly head and many lives were lost. The Jews' entry into the Holy Land was delayed by forty years. The sinners and rebels lost everything they sought. But, regrettably, many thousands of others' lives were also sacrificed as a result of the controversies.

And yet, Moshe remained steadfast. The Talmud teaches (Shabbat 104a), "Truth stands [eternal]!" Whoever is on the side of truth need not fear for his position. If he sincerely pursues the truth, then he is on the right side. Even if he is in error, he will eventually find the truth — through dialogue and honest search, since his intention is only truth. But those who make a mockery of God mislead not only themselves, but many, many others as well. Those who belittle others and their devotions come from the "end of all flesh" (cf. Genesis 6:13). That is, they seek the "end of others" by looking for the bad in people, trying to put them down and/or destroy them. The same is true of all those who seek glory "at God's expense." They are very strong in their persistence to impose atheistic ideals upon others, all the while defending "the truth." However, these people are very distant from truth and will not last. They are compared to a tornado which blows with great fury, then suddenly disappears (see *Likutey Moharan* I, 38:2; ibid. 8:3).

But eventually, "Truth stands eternal!" and Mashiach will be revealed. True leadership will be restored to the Jewish Nation — and to the entire world. The attributes of Judgment and Justice will be universally revealed, and each person will be able to use his sense of judgment properly to arrive at the only possible conclusion — that God reigns supreme!

*

"Chad Gadya — One Kid"

We can now tie the ideas of truth and justice even closer together. Mashiach will be a righteous judge, one who will bring a true sense of justice into the world. And a judge does not need to be a leader, for every person has within himself the ability to judge. The necessity of *true* justice for and by every person can be seen from the following:

> Mashiach's main weapon will be prayer. But one cannot utilize this "weapon" (the arrows of prayer) except through sexual purity (the "bow" which corresponds to sexual purity; see above, Chapters 5,7). In order for a person to attain purity, he must first merit a true sense of justice, with the ability to choose between right and wrong and between extremes. That is, he must know how to wield his weapons and not veer to the right or to the left. He must aim straight for the target and not err. This is the meaning of (Psalms 72:1), "Give the king (i.e. Mashiach) Your judgment" for Mashiach will receive his power of prayer through a true sense of justice (*Likutey Moharan* I, 2:4).

For Mashiach to conquer the world, he must use the power of prayer. Prerequisite to perfecting this principle weapon, Mashiach requires purity and judicature. Purity has a simple connotation: a person is either pure or impure. There is no gray area. (One can repent, but at any given moment one is only either pure or impure.) Judgment, however, has many gray areas. Reaching even a simple decision — right or wrong — requires serious deliberation. One must analyze all the data available, to examine the projected outcome, and then hope that one's decision is a correct one.

> (As we have seen, Chesed [Lovingkindness] and Gevurah [Judgment] are depicted as the right and left sides of the sefirot, respectively. Two alternative terms for the center column, Tiferet [Beauty] are Mishpat [Judgment] and Emet [Truth]. The difference between Gevurah and Mishpat is that Gevurah by itself represents strict Judgment. When tempered with Chesed, it becomes Tiferet, compassionate Judgment [Mishpat], the highest expression of Truth. These three columns correspond to the Patriarchs: Abraham, Isaac and Jacob. They emanate from Daat; see also Appendix B.)

Compassionate Judgment is the center column that represents the perfect combination of the right and left, and leads to absolute truth. The verse thus states (Mikhah 7:20), "Give truth to Jacob," for Jacob corresponds to truth. This truth is an expression of Daat, the expanded intellect that will be revealed in the Future. Therefore, in order to understand "Why hasn't Mashiach come yet?" we must first recognize the importance of judgment. For just as the other aspects of Mashiach are present in each person, so too is the attribute of judgment. When *our* sense of judgment becomes refined, then we can aspire to Mashiach's greater sense of justice. To clarify this, we provide several examples.

> One matter of judgment that one must be extremely careful about is in the area of money and property — especially that which belongs to another person. The Torah commands us (Leviticus 19:35-36), "Do not falsify measurements, whether in length, weight, or volume. You must have an honest balance, honest weights, an honest dry measure, and an honest liquid measure." Our Sages state (Sifri, ad.loc.; see Rashi), "This teaches us that when engaged in business one is called a judge. If a person lies when measuring or weighing goods, it is considered as if he corrupted justice. He is wicked, detestable, despised, and worthy of destruction. He strengthens the power of impurity in the land, causes the desecration of God's Holy Name and the exile of the *Shekhinah* (Divine Presence). He also causes death and exile" (*Likutey Halakhot, Rosh Chodesh* 6:11).

That's a lot of name calling and evil happenings for a little "bad" judging. But that's what happens when one intentionally steals from another. "Intentional" does not always refer to actually stealing from or tricking another person. It also covers the "rationalizations" that we make when adding or subtracting from a contract or a given word. And, since judgment and purity go hand-in-hand, financial rationalizations lead to sexual impurity. This was the lot of the Generation of the Flood. "The world was corrupt before God, and the earth was filled with crime... All flesh had perverted its way on the earth" (Genesis 6:11-12). First the Torah speaks about their monetary corruption, then about their immorality (see *Likutey Halakhot, Rosh Chodesh* 6:11).

> A second area involving judgment is how one views others — their motives and intentions. The Mishnah states (Avot 2:5), "Do not judge your friend until you stand in his place." When we sit down to speak about others, we are

judging them. It is absolutely imperative to judge others favorably. For one cannot ever truly know or understand another person's motives or intentions. The slightest error is a corruption of justice. But if one judges favorably, then he is imitating God, Who judges favorably (*Likutey Halakhot, Rosh Chodesh* 6:11).

Grasping the essence of true justice by using our judgment correctly, we can emulate the justice of the messianic era. For only God can administer true justice, which Mashiach will reveal when he arrives. Any error, even a slight one, can cause massive repercussions. This is illustrated in the poem *Chad Gadya* ("One Kid"), which we sing on Passover night at the conclusion of the Seder.

"A kid was bought and was eaten by a cat. A dog bit the cat. A stick beat the dog. Fire consumed the stick and was extinguished by water. An ox drank the water and a slaughterer slew the ox. The Angel of Death slew the slaughterer. Then God slew the Angel of Death."

The cat did an evil deed. It ate something not belonging to it. The dog administered justice, but, "Who asked the dog to mix in?" And so on. The stick, the fire, the water, etc., all tried to avenge a wrongdoing, but each administered justice according to *its* ideal. Maybe they were right. But then why were they punished? This teaches us that judgment is only God's and it won't be until God slays the Angel of Death (i.e. in messianic times) that true justice will reign (*Likutey Halakhot, Rosh Chodesh* 6:19).

Until then, we must do our best to take care of others' property and to judge others favorably. Then we will have corrected, on our level, the true sense of justice, and will be able to experience this justice even now.

*

As with the other messianic concepts — prayer, the Holy Temple and Daat, the Ingathering of the Exiles, purity, etc. — truth and justice are also prevalent in the world today. They are here, before our very eyes, but still "hovering in the distance." The less "needy" we become, that is to say, the less we feel the need for the approval of others, the more we integrate truth into our lives, the greater our ability to "see and feel" the truth and justice of the messianic times.

* * *

9

Mashiach: the Era of Miracles

The main themes of this chapter are faith and Divine Providence, and how they are connected to the messianic concepts discussed above.

The Talmud opines that the nose is the main facial organ used for the absolute identification of a person (*Yevamot* 120a). The same law applies to Mashiach. His "nose" will be his identification. But how will *we* recognize him?

Truth cannot be attained unless we have faith. Faith is the most important prequisite for achieving truth. The entire world operates on faith. For example, when evaluating merchandise you're interested in purchasing, you ask the price. Do you buy it? If you believe that merchant's price is fair, you do. If you suspect something wrong with the price or the merchandise and don't trust the merchant, you don't. The same rules of faith apply whether we are talking about purchasing a house, commodities and stocks, or milk and bread from the local grocer. How about accepting someone's check? Do you trust that it will be covered? Wherever you turn, you must have faith in the people you deal with — otherwise, no deal. Unless you have faith and trust in others, you cannot survive in business.

"Shema Yisrael... God is One." The truth is one. There can be many lies, but there is only one truth. Anyone who looks for truth will see God everywhere. This, in fact, is man's mission; to seek out the Truth — God — wherever man goes. But this truth must have a foundation. The Prophet states (Habakkuk 2:4), "The righteous man shall live by his faith." That is, faith is *the* foundation of all. With it, we can seek the absolute truth and come to recognize God from and within everything in the world (*Likutey Halakhot, Giluach* 4:1-3).

Faith means many different things to different people. The number of religions in the world today is a fair indication of this. But faith is much more than religion. It is *the* fundamental instrument in the way the world operates. Without faith there can be no interaction between people. A person must have a certain amount of faith and trust in others — if only minimal — in order to carry on social, emotional and financial relationships. But faith is so much more crucial when dealing with matters of religion.

It follows then that faith forms a bridge between people. Partnerships can develop, marriages can blossom, etc. — as long as there is faith. How much more then is faith the bridge when developing one's relationship with God? In fact, faith is *the* pillar of one's commitment to love, awe and respect of God. And since this relationship will be the way of life in Mashiach's days, the spreading of faith becomes *the* paramount objective. Therefore, one of Mashiach's main struggles will be ridding the world of idolatries — of false and misplaced faith and ideologies — so that one can truly develop one's relationship with God.

One who attaches himself to the true tzaddikim has true faith. Mashiach is the true tzaddik. One who accepts Mashiach will receive from him pure faith, and will not have misplaced his faith. Since the tzaddikim of every generation reflect the Mashiach, one who has faith in the true tzaddikim has pure faith and can grow spiritually with it (see *Likutey Moharan* II, 8:8). On the other hand, a lack of faith, especially in the tzaddikim, is a blemish in the Voice of Rebuke (which comes through the tzaddikim). This distances the person from the tzaddikim, and even more so from God. By rectifying and strengthening one's faith, one attunes oneself to listening to the rebuke offered, so that one can draw near to God (see *Likutey Halakhot, Halvaah* 3:2).

*

"Gold and silver gods"

> *"On that day, man will cast away his silver gods and his golden gods, that each made for himself to worship...."*
>
> Isaiah 2:20

There is a plethora of "faiths" today which cover every facet of life — but rarely include God. That is, people have certain beliefs which direct their way of life and are the main motive behind their specific lifestyles and goals. When Mashiach comes, he will turn everything around. Faith in God will abound while all other faiths and idolatries will totally disappear.

But what are the faiths and idolatries that Mashiach must do away with? Certain religions worship idols, which are clearly idolatrous practices. Others have idolatrous traditions, though they might not have idolatrous beliefs. However, the Torah clearly states that one should worship only the One God — anything else is by definition idolatrous. And there are many "idolatries" which are a part of our daily lives, yet these go unnoticed. Among them: avarice, haughtiness and anger.

When Isaiah speaks of man casting away his silver gods and his golden gods he is referring not only to the idols carved by a person; he is also referring to the idolatry of wealth and power — lusts that consume people's entire lives. A person might think that it is his hard work that brings him a livelihood. But actually, it is God Who provides, as in (Deuteronomy 8:3), "Man does not live by bread alone, but by all that comes out of God's mouth." It is also written (Deuteronomy 8:18), "Remember that it is God Who gives you power to become prosperous."

One who truly believes that God oversees the world with Divine Providence also believes that He provides his livelihood. Such a person does not mortgage his life to earn a living. He will work — hard and honestly — but will not devote his entire life to acquiring material possessions. Such a person has faith. However, one who pursues wealth, with the thought that *only by his* efforts will he earn a living, is an "idolator" — who believes in silver and golden gods. And, as idolatry, this is a falsehood. How many people have gone from "rags to riches" and from "riches to rags" overnight? Quite obviously, there is a Divine Hand guiding things behind the scenes.

Virtually every person who runs his own business can readily testify to the hidden presence of God's Hand. Many times a businessman may pursue a certain contract which he believes is "in the bag" — but it might take weeks, months or even longer (and maybe never) before it materializes. Yet, while he is consumed by the negotiations for the contract he is pursuing, he will find business materializing from areas that weren't even explored.

The average wage-earner can also testify to God's Divine Providence. How many times have people examined their finances and said, "There is *no way* we'll make it to the end of the week." Ten years later, people say the same thing! But what happened over the past ten years when they could "never" have made it? In retrospect, it is clear that God provided, even though they cannot explain how it happened. Every person has his "miracles" to relate — even though they may have seemed "natural." To have faith, all that is required is that a person open his eyes and mind — just a little. Then he can see wonders that were there the whole time.

*

Interestingly, the pursuit of wealth and power is rooted in messianic concepts. In the Days of Mashiach, everyone will have abundant wealth. Even the famous names of "old money" — Rockefeller, Mellon, Rothschild, the Royal House of England and so on — which have represented for the masses untold riches, will pale by comparison. Therein lies the reason behind the chase after material possessions.

Mankind was created to pursue a specific goal — God. Thus, man's basic instinct is to seek a goal. But when clouded by evil desires, the quest for the goal becomes deflected. Since wealth will be widespread in the future, man's desire for it is rooted in a worthwhile goal — that of the messianic era. Unfortunately, the pursuit of great wealth today, since it is currently not connected with the service of God, is idolatrous (see *Likutey Moharan* I, 13:1).

Money is important — one has to meet one's obligations. But it is one's *approach* to acquiring wealth that requires direction.

*

The same applies to the craving for influence. Mashiach will be the most powerful person ever to live, for he will rule over the entire world. As "a light to the nations," Jews must influence the entire world to serve God. As part of the ultimate goal, however, power becomes "power play" which is so often misused today for personal gain (see Likutey Moharan I, 54:4).

Anger and haughtiness, extensions of the quest for power, are also major forms of idolatries. The Talmud teaches (see Nedarim 22a), "Anger is akin to idolatry. An angry person is a sinner..." and so on. Anger causes rifts and ill feelings, the opposite of the peace that will reign in messianic times.

Haughtiness is even worse (see Sotah 4b). The haughty person thinks all is "due him" because of who he is or because of his accomplishments. This is the worst kind of idolatry, for it was God Who gave him everything he is and has in the first place.

The problem with the idolatry of haughtiness is that it clouds one's sight. "*I* am", the haughty man says. But how does a person who sees himself as "I" come to recognize the *real* "I [am God]"? (Exodus 20:2). And more problematic, a person's clouded sight — his blemished sense of judgment — gives him a distorted vision of how the world really operates. For example, everyone recognizes that there are forces of nature. Yet, Who created nature and Who put the force behind it? One who believes he is the "I" will not look any further than what is obvious to him. He thinks that everything he achieves through nature is up to him and it's all in his own hands. But one who does seek God realizes that there is much beyond nature. This person can merit to see the Hand of Divine Providence, and witness the miracles of daily life, as will occur in the Days of Mashiach.

[Though the Rambam opines that Mashiach does not have to perform miracles (Yad HaChazakah, Melakhim 11:3), this does not mean that he won't; simply that he doesn't *have* to. According to the *Zohar* mentioned earlier, the miracles of Mashiach's days will far outshine those of the Exodus; Zohar II, 9a.]

The traits of avarice, haughtiness, anger and so on, all lead to strife, annulling any of the gains of dialogue and peace. This is *the* leading cause of the exile, and because of the pursuit of power and haughtiness, we are still in exile today (Likutey Moharan I, 11:8; see below, Part IV; see also *Crossing the Narrow Bridge*, Chapter 10).

*

Divine Providence

Every aspect of life in this world — mineral, vegetable, animal and human — is overseen by God. And it is Divine Providence that dictates that supervision, twenty-four hours a day, seven days a week.

Nature is Divine Providence, in a concealed mode. The laws of nature are a means of concealing Godliness. This is for man's benefit, for God's concealment allows man to exercise free will. When one comes to the realization that all nature is directly controlled by God, one can merit to witness God's open miracles.

> This world is in a state of constriction, the concealment of Godliness (an aspect of Judgment). The reason for this is that man must have free choice (which is discussed below, Chapter 10). But if a person sins, he heightens the concealment of Godliness, causing judgments to dominate and bringing vengeance down upon himself. Thus, the "nature" of Judgment is that it demands punishment. God, Who created reward and punishment, seeks justice. But at the same time, He seeks to show kindness (i.e. a revelation of Godliness), even if not deserved. What is the real miracle? When Judgment is subjugated to kindness! At present, there is concealment, Judgment; and there is also the revelation of God's kindness, even though one still suffers somewhat. In the Future, when Judgment is totally subjugated and great lovingkindness is revealed, then miracles will be the way of life — for there will be no more constrictions (*Likutey Halakhot, Hodaah* 1:3).

Faith and Divine Providence are bound together. When the time came for the Exodus from Egypt, Moshe was given permission to perform several miracles in order to implant faith in the Jewish Nation. Seeing that there was a tzaddik who rose above the material world and revealed Divine Power, the Jews' faith was established. Moshe then performed greater miracles, the Ten Plagues, which defied every force and concept of nature. This was to instill the realization of God's existence within an idolatrous people, in an idolatrous country. But Pharaoh was too much of an idolator to accept that God is above nature. He therefore brought utter destruction upon himself and his fellow idolators.

After the Ten Plagues and the splitting of the Red Sea, the Jews merited to witness the Revelation of God at Sinai. They also lived through forty years of miraculous existence — manna from heaven daily (except Shabbat), a "rolling stone" which supplied them with water, and clouds of glory which formed a protective "magnetic field" around them in the desert. All this was to instill within the nation a deeper faith. These miracles were witnessed by several million people (600,000 men, plus their wives and children), and are recorded in detail in our history. The reason for the miracles and the supersedence of nature was to show us clearly that God controls all, and to instill in us faith to believe that He can perform miracles of the same magnitude at any moment.

Miraculous existence will be the way of life in the Future. Instead of being subject to the forces of nature, man will transcend them. For in the Future, God will no longer be so fully concealed. There will no longer be any need for nature, the constraints of time and space, for man will then see unequivocally that everything is directly under God's supervision. As He is above nature, those attached to Him will also live a supernatural existence.

Miracles, as we think of them now, will be the norm in the messianic era. One with faith witnesses this even today. On the other hand, one who thinks that everything happens in a natural way comes under the jurisdiction of natural laws. Such a person has a narrow range of vision, a narrow mind, for he can view life only in a limited scope. One who so chooses, can openly see that there exists a Controlling Force behind nature — God.

One who has faith and believes that God controls the universe knows that everything has a reason for its existence. Such a person will open his mind to whatever is taking place around him and literally "see" Godliness. Everything that happens will stimulate him further in his search for Godliness. And if he then remains steadfast in his faith he will even understand after a while why God wanted it so. This is faith; this is Divine Providence. They are intertwined. One can taste the future in the present, if one strengthens one's faith accordingly.

*

Daat and faith

But what is the real difference between a person who has faith and one who hasn't? Everything works the same for both — or at least on the surface it seems to. The answer is that one who has faith will eventually *know* empirically whatever he believes in. If one believes in God, one will come to *know* Him. He will understand what he previously only believed. Conversely, for those who lack faith, what type of knowledge can they hope to attain? They can be compared to those who never went to first grade, where all knowledge is gained by faith: listening to and accepting the words of the teacher. They lack the fundamentals to attain the great knowledge of the messianic era that will then be revealed and are destined to remain at the very bottom of the "educational ladder."

For when Mashiach comes (Isaiah 11:9), "The world will be filled with the Knowledge of God." As we have seen (above, Chapter 8), the attainment of messianic ideals (truth, etc.) depends upon a person's efforts to acquire these traits and qualities prior to Mashiach's revelation. Thus, one who believes in God is one who strives for the knowledge of God. Such a person will come to know God and cleave unto Him, thereby transcending the limitations of time, space and nature. For him, everything will be miraculous.

According to the Kabbalah, the reason for this is that Malkhut, God's Kingship, the lowest of the sefirot, filters the awesome spiritual lights of the upper sefirot, especially that of Daat, the external manifestation of Keter (the level of Mashiach). Malkhut also denotes faith, because by accepting God as our King, we are affirming our faith in Him. When the time for the revelation of His Kingdom arrives, those with faith, God's "proven" subjects, will merit the expanded intellect of Daat that will be revealed then (see Likutey Moharan I, 21:14-15).

*

This is alluded to in the account of the Creation (Genesis 1:16; see Rashi): "God created the two great lights; the greater light to rule over the day and the lesser light to rule over the night." But, to begin with, there were "two great lights." What happened to cause the moon to be called *the lesser light*? Why did it become diminished? The moon complained that "two kings cannot use the same crown simultaneously." [People would not be able to differentiate between the sun and the moon.] God accepted the moon's argument and made it smaller (Chullin 60b). Reb Noson explains this allegorically:

> The sun and the moon correspond to intellect and faith. The sun, which shines by day, indicates brightness/intelligence, which can guide a person on the right path. The moon, which shines at night, indicates faith, a "light within the darkness" that enables a person to continue along his path, even without clear visibility. When they were created, God intended that intellect and faith be equal to each other. That is, faith is applicable only where knowledge is impossible. A person's faith should be so strong that, even if he doesn't understand, he will accept with faith what he sees and what is happening around him as coming from God, exactly as if he *understood* it with his intelligence! But faith complained that people wouldn't be able to differentiate between knowledge and faith. Therefore, faith was diminished. Man's battle now is to build and strengthen his faith so that what he believes in, even if he can't understand it, will be as clear as if he sees it with his own eyes. Then the light of the "moon" (faith) will again be equal to the light of the "sun" (intellect) (Likutey Halakhot, Rosh Chodesh 6:2-4).

Then the verse will be fulfilled (Isaiah 30:26), "And the light of the moon shall be like the light of the sun; and the sun shall shine sevenfold as [it did] during the days of Creation, on the day that God heals the wounds of His people."

Amen, may it be His will.

* * *

10

The Wondrous Advisor

> *"A child will be born to us, a son given to us, and responsibility will be upon his shoulders. His name shall be, 'Pele Yoetz' (Wondrous Advisor)... for the realm to flourish, for eternal peace, upon the throne of David and his kingdom, to establish and strengthen it with justice and charity..."*
>
> Isaiah 9:5-6

Mashiach will be kept quite busy working to establish a world of justice and peace, of harmony and love, of respect and spirituality. We are fortunate to be privy to some of the "weapons" in Mashiach's "arsenal" with which he will fight his Armageddon — the battle of the Godly forces against the forces of agnosticism and materialism. And though these "weapons" are crucial to his war, there are others which are equally important.

Several concepts yet remain to be discussed about Mashiach's mission. After these are explained, we will be able to review them all and see how the mosaic of Mashiach's mission comes together in perfect harmony. In this chapter we will discuss why man must have free will and if it will apply in the Days of Mashiach. Also to be discussed is the importance of the Torah in one's daily life and the Torah of the Future — the Torah of Atik — which will be a major "weapon" of the Mashiach to bring people back to God.

*

Free will

God can do everything by Himself. He does not need anyone to assist

Him. When God does everything Himself it is called, *it'aruta de-l'eilah*, "arousal from Above." That is to say, the inspiration for what happens comes from God. During Creation, however, God set up a system whereby man would be the prime mover of action in this world, and this is known as *it'aruta de-l'tata*, "arousal from below." That is, the inspiration for what happens comes from man.

At the time of the Exodus, the Jews were without mitzvot. Regardless, God took them out of Egypt in order for the Jews to serve Him. This is an example of *it'aruta de-l'eilah*. Man wants to serve God. He chooses to serve God of his own accord. This is an example of *it'aruta de-l'tata*. Thus, free will involves exercising one's will and desire, either to serve God or to choose a material life. Choosing the spiritual is an "arousal from below" which, as it were, "forces" God to respond to man's behavior (prayer and good deeds), with bounty. This is as opposed to going against God, which causes suffering, forcing one to respond to His desire.

Free will stems from the fact that God created the world for us to serve Him, then concealed Himself and left us to our own devices to find Him. If He were revealed, then of course free will would be negated — for no-one would choose transitory, material satisfaction over the everlasting pleasures of eternity. So of course, free choice will terminate when the Mashiach comes. Or will it?

*

Free will in messianic times

> "Remember your Creator in your youth before the days of evil come, and [before] years approach of which you will say, 'I have no desire for them'."
>
> Ecclesiastes 12:1

> "...*before years approach of which you will say, 'I have no desire for them'*" — these are the Days of Mashiach, when there is no reward and no punishment.
>
> Shabbat 151b

Our Sages are evidently of the opinion that in the Days of Mashiach there will no longer be "free will," that is, the opportunity to choose between right and wrong. When the beauty of serving God is revealed to all, who would choose foolishness over what is right; who would choose a raw turnip when one could have the choicest delicacies? Who would choose a plug nickel when one could have diamonds, emeralds, rubies? This startling concept gives rise to important questions.

The ARI writes that God created the world to reveal His goodness. The purpose of free will is to enable men to receive reward or punishment for their deeds. If there were no free will, if every action were done instinctively, without the option to choose otherwise, it would make no sense at all for one who performs good deeds to receive any reward for them, or for one who sins to be punished.

As long as we have free will, we have the opportunity to earn reward in the World to Come. But if, in the Days of Mashiach, God is to be revealed, and free will is negated, then what will be the purpose of our existence? How will we rectify ourselves, when we will be "preprogrammed" to behave as we will, without the choice to behave otherwise?

Furthermore, what if a person isn't worthy when Mashiach comes? "If I'm not worthy," the person may claim, "if I've sinned or rebelled against God, then my rectification can't be worth very much. How can I be entitled to the delights of the messianic era if I've caused so much damage that only Mashiach can rescue me from myself? If free will is negated, then my devotion to God will be an arousal from Above. If so, I'm probably not entitled to anything!"

Is this what the messianic delights are all about? Only a select few will reap full benefit while the vast majority of mankind will hide in the humiliation of their unfulfillment? Is the idea of a Mashiach that humanity will drown in shame and embarrassment for its wrongdoings? Certainly not! But then, man must be able to rectify himself. Free will must exist in order for man to be able to choose correctly. Yet this contradicts our Sages' statement that "In the Days of Mashiach there will be no reward and no punishment," for free will will have been negated. There must be more to this "rectification" than meets the eye. And there is.

*

"I will place My spirit within you, and I will cause you to follow My decrees..."

Ezekiel 36:27

One must be an expert in *halakhah* to know how to walk in the ways of God. *Halakhah* is translated as "the Codes," which means that one must study the Word of God to know how to serve Him. But *halakhah* also means "to walk." A person must be an expert in knowing how and when to walk forwards and how and when to hold back (see *Likutey Moharan* I, 6:4). That is, people attempt to serve God, but they face obstacles and encounter doubts which discourage their efforts. This is depressing and they may stop trying altogether. Therefore, those who want to serve God must know how to strengthen themselves at all times. They must know when to move forward and when to restrain their efforts, so that their lives are balanced — then they can enter into holiness.

The great tzaddikim have experienced all sorts of ascents and descents while serving God. Having succeeded, they are experts at knowing what to do — and how and when to do it — in order to truly serve God. Further, they try to imbue others with this expertise. Now, the great tzaddikim are far beyond the conception of the human mind. They are like "the sun," which is far too bright to gaze upon. Their teachings must be filtered down to us through their disciples, who correspond to "the moon" — which reflects the light of the sun. As the world becomes enlightened and the teachings of truth spread [through dialogue and peace, as discussed above], everybody will come to know *what, how* and *when* to do what is proper.

Even when Mashiach comes the evil inclination will still exist and people will have free will to choose between right and wrong. If there is no evil inclination, Mashiach will not be able to rectify the world. For a person who has no evil inclination is as if he were dead, with no free will and no means of repentance and rectification. Therefore, even after Mashiach comes free will *must* exist [due to the existence of the evil inclination]. But Mashiach will be an expert in knowing *what, how* and *when* to do what must be done. That is, he will be able to draw on his knowledge to instill the same expertise into every person according to his level until *everyone* will be aroused to serve God — even those who are very, very distant from Him! This is the meaning of the verse, "I will place My spirit within you, and I will cause you to follow My decrees..." "I will cause," means that God will cause — *something*. Through that *something*, "you will follow My decrees" (*Likutey Halakhot, Birkhot HaPeirot* 5:17).

That "something" is Mashiach. Mashiach will have the ability to attract people by drawing them close to God. As an expert in serving God, he will instill in people the desire to serve God so that even the very distant — those floundering in the lowest levels of materialism — will *want* to serve Him. He will be able to do this because he will have the right advice to offer each person. Thus, each person will rectify himself by knowing *how* to exercise his free will to grow spiritually through his own good desires and deeds. The question is: What happens next?

The free will of which we have been speaking is intimately bound up with overcoming the evil inclination. As Reb Noson stated categorically above: "Even after Mashiach comes, the evil inclination will still exist and people will have free will to choose between right and wrong," and "Therefore, even after Mashiach comes, free will must exist [due to the existence of the evil inclination]."

What, then, will happen when there is no longer an evil inclination? What kind of free choice will exist then?

This is the subject of our Sages statement in the Talmud (*Sukkah* 52a), "In the Future the evil inclination will be slain." Obviously, the time must come when there will no longer be any evil inclination to sway a person away from God. But at the same time, the Talmud there speaks about the "death of Mashiach ben Yosef." We have seen earlier that Mashiach ben Yosef represents all the tzaddikim who strive to bring knowledge of God to everyone (Chapter 4). When this knowledge is instilled in all people, then there is no longer a "battle" to teach people about God — hence, there is no longer a "need" for a Mashiach ben Yosef to do battle. The war is won.

The resolution of our problem is this: At the onset of the revelation of the Mashiach, the battle for truth against falsehood and good against evil will still be waged. As Mashiach's influence spreads, however, people will be drawn to him and will exercise their free will to seek God and become rectified. It is about the time following this rectification that

Ecclesiastes spoke of "years of which you will say, 'I have no desire for them'." All humanity will then see the awesome beauty of serving God and the incredible delights awaiting those who did serve Him. Everyone will share in the joy and excitement of those days, for then there will no longer be an evil inclination and free will. There will be no need, for man will be rectified!

*

The Eternal Torah

We have just seen that Mashiach will be able to reveal to everyone the "what, how and when" of serving God. The next obvious question is, "What does this mean?" "How and when" mean how and when to strengthen ourselves — "to do or refrain from doing, to move forward or wait and be patient, etc." But, *what* directives will there be? The answer is, the Torah. The Rambam writes:

> This Torah — its laws and directives — is eternal, forever and ever. One cannot add to it, nor can one subtract from it (*Yad HaChazakah, Melakhim* 11:3).

The word ToRaH, comes from the root *ToReH*, which means "to teach" or "to reveal" — and in this instance it means "to show" which path is the right one to walk when serving God. Thus, the Torah can show us *what* we must do in order to come close to God. The Torah is eternal and has guided the spiritual search for God since Creation. The Talmud teaches that Adam, Noah and the Patriarchs studied and observed the Torah ((see *Eruvin* 18b; Rashi, Genesis 7:2; *Kiddushin* 82a, etc.). However, it was concealed then from most people. This is why the world was in a state of chaos for its first two thousand years.

Beginning with the Patriarchs there was a continual rise in spirituality, until Moshe was able to bring the Torah to all of us at Sinai. And just as the Torah was valid in the past and is effective in the present, it will continue to be inspiring in the future. The question remains, though: The Torah was already given to us. Since, even though we have possessed the

Torah for thousands of years, we have been unsuccessful in serving God properly until now, *how* will it be able to help us more in the future?

The Torah is known as the *"taryag itin d'Oraita* — the 613 counsels of the Torah" (Zohar II, 82b; see Likutey Halakhot, Eiruvei Techumin 5:6). That is, the Torah with the 613 mitzvot that God commanded us to observe is good advice. It is so called because, by observing the commandments properly, one can successfully navigate the material world and reap the eternal, spiritual rewards of the World to Come.

On a deeper level, the reason we need the Torah to advise us is because Adam sinned by accepting the Serpent's advice and eating from the Tree of Knowledge. Advice, in Hebrew, is *EiTZah*, which is etymologically related to the word *EiTZ*, tree. Adam was supposed to eat from the Tree of Life ("advice that brings eternal life"). Instead, he partook of the fruit of the forbidden tree, seeking the material (see Likutey Halakhot, Yom Kippur 2:4). He lost his standing and was banished from the Garden.

Conversely, Mashiach, whose mission is to elevate us to the realm of spirituality, will have wondrous advice (as we shall now see), which will strengthen his dominion over mankind. This is because the Hebrew for "taking counsel" is *niMLaKh*, similar to MaLKhut, kingship. A government can rule effectively only with good counsel (see Likutey Moharan I, 18:4). Thus, in order to establish his dominion over the world, Mashiach must have a never-ending supply of wondrous advice (see Likutey Halakhot, Sukkah 7).

*

The Written Law and the Oral Law

The Torah is divided into two parts: the Written Law (the Bible) and the Oral Law (Talmud, Codes, Midrash, Kabbalah, etc.). We can easily read the Written Law but, without the Oral Law to explain it, we would never be able to understand from it how to perform the mitzvot. The Oral Law is transmitted from one generation to the next by its leading scholars. Because the Jews have faithfully adhered to the words of their teachers, the true tzaddikim of each generation, they have remained viable as a nation throughout the ages (see Likutey Moharan I, 7:3).

Jewish history shows us that whenever deep rifts developed in the nation and people left the faith, it was because they contested the rabbis and strayed from the Oral Law. Witness the Sadducees, the Karaites, the various apostates of the Middle Ages (who provoked disputations and the public burnings of the Talmud), the Shabbatean, Frankist and Enlightenment movements, etc., all of which spawned a departure from faith which eventually led to a rejection of Jewish practices and ultimately to assimilation. The reason for this is that all sins stem from receiving bad advice — from Adam having accepted the counsel offered him by the serpent. Therefore, one must seek good advice, that which comes from the Oral Law, from the tzaddikim (see Likutey Halakhot, Taanit 4:2).

Taking this a step further, we find that the Oral Law corresponds to Malkhut (Tikkuney Zohar, Introduction, p.17a). This is because the Oral Law is the final word in Jewish law. Therefore, the rabbis who have mastered the Oral Law possess authority, i.e. Malkhut (Gittin 62a). In the Kabbalah, Malkhut refers to God's Indwelling Presence. As we shall see (below, Parts V-VI), all interaction between God and man is through Malkhut, the acceptance of God's Kingship. Thus, those who distance themselves from the Oral Law are actually distancing themselves from spirituality. The Oral Law is the ultimate manifestation of Godliness, and without it one cannot expect to truly find God.

When Mashiach comes, everyone will accept him as their expert guide. As the leading authority, his teachings and advice — all 613 of them based on the Oral Law — will be accepted and adhered to. The Torah will once again reign supreme.

*

The "New" Torah

"A [New] Torah will come forth from Me..."
Isaiah 51:4; Vayikra Rabbah 13:3

The Torah was given to us as a spiritual guide for a material world.

Since in the world of the Future we will be living on a spiritual level, of what avail will this Torah be? Once Mashiach arrives and the evil inclination is slaughtered, the spirit of impurity will be removed from the earth (cf. Ezekiel 36:26). What then does it mean that the Torah is eternal?

We have seen that the level of Mashiach is that of Keter, the highest of the five divine personae (above, Chapter 4; see below, Part V). The soul of a person also has five levels: *nefesh, ruach, neshamah, chayah* and *yechidah* (soul, spirit, Godly soul, living essence and unique essence). These five levels parallel the divine personae. The Torah itself, with its five books, also corresponds to these five personae and comprises five levels in itself. These are: *p'shat, remez, drush, sod* (or *razin*) and *razin d'razin* (simple meaning, allusions, homiletics, mysteries and hidden mysteries) (see Appendix B; see also *Innerspace* by Rabbi Aryeh Kaplan, Moznaim Publishers, and *Anatomy of the Soul* by Breslov Research Institute, for detailed descriptions of the soul and the corresponding divine personae.)

The Kabbalists explain that the Torah we have received contains all these five levels. However, for the past several millennia, we have only been able to delve into the Torah on four levels: including the Kabbalah. But, just as Mashiach's level has yet to be revealed, so too the level of the hidden mysteries of the Torah has yet to be revealed. This awesome level of "hidden mysteries" is called the "Torah of *Atika Stima'ah*" ("Torah of the Hidden Ancient One") or simply, the "*Torah of Atik*" that will be revealed in the future (see Zohar III, 152a).

Throughout our history, the Torah of Atik has been concealed, with rare revelations made by our Prophets and Sages, as when they foretold the Days of Mashiach. They were given "a taste" of the Torah of Atik, experienced the messianic era, and shared it with us (see Zohar III, 110a). They glimpsed the "New Torah" which will be revealed in the Future. It is the same Torah as we have today, but in its deepest form. The same laws will apply — not one iota will change! But its application to our daily lives will bring a much deeper understanding, through which we will be able to experience the Divine (*Likutey Halakhot, Eiruvei Techumin* 5:22).

It *is* possible to taste and experience this Torah of Atik even today.

Praying with self-sacrifice, whereby the person negates himself totally before God, is known as *hitpashtut hagashmiyut* ("the shedding of corporeality"; prayer is *the* means of binding oneself to God, as explained above, Chapter 5. When one prays with the negation of one's material self, one "loses" oneself and feels that incredibly strong bond to Godliness, spirituality.) One who prays in this fashion relinquishes his corporeality, that which confines him within a "limited body." Transcending the material, he is now without limitation — and can merit the Torah of Atik, which is also beyond any limitation! (see Likutey Moharan I, 15:4, see also note 29).

It is told of Rabbi Eliyahu, the Gaon of Vilna, that after he passed the age of forty he would study only from a *TaNaKh* (Bible). That is, he was able to see every item of the Oral Law in its source, the Written Law. In the same way, the Torah of Atik must also be found in the *TaNaKH*, though we do not know yet how. If a person studies and tries to learn from his studies how to come closer to God, he is, in a sense, seeking the counsel of Torah as will be revealed by Mashiach. Mashiach will reveal the advice in Torah as it applies to each person. Thus, studying Torah with the intent of finding God and Godliness can give a person a taste of the Torah of Atik (see Likutey Moharan I, 61; Likutey Halakhot, Taanit 4:2).

As we have shown, our Prophets and Sages were privy to the Torah of the Future. There are also writings today from the tzaddikim of previous generations, most notably the followers of the Baal Shem Tov, which speak about the Torah of Atik (or *Atika Stima'ah*). One can be assured that those tzaddikim who discuss it in their works were also privy to that aspect of Torah. By studying their writings one can also glimpse a little of the Torah of Atik. Furthermore, Rebbe Nachman teaches that accepting advice from tzaddikim is the most viable means of finding out the truth (Likutey Moharan I, 7:3). Thus, seeking the teachings of the tzaddikim and accepting their counsel (i.e. the Oral Law) brings one to the messianic revelation of truth and great Daat — to the Torah of Atik!

*

The "New Testament"

Having seen that the Torah comprises "613 counsels," we can now understand how Mashiach, with the revelation of the Torah of Atik, will be able to direct people's free choice towards the will of God. The Torah that we know today, that was revealed to us at Sinai, was given to us at a time when the world was not yet free of evil. Man was still left to his own de-"vices." To anyone adhering to the mitzvot, the 613 counsels become "advice," helping to direct him towards a spiritual life. But man must still seek this advice from the true tzaddikim, those who have mastered the study of these counsels and have also mastered the evil inclination. They, with all their special experience, *know* how to apply the Torah's advice so that every soul can glean spiritual growth from it.

However, faced with an ever growing array of counter-advice by one's evil inclination, man must heed the tzaddik's advice carefully. As each generation spawns its own forms of materialistic foolishness, the eternal Torah must combat the new attacks upon it from fresh perspectives. This places increasing pressure upon those who sincerely seek the Torah's advice — the mitzvot — for the world at large today tends to view the traditional as being less than relevant in today's "enlightened" atmosphere. Religions, cults, secular mystics and gurus are often sought by those who reject a Torah life. Historically, Jewish suffering fed exasperation to the point of despair. All this has led to an unprecedented alienation from God's guiding light, the Torah.

We can now understand the universal pursuit of "news" and new approaches to life. When Mashiach comes there will be ever greater revelations of spirituality, and this will be the *real* news, as in (Jeremiah 31:21), "God will reveal *newness* in the world..." The Targum translates this as the search for new Torah teachings. Thus, the search for new revelations and ideals is rooted in the Future, along with the other messianic concepts. But, when sought out before their time, or out of place or context, the "new" paths become distorted and eventually lead people away from God. Rashi explains that the Torah's use of the word "today" is to teach us to look daily at the Torah with a fresh view (Deuteronomy 6:6; ibid. 26:16); that is, to look at the Torah as it is — an enduring entity. Examining it with a fresh approach leads us ever closer to God. On the other hand, looking "outwards" for something "new," something that is not enduring, is not beneficial for our spiritual growth. This includes all the *new testaments* and *spiritual teachings* which promise fast salvation and enlightenment, but which dissipate after several centuries or decades, if not sooner.

The Prophet Jeremiah lived during the time of the destruction of the First Temple. He witnessed the destruction and exile of his people, whom he had sought throughout his life to lead away from sin and back to God. The people rebelled against God, against the Torah and against Jeremiah, the tzaddik — hence they suffered terribly. Yet Jeremiah was so great, he still spoke lovingly to his nation and tried to console them. He foresaw that the time would come when they would accept the Torah and return to God.

> *"Behold! Days are coming, says God, when I will make a 'new covenant' with the House of Israel and the House of Judah. Not like the covenant that I made with their ancestors, when I redeemed them from Egypt, which they violated... This is the covenant... I will place My Torah within them and inscribe it upon their hearts..."*
>
> Jeremiah 31:30-32

There are those who have chosen to misinterpret the Torah, thereby misleading their followers. Many have made their own bibles and testaments, others have misrepresented the Torah's meaning. Mashiach will reveal the truth, the real "New Testament," the new covenant that God will make with His People — for Mashiach will be able to reveal the deeper meaning of every facet of Torah.

The tzaddikim of all the generations have had to battle with every foolishness that arose during their lifetimes. As the years wear on, the "new approaches" to life become transparent, revealing the absolute nonsense that they are. People tend to tire of the insanities around them, especially when they see that the advice given by the tzaddikim provides stability in chaotic surroundings and stands up to the ravages of time. But the pattern has been that when the war for spirituality appears to have been nearly won, new nonsensical ideas are spawned which demand a fresh approach on the battlefield.

These nonsensical ideas are represented by Amalek, the Jews' eternal enemy who has always tried forward-and-flank attacks to weaken and destroy us, especially when we are lax in our adherence to Torah (cf. *Sanhedrin* 106a). Other attacks by Amalek include his "cutting off the 'tails' (weakened Jews)" — trying to cut off the inattentive Jew from his community (cf. *Tanchuma, Ki Tetze*). This also alludes to Amalek's cunning in getting the Jews to set people of no value (i.e. tails) at their helm (see *Likutey Halakhot, Shabbat* 5:9). These "leaders" lack sensible advice and mislead the Jews when they espouse their ideals — to begin with their interpretations are based on falsehood. The deviousness of Amalek in shunting the Jews away from God and Torah arises anew every generation. This is the major battle to be fought by the tzaddikim of each generation, and ultimately by Mashiach.

But Mashiach is the true leader, a leader of stature. He will not be misled, nor will he mislead through false interpretations of the Torah. On the contrary, he will reveal advice offered in the Torah of Atik — the same, eternal Torah we study today with its 613 counsels — which transcends anything that Amalek could proffer. The advice Mashiach will dispense will be more than adequate to counter any foolishness that arises. Thus, Amalek, the evil inclination, will ultimately be defeated. And man, because of the revelation of the Torah of Atik, will learn and know how to repent — to rectify all his wrongs and recognize God (see *Likutey Halakhot, Eiruvei Techumin* 5:13).

This is why Mashiach is called *Pele Yoetz*, "the Wondrous Advisor." Kabbalistically, *Pele* (Wonder) stands for Keter (*Tikkuney Zohar* #70, p.135a). Mashiach's advice stems from Keter, the Torah of Atik, the 613 wondrous counsels. And he will be able to dispense this advice to each and every person, according to his effort and ability to serve God. The verse thus states (Isaiah 11:2), "Upon him [the Mashiach] will descend a spirit of God; a spirit of wisdom and understanding, a spirit of *advice* and strength, a spirit of knowledge and fear of God" (*Likutey Halakhot, Eiruvei Techumin* 5:22).

May he come speedily, in our days, Amen.

* * *

11

My very own Mashiach!

The objective of this book is to relate the messianic ideals to our daily lives. It is taught that "Every person has a portion of Mashiach within" (Likutey Moharan I, 78). By understanding the messianic ideals, we can relate to Mashiach in a sensible and mature manner, bringing out the Mashiach within ourselves and bringing Mashiach closer to us — for the benefit of all mankind.

The messianic concepts — who he is and what his mission is — are many. We are now ready to discuss *why* Mashiach is necessary and *how* he will accomplish his mission. But before we proceed, it would be very beneficial to review what we have learned to this point. In this chapter, we will bring together the ideas discussed thus far, so that instead of looking at different segments of the messianic mosaic, we can begin to see how they all tie together and enable us to better understand the "who and what" of Mashiach.

*

Mashiach is someone who will bring peace and tranquility to the entire world. Since the world today is nowhere near that stage — or so it seems — Mashiach must be an extraordinary person. In order for him to conquer the entire world, which is armed with so many terrible weapons, both conventional and non-conventional, an extraordinary Mashiach requires exceptional weapons.

The weapons found in Mashiach's arsenal are: prayer, fear of God, Torah, faith, truth, a Voice of Rebuke and sexual purity. Through the wise use of these weapons, Mashiach will be able to gather in the exiles, build the Holy Temple and advise people on how to search for God. He will spread the knowledge of God, revealing great levels of transcendental intellect. Mashiach will reveal Divine Providence, that all of nature is actually Godliness, will adjudicate honestly and will bring healing and wealth, peace and goodwill, to all. Let's see how.

*

The messianic ideal

Mashiach's spirit stems from "the nose" of Arikh Anpin, the level of Keter. Arikh Anpin in turn is rooted in Atik, the highest level of all the divine personae of Atzilut. Keter represents the highest level at which man can currently relate to God. (Since God is *Ein Sof,* "The Infinite One," there will always be ever greater levels of Godliness to be revealed. But for now, we can only refer to Keter, which is itself far beyond our conception.)

As the major organ of breathing, the nose is controlled by the mind. So too, Mashiach, as represented by "the nose," is rooted in the exalted levels of Keter. Since this transcends all levels known to us, we have no conception of who Mashiach really is. However, we do know that his intelligence and ability — due to this exalted level — will be tremendous.

Keter reflects the Torah at its highest level. When Mashiach comes he will reveal the level of Keter, the reality of Torah and how it is vitally pertinent to each person, Jew and non-Jew alike (see Likutey Moharan I, 21:15). Then every person will have the correct advice he needs to serve God (i.e. the "613 counsels of Torah"). This is because Mashiach is called "*Pele Yoetz*" ("The Wondrous Advisor"), and can draw on his incredible wellsprings of knowledge to advise all of mankind as to how they are to proceed, each on his own proper path. Man's free will, until that time subjected to immense pressure from ever-unfolding quarries of foolishness stemming from the evil inclination, will then be exercised to serve man's spiritual benefit.

With Mashiach's advice, people will be able to translate that supernal knowledge into prayer. The nose indicates breathing, which is each person's life-force. The nose also corresponds to prayer; thus with each breath, we will praise God. This is because Mashiach will reveal an awareness of God which we will feel at all times. God's exaltedness will become very real to each and every human being and, out of awe and respect, everyone will honor God through prayer. This is why the nose also corresponds to the fear and awe of God which will be greatly increased then. This will lead to greater knowledge and awareness of Godliness, the exalted levels of Daat.

This Daat of Atik represents pure kindness, with no admixture of judgment. The ARI explains that Daat is the external manifestation of the hidden Keter. Hence, the Daat that will be revealed in the Days of Mashiach is actually the revelation of Keter, where only goodness and kindness reign. This is the great Knowledge that will be revealed in Mashiach's time. Thus, the Torah of Atik corresponds to a high level of Daat, wherein peace is dominant. This is because great Daat can combine (i.e. make peace between) two opposites, as is found in Torah — for example, the opposing views of two sages are both rooted in one single Unity, God (see Eruvin 13b). When this great Daat, the Torah of Atik, is revealed, peace will abound (see Likutey Moharan I, 105).

Prayer is the ultimate recognition of the fact that God is Master of the Universe and that everything functions under His direct Divine Providence. Recognizing the Creator as great and awesome will instill in humanity an appreciation of, and respect for, His exalted greatness. Mankind will acknowledge this by offering sincere praise to God. Recognizing God and praying to Him will effectively bring about the end of idolatry and the spread of true faith. When one attains faith, one begins to see how the entire world is directed through Divine Providence, that every *natural event* is a miracle.

With the spread of knowledge of God, Mashiach will gather in the exiles and build Jerusalem (fear of God) and the Holy Temple. This is because (Isaiah 2:3), "Torah will go forth from Zion" — the Torah of Atik. The Temple signifies Daat, which each person helps to build through his prayers and good deeds, by searching for Godliness in everything in Creation. Mashiach also establishes harmony and peace between individuals, by judging (and teaching mankind to judge) everyone favorably and seeking the good points in everyone. This leads to universal peace.

Peace in itself alludes to many ideas. When one suffers illness, it is because one's organism is out of balance. This denotes strife and argument. But with the advent of a greater peace in the world, "peace in one's body" also becomes a reality.

By heralding an era of peace, jealousy and hatred will disappear. The immense resources of wealth that exist in the world will be open to all — with no-one encroaching on the needs of another. Everybody will have enough. (There are significant reasons for the great wealth we will have then, and these will be discussed below, Parts IV-VI.) Furthermore, the Hand of Divine Providence will dispense abundant blessing, enabling people to receive their livelihood without even lifting a finger.

A person's sense of smell can detect foul odors. So too, the "Mashiach within us" (i.e. our own "nose," or ability to sense right from wrong) will be able to detect what is decayed and corrupt. Most people do not want to fall victim to sin, yet many times they cannot help themselves. When Mashiach comes, falsehood and crime will be eradicated. Immorality, the bane of every civilization, will no longer exist. Thus, every person, smelling the sweet fragrance of purity and honesty, will be drawn to Mashiach, who will advise him on how to extricate himself from his evil traits and actions and assist him in his efforts. His advice will radiate from a Voice of Rebuke that speaks only truth. But, instead of "the truth hurting," this Voice of Rebuke will invoke the sweet smell of the Mashiach, of rectification, and draw a person close to God.

All the above reflects the messianic powers that are available to each person on his own level. But each person also needs his "own" present-day Mashiach — reflected in his attachment to the tzaddikim of the generation. By binding ourselves to the tzaddikim, we bring ourselves closer to that aspect of Mashiach, making it easier for us to recognize him and his qualities.

*

Mashiach and the tzaddikim

Godliness is an awesome spiritual light. It is too intense for the average person to benefit from. (Just how intense it is will be seen in Part V.) Therefore, in order for a person to experience it, it must be filtered down to the appropriate level. The filters of Godliness are the tzaddikim, Torah and mitzvot, prayer and faith.

We have seen that Mashiach's name is an acrostic for Menachem, Shiloh, Yinon and Chaninah. These names also reflect the powers of Mashiach.

> Menachem translates as consolation, and in the main, consolation is dependent upon knowledge. Understanding why one has suffered is a most soothing consolation for suffering (Likutey Moharan I, 21:12). (One who is bereft can be consoled with the knowledge that better times will come. This is another example of Daat as the main consolation.) Thus, Mashiach is "Menachem" who will reveal great knowledge — the Torah of Atik.
>
> Shiloh is Moshe (see Chapter 4), the paradigm of a true leader, a righteous judge and a tzaddik.
>
> Yinon translates as Malkhut, Kingship (Rashi, Psalms 72:17), which alludes to faith. Before one can arrive at the gates of sublime Daat, one must have faith that such exalted wisdom exists. Thus, Mashiach represents pure faith (see Likutey Moharan I, 1:2).
>
> ChaNaNyah is from the root word, l'ChaNeN, to plead, indicating prayer.

All these concepts represent either the ideal tzaddik and leader (i.e. Mashiach), or the other main pillars upon which Judaism rests: Torah, truth and righteousness (i.e. the mitzvot), prayer and faith. The Torah, until now, revealed — yet constricted — Godliness. When Mashiach comes, the constrictions of sublime knowledge will be expanded to reveal ever higher levels of Godliness and take on a newer, fresher meaning, as the Torah of Atik unfolds before us (see also Vayikra Rabbah 13:3).

But in a certain sense, prayer is even more exalted than the Torah (see Likutey Halakhot, Rosh Chodesh 5). This is because Torah itself is a constriction. The depth of knowledge contained therein is so intense that it must be restricted in order for a person to be able to understand it. In prayer, on the other hand, a person transcends any worldly form or shape. His desire is raised to a level beyond any description, as he attempts to ascend into total spirituality. Therefore, for all the exaltedness of the Torah of Atik, prayer will be Mashiach's main weapon. For it can transcend even the level of Atik by the person's desire to be included in the Infinite! (Atik, the Keter, corresponds to pure desire, and will be explained below, Parts V-VI.) And prayer is uttered with a voice, corresponding to the "Voice of Rebuke" which will arouse all to the service of God.

*

Torah and prayer

> *"One day will be known as God's day, neither day nor night; towards evening it will become light... On that day, God will be King over the entire world..."*
>
> Zekhariah 14:7-9

We have seen that Mashiach is the tzaddik who will reveal the Torah of Atik and the power of prayer. The Torah offers us the correct advice to follow, while prayer gives us the freedom of expression to attain, internalize and fulfill those teachings. This shows us that at their source, Torah and prayer are closely related. The Torah can be understood if studied through the "Thirteen Principles of Torah Interpretation" (*Sifra*). The ultimate prayer is when one is able to pray to God, pouring out one's heart in true supplication and arousing the Thirteen Attributes of Mercy, as Moshe did (Exodus 34:6-7; see *Zohar* III, 62a). Thus Moshe, though the paradigm of Torah, also embodies the power of prayer.

King David authored the Book of Psalms, which consists of prayers and pleas to God to provide him with all his needs, both the physical and, even more, the spiritual. When he wrote Psalms, King David divided them into five books, corresponding to the Five Books of Moshe. For King David turned his studies into prayers, pleading with God to be able to fulfill the Torah. Thus, both Moshe Rabeinu and King David, the paradigms of Torah and prayer, drew upon one another's qualities to enhance their spirituality (*Likutey Halakhot, Rosh Chodesh* 5:6-7).

This is Mashiach's assignment, to inspire us to draw upon the spiritual energy of whatever we study and pray that it brings us closer to God. We can do this even today, and repent with a full heart. By studying Torah, a person comes to see what good he has done and which sins he has committed. By confessing these sins before God, he converts his Torah (i.e. his studies) into prayer! (Likutey Halakhot, Rosh Chodesh 5:25). Praying to God by enumerating one's sins and asking to follow the Torah instead of disobeying it is a taste of the messianic prayer, that prayer which is Mashiach's main weapon.

Mashiach is represented by Moshe, Joseph and David, for all three combined represent the strength of Mashiach. Moshe stands for Torah while King David stands for prayer. Joseph, "the tzaddik," combines Torah and prayer. This is because the tzaddik can teach Torah and is also capable of teaching us how to turn our studies into prayer — i.e. to pray to God to fulfill that which we have studied. Thus, if we examine the numerical values of their names, we will find that Moshe-משה (345), Joseph-יוסף (156) and David-דוד (14), are equal to the word *tefilah*-תפלה (515). The combination of the powers of these tzaddikim forms the weapons of Mashiach (Likutey Halakhot, Rosh Chodesh 5:20; see Appendix B).

*

And yet, in contrast to our earlier statement that Torah is a constriction and prayer can transcend it, we also find that Torah corresponds to day (brightness, intellect) while prayer corresponds to night (constrictions, need). This is because one might study and gain spiritual knowledge, but because of one's physical needs one's prayers are, in essence, materialistic. However, when one combines Torah and prayer, using one's prayers for *spiritual* pursuits as will be in the Days of Mashiach, then there is "neither day nor night." It is "God's day," in which night and day — Torah and prayer — are combined and shine brightly. For the powers of the Mashiach as revealed through the tzaddikim can combine Torah and prayer to reach a level which transcends anything we can imagine (Likutey Halakhot, Rosh Chodesh 5:21).

Before his passing, Moshe Rabeinu exhorted the Jews to strengthen themselves with faith in God. How were they to do this? By transforming the Torah that he gave to the Jews into a prayer, the "Song of *Haazinu*" (Deuteronomy 32). Strengthening themselves with Torah and prayer will carry them through the difficulties of the "End of Days." Then, on that day, "God will be King over the entire world..." (*Likutey Halakhot, Rosh Chodesh* 5:30-31).

*

"V'naharu eilav... all the nations will flow to it"
Isaiah 2:2

"The River flows from Eden and waters the Garden..."
Genesis 2:10

"Eden" represents prayer; like prayer, Eden is beyond conception (cf. Isaiah 64:3; Berakhot 34b). "The Garden" represents the Torah (*Tikkuney Zohar* #14, p.29b). "The River" refers to drawing the power of prayer into the Torah, so that people will fulfill the mitzvot (see *Likutey Moharan* I, 8:7). Furthermore, "the River" refers to the Voice of Rebuke (as above, Chapter 7). The Voice of Rebuke is present in the Mashiach, represented by the tzaddikim who reveal the pathways of spirituality. And this Voice can be found in the Torah — the Torah of Atik — as our Sages' state (*Kiddushin* 30b), "The Torah is a spice against the evil inclination." That is, the Torah is that sweet-smelling spice which emanates from the Voice of Rebuke, bringing all back to God (see *Likutey Halakhot, Arev* 4:10).

The Mashiach of each generation (i.e. the tzaddikim) are those who draw the power of Eden (prayer) into the Garden (Torah), giving form and shape to that which is beyond conception. This is their awesome power, and this is why they can reveal Godliness — for they are able to reveal the mitzvot and advice with which we can relate to God. This is why the tzaddikim are called "the Voice of Rebuke," "the River." In Hebrew, river is a *nahar* (נהר). When *NaHaR* is expanded (נון הא רש) — *NUN, HE, ReSh*), the numerical value of its letters is 612 (see Appendix B). Adding one more to the sum for the word itself, it numerically equals 613, the number of mitzvot in the Torah. These 613 mitzvot are the 613 counsels of the Torah to be revealed in the Future, the Torah of Atik, the level of Keter. Thus, the tzaddikim, the Voice of Rebuke, parallel the revealing of the level of Keter in the Torah! This is why cleaving to the tzaddikim — to Mashiach — is crucial. Without it, one cannot hope to combine the aspects of Torah and prayer, and thereby come to recognize God.

*

We can now relate the Voice of Rebuke to faith and to the Song of the Future. The Jews are called *IVRim*, because they have been able to *oVeIR* (pass over or endure) the challenges to their faith, *with* their faith (Likutey Moharan I, 64:2). Faith is what has carried them through their long sojourn in exile.

> Every wisdom has its own song, as in (Psalms 47:8), "*Zamru maskil*" ("sing, wise one"). Even heresy has its own song, as is evident by hymns sung during idolatrous practices. Faith, too, has its own melody. The greater the faith in God, especially as the *Ein Sof*, the Infinite One, the loftier the level of this melody. Alluding to the Future, when all will come to recognize God, we are told (Songs 4:8), "Come, sing from the heights of [Mount] AMaNaH" (which is like *ÆMuNaH*, faith) (Likutey Moharan I, 64:5).

The Voice of Rebuke is the Song of the Future, which itself corresponds to the revelation of God's Name (see above, Chapter 7). What a person is able to understand does not require faith. What is beyond the person's ability to grasp requires faith. At the level on which only faith applies, questions can have no empirical answers. Faith therefore requires silence. However, though one cannot answer questions in these areas, one *can* think silently — and hum a tune. This is because "answers" require a format while melody has no actual corporeal form. For melody does not contain speech, only thought. Since faith is so lofty a level, those who merit faith will "feel" a revelation of God, hence their melody is comparable to the "Song of the Future." Thus, those who have faith can merit even now to hear the Voice of Rebuke, the Song of the Future, the revelation of God's Name, even in material surroundings.

*

The verse states (Deuteronomy 17:15), "You should appoint a king over yourself…" Our Sages teach that even when you are in exile, you should appoint a king over yourselves. That king is God (Tikkuney Zohar #21, p.60b). As mentioned above (Chapter 5), each person has to build his own Holy Temple, his own Sanctuary. This is accomplished by drawing near to the tzaddikim, by speaking truth and acting in purity, by engaging in prayer and Torah study and by strengthening one's faith. By searching for God, a person builds Jerusalem, his fear of God, and transforms himself into a Sanctuary, a Holy Temple, where his mind becomes a vessel to receive great perceptions of Godliness. This is the great Daat that will be revealed in the future. This is every person's very own Mashiach, one that he can relate to even now.

Then, in the Days of Mashiach (Zefaniah 3:9), "I will imbue all peoples will a *saphah brurah*, a pure tongue; that they may call in the Name of God and all serve Him in one manner." The word *saphah* (שפה) is numerically equal to 385, which is the same sum as the word *Shekhinah* (שכינה), the Divine Presence (Tikkuney Zohar #21, p.62a). When one calls out truthfully to God, one merits a revelation of God, as will occur in the future, when all nations will call out to God.

*

Then the *NaHaR* (the River, i.e. the Voice of Rebuke) will transform into *RiNaH* (joyous song). Great joy and happiness will abound in the world and all those who cling to God will rejoice greatly. Isaiah's prophecy will then be fulfilled:

> "And the exiles of God will be redeemed and return to Zion *b'rinah*, in joyous song, with eternal joy upon their heads; they shall attain joy and gladness — and sorrow and sighing will flee" (Isaiah 35:10).

Amen, may it be His will.

* * *

Part IV

Mashiach:

Why?

In this section we will discuss the reasons for the delay in Mashiach's immiment arrival. The ideas presented here are based on the ideals and goals of various "groups" in Rebbe Nachman's classic story, "The Master of Prayer" (the entire story has been included as Appendix A). *Our discussion will focus on the major qualities that characterize mankind at the present time, and their implications for the messianic future.*

12

Why hasn't Mashiach come yet?

There are many "Why?" questions we can ask about the Mashiach.

Why should there be a Mashiach at all? If the idea of free will is for each person to receive reward or punishment according to his deeds, why have a Mashiach to rectify mankind? Let everyone reap the consequences of his deeds (see above, Chapters 8,10). However, if Mashiach is going to rectify the world anyway, why put people in the position of being tempted by and perhaps succumbing to sin in order to earn their reward in the first place?

Why should Mashiach undertake such a job? Ever try to keep one small congregation united in peace? Just thinking about it can give a person a headache. Imagine then, trying to get the whole world together "under one roof!"

And why, if Mashiach wants to come and redeem us, hasn't he already done so?

We have been hearing for nearly two millennia that Mashiach is going to come. In fact, he's "in the air" already. These are the days of the *Ikv'ta d'Mashicha* ("The Footsteps of Mashiach") and, as we have shown, many of the ideas and ideals of messianic times are being revealed to us as never before (see above, Parts II-III). Naturally, we all want Mashiach to come. Who needs drugs, crime or illness; who wants enslavement to work, alcohol, strife or war? Who doesn't want good health, great wealth, peace and the ability to bask in God's Light? If so, since we really want Mashiach, what is holding him back? Why hasn't he come?

*

To provide anything approaching a *complete* answer to the question of why Mashiach is necessary or why everyone must earn his own reward would require several volumes. However, for our purposes, we need only understand that God created the world through His mercy, to bestow His goodness upon mankind. It is human nature for a person to feel guilty or embarrassed if he receives unearned gifts. Thus, God created the material world so that mankind could be subjected to external and internal pressures, yet seek the greatest spirituality possible. In this way, humanity would earn its own eternal reward and usher in a world of spiritual joy and delight. Were there no "free will" — i.e. no evil inclination — mankind could never earn its everlasting reward.

Yet if mankind failed and did not earn any reward, what purpose would life on this planet have served? What benefit would God have had in creating us? How could God ever bestow His goodness upon us?

A human being cannot know beforehand how his handiwork will turn out. He must experiment several times before perfecting an invention. This is not so with God, Who knows beforehand what the outcome will be. He created every soul with the express intention of eventually rewarding all of them. But He also wants us to *earn* our rewards. Therefore, God created the world with a Mashiach who will instill in all mankind the desire to serve God. Everyone will thus serve God, even if only a little, and for this he is entitled to some reward. This way, no person who has ever lived will have lived in vain. This includes *everybody*, except for a few so evil that they must be totally destroyed (see *Sanhedrin* 104b), and even they serve a purpose in the world, as will be discussed below (Parts V-VI; see also *Rosh HaShanah* 17a).

*

Why should Mashiach undertake such a job? What's in it for Mashiach? Frankly speaking, Mashiach doesn't have much choice. He was chosen for his job even before the world was created (see *Pesachim* 54a). But there's far more to it than that.

Tzaddikim are those people who negate themselves completely for the sake of God's will. Their entire existence is devoted to serving God and giving Him the satisfaction of receiving *nachat* (pleasure) from His creation (as a parent seeks from a child). Therefore, the tzaddikim do not live for themselves, but rather extend themselves to draw as many people as they can to God. The foremost example is Moshe who drew not only the Jews but even the Mixed Multitude to God. Moshe lived a life of total self-sacrifice on behalf of his people. Still, this was his heartfelt enjoyment, because he knew that he was bringing God pleasure. Mashiach, who will be the greatest tzaddik of all time, will take special delight in each soul as it draws near to God. His life's pleasure is his mission to reveal Godliness, so that everyone can partake of God's spiritual delight. Thus Mashiach will readily accept the mission — and do it well — for drawing people to God, no matter how formidable the task, is his own fulfillment.

If Mashiach wants to come and redeem us, why hasn't he already done so? We have been told for nearly two millennia that Mashiach is going to come. Why hasn't he come? Where is he already? Rabbi Zvi Aryeh Rosenfeld (1922-1978) asked this question of his mentor, Rabbi Avraham Sternhartz (1862-1955). The answer? "It is not that Mashiach isn't coming. He is always getting nearer. If we stood our ground Mashiach would have been here long ago. *We* are the problem — for we continually regress."

*

The 974 generations

> *"Mashiach will come in a generation that is either totally worthy or totally guilty."*
>
> Sanhedrin 98a

The following story is told about an encounter the Baal Shem Tov had with the Satan.

> "You are holding back Mashiach," the Satan said to the Baal Shem Tov. "'Mashiach will come in a generation that is either completely pure or totally impure.' As long as I am still able to do my job, the generations will never be completely pure!"
>
> The Baal Shem Tov replied, "You are holding back Mashiach. There can never be a generation that is totally impure for each generation has at

least thirty-six tzaddikim (see *Sanhedrin* 97b). Therefore, you are the one who is detaining Mashiach!"

It is not that Mashiach doesn't want to come. On the contrary, his whole existence demands that he come as soon as possible. So we have the answer to our question, "Why hasn't Mashiach come yet?" — because man is still succumbing to the evil inclination. But we are all part of a Greater Plan for each and every person to attain perfection. Thank God, not everyone is impure. In fact, as we have just seen, that would really be an impossibility. But then again, we can't really say that we've reached a stage of perfection! What prevents us from being worthy of the Mashiach?

The Talmud teaches (*Yoma* 38b), "God saw that tzaddikim are few in number; He therefore spread them out so that there are always some in each generation." It further states (*Chagigah* 13b-14a), "The Torah was to be given after 1,000 generations. But God saw that the world could not exist without the Torah so He skipped over 974 generations and gave the Torah to the 26th generation, that of Moshe. What happened to the souls of those people who were of the remaining 974 generations? They are the brazen-faced people (who live without Torah). They were spread out so that there are always some in each generation" (see Rashi, *Chagigah* 14a).

Reb Noson writes that this is the meaning of the statement of our Sages, "Mashiach will come in a generation that is either totally worthy or totally guilty." Either the generation will repent and be worthy and thereby merit the Mashiach. Or the impurities will be so great that Mashiach will have to come despite our sins. For when God is so concealed, then He *must* reveal Himself (see *Likutey Halakhot, Rosh Chodesh* 3). Thus, there are always tzaddikim who try to bring us near God. And there are the brazen-faced people who try to conceal the light of God and Torah.

In these coming chapters, we will view Judaism as it was given to us at Sinai and its "evolution" to its present form. We will examine several character traits — both positive and negative. We will define the brazenness *within us* that distances us from God, and we will see how these *very same* characteristics are powerful enough to bring us near to God.

* * *

13

The Master of Prayer

This chapter contains excerpts from Rebbe Nachman's story, "The Master of Prayer." We have limited our discussion to the opening passages about the Master of Prayer and the people of the Land of Wealth, and have included the storm wind which upset the entire world and the groups mentioned by the Rebbe. We have also included several other pertinent ideas. The entire story appears in Appendix A.

*

Once there was a Master of Prayer. He was constantly engaged in prayer and singing songs and praises to God.

He lived far from civilization. He would visit inhabited areas regularly in order to have heart-to-heart discussions with the people about the purpose of life. He would explain that the only true purpose was to serve God and sing His praise....

He would speak to an individual at great length, motivating him, so that his words entered the other's heart. As soon as the Master of Prayer convinced the individual to agree with his ideals, he would bring him to his isolated place.

It is for this purpose that the Master of Prayer had chosen for himself a place far from civilization. There was a river there, as well as fruit trees, which provided food for him and his followers. He was not at all concerned about clothing.

The only activities of those he brought home would be praying, singing praise to God, confession, fasting, self-mortification, repentance and similar occupations. He would give them his books of prayers....

Eventually, his teachings began to make an impression, and his activities became well known. People would suddenly vanish without a trace; no-one knew where they were. But finally people began to realize that all this was due to the Master of Prayer, who was attracting people to serve God....

*

The Land of Wealth

Meanwhile, there was a land in which everyone was wealthy.

This land, however, had very strange customs, since everything was dependent upon wealth. Thus, a person's status were determined solely on the basis of his wealth. One who had a great deal of money had a certain rank, while others who had smaller amounts had lower rank. The entire order of social rank was thus determined by the amount of money that each one had. According to their constitution, the one with the most money was king....

Rank was determined in the following manner: If a person had a certain amount of money, he was considered an ordinary human being. If he had less than this, he would be considered a bird or a beast. If a person had only a small amount of money, he might be considered a human lion or the like.

News of this land began to spread. The Master of Prayer sighed and said, "Who knows how far they will go because of this and what great errors they will make!..."

Around this time, the people of the land agreed that they wanted to establish the ranks of "stars" and "constellations." If a person had a certain agreed-upon amount of wealth, he would be a star.

Eventually, they also established the rank of "angel." This too depended on a person's wealth.

Finally, they also agreed to confer the rank of "god." If a person had a huge amount of wealth as stipulated in their rules, he would be a "god."

Since God had granted him such great wealth, that person would also be a "god...." They used "angels" for transportation. Their horses were bedecked with so much gold and treasures that their ornamentation alone would be enough to confer upon them the status of "angel."

Guards were stationed far from the mountains where they lived to prevent strangers from approaching them. They lived in the mountains and abided by their customs.

These people worshiped many gods who were appointed on the basis of wealth. They thus institutionalized their belief in wealth. They had services, sacrifices and incense which were used to serve the extremely wealthy people who were their gods.

Nevertheless, there was much killing and stealing in the land. People who did not believe in their religion became murderers and thieves in order to amass wealth. With money, one could buy anything: clothing or luxuries.

Sometimes an animal would become a human being or vice-versa. If a person lost his wealth, he would become an animal. Similarly, if an animal amassed wealth, he could become a human being. This was true of all ranks.

These people also had images and icons of the wealthy people who were their gods. They would embrace these images and kiss them. This was part of their religious service.

*

The Master of Prayer was unaware of the caste system that the Land of Wealth had established. Later he heard that the inhabitants of the land had made themselves into gods. The Master of Prayer said that this had been his original concern. He had great pity on these people and decided that he himself would go there, since he might be able to make them abandon their erroneous ways....

*

The Holy Assembly

Rebbe Nachman now introduces another main character in the story, the

Mighty Warrior, who was intent on conquering lands. He met up with the Master of Prayer who was trying to help the people of the Land of Wealth see the folly of their ways. The Mighty Warrior did not seek power but had an ulterior motive of seeking the ten members of the Holy Assembly. The Holy Assembly consisted of a King, and a Queen who had a Daughter. This Daughter married the Mighty Warrior and they had a Child. The King's inner circle included a Master of Prayer, a Faithful Friend, a Treasurer, a Bard and a Wise Man. These ten were dispersed during a hurricane that engulfed the entire world, and the Mighty Warrior went looking for them.

Meanwhile, there was a Mighty Warrior. Many other warriors had joined him and he and his men had conquered several countries. He demanded only subjugation. If the citizens of a land subjugated themselves to him, he would spare them; but if not, he would destroy them. He did not want any wealth, only subjugation (in order to find the King and the other members of the Holy Assembly). Because...

Once upon a time, there was a powerful hurricane. It transformed sea into dry land, and dry land into sea; desert into inhabited land, and inhabited land into desert.

When this hurricane struck the King's palace, it did not do any damage. However, it carried away the Child of the Queen's Daughter. The Queen's Daughter and the King and Queen ran after the Child. They became scattered, and no-one knew where they were. When the other members of the Holy Assembly returned, they could not find them....

*

At the time when the Mighty Warrior was approaching the Land of Wealth, the Master of Prayer was present. Knowing of the approach of the Mighty Warrior, he went to his camp and spoke to one of his guards in order to determine if his master was his old friend, the King's Mighty Warrior. The Master of Prayer asked him, "What is your occupation? How did you join up with this Warrior?" The soldier replied with the following story:

The chronicles

It all happened in this manner:

In our chronicles it is written that there was a great hurricane in the world which turned the whole world upside-down. Sea was transformed into dry land, and dry land into sea. Desolate areas became inhabited, while inhabited areas became desolate.

After the panic and confusion, the people of the world decided to elect a king. They delved into the question of who would be most fitting to be elected king. Upon deliberation, they finally said, "The most important consideration is the goal of life. Therefore the person who strives the most toward the goal is the most fitting to be king."

But then they had to determine the goal of life. Regarding this question, there were many factions.

One faction said that the main goal in this world is honor. If a person is not given proper honor, or if people say something that impinges on his honor, he is so offended that he can even commit murder.

Even after death the main consideration is honor. People are careful to honor one who is dead, burying him with honor. They even say to him, "Whatever is being done is being done for your sake, for your honor," even though the dead have nothing more to do with wealth or pleasure. Therefore honor is the main goal of life. They also had other confused, foolish "logical" reasons.

They also pursued honor. Such an "honored man" would be one who pursued and gained honor. If he already had honor, then, when he pursued it, his nature would help him attain it. In their foolish and confused opinion, such a man would be most fitting as king.

They went out to find such a man and finally discovered an old gypsy beggar who was being carried and followed by some five hundred gypsies. The beggar was blind, crippled and mute, and the people following him were all members of his clan. They were his brothers and sisters, as well as the children that he had sired.

This beggar was very particular about his honor. He had a nasty temper and was always scolding them. He constantly ordered different people to carry him, and then became angry with them.

Obviously, this old beggar was a highly honored person. He also pursued honor, since he was so particular about it. This faction therefore felt that it would be best to accept him as their king.

The land itself also influenced the goal. Some lands had an influence that was particularly conducive to honor, while other lands were conducive to other traits. Therefore, the group which had determined that the main goal was honor sought a land conducive to honor. When they found such a land they settled there.

Another faction decided that the main goal was murder. It is obvious that all things in the world, whether herbs, plants or people, deteriorate and decay.

Hence, a murderer who kills people and destroys lives is doing very much to bring the world to its goal. This group therefore concluded, according to their warped opinion, that the man most qualified to be king would be a murderer who was easily provoked and was fiercely jealous.

While seeking such a person, they heard an outcry. "What is this loud outcry?" they asked.

They were told, "A man just slit the throats of his father and mother!"

"Could there be a murderer with a harder heart or a fiercer temper than this?" they exclaimed. "Here is a man who killed his own parents!"

According to their opinion, this man had attained the goal of life, and they accepted him as their king.

They then chose a land that was conducive to murder. It was a hilly, mountainous land inhabited by many murderers. They settled there with their king.

Another faction maintained that the person best qualified to be king would be one who had an abundance of food, but who did not eat the food of ordinary people butm rather, ate highly refined food such as milk.

They could not, however, immediately find such a person. They therefore chose as temporary king a wealthy man who had an abundance of food. He would rule until they could find the kind of person whom they desired.

They accepted this man as a temporary king and settled in a land that was conducive to their goal.

Another faction maintained that a beautiful woman was most qualified to rule. They held that the main goal was that the land be populated, since it was for this reason that the world was created. Since a beautiful woman arouses the desire to populate the world, she brings about the goal.

They chose a beautiful woman and she became their queen. They then sought out a land conducive to this, and settled there.

Another group maintained that the main goal was speech. The primary advantage that man has over animals is that he is able to speak. They accordingly sought an orator who was expert in language, who knew many tongues, and spoke them all the time. They found a demented Frenchman who was constantly talking to himself.

According to their foolish, confused opinion he had reached the goal. He was a master of language and knew many languages. Moreover, he was constantly talking to himself. He was ideal in their opinion, and they accepted him as king. They also chose for themselves a land that was conducive to their concept, and they settled there with their king. One can be sure that he led them in a straight path!

Another faction maintained that the main goal was joy. When a child is born, when there is a wedding, when they conquer a land, they are joyous. They therefore sought a man who was always happy.

They found a heathen wearing a filthy shirt and carrying a bottle of whisky. A number of heathens were following him. Since he was very drunk, and therefore very happy, they accepted him as their king. One can be sure that he led them in the straight path!

They also chose a land which was conducive to their concept. It was a place of vineyards, which they could use to make wine. Out of the seeds they made brandy, so that nothing was wasted. Their main goal was to become drunk and thus always be happy. Actually, of course, this had nothing to do with their concept of joy, since they had nothing for which to be happy. They chose a land conducive to this, in which they settled.

Another faction maintained that the most important thing was wisdom. They sought for themselves a very wise man and made him their king. They also sought a land which was conducive to wisdom and settled there.

Another faction maintained that the main goal was to pamper oneself with food and drink, and thus develop large muscles. They therefore sought a man who had large muscles, and who exercised to enlarge them, since such a person would have large limbs, thus having a greater portion in the world, taking up more space in the world.

They found a very tall athlete, with large limbs, and accepted him as king. They also sought a land that was conducive to this, and settled there.

There was another faction who maintained that none of these could be the goal of life. The main goal was to pray to God and to be humble and lowly.... They sought for themselves a prayer leader and made him their king.

*

The soldier told all this to the Master of Prayer.

The soldier explained that those who had joined the Mighty Warrior belonged to the faction of body builders. The soldier concluded, "He is the Mighty Warrior with whom we are now conquering the world. But he said that he had an ulterior motive for wanting to conquer the world. His intent is not that the world be subject to him. Rather he has a completely different motive." When the Master of Prayer heard this, he realized that this was certainly the Mighty Warrior who had been with his King....

When the Master of Prayer asked to meet with the Mighty Warrior who was their king, they replied that they would have to speak to the Mighty Warrior. The Mighty Warrior agreed to the audience.

When they met, they immediately recognized each other. They were both very happy at being reunited. Their joy, however, was intermingled with tears when they remembered the King and his men. The Master of Prayer and the Mighty Warrior then discussed how they had come to their present situation...

The Master of Prayer spoke to the Mighty Warrior about what could be done with the people of the land who had fallen into the desire for money to such an extent that they made the wealthiest citizens into gods. He told him about all their foolish beliefs.

The Mighty Warrior told the Master of Prayer that he had heard from the King that when a person becomes entrapped by any desire, it is possible to pull him out. However, if somebody becomes trapped by the lust for wealth, it is totally impossible to extract him. Therefore nothing can be done for these people. It is totally impossible to pull them away from their error... except through the path to his sword... which includes eating certain, specific foods....

*

Rebbe Nachman continues his story with the Treasurer meeting with the Mighty Warrior and the Master of Prayer, who together go to seek the King and the remaining members of the Holy Assembly. During their travels, they come across each of the aforementioned groups who have chosen as their goal the materialistic pursuit of the characteristics described above. As the story unfolds, we find that although each group chose an unworthy leader, they eventually found someone who was pure and capable of guiding them — steeped as they were in their false beliefs and interpretations of the true goal. For each of these groups ultimately chose a different member of the Holy Assembly as their leader.

As the trio began their search, they began to meet up with the other members of their Assembly. This greatly enhanced their search and encouraged them further in their search of the others until they were all joined together again. Then the Master of Prayer was sent to each group to rectify them. And even during the search, especially for the group pursuing immorality, the Master of Prayer did his best to help the people improve their lives and concentrate on the positive — and spiritual — aspects of their goals.

And then, the King ruled over the entire world. The whole world returned to God, and occupied itself only with Torah, prayer, repentance and good deeds.

*

After telling the story, Rebbe Nachman spoke of the ten main characters of the Holy Assembly as symbolizing the World of Rectification (i.e. the Ten Sefirot). By inference, we understand that the groups which were misguided in their approach to the true goal represent the World of Desolation. In the following chapters, we will begin to examine the implications of these groups in our contemporary lifestyles and try to find the answer to, "Why hasn't Mashiach come yet?"

* * *

14

The Holy Assembly

"The Master of Prayer" offers many ideas for discussion. However, for the purposes of this book, we will concentrate on the ten factions. The characteristics of these groups define the basic needs and lusts of life which a person can develop either as ladders upon which to climb to the heights of spirituality, or as tasteless characteristics through which to descend to the depths of materialism. In each case, we will see the free choice that man has and how he can make use of his "sense of true judgment" — in order to develop his own "Mashiach" and help prepare the world for *the* Mashiach.

The ten main characters are: the King, the Queen, the Queen's Daughter, the Child, the Faithful Friend, the Bard, the Wise Man, the Treasurer, the Mighty Warrior and the Master of Prayer, and are called the Holy Assembly. The ten factions were those who sought honor, endorsed murder and waste, sought special foods, sought to eat a lot (body building), had lust for wealth, sex, speech, joy, wisdom, and prayer.

*

History shows us that people who migrate lose their identity. To be sure, there are groups in North America that display their roots proudly: French-Canadians, Italian-Americans, Polish-Americans, Afro-Americans and so on. This can be easily understood because, first of all, the countries of the Western Hemisphere are only several hundred years old and many groups have immigrated far more recently. Secondly, and more importantly, very few groups — if any — retain ties with their ancestral homes.

The Jewish Nation has been in exile for two millennia. Yet, wherever we've been, we've managed to maintain our identity as Jews. This has been due exclusively to our acceptance of, and adherence to, the very Torah that originally forged us into a nation (Exodus 19:5-6). Nevertheless, our sojourn in exile has taken its toll. For as a proud and "stiff-necked people" (cf. Exodus 33:5), the way in which we have adapted to the exile is very similar to that of the ten factions in the story, "The Master of Prayer."

Let us transport ourselves back in time to when the hurricane caused the dispersal of the royal family (above, Chapter 13), and apply it to our pursuit of the future, the messianic era.

*

The storm wind

The king's group consists of ten people who kabbalistically correspond to the Ten Sefirot. The Ten Sefirot are Divine Qualities or Attributes with which God directs the world. Each has a separate name, and a purpose that reflects its function. For example, there are sefirot known as Chesed (Lovingkindness) and Gevurah (Judgment). When God bestows bounty upon the world, this is when He is employing Chesed. When Judgments reign, then God is using the sefirah of Gevurah. (The names and array of the Ten Sefirot are found in Appendix B; see also Part V, Chapter 18). The Ten Sefirot correspond to *Olam HaTikkun* ("The World of Rectification"). That is, when the Ten Sefirot are properly aligned, they bring bounty and good health to the entire world, and reveal spirituality at the highest levels. When man sins, he causes disarray of the sefirot. Upsetting the normal plan with which the sefirot operate causes "hurricanes" — chaos and confusion — which lead to illness and poverty, etc., for the World of Rectification is shattered.

The hurricane represents the "Shattering of the Vessels" (explained below in Part V), i.e. that moment of Creation when chaos and confusion ruled (cf. Genesis 1:2). Adam's fall also parallels the Shattering of the Vessels and his eating from the Tree of Knowledge is what caused both the physical and spiritual exile — the transformation of desert to civilization and civilization to desert, etc. Alternatively, we can compare the hurricane to the destruction of the Holy Temple, when the dispersion of the Jews to all the corners of the globe began. All three of these are examples of a Shattering of Vessels.

The hurricane transformed desert into inhabited land and dry land into sea. People view civilization as the sum total of life. In reality, a simple look around tells us that our values are quite confused. What to some is "a desert" is to others "real civilization," and vice-versa. In the story, the hurricane (exile) took a very heavy toll, and the people forgot what life had been like under the rule of the King (i.e. God). *Their* civilization was turned topsy-turvy and, finding themselves in unfamiliar surroundings, they began to search for a new meaning in life. They were all aware that life has a purpose and began their search for *the* goal, a very commendable step. However, confusion reigned and disputes arose. "What is that goal?" This is where the people exercised their sense of judgment in choosing their goal. This is exactly why Mashiach must bring into the world an unerring sense of judgment, so that man exercises his free will properly.

We can now examine some of the distorted reasoning behind each of the ten groups as outlined by Rebbe Nachman in the story, and explained by Reb Noson in *Likutey Halakhot* (Tefilah 4). In the following chapter, we will see how these ten groups make up a composite picture of Judaism today. Then we will show how they actually provide the basis for the powerful return to Torah which is necessary in order to merit the imminent redemption.

*

Seeking honor

> **Everything God created was for the sake of His honor.**
> Yoma 38a
>
> Honor is the source of all Creation, as in (Isaiah 43:7), "For My sake and honor I have created it..." Honor is an integral part of the Creation and

we can reflect this honor by honoring God, His Torah and the true tzaddikim. To truly honor God, one must minimize one's own honor and actually flee from prominence. This is done by realizing one's insignificance vis-à-vis God's awesomeness. In return for this, one merits to bask in God's honor and glory as in (Isaiah 58:8), "God's honor will gather you in," and as in (1 Samuel 2:30), "I will honor those who honor Me" (*Likutey Halakhot, Tefilah* 4:3).

But the fury of a "hurricane" prevents one from focusing clearly on what is right. The desire for honor, rooted in the honor of God, becomes a very real focal point for the average person. People can become *mortally* offended if their honor is impugned — even to the point of committing murder! In fact, many people who strive for wealth do so for the honor and power it brings. And the same is true in Judaism today.

Many search for honor with a zealousness that guarantees the loss of their World to Come and consumes their life in This World — for the sake of some dubious glory that may or may not endure. Some seek wealth in order to be honored among the rich. Others yearn for glory so they can be recognized amongst the "power players" of their city or country. Others seek glory in their studies and education to become a rabbi or Jewish leader in a large community or city… But all this is wrong, for a person must see that all honor is bestowed only to glorify God (*Likutey Halakhot, Tefilah* 4:13).

Our Sages denigrated those who study or otherwise use Torah for honor, money or other personal benefit. "Do not use it as a crown for self-aggrandizement, nor as an axe with which to hew" (*Avot* 4:7). And that was two thousand years ago! In our day, honor is a most powerful drawing card. Everyone screams about the honor due them, like the blind, gypsy beggar of our story who was very particular about his honor. Interestingly, as particular as he was about his own honor, he was just as nasty and angry at everyone around him, belittling the honor of all but himself (see above, Chapter 13).

Moshe, the paradigm of Jewish leadership, was humble beyond compare (see Numbers 12:3). Everything he did was for God's honor and he negated himself in every way for this goal. But those "leaders" who seek glory harm not only themselves; they do a terrible disservice, and even damage, to our people.

> Haughtiness is a despicable trait which everyone recognizes as such. Therefore, those who aspire to honor are ashamed to display their craving. Instead they portray themselves as humble people, but in reality their humility is only in order to receive honor! Remember, the Jewish People were exiled because of their idolatrous behavior, and "Haughtiness is akin to idolatry" (see *Gittin* 88a; *Sotah* 4b). Therefore, we must first rid ourselves of haughtiness before we are able to return from our exile to the Holy Land (*Likutey Moharan* I, 11:8).

As a humbled and broken nation following the Holocaust, the subsequent return to the Holy Land seemed to herald the messianic promise of the Ingathering of the Exiles from the Diaspora, part of which had already begun. But pride can take a terrible toll. Strife arose among those fighting for the right to save the remnants of world Jewry — with each individual or group exerting its influence to save them according to their ideals. That strife claimed more than its fair share of victims and continues until today.

Conversely, humility is a most powerful trait. The more humility a person shows, the greater his capacity to recognize God, Who is called *Ein* (Nothingness, meaning totally beyond any Something we can imagine). Knowing himself as "nothing," a person has a greater capacity to accept what is above and beyond himself. This is why humility will be one of Mashiach's most powerful weapons. The more a person strives for it, the greater will be his appreciation for the Mashiach and the greater his yearning for the return to Zion and Jerusalem.

*

Murder, Incorporated

There was a group which felt that since everything must come to an end, then murder is a worthy goal to be pursued. It seems very remote — even bizarre — to think that people could reach such a conclusion. But, as is evident today, murder is not as far-fetched a goal as we would like to believe. Where does the idea come from?

"God is jealous and vengeful."

Nachum 1:2

There is an anger and vengeance that is considered holy. This comprises capital punishment and other penalties which the courts are empowered to implement when a situation warrants it. There are four types of capital punishment, which correspond to the four letters of God's Holy Name *ADoNaY* (אדני) — which implies *DiN* (דין-Judgment). When capital punishment is called for and implemented, it brings about great unifications Above (*Likutey Halakhot, Tefilah* 4:4).

Thus, in holiness, the idea of bringing an end to evil and evildoers is very exalted. But when this goal descends to the level of the mundane, it becomes warped, malicious and murderous. We see this most often in people who become enraged or jealous and subsequently commit the most heinous crimes. "I want it, and I want it *now*, regardless of the consequences, and will even kill to get it" — a common sentiment found among drug addicts. Others go through life with an attitude that nothing matters, since everything must come to an end, and all will eventually go to waste. And it all does, for those people "kill time" freely and literally waste their lives!

In our story, this group chose a man who slaughtered his father and mother. "Since this man has a hard heart and a fierce temper, who is more fit than him to be the leader?" Kabbalistically, "father and mother" correspond to Chokhmah and Binah, one's mental faculties (see Appendix B). Only one with a blemished and warped mind can accept waste and destruction as a goal. But it happens daily, as we witness in drunk driving accidents, gun accidents, gang wars, the mafia, the drug lords and in nearly all dictatorships. This mentality is even found in your average "democratic" politician, who will do his utmost to undermine and denigrate an opponent. Your common, everyday mugger also has no consideration for human life.

This destructive tendency is manifest far too much in our daily lives.

There are people who turn angry and bitter. They become enraged, will hate others and become involved in fights, to the point of killing someone, financially or even physically. There are those who will do anything they can to destroy another's reputation. And our Sages teach that humiliating another publicly is akin to murder (Bava Metzia 59a). Tensions at home or in the office are more than likely to provoke anger and cause someone embarrassment. So we see that "murder" is not as remote a concept as we would like to imagine. The society that thinks nothing of — or even condones — the public humiliation of others, in the office, through the media, or even at home in front of other family members, can expect this anger to culminate in one kind of murder or another.

Furthermore, we lose patience waiting for our salvation — on a personal or national level. Many times we force an issue when there is no need, because we lose patience with ourselves, our spouse, our friends, our community, etc. Indeed, much sin comes about through impatience. If people could learn to restrain themselves, many a sin could be averted. In the process of battling the evil inclination, however, we lose our composure and the patience to wait out the urge. By learning to "wait things out," we would be invoking the messianic trait of patience (see Likutey Halakhot, Toen v'Nit'an 3:2).

Such patience is a great virtue. By controlling one's anger, one can transform it into compassion (see Likutey Moharan I, 18:2). With patience, we can overcome all the obstacles and problems that life throws at us. We would have the fortitude to wait out the difficult moments until relief and respite arrive. It is not at all easy, as mounting pressures prevent us from seeing beyond our present difficulties. But everyone can testify to some moment in life when, after all his efforts and rages accomplished nothing, he just *had to wait* for salvation — and it came.

Interestingly, the Rambam writes that man should always choose the middle path in each characteristic: not to be too joyous or too depressed, neither too stingy nor too extravagant, neither too loquacious nor too reticent, and so on. When it comes to haughtiness and anger, on the other hand, one must distance oneself to the extreme (Yad HaChazakah, Hilkhot Deot 2:3), for these characteristics are considered idolatrous and despicable.

In addition, both one's soul and one's wealth are rooted in the same exalted place on High. One who is careful not to become angry, merits wealth. On the other hand, one who becomes enraged, "tears up his soul" (Zohar II, 182a). This causes the person either to "tear up" any bounty due him, or to lose the money he already has (Likutey Moharan I, 68). Thus, patience and wealth come hand in hand, while anger causes one to waste one's life in the pursuit of wealth.

Moshe was the paradigm of a Jewish leader, for he was humble, patient and able to restrain his anger (Rashi, Numbers 12:3). Yet, even he succumbed to anger when he struck the rock to obtain water in the wilderness. As a result of his impatience, he was prevented from entering the Holy Land (Numbers 20).

In Torah literature, we find that "short-tempered" or "long-suffering and patient" are both related to the nose, Mashiach's source of vitality (see above, Chapter 5, 7) One of Mashiach's responsibilities is to gather in the exiles to the Holy Land. It is taught (Likutey Moharan I, 155), "One who exercises patience breaks the attribute of anger and merits the Holy Land." And patience with our fellow man leads to peace between people. It is thus taught (The Aleph-Bet Book Faith A:50), "Through unity among the Jews, Mashiach will come."

*

"Be fruitful and multiply"

To populate the world is the very first mitzvah of the Torah. It is *the* means of transmitting the glory and knowledge of God, for without offspring, civilization ends. The verse thus states (Psalms 145:4), "Generation to generation will praise Your works..." God therefore formed man and woman in such a way as to create an attraction between them. In the Kabbalah, the union of husband and wife is extremely exalted, because it parallels the unification of the sefirot and of the supernal universes (see Likutey Halakhot, Tefilah 4:5; below, Chapter 18).

The Holy Assembly / 141

The very first mitzvah in the Torah is "Be fruitful and multiply." We have seen (above, Chapter 10) that the main test of being human is in using our free will to choose to serve God. The Torah commands us to be fruitful and multiply in order to increase our reward, because the more people that exist, the greater amount of choices there exist for choosing between good and evil. For example, Adam did not sin when he was alone, only later when he was with Eve. Thus, there is a greater reward when one chooses the truth.

The ultimate purpose for all of Creation was so that man could come to recognize and serve God. Those who recognize God are considered human. Those who do not are considered animals in a human form (see *Likutey Moharan* II, 7:2). As we shall see (below, Part V), Adam's soul was comprised of all the souls of all future generations. Populating the world is the means of bringing forth all those souls that are part of Adam. Only by being born in this world can they all attain their perfection. The goal of the group that advocated populating the world was ideal, but they were misguided in their endeavors. Pursuing this goal on a material level caused them to descend to the depths of sexual immorality and depravity — "an animal in human form."

In our story, after all the members of the Holy Assembly were reunited, the Master of Prayer was sent to rectify all the other groups by returning them to the service of God and a spiritually rich life. The Queen's Daughter, who ruled over the land of immorality, was the only ruler of the ten who requested of the Master of Prayer that he purify her subjects of their lusts prior to the gathering together of the Holy Assembly. This is because Mashiach represents purity and one who is steeped in immorality cannot begin to get even a whiff of Mashiach ("the nose").

The source of an *obsession* with sex is depression, which then steers a person into greed (see *Likutey Moharan* I, 23:2). This is because such a person always craves fulfillment. What is not attained legally will be sought through immorality and sometimes other illegal means. Any honest survey will reveal that those engaged in immoral relationships are depressed, for they are an "enslaved people," enslaved to their fantasies. Furthermore, the exile corresponds to depression while joy represents an end to the exile. A joyous mind has freedom of thought, which develops into freedom of speech and action (Likutey Moharan II, 10). This is because a person who is joyous doesn't feel the constraints of an exile — a society enslaved to sexual abnormalities.

Mashiach represents purity at its zenith. At his level (i.e. that of "the nose"), even a slight whiff of immorality is intolerable. Therefore, anyone who truly seeks the messianic era must purify himself completely from any aberrations that influence his thoughts and deeds (see Likutey Moharan II, 32). Since we all have a "little of Mashiach" within us (see above, Chapter 11), it is our deeds that invoke his spirit of purity to bring the world to its rectification. As part of his job, Mashiach must bring us to the Holy Land. Regarding immorality the verse states (Leviticus 18:28), "[Do not commit any of these perversions] lest the Land vomit you out as it vomited out the people that preceded you." But purity brings us back to the Land and enables us to experience the messianic age.

*

"To eat, or not to eat...?"

There were two groups which chose eating habits as a goal. One was the group which had abundant food, yet did not eat the same food as ordinary people, only "highly refined foods." The second was that of the "body builders," whose goal was to enlarge their bodies and make their physical presence felt.

Eating is actually a very exalted activity for it is *the* means to keep body and soul together. Concerning the Generation of the Exodus who broke their lust for food and ate only to serve God, it is written (Psalms 78:25), "Each man ate the bread [manna] of the mighty angels." Those who follow in their footsteps are also considered worthy of partaking of the heavenly manna.

There are also times when it is a mitzvah to eat, as on Shabbat and the Festivals. It is written (Proverbs 13:25), "A tzaddik eats to satisfy his soul," for eating can elevate a person to the highest of levels — to the level of Keter (Mashiach's level) (see *Likutey Moharan* II, 7:10).

But there are those who train themselves to eat very little, as if to show the world they are "spiritual people" and not possessed by gluttony. They *can* eat, and have a strong desire to do so, yet abstain for the sake of honor and haughtiness or other silly reasons (*Likutey Halakhot, Tefilah* 4:6). Others are perennially obsessed with diets, for material reasons only, that have no bearing whatsoever on their spiritual growth. Dieting has become an idolatry. This is because the desire for prohibited foods and bad eating habits stems from the First Sin, Adam's *eating* from the Tree of Knowledge of Good and Evil, thereby blemishing the exalted act that eating was meant to be.

The other faction that maintained that eating regularly, and body building foods at that, is the goal, also has a holy source in the pleasure found in the meals of Shabbat and the Festivals. One must also keep one's body healthy, for it is the most basic vessel with which one must serve God. We also find that Abraham (*Joshua* 14:15) and Moshe (see *Berakhot* 54b) were tall and impressive in their looks. A requirement of the members of the *Sanhedrin* (the Jewish Supreme Court) is that they be "men of stature" (*Sanhedrin* 17a). This requirement was meant to increase people's awareness and awe of the spiritual. But this ideal too has become corrupted, and physical health has become an obsession — at the expense of our spiritual health (see *Likutey Halakhot, Tefilah* 4:10).

The Torah permits eating kosher food — such as animals or fowl that have certain features and are ritually slaughtered. Fish do not require slaughter, but must be of a kosher species. Virtually all vegetation is permitted, save for poisonous plants, which are deemed unfit because of the danger to life they pose. Insects are forbidden, and all legumes, fruits and vegetables that might be infested should be inspected for bugs. Meat must be salted to remove the blood, meat and dairy cannot be cooked together and foods may not be cooked on Shabbat. And so on.

However, many people today allow themselves to be guided by the effects of the food advertisers — whoever is better at selling their "health" product — rather than by the kashrut of the food. A simple, balanced diet, without pills, drugs, cigarettes or alcohol will guarantee as healthy a life as possible. And there is plenty of latitude in choices of foods, for a person may eat a large variety of foods. But a spiritual life becomes very difficult if one does not adhere to the laws of kashrut. The verse states (Leviticus 11:43), "Take care not to eat the unclean, [otherwise], *V'NiTMeiTeM bam*, you shall be defiled by it." Our Sages teach (Yoma 39b), "*V'NiTaMTeM bam*, you shall become foolish because of it."

Of all sins that a person can commit, only food can actually enter into the body. When nonkosher food is ingested, it is absorbed by the bloodstream and spreads throughout the entire body, including the heart, the mind and so on. Since "we are what we eat" — because the food becomes part of the organism — the body assumes a "nonkosher" personality. Each person is directed by his heart and mind — therefore a "nonkosher" body adversely affects one's ability to seek spirituality. Thus, eating nonkosher food causes foolishness and leads to sin.

Physical fitness is important, because good health is important. Furthermore, in our story, the main rectification of the country of wealth came about through eating (see *Likutey Halakhot, Rosh Chodesh* 7:35, 39). Thus, in the Days of Mashiach all food will be healthy. Furthermore, all foods will be delicious. And (Isaiah 30:20), "Man will be sated with bread and water alone, for God will not hide and man will see his Master." Man will have the best of two worlds. Partaking of a minimum of food, man will experience the sweetest and finest tastes in all that he eats.

*

"To speak or not to speak...is that a question?"

Another group chose articulate speech as its goal. Of the four levels of Creation — mineral, vegetable, animal and human — man is exalted above all the others because of his ability to speak. Speech is very great, for with it people can articulate their thoughts and feelings in a coherent fashion. But this group chose "a demented Frenchman who knew several languages, and he most certainly led them on the right path!"

The Hebrew word for oration is *melitzah*. This word can be translated several ways, all of which are germane to our text. It can mean rhetoric, lyrical language, phraseology, a flowery speaker, an advocate, an interpreter, etc. In short, it refers to a "master of language." Language is an art, an important discipline — when used properly. For the concept of language is rooted in the highest spiritual levels.

A *meilitz* is an advocate. When a person is judged in an earthly court, his hopes depend upon the defense counsel's ability to present his case convincingly. The same is true when a person is judged in the Heavenly Court (e.g. on Rosh HaShanah). He has the merits of good deeds which stand in his favor, which he knows he performed and seeks to use on his own behalf. Heaven is also aware of these merits. What can he do to enhance his position? If he is a master orator, he can compose supplications that frame his pleas into a beautiful prayer. Enhancing one's merit through language brings forth the beauty of the act that was done, and arouses mercy. Thus the power of speech can literally save a person's life, depending upon how it is used. If a person is truly sincere in his pleas, however they are phrased, this will also have a powerful effect, and will be reflected in his speech.

Furthermore, *melitzah* can be applied to Rebbe Nachman's teaching of *hitbodedut*. *Hitbodedut* is a prayer that one offers in one's mother tongue, in which one feels closest to the spoken words. It is a meditative practice, where one sets aside time for personal prayer and introspection, to contemplate the past and the future, and to take strength in the present. Whatever good a person has experienced is recognized, thereby giving hope for a better future. What has been done, right or wrong, is analyzed and then verbalized before God — to repair past damage or to enhance the good performed. Afterwards, one prays to God asking for one's heart's desires — physically and spiritually. Knowing how to articulate one's thoughts and feelings enhances one's ability to practice *hitbodedut*. It draws one closer to one's prayers, and the prayers closer to his heart. And interestingly, even if a person is not a master of language, as long as he is consistent in his *hitbodedut*, he will see how God Himself "places" the words in his mouth to offer a beautiful prayer (Likutey Halakhot, Tefilah 4:7; for more about *hitbodedut* see *Outpouring of the Soul*; *Under The Table*, Chapter 6; *Crossing the Narrow Bridge*, Chapter 9; and *Jewish Meditation*).

The mouth is called "a palace," which in Hebrew is "*heichal.*" The numerical value of *HeIChaL* (היכל) is 65, the same as that of the Holy Name, *ADoNoY* (אדני), which corresponds to Malkhut, represented by the mouth (see Appendix B). The verse states (Psalms 29:9), "In His *heichal*, everyone speaks His glory." By purifying one's tongue, i.e. one's language, one can ascend to a level (as will be in messianic times) on which every word one speaks will reflect the glory of God (Likutey Moharan I, 55:7). This mastery of language draws a person closer to God.

But language, when not used in holiness, leads man astray. King Solomon taught (Proverbs 18:21), "Death and life are in the hands of the tongue." For just as the tongue can draw a person closer to God, it can also distance him. An author can compose a novel or an essay that can powerfully influence people, either for good or for evil. Poetry, the theater and all kinds of literature, beckon us. This is because speech, i.e. the mouth, is a form of Malkhut, conveying the implication of an edict, which is enforceable. Thus, even a single word carries with it tremendous impact, which can direct, or misdirect, a person's entire life. Do we have the ability to "read between the lines" to define spirituality? Do we choose a "demented Frenchman" to guide us, or will we use the power of speech for more exalted purposes? Consider the following:

> Conceptually, speech is associated with the "breath or spirit of God," as in (Psalms 33:6), "With God's word (*bid'var HaShem*), the heavens were made, and with the breath of His mouth (*u'vruach piv*) all their hosts." The power and authority of human speech emanate from God's "speech," His Malkhut. This is seen in a king whose word is law.

Speech and Malkhut are thus both related to the Divine Name, *Adonay* (see Appendix B). When speech is rectified and perfected, then (Psalms 51:17) "*Adonay*, open my lips." That is, "my lips will open with Godly speech and the Malkhut of God will be revealed to all." When one blemishes one's speech — with profanity, falsehood, and especially with unfounded condemnation of others — then one has taken speech, the "spirit" of God, and transformed it into a *ruach se'arah*, a storm wind.

The letters of the word *Se'ARaH* (סערה) can be rearranged as *SaH* (סה) and *RA* (רע). SaH equals 65, the numerical value of *ADoNaY* (אדני). *RA* means evil and is numerically equal to 270. This number is the product of the twenty-seven letters of the Hebrew alphabet (22 letters and five final letters) multiplied by 10, the number of vowels (9 vowel points and one silent pronunciation). Thus, one who utters blemished speech causes a "force 10" storm wind (as in our story) — blowing a hurricane that causes terrible damage, uprooting civilization by destroying lives and property. These people come from (Genesis 6:13) "the end of all flesh," for their objective is to bring mankind to an end! But positive speech reveals Godliness (*Likutey Moharan* I, 38:2).

Reb Noson adds that all blemished speech stems from arrogance (*Likutey Halakhot, Chezkat Mitaltilin* 4:9). Simply put, were a person not to think of himself as better than another or "holier than thou," he would have no reason to speak negatively against anyone else. Furthermore, he would recognize his own failings and take better care of his choice of words.

With the ingathering of the Jewish People comes free speech (see *The Breslov Haggadah*, Appendix A, p.8). By concentrating our efforts on abstaining from slander, profanity and other forbidden speech, and by using language beneficially — i.e. in Torah and prayer, offering encouragement and kind words and by judging others favorably — we merit the final Ingathering. And then the prophecy will be realized (Jeremiah 31:6), "Sing with gladness for Jacob, and shout on the hilltops of the nations: Declare, praise and say, 'God! Save Your People!'"

*

"Let's party..."

Joy is *the* main vehicle through which to serve God. The exile and subsequent punishments are the results of not serving God with joy (cf. Deuteronomy 28:47). Conversely (Psalms 19:9), "The teachings of God are upright; they bring joy to the heart."

"I commend joy, for man has nothing better to do in life than to eat, drink and be merry..." — "This refers to Torah and good deeds" (Ecclesiastes 8:15, see Rashi). Whoever has faith, each according to his level, can rejoice every single moment of his life. He can rejoice in the knowledge that Moshe Rabeinu instilled faith in us that there is a God — and that we can observe the Torah and perform His mitzvot, every single day! He can rejoice in the fact that we believe in the Living God, the Eternal God, Who is exalted above all conception. But there is also a negative side to joy, as in (Ecclesiates 2:2), "What point is there in joy?" Our Sages comment (Shabbat 30a), "This is joy that is not associated with good deeds" (Likutey Halakhot, Tefilah 4:8).

One of the groups in our story chose joy as a goal and picked an alcoholic to lead them. Joy is an emotion, "spiritual" in character. When joy is experienced as a spiritual pleasure it endures — as opposed to joy from materialistic pleasures, which is only temporary by nature. The pursuit of these "joys" leads to alcoholism and other "highs" which actually negate joy. The Talmud thus teaches (Yoma 76b), "Wine has two powers: one who is meritorious will flourish [through drinking]; one who is not meritorious will decline [through drinking]."

Even drinking wine (though not alcoholism) is a messianic concept. This is because wine is associated with joy, which will be widespread in messianic times. Then, we will be able to taste the oldest vintage wine in existence, the wine of the Garden of Eden, "Wine preserved in its grapes from the Six Days of Creation." (Berakhot 34b). This is because wine, *YaYiN* (יין), is numerically equivalent to *SOD* (secret-סוד) (70), corresponding to the mysteries of the Torah, the Torah of Atik. This wine (the "seventy") was made to combat the influence of the evil characteristics of the "seventy nations," which consist primarily of immorality (see Likutey Moharan I, 36:2; see also Likutey Halakhot, Pesach 5:1). This is why most partying culminates in immoral behavior.

We have seen that joy is of paramount importance, for without joy we could not serve God properly; we could not even make it through the week. But true joy is actually a joyous state of mind — which impoverishing ourselves, through a night of drink, leisure and "enjoyment," doesn't help. Rebbe Nachman once said (Likutey Moharan II, 108), "For a pleasure of a quarter of an hour, one can lose all of This World and the Next!" On the other hand, through spiritual joy, one can defeat the *kelipot* (forces of evil; depression and melancholy) and soar on the wings of joy to the loftiest heights. In fact, it is the joy of serving God in the messianic era that will vanquish the *kelipot*, and they will cease to exist (Likutey Moharan I, 24:10; see below, Chapter 28).

When we attain true joy, the exile will automatically come to an end. Then the verse will be fulfilled (Isaiah 55:12), "For you shall go out [of exile] with joy, and with peace you will be brought in [to the Holy Land]; the mountains and the hills will break forth before you in song, and all the trees of the fields will clap their hands."

*

The People of the Book

There was a group which chose the pursuit of knowledge and wisdom as its goal. This was a "wise" decision because (Psalms 104:24), "You made the entire world with wisdom." Furthermore, wisdom is the source of all life, as in (Ecclesiastes 7:12) "Wisdom gives life." But the main wisdom is to serve God.

> *"The beginning of wisdom is the fear of God, it imbues good sense to all who do them [the mitzvot]. May His praise endure forever!"*
> Psalms 111:10

> *The goal of wisdom is repentance and good deeds. This, because a person should not become learned and then rebel against his parents, rabbis and others who are greater than him. It is written, "The beginning of wisdom is the fear of God, it imbues good sense to all who do them." ["Them" refers to the mitzvot of the Torah.] Thus, it is not written, "...for all who study them" but "for all who do them."*
> Berakhot 17a

The most important knowledge a person can attain is Knowledge of the Infinite. This translates into realizing how distant one is from true wisdom, from God, Who is Infinite. This is the idea of Transcendental Intellect. Before we study, all knowledge is transcendental. As our knowledge grows, we transform "transcendental" knowledge into "immanent" knowledge. But since God is Infinite, no matter how much we've studied and gained knowledge, we haven't yet even begun to *know* God. Thus, "the beginning of wisdom is the fear of God" — to have faith and perform the mitzvot which gives a person the Knowledge of the Infinite (see above, Chapter 7). By performing mitzvot, a person is fortified with fear of God to know that he has yet infinitely more levels of knowledge to attain. This person, who always strives for Knowledge of God, will come to know Him, as in (Deuteronomy 4:39), "Know this day and bring [this knowledge] into your heart that God is the Supreme Power in heaven above and on earth below — there is no other!" (Likutey Halakhot, Tefilah 4:9).

On the other hand, concerning those who study Torah without observing the mitzvot, it is written (Jeremiah 8:9), "They rejected the Word of God; what wisdom do they have?" Our Sages comment (see Sanhedrin 99a), "If they do study Torah, why are they considered as having rejected the Word of God? Because they despise His commandments and do not observe them." For there is nothing more foolish than a person thinking he can grasp divine knowledge and an understanding of God or His thoughts! How can mortal man believe that he can understand a God Who is exalted and awesome beyond anything that the human mind can conceive? King Solomon said (Proverbs 26:12), "Have you seen a man who is wise in his own eyes? There is more hope for the fool than for him!" Thus, those who study Torah as an intellectual pursuit, but not for the purpose of seeking God and performing His mitzvot, literally separate wisdom from its Source — God. Since the mitzvot are the channels through which one can perceive Godliness, they deflect the Godly wisdom away from themselves and cannot receive it (see above, Chapter 7). This type of Torah study leads them away from God, for they have separated themselves from the Source. This approach leads people yet further astray, for they begin to equate Torah, a spiritual intellect, with secular intellect, and lose the ability to define the difference between the sacred and the secular. This separation from Torah eventually serves to disconnect people from God altogether (see Likutey Halakhot, Tefilah 4:9).

As we shall discuss in the following chapter, nowadays, everyone has ideas about wisdom and education. The problem is that some of these

The Holy Assembly / 151

ideas can be very misleading — even devastating — for both spiritual and materialistic lifestyles. Still, the pursuit of knowledge is a messianic gift, for in the Days of Mashiach, "The world will be filled with the knowledge of God." Its manifestation in this world can be found in our ability to filter out all unnecessary wisdom and to concentrate upon the Godly. Then, even our mundane wisdom will be of use in finding God.

*

Wealth

The community not mentioned as a separate faction is the group that sought wealth as a goal. In holiness, wealth is of great benefit. Charity helps others, funds promote Jewish education, and make it possible to purchase kosher food and other things related to mitzvot (e.g. tzitzit, tefilin, mezuzot, Torah educational material) without difficulty. The Mishnah teaches (Avot 3:17), "If there is no flour (i.e. livelihood), there is no Torah." Without an income to pay for one's material needs, one cannot concentrate on one's spiritual growth (see Likutey Halakhot, Kiddushin 3:12).

In a deeper sense, wealth is a *tzimtzum* (constriction), for it is God's bounty that has spiraled downward to the world into a gross material form. As we have seen with fear and with the mitzvot (which are also constrictions; see above, Chapter 7), these *tzimtzumim* allow us to perceive Godliness. Through this constriction, one can come to perceive exalted levels of spirituality (Likutey Halakhot, Melamdim 1:1). Therefore, the greater the level of fear of God and purity of deed one attains, the greater one's ability to absorb this wealth in a beneficial manner (see Likutey Halakhot, Pidyon Peter Chamor 2:6).

But all too often, the desire for wealth becomes an obsession. The criterion for ascertaining whether we are members of this group is the definition of our assessment of people. In our story, one who had a minimum of money was considered "an animal or a bird" — a person with little stature and unworthy of our consideration — unless we wanted a little attention without having to return too much. ("Be a good dog. Give me your love and devotion and I'll buy you a delicious bone!") One with a large amount of money was a "star," perhaps even a "whole constellation" or an "angel." Those with excessive wealth became "gods." The modern-day counterparts of those people who sacrificed themselves to and for these "gods" are to be found in those who sacrifice themselves, their families and their integrity in their worship of wealth or of a person with wealth.

But their lives were lived in vain, for only God can provide income. One has to be engaged in a livelihood and must deal honestly and honorably. Still, one must set aside ample time to learn and pray and devote oneself to God. Otherwise, one fritters away one's life — and for naught (see Likutey Halakhot, Tefilah 4:11).

The desire for wealth is rooted in the messianic era, since then everybody will attain great wealth.

> All the Prophets were wealthy. Moshe Rabeinu, who received the Torah, Rabbi Judah the Prince and Rav Ashi who compiled the Mishnah and Talmud respectively, were also extremely wealthy. This is because there are paths of Torah which require deep understanding and can be attained only with great wealth. The Mishnah teaches, "If there is no flour, there is no Torah." If flour is necessary even for a basic understanding of Torah, then for the Torah of Atik that will be revealed in the Days of Mashiach great wealth will be required (see Likutey Moharan I, 60:1).

But that wealth will be messianic wealth — the antithesis of the kind of wealth that people lust after. If we strive to control our lust then the following prophecies will come true. "I will lay your stones with shining colors and your foundations with sapphires. Your windows shall be rubies, your gates of beryl and carbuncle, and all your borders of the choicest stones..." (Isaiah 54:11-12). "In place of copper I will bring gold; in place of iron, silver... peace and righteousness... and the days of suffering shall end" (Isaiah 60:17,20).

*

The prayer group

The ARI writes that the main rectification of fallen attributes is through prayer (cf. Shaar HaKavanot, Tefilin 5). This is why prayer should be offered in "a quorum," a group of ten. There are ten attributes, Ten Sefirot, which complete the World of Rectification. One's prayers to defeat the evil characteristics and to attain spirituality correspond to the "ten rulers" who rectify all the evil goals. Thus, it is prayer, Mashiach's main weapon (see Chapter 6), that will be used to rectify the downfall of man which came about through misguided choices of goals.

In the story, the Master of Prayer passed through the lands of all the groups, but was unable to find the true leader of each group. Therefore, he left and made a life for himself. It wasn't until the people of each group themselves eventually realized the disgrace of their materialistic pursuit and the futility of their chosen goals that they were willing to accept a spiritual leader. This was the beginning of their rectification on a minimal level. But only after the Holy Assembly reunited did all the groups understand that they required prayer for their rectification. The Master of Prayer (Mashiach) was then able to enter all the lands — i.e. to reach out to all humanity — and help it attain perfection.

*

In this chapter, we have reviewed the basic characteristics that give man the capability for either good or evil. All these characteristics are interrelated. Honor and wealth are connected, as are honor and knowledge (which is power). Immorality and joy are intertwined, and wealth has its influence upon these too. Wealth and anger go hand in hand (rarely does one see a rich and powerful person acting humbly). Athletics, physical fitness, wealth and honor are also connected, and so on. Each person has within him a little of each characteristic, but each also has a greater tendency to lean towards one of the (evil) characteristics. Whoever can get his act together — i.e. learn to direct each of his characteristics towards spirituality — has "accepted" the King's Holy Assembly as his "leaders." Then he will feel the necessity to pray to God, and will attain his perfection.

Having discussed the story of the Master of Prayer and the basic ideas behind the groups and choices of lifestyle, we are now ready to see how these "goals" are manifest in our day and age, and how they are the main reasons for "Why hasn't Mashiach come yet?"

* * *

15

Judaism today: A fashionable look at the Emperor's New Clothes

Each of the ten factions in our story represents a unique characteristic, and each had its own compelling reasons for choosing its particular lifestyle. Each truly felt that its chosen path was a goal of life. Frankly, it was — or would have been — had the goal been developed positively. Our Sages teach (see Rashi, Numbers 13:27), "All falsehood that does not begin with some truth will not endure." Thus, each of the lifestyles chosen by these groups was rooted in the highest realms of truth and spirituality (as above, Chapter 14). But as mankind allows the "wool of the emperor's new clothes" to be pulled over its eyes, the focus is lost, while the frivolities of life remain. Thus it is with the modern counterparts to each of these factions.

Every human being reflects the archetypal characteristics mentioned in our story. We are all made up of all these characteristics. Of course, for some of us, the desire for honor will be strongest. Others will seek a life of joyous, carefree leisure. Some will take education very seriously and still others, physical fitness... (see *Likutey Halakhot, Tefilah* 4:13).

An interesting factor in our story is that the pursuit of wealth runs throughout and yet is not mentioned in the chronicles as a separate group that sought a goal. This is because the pursuit of wealth hardly makes sense as a goal unto itself. Rather, having wealth makes all the other "goals" accessible. Still, before people attain their other "goals," pursuing wealth is a compulsive, overpowering disorder — which can easily distort anyone's view of the goal. Certainly, "a person must have money to pay his bills." But once one's view on life is even slightly distorted, a host of other distortions immediately make themselves apparent — as if they were waiting in the wings the whole time (see above, Chapter 8). The desire for wealth is an open invitation for a person to confuse a "fool's paradise" with a real, enduring Paradise — spiritual delight.

"Why hasn't Mashiach come yet?" The answer is that we have allowed ourselves a little too much "over-indulgence." Ask any Jew from any persuasion — Orthodox, Conservative, Reform, non-committed, etc. — about his spiritual endeavors. Nearly everyone will reply that he is focused on Judaism, on spirituality, on God. And all truly believe it, each on his level, each according to his beliefs, his knowledge, his emotions. But we are left with a gnawing feeling. With all the choices of direction that can lead us to God, perhaps we have chosen a well-meant yet misguided path, as did those in the story of "The Master of Prayer." Perhaps we all believe that we are following the true path when all we really have is "the emperor's new clothes."

*

The Emperor's New Clothes

Most people are familiar with Hans Christian Andersen's famous tale, "The Emperor's New Clothes." Briefly, the emperor wanted new royal robes. A couple of con artists arrived in town and "wove" the emperor a "yarn" about a very special material that they possessed, which would only be visible to those who were worthy. The only defect in their material was that it did not exist. Still, the thieves wove a magnificent "fabric" and convinced the emperor of its beauty.

The weavers took the emperor's measurements and began "spinning their yarn" — for the sleeves, robe, garment and so on. Occasionally, they would call in the king for a "fitting," assessing their progress. Everyone would admire the beauty of the robes and how magnificent the emperor looked in them. No-one would admit that he could not see them, for fear that it might expose his unworthiness. Finally, the day came for the emperor to don his new apparel. The weavers went through all the motions of dressing the emperor in his new clothes and everyone expressed his amazement at their beauty. Paid in full — for nothing — the thieves fled.

The royal entourage declared a national holiday and organized a parade for the emperor to display his new clothes. People gathered and lined the streets, waiting for hours for the emperor to appear. Finally he arrived, standing tall and proud in his "new robes." Everyone fell under the spell of the "beauty of the clothes," and applauded his majesty of his new robes.

"Ooh! Ah!" "What beautiful robes!"

"Ooh! Ah!" "What exquisite clothes!"

This went on for some time until... a little boy standing near his mother asked her what was going on. She replied that the emperor was displaying his new clothes. "But," said the boy with the innocence of youth, "the emperor has nothing on!"

*

King Solomon taught (Proverbs 16:18), "Pride comes before a fall." The emperor and his entourage, as well as all the people in the parade, were proud. They saw nothing of their emperor's new clothes, but refused to admit it, for fear of being thought unworthy. They allowed their pride to cloud their judgment. Everyone, from the emperor to the beggar in the street, allowed himself to be taken in. To conceal a minor embarrassment, they permitted a major catastrophe. And, if we examine the groups of our story we can easily — and unfortunately — see how today's Judaism bears a remarkable resemblance to the "emperor's new clothes."

Author's note: The ideas presented in this chapter occurred to me a few years ago after reading several articles over a period of time presenting Jewish ideas, with several perspectives offered on each idea. One article was about rabbis for human rights who paid condolence calls to those Arabs whose children were accidently killed by Israeli gunfire during intentional Arab attacks against the Israeli Army! Another article spoke of some novel views about the circumcision rite, including the right of Jewish female infants to have a *britah* ceremony — just as a male child has a brit! Yet a third article mentioned

Judaism today: A fashionable look at the Emperor's New Clothes / 157

the need to modernize the wedding ceremony. "It must be a meaningful ceremony!" was the claim of the writer. I was awed by the idea. Contemporary couples who seek new, "meaningful" ways to get married, rarely put in meaningful effort to stay married and are divorcing at almost the same rate as they are marrying. I had difficulty understanding why they don't make a "meaningful" divorce ceremony, instead of the traditional slugging it out in the lawyer's office?! Voilà! The "emperor's new clothes!"

All one would need in order to write a book on "Judaism and the emperor's new clothes" would be to collect articles from the world-wide glut of Jewish newspapers — Orthodox, Conservative, Reform, Reconstructionist, Zionist, Anti-Zionist, Bnai Brith, committed, uncommitted, anti-committed, and so on. What we do to ourselves in print, no non-Jew would dare, for fear of being labeled an antisemite. In fact, that's why I made a decision not to collect the articles. Instead, presented here are several of the more prominent issues faced by world Jewry today, along the lines of the "ten groups" found in our story.

The author begs the reader's indulgence for his flippant tone, but it is difficult to restrain oneself when one sees such a brilliant nation parading itself around "stark naked" — wearing the "emperor's new clothes." The presentation is satirical in nature, based upon observations of everyday "Jewish" life from the author's experiences in Israel and the USA, as well as in several other countries he has visited.

*

Our Sages teach (Bereishit Rabbah 16:4), "The Egyptian exile included all the subsequent exiles." Thus, in Egypt, many things paralleled what is taking place now in our present exile. For example, Egypt was the world's most advanced civilization at that time: from Midrash and from history we see that it had educational facilities, great wealth, and all the various goals mentioned in the story of "The Master of Prayer."

Jacob and his family came to Egypt not out of desire, but because they were forced to. But Jacob's children became comfortable in their surroundings and began to adapt to their alien culture. Pride got the best of their egos and they began assisting Pharaoh. As Jews, they did their best, as they always had. However, it was not until Jacob and his children passed away that their descendants fell under the spell of the Egyptians. Before long, they discovered that they had become slaves. Working from sunup to sundown under back-breaking conditions, they were forced to sleep in the fields. The Egyptians forced the Jews to switch roles — men did women's work and women performed men's labor. Their children were abducted and cast into the river, and so on. (See *The Breslov Haggadah*, Appendix A, for a stark description of the exile and bondage.)

Sound familiar? No? Well then, let's take a look at today's world. Nobody moves from comfortable and/or familiar surroundings unless forced to, which is why the continual pogroms of the 19th century and the Holocaust of the 20th century led to the mass migrations of European Jewry to their current homes. At first, the adaptation was difficult. As the image of "Jacob," i.e. their grandparents and parents, faded, the desire to be part of their new, surrounding culture, took root. Soon, the Jews were advancing rapidly in progressive cultures — working long hours in the sweat shops under back-breaking conditions — all for the "privilege" of belonging to an advanced society. The sweat shops may have disappeared, but somehow the hours haven't changed. People work the same long hours, many times even "too busy" to return home at night. Children are cast away — no one wants them any more. If they do have children, parents try to devote no more than a few hours a week of "quality time" to building and moulding a child — a human being and a future adult with adult responsibilities — with good characteristics and so on. When the teenage child feels abandoned and ends up as a runaway in cults or on the streets, or at least with many opinions on life that are different — and frightening — from the parents' point of view, the parents are horrified. Furthermore, in contemporary civilization, traditional roles have changed. Women take men's places, men assume women's roles and so on. It's fantastic! Now we've all ended up with identity crises! "Who are we?" "Who am I?" It's no wonder people have difficulties with their gender identity and why immorality, abominable acts and violent crimes proliferate at an alarming rate.

Thus, we are in the "Egyptian Exile" all over again, but with different twists. Our hope and salvation is "a Moshe Rabeinu" who will save us from our "self-destructing" ideas and lead us to "Mount Sinai," a revelation of Godliness and the Torah of Atik. (For more on the exile see Part VI.) Meanwhile, let us take a closer look at how our current "Jewish" lifestyles mimic the "emperor's new clothes."

*

"Honorable indeed"

We live in an era in which many consider themselves "Jewish spokesmen" or perhaps even "Jewish foreign ministers." Even those who have never studied the bare basics of Judaism — a religion and culture some 3,500 years old — are quick to offer opinions as to what Jews and Judaism are all about. Never mind that the facts are distorted; most others don't know the facts either, and certainly not the non-Jews. So an "honorable individual" establishes an "honorable group" which establishes committees and agencies to represent Jewish issues, as do other "honorable groups" and still other "honorable groups" — whatever is convenient for *them* at the moment. Each claims to be *the* representative of the Jewish People, while each group knows that it represents only those few people who, at that particular time, happen to agree with that group's ideas. But then, another group makes the same claim, as does a third, fourth, fifth, fiftieth, and so on. Ever count how many educated, sophisticated and authorized opinions there are on one issue? Ever count the stars in the sky? God forbid that any one group should defer to others and work together for the common good! It sometimes seems that these "honorable, Jewish representative groups" multiply faster than rabbits. Or perhaps they *divide* — faster than amoebas?

Wearing the "emperor's new clothes" can be a chilling experience. We "expose" ourselves to the debasement of our nation, and for no justifiable reason — only that "my honor" remain intact, or at least that it not be smeared. Yet, our "honorable leaders" (like the blind beggar in our story), continue to reign. Like their prototype, they scream, yell and heap abuse upon others, all for the sake of "Jewish ideals and honor," which, for some strange reason, fails to bring honor. Will wonders never cease?! Will the emperor ever get properly dressed?

This "honorable group" (those who pursued honor) ended up with the King, the leader of the Holy Assembly, as its ruler. This teaches us that the pursuit of honor — with its sister traits, arrogance and haughtiness — is actually the worst of all characteristics. For it required the highest level, that of the King, corresponding to the sefirah of Keter, to combat the evil influence of haughtiness and the desire for honor.

One of the main reasons for our seeking honor is rooted in Jewish pride. And this pride is rooted in our spiritual connection to God. The Midrash teaches (Vayikra Rabbah 36:4), "The world was created for the sake of Israel." This being the case, we certainly have much to be proud of. We were first and foremost in God's initial plans for the world! Just as Godliness permeates every area of Creation, this connection to God's initial thought is present in every facet of our lives (see Likutey Moharan I, 17:1). We can be proud that we are Jews, coming from a dignified heritage which boasts many major contributions to life as we live it today. This is due to our having remained firm in our connection to God.

Alas, we find our pride in being Jewish today in every kind of material achievement. Instead of looking *upwards* towards our Source, our great spiritual accomplishments and our moral contribution to contemporary civilization, we tend to look downwards and measure our success from our lowly material achievements. Is one more proud of climbing a small hill or of climbing Mt. Everest (or Mt. Sinai)? But we "pride ourselves" in petty triumphs. Thus Jews are found in the forefront of every group that is spawned — religious, anti-religious, liberal, conservative, moral, immoral, and so on. They display their Jewishness up front, getting Jews involved in causes that many never even knew existed, only to debase the entire nation at a later stage (witness the Marxists and socialists). "It was a Jewish ideal! We were proud of it!"

But (Proverbs 16:18), "Pride comes before a fall," and this false sense of pride, gleaned from materialistic goals and attainments, is as detrimental to the individual as it is to the nation as a whole. In general, false pride leads to depression, an unfulfillment of any goal. It is false, and was false to begin with. And, the distortion, even slightly, of one's goal tends to further cloud one's vision of the goal, further distorting the goal until one falls deeply into the abyss.

Conversely, true Jewish pride is found only in our connection to God. Every single person has within himself "good points" — favorable characteristics or good deeds of which he can be proud. One who is truly happy can be so because he has good feelings and joy. This person can feel the pride of his accomplishments, for every good deed performed becomes a fundamental pillar in his makeup, adding reasons for joy and good feelings. It doesn't take much to do a mitzvah, for many opportunities arise: prayer, study, charity, helping another, a kind word and so on. A person can amass a long list of mitzvot daily without even realizing it. Then he can feel proud of himself, proud of his heritage, proud of being born into a nation which has contributed so much to humanity. (The publication *Azamra!* speaks about this topic in detail.)

*

What a waste!

We have seen that the attributes of anger and jealousy stem from an exalted level. But when they are misguided or misused their corruption becomes murderous (Chapter 14). The manifestation of misguided anger and vengeance evolves into a "holy war," a battle for the sake of God. Today there are many views of Judaism: Chassidic, Lithuanian, Modern Orthodox, Traditional, Conservative, Reform, Reconstructionist, secular humanistic, atheistic, etc. You name it, we've got it. And everyone is engaged in "God's battle" (even atheists!) to prove their legitimacy. Everyone sticks to his view, which might be justified if nobody got hurt in the process, for "Words of truth are recognized" (Sotah 9b; see above, Chapter 8).

It is incredible when we think about it: everyone is only fighting with the other because of the truth! That is, *his* truth — because that's all anyone wearing blinders can see (Likutey Halakhot, Ribit 5:20). So let everyone do his own thing and whoever wants the truth will find it... but that's not how life works.

Our Sages teach (cf. Shabbat 138b), "Before Mashiach's arrival, the Jews won't be able to reach agreement on matters of law" (or almost anything else either). The "Jewish emperor's new clothes" has provided apparel which we can all hide behind. It is a cloak of "truth, Godliness and cynicism," all woven together in one garment. A person can demand whatever he wishes, in the name of God, religion or pluralism — because everything is Jewish or Judaic — and try to impose his will upon others. The result is always the same: an unending series of arguments which leads to further division among our people. The trend began with Joseph and his brothers, continued with Korach against Moshe, and has an "unbroken tradition" to this present day. At least the early generations were tzaddikim whose arguments were solely for God's sake — which was bad enough in itself. Look at the aggravation and suffering Jacob endured because of it.

> "Jacob settled in the Land." "He wished to live in peace but his suffering from Joseph assailed him" (Rashi, Genesis 37:2). Jacob suffered from Laban, then from Esav. Eventually, he settled in the Land and thought he would have peace, but the conflict between Joseph and his brothers began and Joseph was sold into slavery. This refers to the battles between good and evil that a person faces, between Jacob and a Laban or an Esav. When this battle between good and evil is settled, the good thinks it is now a permanent fixture. But this is not so, for then, even between the righteous, battles break out.
>
> On the other hand, we find that God chose Moshe to lead the Jews out of Egypt. His elder brother Aaron was then the leader. Yet, when Aaron was informed of his younger brother's mission and position as leader, he greeted him happily and assisted him in all his endeavors (Likutey Halakhot, Rosh Chodesh 7:43).

Consider: Aaron was the leader of the entire Jewish Nation. He suffered with them in Egypt throughout their slavery. Moshe was an unknown entity to the Jews, having spent some sixty years in exile after fleeing Pharaoh's sword. One day he shows up, unknown and unrecognizable, and says, "Here I am, your leader, and I'm going to take you out of exile!" Who would believe him? Accept him? You? Me? Not much chance. But Aaron, his elder brother, does. And not only that, Aaron places himself *under* Moshe's leadership, giving up his position and canvassing to convince the Jews that Moshe is their leader! Can we picture this happening today? Which "leader" would even think of deferring to another? Who would give up his position without a fight, knowing how many sacrifices fall victim to the "truth" which is being fought over? In contemporary terms, which leader today would accept Mashiach, a total stranger, and bring his followers to accept their new leader?

And it is much worse today, for as the levels of the generations plummet, the ideologies plummet with them and the claims of "battling God's war" become more questionable — even ludicrous. "This murderous trait of strife is the battle of Amalek in every generation. It delays the arrival of the Mashiach" (*Likutey Halakhot, Matanah* 3:4-5). Furthermore, the character traits of haughtiness and anger denote a constricted mind (cf. *Pesachim* 66b). These traits are manifested in continuing strife and petty arguments. Thus, since Daat is a feature of the Days of Mashiach, anger and arrogance hold back Mashiach.

Thus, each of us thinks that we are engaged in a battle against an "Esav," or a "Laban"; or maybe we'll be nice and call the other guy a "Joseph" or a "brother." "I'm on the *right* side and must battle against the evil of those who oppose me and my views! Why make peace if we can have war?!" We waste our time, we waste our energy, we waste our resources fighting each other, thereby wasting ourselves and our lives — and for what? We need only to examine the results of our labor. And we think it bizarre that there's a group which considers murder a goal? The "emperor's new clothes!"

*

Marriage: a family "institution"

> "Another group maintained that the main goal was for the world to be populated. Since a beautiful woman arouses the desire to populate the world, she brings about the goal."

The feminists were not consulted by this group. The nerve! But then, don't certain magazines extol beauty just for sales and advertising revenues? But then again, why the obsession with sex? Just because the world must continue? But nobody wants children anymore! Where would we be today if Adam and Eve thought like us?

Marriage is a family institution. It has held the Jewish community-in-exile together and kept our nation flourishing even under the most brutal conditions. But the spawning of "new marriage ideals" has turned the institution of marriage into a type of "institution" where most people feel forcibly locked in. The Talmud relates (Berakhot 8a) that when a person married, those gathered would ask him, "Have you *found* or do you *find*?" They explained: One verse states (Proverbs 18:22), "He that has *found* a woman, he has found good." Another verse states (Ecclesiastes 7:26), "I *find* the woman more bitter than death." People used to approach marriage knowing that, despite the difficulties of life, there is a shared responsibility to raise a family and instill values in their offspring to do the same. Today's materialistic leanings do nothing of the sort. Thus, those who have *found* — look to past values to sustain their present and future goals — have found a good life, despite the difficulties they face. But those who seek contemporary ideals upon which to build their marriage, will *find* nothing concrete to build upon, hence their need for an "institution" when faced with the daily grind of life.

Without strong family values — respect and love, etc. — immorality sets in. It begins very subtly, and ends with the immoral person plunging into an abyss. "For the pleasure of a quarter of an hour, a person can lose This World and the Next!" (Likutey Moharan II, 108). People sacrifice their wives or husbands, children, families and even their wealth (sometimes just in divorce proceedings, lawyer fees and child support!), all for the sake of a brief encounter. And if it lingers, it only becomes worse.

Today's "emperor's new clothes" have civilization(?) and society(?) condoning and even supporting: childbirth out of wedlock, pornography, masturbation, transvestism, homosexual and lesbian relationships. These have all increased the number of divorced and abandoned spouses, unwed teenage parents, pedophilia, child abuse and bestial relations. For once the gates of sexual aberration are opened they can lead only in one direction — down. Instead of building floodgates to stop the tide, "society" continually demeans itself by lowering the level of its morals. Then, after accepting and condoning abominations, they "wonder" why cases of pedophilia and child abuse, rape and other violent crimes, are on the rise!

It is an admission to donning the "emperor's new clothes," that even in Jewish circles — where the family has been the foundation of our history — the breaches in society have become part of our lives. Divorce and single parenting are growing. This is because misplaced pride (e.g. honor, status, regardless of the spouse or children, etc.) and immorality go hand in hand (Likutey Moharan I, 11:3). And this casual attitude becomes truly frightening when one approaches the roots of this group, i.e. the goal of populating the world with *human beings*. Instead of "being fruitful and multiplying," we find that just the thought of having children becomes a difficult decision. "We can't afford it yet." "It interferes with my career." If the thought of a child is somehow acceptable, then "quality time" — a few hours a week — is set aside to raise that child. This is unfortunate, because the child isn't always prepared during those few moments the parent sees fit to offer it! Offering children time based on their needs would most certainly interfere with work schedules. Yet parents expect their children to be human beings? Then again, maybe only those who appreciate life will continue to pass it along to others. Barnum and Bailey couldn't put on a better circus! Wearing the "emperor's new clothes," we can all attend the royal weddings and have a ball.

*

The anorexic heavyweight!

> "One faction maintained that the person best qualified to be king would be one who did not eat the food of ordinary people but, rather, ate highly refined food..."

The reason food and drink are such an obsession in our lives is because Adam and Eve ate from the Tree of Knowledge of Good and Evil, blemishing the concept of eating. Food was originally intended to enable man, as a material being, to live a spiritual existence — by keeping body and soul together. Adam sinned through eating and forced humanity into exile (see *Likutey Halakhot, Pesach* 6:6). In fact, in the main, all exiles are a product of obsession with food — traveling to work for our livelihood or forcing a trip to the local supermarket or the 24-hour convenience store.

But there's more. Today we are blessed with a plethora of eating habits, diets and disorders. There are no-fat, no-cholesterol, no-caffeine, no-salt and no-taste diets. There are literally hundreds of "approved" diets — all "guaranteed" to make money for the authors, doctors, dieticians and so on. Then we have junk food paradise, and vegetarian meats, together with the "true veggies," organic mavens, macrobiotics and weight-watchers. Add to this bulimia and anorexia, among our other infatuations, and we have a comprehensive picture of humanity with "obsessive/compulsive eating disorders."

We've got to watch the chemicals and DDT found in our food. Our fruits, vegetables, water, milk, meat: everything carries chemicals and pesticides which inspire dieticians, laboratories and the advertising industry which take up the banner of "popular causes" to save humanity. It can be an absolutely frightening experience to eat these days — especially in a generation when people are living longer, healthier and better than they have for many centuries. Good health requires that we choose a healthy variety of simple, well-balanced meals (according to our individual body requirements). Life would be so much easier if we just ate like human beings should eat... and avoided cigarettes, alcohol and drugs. There is nothing wrong with eating — we must eat if we are to survive. But the "emperor's new clothes" may not fit properly if we don't watch our food intake...!

*

Another group held that eating regularly, and body building foods at that, is the goal. Eating for physical strength was meant to increase one's awareness and awe of the spiritual. But we have successfully turned ourselves around so that the body itself has become a goal and a focus of idolatry. As with the other goals, physical fitness has been taken to the extreme, in the form of sports and exercise. It's amazing what body building and competitive sports can do for us, and how much time and energy we spend on the body. This is aside from the adulation given to sports figures which, for many of our youths, borders on idolatry. The "emperor's new clothes" comes in many uniforms! (But don't worry. The Talmud teaches (Megilah 6a), "In the Future, sports stadiums, theaters and circus arenas will be transformed into Torah study centers!")

Regular exercise and meals are the best way to stay healthy. Having a strong body is one of the great benefits of living in the messianic era, with no illness and only good health. But the purpose of good health then, as should be now, is to be able to better serve God. For when Mashiach comes, Scripture tells us (Isaiah 35:3-6), "Strengthen the feeble hands and weak knees... the eyes of the blind will open and the ears of the deaf will hear... the lame will jump as a deer and the tongue of the dumb will speak..." speedily, in our days, Amen.

*

Freedom from speech!

Speech, when used in holiness, leads man to God. Speech, when not used in holiness, leads man astray. King Solomon taught (Proverbs 18:21), "Death and life are in the hands of the tongue." For just as the tongue can draw a person to God, it can also distance him. Herein lies the scourge of today's spiritual life — the way speech is used. And nobody is as successful in abusing the power of speech as the media.

There's television, radio, magazines and newspapers. We have cellular phones, faxes and electronic communications. We are fortunate — some consider this a "privilege" — to be inundated incessantly, twenty-four hours a day, seven days a week, with information that others consider important for us to know (unless we observe Shabbat — in which case we have one day less of this nonsense each week!). Novelists, the theater, Hollywood and Madison Avenue all present "meaningful" ideas that are intended to impress us with relevance to our daily lives.

Perhaps ludicrous is too nice a word to describe the serious presentation of the news and information reaching us every day — but we must give credit where credit is due. It takes masters of language to present *raw sewage* as important information. And with it, the media —

conventional and electronic — have successfully captured the hearts and minds of the people. Democracies scoffed at the communists who controlled the minds of their citizens through the media. But somehow, this attitude was lost on the democracies which themselves are controlled by the press!

Our enthusiasm for news is rooted in the messianic era, when new revelations of Godliness will be unearthed every moment. This explains the drive of readers, newscasters and writers (of novels, plays, poetry, etc., as well as reporters) to seek something new at all times. But as mankind has plunged to the depths of depravity, it has taken its language with it. Profanity and immorality, along with stories that would make Alfred Hitchcock blanch, have become a staple of life, all in the name of "It's in the public interest!"

The "emperor's new clothes!" We have a Torah that has remained the same since it was given to us at Sinai over three thousand years ago. Yet, in every generation, the *very same words* give forth new teachings and are a source of inspiration for a whole nation! How tragic that instead of expressing our ideas in Torah terms, we spend our time staring through "the looking glass" (TV) or reading an educated guess from someone who gets paid to write *his* opinion! We have allowed ourselves to be integrated into a "freedom of speech" culture that has found it imperative to censor its own films, television programs, the profane language of its musicians and the pornography of its arts and artists! Worse, we have allowed our "freedom of speech" to support symposiums and programs that teach blasphemy and atheism, which distance us from God.

As a goal, especially a messianic goal, *melitzah* (expression through speech) is a very authentic one. While the Jews were in Egypt, Moshe was said to be "a stutterer" (Exodus 4:10). The ARI teaches that speech itself, i.e. Malkhut, was in exile. This alludes to prayer (as above, Chapter 5). This is why we find that the Jews' prayers then were only cries and sighs (Exodus 2:23-24). But after the Exodus, they attained "free speech." *PeSaCh* (Passover), which represents the Exodus from Egypt, comprises the words *Peh SaCh*, "a mouth that speaks." As long as speech promotes profanity and immorality, we are in exile, enslaved to alien cultures. When we turn our speech to the glory of God, this is the beginning of the end of the exile. Furthermore, when the verse states (Numbers 14:20), "And God said, 'I have forgiven, according to your word,'" this means that God's pardoning a person for his transgression is according to *how* he speaks! (Likutey Halakhot, Yom Kippur 1).

There is a difference between "freedom of speech," and "free speech." Under the banner of "freedom of speech" anyone can say or publish anything, right or wrong: profanity, falsehood, ethnic insinuations, blasphemy, and so on. But its impact on society is extremely detrimental. "Free speech" indicates that words can flow freely, without offending anyone. In addition, speech is *the* tool of dialogue, that messianic ideal which leads to peace — not to neuroses and psychotic behavior caused by the panic imposed upon us by reporters, artists and advertisers. This "free speech" is truth, the truth that will be spoken when Mashiach comes, and the truth with which we can engage in dialogue, today (see Likutey Moharan I, 38:3).

*

"That's entertainment!"

> "Yet another group chose joy and merrymaking as their goal. When a child is born there is joy. At a wedding, there is joy. Every conquest brings joy. So joy must be a worthy goal. They found a drunkard who appeared not to have a worry in the world. He was always joyous. So he became their leader. One can be sure that he led them on the straight path!"

Thanks to modern technology, life has been made very comfortable and leisurely. People can relax in comfortable chairs, drive in comfortable cars, dine in comfortable and elegant surroundings, and fly in a few hours to a comfortable resort for a few days of comfortable vacation. We are in an age where leisure, a most sought-after luxury, has become a necessity, as merrymaking and partying have become a dominant theme in life.

Life is portrayed in the media as if everyone has a beautiful home that may lack only a few accessories to help redecorate or refurnish. So there's plenty of time and money for fun. And in dramas we are presented with challenges and solutions that have an astonishing way of solving all life's problems in an hour (with about a third shaved off for advertisements!). Therefore, there's plenty of time for rest and relaxation. And this leads us to the "good life." But, if so, why are alcohol and drugs such a growing problem?

"Who is wealthy? One who is satisfied with his lot" (Avot 4:1). This applies to every area of life. One who is happily married will not seek "enjoyment" elsewhere. One who is satisfied with his finances will appreciate his home, family and possessions. Conversely, one who always wants more than what he has will always have a craving and an empty feeling. Our *craving* for leisure stems from discontentment, from a false sense of security and a mistaken feeling of joy and happiness. Let us examine this idea.

On Shabbat, work is forbidden. It is a day of rest, of leisure, of enjoyment. One spends time in the synagogue in prayer and then spends leisure time with the family. A sumptuous meal is served, songs are sung and people have time to sit relaxed at the table and catch up with family and friends after a week of bedlam and drudgery at work. Shabbat as a day of leisure thus serves as a time when one can abandon busy schedules and focus on oneself, one's family and environment. "Have I grown this week?" "Have I accomplished anything this week?" "What about the family?" "Where am I headed?" "Where are we headed?" In short, we eat, rest, enjoy and contemplate our life situations. We have ample opportunity to reflect on each week as it passes by.

But Shabbat alone is not sufficient for total leisure. Man faces many trials during the year. So we have Festivals that occur every few months where the same opportunities present themselves, albeit in different ways. There's a full week of Chanukah, of Passover and Sukkot, and there are other days here and there that call for reconnecting with God, with our familes and with our selves. On some days we are forbidden to work, on others we are permitted — each festival calls for a different way of recognizing and assessing our situation. The overall effect is that man is presented with "time off" from his burdens to take a good look at himself and his life. So obviously, the Torah's view of rest and recreation is reflected in days such as Shabbat and the festivals, when one has the time and opportunity to reflect on oneself and one's attainments.

And as for other types of relaxation and entertainment, the arts and music can also be very beneficial. Music is a very powerful medium and is the source of prophecy (see Zohar III, 68a; Likutey Moharan I, 3). The same can be said for the appreciation of art. The architectural beauty of the Holy Temple had no equal (cf. Bava Batra 4a), while the Sanctuary and the Holy Temple, with their art work and design, were built in such a manner as to manifest the aura of Creation and the Garden of Eden and to reveal, literally, the beauty of God (Tikkuney Zohar Introduction, p.13b; see also Likutey Moharan II, 1:14). In the Temple, the Levites would sing and play musical instruments, combining the "arts" under one roof. Those who attain a true appreciation for the power and beauty of music and art in holiness can ascend the spiritual ladder with great ease.

But now let's take leisure as presented by modern day "leisure experts." (Incidentally, "leisure studies" are acceptable as credits for university degrees in several institutes of higher learning!) One requires time off from a heavy schedule, but one can never really remove oneself from one's environment. The car needs fixing, the lawn needs mowing, the TV stays on, newpapers and magazines inundate us, the telephone is kept busy, etc., so that we never have the chance for introspection and to connect with ourselves. Is it any wonder we need a five o'clock martini *and* a nightcap? (aside from the after dinner cocktail and/or the red wine before lunch...!). Is it any wonder, never having taken time off to find out "who I am," that people turn to insubstantial "substances" for their "high" of the day? The more people crave something beyond what they have, the more the empty feeling gnaws at them. And the more people turn to outside stimulants to help them through their difficult times, the more dependent they become. And those who present music and the arts in an immoral, impure and profane manner, bring tremendous blemish upon themselves as well as their followers. This is because, "An irresponsible drunkard leads us on the straight and narrow path!" (from our story, Chapter 13).

*

The ultimate leader of the group of joy and entertainment was the Faithful Friend of the King. And herein lies another reason for our pressing requirement for leisure time: friendship.

People require friendship and companionship, and by this is meant a reliable friend — "a rock" that one can rely upon — to listen and understand what "I'm all about." Today, however, friendship translates as a relationship with a therapist to whom we go to for a "quick fix" of a few minutes, talk our heart out, listen to some textbook advice and, on top of it, pay a small fortune for the privilege. Never mind that "the expert" has many similar hangups of his own and needs his own therapist to work them out! Most relationships today are so shallow that one rarely bares one's heart to another, for fear of that person betraying him and publicizing the innermost feelings of his "friend."

"Cover up" is the word. We have become so inwardly conscious about our shortcomings that to cover up our fears and insecurities we always put on the façade of joy and friendship in public. Since there is a fear of establishing long-lasting relationships, we make sure that our time is taken up with frivolities so that serious conversation can never take place. Anger builds up, honor is slighted, arguments become frequent and our only refuge seems to be those few moments of entertainment! (Here we see how speech, joy and anger are interconnected. Actually, all the goals — in holiness or unholiness — are interconnected and have bearing upon each other.)

Dialogue and peace will be the mainstay of all life in the messianic era. But currently, finding it too difficult to bare one's heart, one somehow feels more comfortable dressing oneself in transparent clothing instead. Mankind is suffering from the "chills" — from frosty and unviable relationships with our fellow man. Voilà! The "emperor's new clothes!"

*

Higher? education

> *During the Exodus, Moshe split the physical sea with his staff. For the final redemption, the staff will split open the "sea of wisdom."*
>
> Tikkuney Zohar #21, p.43a

The commentaries point out that the *Zohar's* teaching refers to the revelation of deep Torah knowledge (i.e. the Torah of Atik) which will be revealed in the Future. During the final redemption the staff, which is the quill — the written revelation of these deep mysteries — will split open the "sea of wisdom" for all mankind to perceive Godliness (cf. *Likutey Halakhot, Pikadon* 5:40-42).

The Torah is God's gift for us to use as a pathfinder to Godliness. At the time of the Revelation at Sinai, God offered the Torah to all of mankind. All the nations, save the Jews, rejected it (*Avodah Zarah* 2b). Rabbi Yisrael Meir Kagan, the *Chafetz Chaim* (1840-1933), used to say: "At the time of the Revelation, there were many non-Jews who wanted to receive the Torah, but their compatriots refused. These souls converted to Judaism over the generations. On the other hand, there were Jews then who did not wish to accept the Torah. These are the Jews who later in history rejected Judaism and became apostates." (More about the Jews and non-Jews and their rectification in Part VI).

The Torah is *the* means by which to be able to recognize and serve God. This is what Torah study is all about and what our Jewish educational system is all about. Throughout the ages, under all types of difficulties, the Jews managed to maintain their values for Jewish education and Torah study, which is why we are known as "The People of the Book." And this is what today's Jewish schools, yeshivot, the rabbinate and Jewish leadership are all about. Or should be.

But lo and behold! The People of the Book, whose educational endeavors have never waned — despite two millennia of exile, poverty, physical and psychological abuse, blood libels, expulsions, wanton murder and holocaust — have exchanged the mantle of their glorious heritage for the "emperor's new clothes." Not only has the purpose of the study of Torah been misguided, but the idea of what Jewish education should be today is totally misdirected.

The modern trend began with the enlightenment in the late 18th century, when the Jewish Nation, masters of Torah, began in large numbers to focus their educational pursuits elsewhere. Secular education was imposed upon the Jewish school system by parents and educators. These educators decided that the knowledge of how many tails certain parasites have and where Central Africa is on the map was more important than the Jew knowing what Judaism is all about (see Likutey Halakhot, Geviyat Chov MeYetomim 3:5). When the walls of the ghettos — and the bastions of religion — began to crumble, European universities began to admit Jews into institutions of "higher education." The trend continued throughout the nineteenth and early twentieth centuries until, by the 1960s, a large percentage of Jews in the world were either university graduates or students. What an intelligent nation! What a bright future must be in store for them! The benefits of striving for this "higher education" must have done wonders for us as a nation. Or has it? Let us examine the facts.

The percentage of Jews found in the fields of medicine, law, accounting, the sciences, etc., is far greater than that of any other group. The basic underlying reason is that, because our ancestors accepted the Torah (i.e. wisdom) at Sinai, the Jew has a remarkable affinity with wisdom and knowledge. Statistics bear this out in the ratio of achievements and awards (e.g. Nobel prizes) earned by Jews as compared to other nations. But has this intellectual pursuit affected our nation positively or negatively? Considering the financial plight of European Jewry in the past centuries it certainly appears that the opening of universities to Jews has had a positive effect. People are educated in many areas: health, social welfare, the sciences, human rights and so on — which have all contributed greatly to better living conditions. And, parents do have an obligation to teach their children a trade or profession (Kiddushin 29a). Still, unfortunately, the overall effect of this pursuit of higher education has taken far more than its toll on our people. For it is obvious that the Jewish venture into the realms of "higher education" has been at the expense of Higher Education.

The Jew no longer invested significant time or effort in spiritual studies and Judaism was shunted aside. Many communities established a Jewish day school system, whereby one studies Judaism — as one studies any secular subject — for half a day, while the main emphasis is on secular studies. Others "fooled the emperor" even more and sent their children to secular schools with only an hour or so a day given over to God. Still others felt this too much and instead enthusiastically endorsed an hour or two a week so that their children can be "fully" apprised of Jewish history, heritage and ideals. After all, an hour a week of Jewish studies is surely sufficient to implant 3,500 years of Judaism into our youth. And if the child intermarries, or wants nothing at all to do with his temple or his people, then the question is asked, "How could this happen to us? Haven't we given our child the *best* Jewish education possible?!" The Midrash describes this long exile as the abyss (Bereishit Rabbah 2:4). Reb Noson adds that this abyss is manifest in the inculcation of Jewish youth with secular cultures, at the expense of their Higher Education (Likutey Halakhot, Chezkat Mitaltilin 5:16). We're there, we're in it, and we are no longer even capable of gauging its effect upon us.

In short, our "higher" education has given us the ability to become smart and wise — beyond our years, beyond our abilities, beyond common sense. We've become so brilliant that we can rationalize the sacrificing of one's self and family for the idolatry of wealth, the desecration of Shabbat, kosher-style foods, and assimilation — all in the name of Judaism!

*

The fundamental of all wisdom is the fear of God (as above, Chapter 7). Obviously, the purpose of Torah study is to instill fear of God and knowledge of Him. So our Sages teach (see Shabbat 31a): "Fear of God is the key to the outer gate [of recognition of God]. Torah is the key to the inner storehouse. One who studies Torah without fear of God is compared to one who has only the keys to the inner storehouse, but not the keys to the outer gate." The function of "the rebbe" or rosh yeshivah is to speak to his flock and advise them on how to draw near to God. He must teach fear of God as well as Torah and its meaning. This is Mashiach's mission and, as each tzaddik reflects Mashiach (as above, Chapter 9), this should be the function of each Jewish leader.

We are very fortunate in this generation to have houses of study where people can, and do, study Torah. There is a growth of yeshivot where people can *kvetch de beink* ("press the benches") for many years

— from play school through high school and into the *batei midrashim*. The Torah world is growing and coming into its own. But the "emperor's black hat, coat and shtreimel" are as transparent as his other royal robes. In the *yeshivishe* world, the students are all cloned to wear the same "emperor's" uniform while the underlying purpose of Torah, to recognize God in every facet of life, is as often distant as ever. And, would you believe, a men's store in a religious neighborhood of Brooklyn once advertised "*Chassidic fashions*"!!! The Baal Shem Tov would have great difficulty identifying with the movement he started. An elderly Jerusalemite I know commented on several contemporary extremist trends in religion: "Moshe Rabeinu would not be able to recognize the Torah he gave us!"

But the material apparel with which we've succeeded in "clothing" our religion has led us all to seek materialism from our leaders. We all need good health, financial security, good marriage partners, along with a peaceful home and *nachat* from our children, etc. But we have "succeeded" in directing our spiritual leaders to concentrate their efforts on our material needs. The proof is: how often is a rabbi, rosh yeshivah or rebbe approached for spiritual guidance? How many people run to their rebbes to complain that their prayers lack concentration and feeling? When does one ask one's rosh yeshivah advice on how to improve and increase one's studies? How many times do people seek advice in order to increase their joy when performing mitzvot — e.g. receiving Shabbat, the festivals, sukkah, etc.? Or, as too often happens, is the rabbi only sought out when a burial must take place?

In earlier generations, Torah was studied as a means to define the law and direct us towards observing the mitzvot. One need only study a little of the *Rishonim* — Rashi, Rambam, etc. — to see that their writings concentrate on the law at hand to bring it to a definitive, *halakhic*, conclusion. The early Codifiers all followed this path. But rarely does contemporary Torah education "bring the study to its *halakhic* conclusion" (see Yoma 26a). After a decade of Talmudic study, one rarely knows the law that one spent so much time studying. The actual study is in itself extremely important, but the main point is to know what to do *and to do it*, in order to come close to God (see *Likutey Halakhot, Netilat Yadaim Li'Seudah* 6:91).

There is a need to strengthen Jewish education, an education which teaches our youth and ourselves to recognize Jews and Judaism for what they *really* are. The history of the Jewish Nation extends over 3,500 years — a history rich in tradition, law, education, moral values and dignity, even under the most stressful conditions — which cannot be encapsulated in a few hours' study, let alone an hour a week. Torah is truth, and has survived every feasible attack upon it and still endures, as truth will always endure.

Everyone, from ultra-educated to those ignorant of Jewish values, must seek to study Jewish thought and Judaism. We must seek authentic Jewish books, legitimate Jewish values and true Jewish education, in order to reach the messianic goal of attaining Daat of God. We have to encourage one another to study Torah books and then "Words of truth are recognized." Each person will recognize the truth from his perspective and draw near to God from the angle that suits him best. Then (Isaiah 11:9), "The world will be filled with knowledge — Knowledge of Godliness — as waters cover the earth."

*

Money makes the world go 'round

The group which runs through the entire story is the one which sought wealth as a goal. This is because all the above-mentioned groups also have wealth as a goal. It is just that their perverted goal overshadowed their desire for wealth. Still, there are those who have little use for other desires. Instead, their entire being "screams" for wealth and material possessions. And they will steamroll over anyone who tries to get in the way of their obtaining that goal. They'll lie, cheat and steal, plunder and murder, all for a few dollars, as we've seen in our story — and as is evident in today's world. Nice, friendly bunch of guys, don't you think? And they live among us. It has been said, "We have met the enemy and they are us!"

Interestingly, the source of this deep obsession with wealth is rooted in a very exalted place. Our Sages teach (Nedarim 38a), "All the prophets were extremely wealthy." It simply wouldn't do to have a pauper walking around with a big sign, "Repent! The sky is about to cave in!" But as for a wealthy man — "one who's made it" — people listen when he talks.

On a more serious note, the spiritual root of money is the same as that of prophecy. Today, "Prophecy has been taken from the prophets and given to fools," for the meaning of "*vayitnabeiy* (prophesied)" is "*v'ishtateiy* (became foolish)" (see Targum on 1 Samuel 18:10; Bava Batra 12b). The same applies to wealth. Since prophecy has fallen to the depths, wealth — its concept and power — has also fallen and has been given to the fools who pursue it passionately (Likutey Moharan II, 64).

> "...The people used 'angels' for transportation. Their horses were bedecked with so much gold and treasures that their ornamentation alone would be enough to confer the status of 'angel' upon a person" (from our story. See above, Chapter 13).

And so it goes. He made it! A Cadillac. A Mercedes-Benz. A Porsche. A Rolls Royce. Why not one of each?! "What good is my wealth if I can't flaunt it?" And so, our heroes of today are those with the big bank accounts. For example, our synagogues, day schools and other charitable foundations make fund-raising dinners. "We are pleased to welcome the honorable so and so..." because today we need his money and his influence. This is how our model institutions of Judaism and Judaic studies instill "proper Jewish values" into our children. And we wonder where today's youth learned to be greedy?!

Rabbi Akiva was a pauper and an ignoramus. His wife Rachel was the daughter of one of the wealthiest men of the generation, Kalba Savua. Against her father's express wishes, she married R. Akiva, because she had faith in his potential. Her father was so enraged, he banished her from his home and excluded her from his estate. Eventually, Kalba Savua regretted his action and accepted the couple back in his home. Meanwhile, Rabbi Akiva had become *the* leading scholar of the generation, and a very wealthy man in his own right. Yet he never forgot his humble beginnings (*Nedarim* 50a).

Contrast this with today's bargaining during a *shidukh* (marriage match). Have there ever been such serious negotiations in the annals of Jewish history? After all, he's going to be sitting and learning! He needs a Volvo and a house and a few trips to Israel...!" Maybe we should include in the marriage contract an additional line or two, "Whatever you get, you have to give at least the same to your future son-in-law!"

A person strived and sacrificed himself for God, ascending the ladder of spirituality until he merited to the level of a Prophet. Then, as a prophet, he was given great wealth. Today, as we have seen, money is from the "fallen wealth" of the prophets. Those would-be "seers of Torah" who seek wealth in a marriage prior to obtaining any level of spirituality have a somewhat odd view of what religion and spirituality are.

And the shame of wearing the "emperor's new clothes" is more evident in how we've managed to turn a family *simchah* into a horror story. "When a child is born, there is joy. At a wedding, there is joy..." We've literally made a study of how to go berserk and spend months, even years, and fortunes, in preparations and celebrations. (I've met people who begin preparing for a bar mitzvah two or three years in advance!) "Who sits at which table?" "What color scheme?" "Should the chopped liver be shaped like a spaceship, a football or maybe like a pair of tefilin?!" We mortgage our lives for an evening of food and drink, dance and song for a thirteen-year-old?! Which businessman would make such an investment? In these very important moments of our child's life, we engage in an excessive display of opulence — all in the name of "religion"! The "emperor" would have been ecstatic to dress up in the levels of absurdity that we have reached!

The criterion for finding out if we are "members" of this "elite" group is our assessment of others. In our story, one who had a little money was considered "an animal or a bird" — someone with little stature and unworthy of our attentions. One with a lot of money was a "star," perhaps even a "whole constellation of stars" or even an "angel"! Others were god-like creatures, those with enough money so that one could count, ogle at and forever admire this ethereal wealth. People sacrificed themselves to and for these gods. They gave up their lives for wealth and for other people with money. And so it is today. The more we seek wealth, the more we "sacrifice" ourselves to those gods who have money.

The Torah does not require this of us. Not at all. In fact, it rejects this extravaganza (which may be why many reject Torah!). On the other hand, there are those who merit wealth and act very honorably with it. In the early 1990s, a very wealthy man in London made a bar mitzvah celebration for his son and invited many guests. Anticipating the gifts from well-wishers, he added a note to his guests: "Instead of a gift for my son, please support a charity. My favorite is...." Incredible! And in this day and age! Maybe Mashiach isn't as far away as he seems.

A meal at a time of joy and celebration, like Shabbat, a brit or a wedding, is a tremendous mitzvah and a time of great rejoicing. We *can* spend and be happy. But we have to realize that there *is* a God and that it is in His honor that we should truly be joyous and honored to *really* dress up for the occasion!

*

The main goal: prayer

Mashiach's root is from a very lofty source. Since prayer is bound up conceptually with Mashiach, it follows that prayer itself is extremely lofty. Indeed, our Sages teach that "Prayer stands at the very heights of the universe" (Berakhot 6b). Since Mashiach and prayer are connected, and since Mashiach can come at any moment, prayer — as a messianic manifestation — should be a major factor in our daily lives. And it is, *but*....

Our Sages also teach that prayer is very neglected (Rashi, Berakhot 6b, s.v. devarim). As we've seen (above, Chapter 5), prayer corresponds to Malkhut, Kingship. Thus, the neglect of prayer is synonymous with the decline of true leadership and authority. Therefore, it is up to us to raise the significance of prayer to its rightful level.

"And there was one group which maintained that none of the above could be a goal in life. The main goal was to pray to God and serve Him, to be humble…"

All the groups we have studied used sophisticated ideas to define their chosen goal, but as we have seen, they distorted that goal. Now who looks at, or listens to, a little boy? Yet, in the "emperor's new clothes," all the sophisticates turned out to be fools while only the little boy had *sekhel* (intellect). This "boy" can be seen as the group which chose prayer and humility as the goal of life. Nobody notices or cares about them. But somehow, they endure. And eventually their ideas will spread to help all others make a break from the foolishness of contemporary civilization.

*

Prayer is extremely exalted. Unfortunately, it is demeaned by many who don't have an inkling of its greatness and power. Consider the following:

> There are three types of prayer. One is for material benefits alone. This is a bad prayer — a "wasted" prayer — because all materialism eventually goes to waste. There is prayer for material benefit, so that a person will have good health and a livelihood, etc., in order to be able to study Torah, perform mitzvot and otherwise serve God. This is a good and beneficial prayer, for it has spiritual overtones. However, this prayer is far below the level of Torah. But there is a third type of prayer, very exalted, which is equal to, and in certain ways even greater than, the Torah. This is a prayer that a person understand the Torah and be able to perform the mitzvot in the proper manner. This prayer is totally spiritual in nature and is *the* vehicle through which a person can draw close to God (Mashiach's main weapon).
>
> We have three vehicles through which to seek spirituality. There is the Written Law, which is the source of all Torah, but by itself does not explain any law at all. There is the Oral Law, which is completely rooted in the Written Law and contains all the laws and commentary on the Torah and the mitzvot. And there is prayer, which has the power to draw the person near to God. When a person engages in prayer as a means of drawing close to God, he forms a unification between the Written Law and the Oral Law. That is, the various parts of Torah unite. As a single unit, Torah

(unified through prayer) is able to reveal itself to that person and illuminate the path that is right for him — each person according to his level.

Kabbalistically, Jacob is called the Written Law (for he corresponds to Tiferet; see Appendix B). Rachel parallels the Oral Law. Rachel in Hebrew is a sheep, whose wool is shorn. So, too, the teachings of the Oral Law are "clipped and shorn" (i.e. discussed and mulled over) until people understand the law. Furthermore, Rachel was very attractive (Genesis 29:17), for everyone can readily see the beauty of Torah. But "Leah had weak eyes." Leah was afraid that she might have to marry the wicked Esav. Therefore, she prayed and prayed, to be saved from such a marriage (Rashi, Genesis 29:17). Leah signifies prayer, but her beauty was marred and hidden.

Jacob knew he was destined to marry both Rachel and Leah. His first thought, though, was that one must first study the Oral Law so that the Written and Oral Law can complement each other. Therefore, his agreement with Laban was to marry Rachel first, and then, with the knowledge of Torah, he would attain understanding of the awesomeness of prayer and know what to pray for. On the other hand, Laban was so steeped in materialism that he couldn't even conceive the greatness of prayer. His intention was to stop Jacob from unifying the Written and Oral Law. So he fooled Jacob by giving him Leah first. But this was God's plan, for only He knows how great prayer is. And the Torah itself complied. Jacob suspected that Laban might fool him and he and Rachel devised identification codes. When Rachel saw that Laban was going to give Leah to Jacob, she transmitted the codes to Leah! (Rashi, Genesis 30:22). Thus, Rachel, the Oral Law itself, revealed to Leah, prayer, the way to interact with the Written Law, so that Jacob, the one who wants to draw near to God, will know how to properly interpret the Torah (Likutey Halakhot, Rosh Chodesh 5:30).

*

Prayer: the feminist movement

Like all the others who wear the "emperor's new clothes," the gender battle of today's world is as transparent as it is incredible. As in the Egyptian exile, when women were forced into a man's domain and men were forced into doing the traditional work of women, today, we've reached that same stage. Men have paternity leave to care for newborn children while the brand new mother can return immediately to the work force. Motherhood, the moulding and building of a human being, has become a much maligned career. It is amazing how we resent work given to us by the boss that really should be performed by others. Yet, we rush to take upon ourselves roles that have traditionally been reserved for others. Had this been the salvation of mankind, "*nu!* Okay." But, as studies show, more women are suffering from neuroses than ever before, while divorce and other — worse — abuses of this free-wheeling "equal" society have created greater pressures and even more difficulties for women. Somehow, the feminist battle for equality has led to a deeper chasm.

When viewing the feminist movement of today we must ponder this phenomenon. Why has the garrulous woman remained silent over her plight for so many thousands of years? It's not as if she's had nothing to say! And why has woman over the past century become so vociferous — even violent — in demanding equal rights? Don't these extremes, seen over such a short period, seem odd? What is really the underlying drive for "equal rights?" It becomes easy to understand in light of the above and following teaching.

Torah is parallel to Man, as in (Numbers 19:14), "This is the Torah, Man..." Woman corresponds to prayer and praise, as in (Proverbs 31:30), "The woman who fears God, she will be *praised.*" Torah and prayer were created with equal importance. Torah teaches the way of God and how to pray in order to attain it. Prayer brings a person to understand Torah and fulfill it, thereby opening the way to ever higher levels of Torah, of Godliness. Each is distinct. Each is a separate idea and world unto itself. But one cannot endure without the other.

Like the sun and the moon, Adam and Eve were created as equals. But Eve was the first to be tempted by the Serpent into eating from the Tree of Knowledge, causing her role to be diminished. This is because woman parallels Malkhut, i.e. the moon, which was diminished (cf. Rashi, Genesis 1:16; see also Appendix B). But equality *must* be attained if the world is to reach perfection. Malkhut will then be restored to its former glory, since Mashiach will arrive and bring the world to perfection.

Malkhut is currently downtrodden, indicative of the state of the holy Malkhut, represented in the Kingdom of King David, the paradigm of prayer, by the Mashiach. Therefore, woman's status has been a subordinate and downtrodden one. Currently, as we enter the final stages before the arrival of the Mashiach, whose main weapon is prayer, the status of Malkhut, of prayer, is on the rise. But the way to equality is through prayer, not through battle.

Prayer means everyone going to the synagogue with the intention of praying, rather than talking. Prayer means everyone showing the respect due to prayer, as one should show respect to one's wife. Prayer means everyone engaging in prayer — talking to God (*hitbodedut*), thanking Him for the good moments and asking for a better and brighter Future. With this deeper kind of connection to prayer, all will see its beauty, and sing and praise God.

And then (Isaiah 35:10), "Those redeemed by God shall return and come to Zion with song, with everlasting joy upon their heads; they shall attain joy and gladness, while sorrow and sighing shall flee." Speedily, in our days, Amen.

* * *

16

So why hasn't Mashiach come yet?

It's quite obvious, isn't it? Anybody wearing the "emperor's new clothes" would be embarrassed to appear in a public ceremony. Just as we wouldn't want to look at our king in "the emperor's new clothes," similarly, Mashiach doesn't want to see us in humiliating circumstances. He's giving us a chance to really get dressed up for the ball!

All the exiles are symbolically contained in the Egyptian exile. In Egypt, the Jews descended to the lowest of levels, to the 49th degree of impurity. Had they remained in Egypt any longer, they would have descended to the 50th level of impurity, from which there could have been no escape: at least not then. The reason is that the Jews had not yet received the Torah, their spiritual direction. Today, however, we have the Torah in our hands and its power is such that it can help us climb out of even the absolute lowest level of impurity. Thus, although man's degradation seems to have reached its lowest ebb in our time, there is great hope. There is always hope. As Rebbe Nachman once called out, "Never despair!" (Likutey Moharan II, 78). And there is more, as Reb Noson explains:

> Why are the Jews compared both to the "stars in the sky" and to "the sand upon the shores"? When they descend, they descend to the lowest of levels. But when they ascend, they ascend to the heavens!" (Megilah 16a).

Interestingly, the two opposites are very much connected, for the intensity of the descent is determined by the potential for ascent — "the bigger they are, the harder they fall." The inverse is also true: According to how low the nation has fallen, the ascent that follows is that much greater. The Jews in Egypt had sunk to the 49th level of impurity. Having fallen so low, they were subsequently able to leave Egypt and ascend to the 49th level of purity in order to receive the Torah. Eventually, they even merited to enter the Holy Land and to build the Holy Temple. Afterwards, they fell, and badly, too. They were exiled once more, to Babylon and Persia, countries steeped in idolatries and other similar "goals." As the years passed, they descended even further, until they ended up partaking of Achashveirosh's (nonkosher) meal, worshiping idolatry and intermarrying (shades of the 20th century).

The factors contributing to this descent, as with the previous one in Egypt, were concomitant with their responsibility to humanity, as the pathfinders of spirituality. The Jews were destined to receive the Torah. With this powerful medium, they might be able to return the entire world to God and make His presence felt by all. So the evil inclination battled very hard to bring them down. Eventually though, good prevailed: Thanks to their redeemer, Moshe Rabeinu, the Jews merited the Exodus and received the Torah. But their success wasn't complete. A golden calf was made and, as a result, an entire generation passed away in the desert before the Jews entered the Holy Land.

Prior to the miracle of Purim, the Jews also reached an all-time low. After their seventy year exile, they were to return to the Holy Land and build the Second Temple. Since their objective was so great, the evil inclination exerted tremendous effort to thwart them. And, unfortunately, it succeeded. Again, eventually, thanks to their redeemer, Mordekhai, good prevailed and the Jews were able to leave their exile. Just as at Sinai when the Jews received the Torah, so too, after the miracle of Purim, they reaffirmed their acceptance of the Torah (Shabbat 88a). But again, the redemption wasn't perfect. Many Jews opted to remain in exile. For others the assimilation was so much a part of them that they never returned. Nevertheless, some merited to return to the Holy Land and build the Temple.

The same principle applies to an even greater extent to our

generations. We are at the threshold of the Days of Mashiach. Because the ascent of humanity will be so great, the evil inclination has extended itself to its limits in breadth and strength, to bring humanity to the depths of foolishness and depravity. But in the end, good will again prevail. Since Mashiach's mission is so exalted, the opposition he faces is strong and terrible. The depths of human degradation we face in current generations are unconscionable.

But again, the heights of our eventual ascent will be in accordance with the depths of our descent. The future of humanity will be a glorious one — an era of peace and harmony, characterized by patience and humility; an era of love, respect and morality, friendship and Higher Education. An era of joy and happiness. It is because such heights are beckoning that the descent seems insurmountable. But that is just the point: It "seems" insurmountable, but it's not. Each of us can contribute to the ascent, each in his or her own little way, each with his or her good deeds. Therefore, one does not need to be terrified at the formidable task facing Mashiach. He will prevail. Why?

The Baal Shem Tov compared the evil inclination's "last stand" to a warrior who knows his end is near. An enemy who is dying throws everything he has into a last attempt to save the day. But eventually the craziness of the generations will fade away — as witnessed so many times with the "fads and crazes" that have obsessed humanity. All evil as we know it today will simply wear out and disappear, just as each fad passes away. Rebbe Nachman told the following story to illustrate this point:

> A man was attacked by a robber. The man said, "I'll give you all my money if you'll just spare my life." The robber took all the money. Then the victim said to the robber, "How can I go home without any money? I've been away from home for so long now, wandering around. How can I return home empty-handed? I would like to make a request. Take your pistol and shoot a hole in my hat. Then I'll have proof that I was attacked by a robber." The robber did this. The man asked him to shoot a few other holes as well. Eventually the robber said, "I haven't any more bullets."
>
> As soon as he said this, the man said, "You don't have any more

bullets?! Come here!" He took him by the neck, called for help, and overwhelmed the robber (Tzaddik #95).

Rebbe Nachman told this in connection with the Jewish intellectuals who used to visit him in Uman. They considered themselves "enlightened" and used to tell him all kinds of nonsense from the literature they read. The Rebbe said: "Quite soon they will have used up all their stock. It won't be long before they won't have anything more to say." So it is with us today. Every nonsense seems to be shooting directly at us. But very soon now, it will all dissipate and we will be able to overcome any opposition to spirituality which is delaying Mashiach's arrival (see Likutey Halakhot, Beheimah v'Chayah Tehorah 4:34).

*

In the merit of Mashiach, the redeemer, we will *all* leave the exile. In addition, in Mashiach's era, the Jews will again receive the Torah. Our descent may be greater than that of our forefathers in Egypt, but the Torah awaiting us will be a Torah on a much higher level, that of Atik. Mashiach's mission will be to gather *everyone* to the Holy Land, something that was lacking in our past redemptions. This time, Mashiach will succeed, and will build the Third Temple, one that is destined to stand forever (see Likutey Halakhot, Eiruvei Techumin 4).

Indeed, our ascent will be extremely great and this is "Why Mashiach hasn't come yet." There's a lot of work to be done, to establish an eternal foundation that will never be uprooted again. The longer it takes, the more effort the evil inclination extends. But then again, the deeper a foundation is built, the greater the height of the building that can rise on it. Fortunately for everyone, each person can be (and is) part of Mashiach's building. Mashiach hasn't yet come because he is building a most solid foundation. It requires great patience — a messianic trait — to wait out the attacks against civility and decency. And in the end, Mashiach will definitely come.

Speedily, in our days, Amen!

* * *

Part V

Mashiach:

How?

In this section we discuss how Mashiach will be able to accomplish his mission, despite the formidable opposition he faces. We will also discuss the ARI's teachings about the Creation of the world, the fall of Adam (Man), the source of Mashiach's soul, reincarnation and repentance, and the ultimate rectification of all sin.

17

Creation

We have seen *why* Mashiach hasn't yet come. His task is formidable, taking a world that has succumbed to all sorts of foolishness and getting all its inhabitants to realize *by themselves* the absurdity of their idolatries. The next question about Mashiach is "how?" How can Mashiach take such a complicated and confused world and turn it aright? It certainly doesn't seem possible.

To understand this, we must go back to the first sin: even before that — to the beginning of Creation — and even before that! Knowing how the world was created and how it is structured will give us a clue as to how sin was made possible — for how is it possible for man to rebel against God? It will also give us a clue as to how it is possible for any sin, even the gravest, to be rectified.

*

> *"The world will last six thousand years. For the first two thousand years the world was desolate. The next two thousand years are those of Torah. The final two thousand years are the Days of the Mashiach."*
>
> Sanhedrin 97a

This world, as we know it, was created to last for six thousand years. The first two thousand years the world was "desolate," for it was without Torah, without spiritual direction. The Patriarch Abraham was fifty-two years old when the world turned two thousand. At that point in his life, Abraham began spreading the Word of God, thus initiating the two-millennia period of Torah. Shortly after the redaction of the Mishnah, the two-millennia period of Torah concluded. Thus began the final two-millennia period, the period of the Mashiach. Once the Torah reached its state of "maturity," the world became ripe for redemption. Having acquired the necessary tools, man must now make use of those tools to strive for his — and the world's — rectification. But is man up to the task? In a word, NO! We need only look at the world around us to judge our state of readiness.

We find in several instances that the souls of certain tzaddikim were prepared long before their birth to fulfill a special mission in life. In the account of the Creation, the verse states (Genesis 2:7), "God created *HaAdam* (the Man)." The Midrash teaches (Bereishit Rabbah 14:6), "*the* Man," refers to Abraham. Then why wasn't Abraham the First Man? Because "if Adam sins, Abraham will be able to rectify the damage." The Midrash also teaches that Moshe was prepared as a redeemer. Jeremiah was told (Jeremiah 1:5), "Before you were created in the womb you were destined to be a prophet." Mordekhai was prepared for his mission, and so on (Bereishit Rabbah 30:8; Bava Metzia 86a). And Mashiach was prepared for his mission — to rectify the entire world — long before it was created (Pesachim 54a).

But how will Mashiach be able to accomplish this?

*

The origins of Creation

"In the beginning, God created..."

Genesis 1:1

When they were created, Adam and Eve were placed in the Garden of Eden. Though created in a corporeal form, their life was to have been one of spiritual delight. They had access to all types and tastes of food and lacked nothing. All Creation was made to serve them. But they transgressed. They partook of the Tree of Knowledge of Good and Evil, plunging mankind into a materialistic existence. To rectify their mistake, and not only to regain their former status but to go beyond it, they would now have to work very hard under these new and strange circumstances.

The difference in Adam before and after his fall can be compared to an exquisite and expensive crystal vessel which is thrown from a great height. The glass shatters into thousands of tiny pieces which are scattered over a large area. Adam, God's most exquisite handiwork, was created in holiness. His fall shattered that holiness into innumerable "sparks (fragments) of holiness," scattering them throughout the entire world. It is now man's mission to harness and utilize all his energies to search for and find these sparks, and restore them to their source. This will repair — and even improve upon — the original vessel, Adam.

But for the present, Adam has transgressed and lost his spiritual direction. Though he himself repented, his descendants subsequently plummeted to the lowest depths of idolatry, immorality and avarice, resulting in the Flood which literally wiped out all life-forms on earth except those in the Ark with Noah (see Genesis 6). The enormity of man's corruption dictated such extreme measures. Thus, after the Flood, Noah, his family and a representative sampling of all the different animal species had to reestablish life on earth.

The question glares at us, "Is mankind so different now than it was then?" The sins of the Generation of the Flood involved every form of immorality possible — adultery, homosexuality, bestiality, pedophilia and so on. Other transgressions included the vilification of others, robbery and murder (see Bereishit Rabbah 26:5, 27:3). Just a few hundred years after the Flood a generation of idolators arose who built the Tower of Babel to rebel against God. Bingo! We're back to where we started. Then why hasn't mankind been destroyed again for the same terrible sins?

But those were the first two thousand years of desolation; desolation, because the power of rectification had not yet been brought into the world; desolation, because there were no righteous people who took it upon themselves to reveal spirituality in the world. Several tzaddikim existed: Adam (who had repented), Enoch, Methuselah and Noah, to name a few. However, they kept their spiritual achievements to themselves (see *Likutey Halakhot, Minchah* 7:82).

Beginning with Abraham, the world began its rectification, as the Word of God spread. The Patriarchs began revealing God to whoever would listen and, as a result of their efforts, many repented of their idolatrous ways. But in the end, Abraham, Isaac and Jacob were successful in implanting permanent spiritual values only within their own family, the Twelve Tribes. Similarly, following the Exodus, Moshe was capable of bringing the Torah down to this world in a way that everyone would be able to partake of the knowledge of God. But, as the Talmud teaches, all the nations rejected the Torah and only the Jewish Nation accepted it (*Avodah Zarah* 2b). By the time the two-thousand year period of Torah ended, the path of spirituality was clearly defined. Thus began the era of the Days of Mashiach and the rectification of mankind.

When one studies human behavior during the past two millennia — with all its wars, depravity and other bestial behavior — one can readily challenge the above statement. But as we proceed, the concept of how rectification takes place will become clearer. The reader will understand that the ultimate rectification is commensurate with the depths to which we have descended. Yes, although we ought never purposely sin, it is nevertheless true that the deeper the fall, the greater the rectification.

In the remainder of this chapter and the next, we will examine the origins of the Creation in the light of the ARI's teachings, as well as develop the reasons for the fall of man and his ultimate rectification. Some of these concepts will seem obscure at first; this is because they contain some of the deepest mysteries of the Kabbalah. We have therefore included short review paragraphs after presenting some of these ideas, to point out the main thoughts of the teachings in concise form. In addition, to assist the neophyte reader to visualize these kabbalistic concepts, we have provided an appendix (Appendix B), as well as several charts and illustrations. The reason for introducing these teachings is that they form the foundation for understanding the setbacks that man experiences during his lifetime, especially those that warrant the rectifications of the Mashiach. However, it is not an absolute necessity to study these teachings to appreciate the impact of man's descent and the subsequent rectification that the Mashiach will bring. Those who are overawed by the profundity of the kabbalistic teachings can skip these introductions and proceed to Chapter 19. In addition, we should point out that these teachings are mentioned here by way of introduction to the material about Mashiach, and are not meant as a study of the Kabbalah *per se*. Those familiar with the Kabbalah will therefore recognize several thoughts that are not fully discussed. This is because they were deemed unnecessary for a basic understanding of our text. (For a masterful introduction to the Kabbalah, the reader is referred to *Innerspace*, by Rabbi Aryeh Kaplan, published by Moznaim.)

Let us now examine the Creation of the World and its rectification process in greater detail.

*

The Vacated Space

Reb Noson writes that the Torah is not simply a history book with a set of laws. It is also the ongoing saga of humanity — of each and every individual who ever lived, is living and will ever live (see *Likutey Halakhot, Nesiat Kapayim* 5:27; ibid., *Minchah* 7:78). Thus, the story of Adam, the paradigm of man, is also the story of each of us. This being the case, let us start with the story of the Creation as presented by the ARI.

This introduction to the Kabbalistic teachings relating to the Creation deals with how God contracted His Infinite Light to create a Vacated Space in which to create the world. In the *Etz Chaim* (Chapter 1), the ARI describes this process as follows:

> Before all things were created... the Supernal Light was simple. It filled all existence. There was no empty space which would be characterized as space, emptiness or void. Everything was filled with that simple *Or* (Light) of *Ein Sof*. There was no category of beginning and no category of end. All was one simple, undifferentiated, Infinite Light.
>
> When it arose in His Simple Will to create worlds and emanate emanations, and to bring to light the perfection of His Actions, His Names and His Attributes (which was actually the purpose for the creation of the universes), behold, He constricted [withdrew] His Infinite Essence away from the very centerpoint of His Light. [Of course, since Infinity has no centerpoint, this is only said from the point of view of the Space that is about to be created.] He then withdrew that Light [even further], distancing it to the extremities around this centerpoint, leaving a Vacated Space and Hollow Void from the centerpoint [to the outward extremities of the newly created Vacated Space]...
>
> After this constriction, which resulted in the creation of a Vacated Space and Hollow Void in the very midst of the Infinite Light of *Ein Sof*, there was now a *place* for all that was to be emanated (*Atzilut*), created (*Beriyah*), formed (*Yetzirah*), and completed (*Asiyah*). He then drew a

single, straight *Kav* (Ray or Thread of Measured Light) down from His Infinite Surrounding Light into the Vacated Space. This Kav descended in stages into the Vacated Space. The upper extremity of this Kav touched the Infinite Light of *Ein Sof* [that surrounded the Space], and extended down [into the Vacated Space towards the center] but not all the way to the bottom extremity [so as not to cause the Vacated Space to collapse and merge back into God's Infinite Light]. It was through this Kav [serving as a conduit] that the Light of *Ein Sof* was drawn down and spread out below... Through this Kav the outpouring Supernal Light of *Ein Sof* spreads forth and flows down into the universes that are located within that Space and Void.

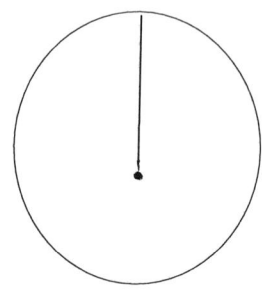

The center dot represents the first Tzimtzum, the very first act of Creation. The circle around it is the Vacated Space, from where God, as it were, withdrew Himself to make room for the Creation. The line represents the *kav*.

*

The Paradox of the Vacated Space

In order to form the so-called Vacated Space, God constricted His Infinite Light. This "constriction" is called the *Tzimtzum*. The reason for the Tzimtzum stems from a basic paradox. God sustains all of Creation. Therefore, God must be found everywhere, even in the Vacated Space — for nothing can exist without His Life-Force. But God cannot be there, because He constricted Himself from the Vacated Space. The paradox is that since God removed His Light from the Vacated Space, it must be empty of His Essence. Still, God must also fill this Space, since (*Tikkuney Zohar* #57, p.91b), "there is no place empty of Him." As Rebbe Nachman masterfully expresses it (*Likutey Moharan* I, 64):

> The Blessed Name created the world out of His deep compassion. He wished to reveal His compassion but, without a world, to whom could He show it? He therefore brought the entire Creation into existence, from the

highest emanation down to the lowest point within the center of the physical world, all in order to demonstrate His compassion.

When the Blessed Name wished to create the world, however, there was no place in which to do so. This was due to the fact that all that existed was His Infinite Essence. [This precluded the existence of anything finite.] He therefore constricted His Light [from what would later be the centerpoint of the Vacated Space] to the extremities. By virtue of this Tzimtzum (Constriction), a Vacated Space was brought into existence. It was then within this Vacated Space that all the Supernal Days and Attributes (Sefirot) were brought into existence.

This Tzimtzum (Constriction) was thus absolutely necessary for the creation of the world, for without a Vacated Space, there would never be a place in which a world could be created. It is for this reason that this Tzimtzum, which resulted in the Vacated Space, cannot be understood or comprehended at all [now], but will be only in the Ultimate Future. This is because we must describe the Vacated Space in two contradictory ways, namely, existence and nonexistence.

For the Vacated Space came into being as a result of the Tzimtzum, from which, to the extent we can express it, God constricted [withdrew] His own Essence. Therefore, God's Essence does not exist there [in this Space]. If His Essence were there, this Space would not be vacated, and there would be nothing besides the Infinite Essence. If this were true, there would also be no place whatsoever for the creation of the universe.

The actual truth, however, is that God's Essence must nevertheless still be in this Space, for it is beyond doubt that nothing can exist without His Life-Force. [Therefore, if God's Essence did not exist in the Vacated Space, nothing else could exist there either.] Thus, until the Ultimate Future, it is impossible to understand the concept of the Vacated Space.

This is *the* paradox of Creation. As Rebbe Nachman explains, this paradox is the source of *all* questions and confusions about God. From this constriction of Godliness emerge the possibility of evil and the desire for a material life, on the one hand, and the free will to choose to serve God, on the other hand. It all stems from the fact that, within the Vacated Space, God's presence is almost completely concealed and undetectable. And, even though God's Light was subsequently reintroduced into the

Vacated Space, its power was greatly diminished to begin with (in order not to overwhelm the Vacated Space), and continued through four major stages of diminution in such a way that the Light was broken down more and more at each subsequent stage. (We shall have more to say about this in the following sections.)

Free will is the key here. Free will must be maintained in perfect balance, on all levels and at all times. Were light (good) outweighed by the breakdown of the light (darkness and evil), or vice-versa, even just a little, man could not be held responsible for his actions. He could not be rewarded for doing good or held accountable for choosing evil. Free will is absolutely necessary for man to receive his ultimate reward (as explained above, Chapter 10)

Thus, the mission of man, who exists in a Vacated Space which is apparently devoid of spirituality, is to find the Godliness that is currently concealed from him. It was with this intention that Adam, the First Man, was created. Adam was to live a spiritual life, on a loftier plane than this lowly, material life of ours. He was to live in the Garden of Eden — the World to Come. However, Adam ate from the Tree of Knowledge of Good and Evil, and not only did he plummet from his exalted spiritual level into material reality, but brought down the rest of Creation with him. Adam became a shell of his former self — a shattered vessel — and must now be rectified.

But how does one go about rectifying and repairing such a shattered vessel, especially one whose pieces were scattered over such a wide area — the entire Creation? And, for that matter, what does it mean that innumerable sparks of holiness were scattered? The answers to these questions will be explained in the following chapters. We must first introduce several concepts concerning the structure of the world in order to understand how Mashiach can rectify it.

*

The Light of the Infinite

> *In the beginning, God created worlds and destroyed them, created worlds and destroyed them.*
>
> Bereishit Rabbah 3:7

Our Sages teach that before this world was established, God created other worlds and destroyed them, then created others still, and destroyed them. What purpose this served is not very clear from the Midrash alone. However, from the ARI's writings and from Reb Noson's commentary, the entire picture of the stages of Creation and Adam's fall and repentance, together with the final rectification through Mashiach, become very clear indeed.

God is *Ein Sof*, the Infinite One. By definition, His Essence and Existence is beyond anything we can conceive. Thus, rather than speaking directly about God, the *Ein Sof*, the Kabbalah speaks of the "Light of the *Ein Sof*." Still, even this Light is described as something far too awesome and brilliant to be experienced by any created being. Therefore, as we have seen, God constricted it in order to create the Vacated Space. He then introduced a measured quantity of that Light into the Vacated Space through what the ARI calls the *Kav* (Ray or Thread). Even this was done in stages so as not to cause the Vacated Space to collapse and merge back into God's Infinite Light. These stages are the various universes the ARI mentions, *Atzilut* (Emanation), *Beriyah* (Creation), *Yetzirah* (Formation), and *Asiyah* (Completion). With each succeeding stage, the Light was further reduced and filtered, until a material world was "completed" which could experience this Light on a much reduced level (see Likutey Halakhot, Minchah 7:22).

Now we can understand why God "created worlds and destroyed them."

God is *the* Master Craftsman. Were He creating a world only for His own purposes, He would have immediately created a perfect world, as He is certainly capable of doing. But His intention in Creation was for mere corporeal man to live in a physical environment, to face temptation and overcome it, and thereby merit awesome rewards for his efforts.

God therefore "had" to filter His light, diminishing it many times over to enable man to interact with Him. This is why "God created worlds and destroyed them." The intention is not that He made a mistake and "scrapped" His first world. On the contrary, that world and all the worlds that followed it were extremely exalted and sublime — too exalted and too sublime. They still revealed too much Light. Many contractions were therefore necessary to filter and measure the light even more. Only after such a step-down devolution could the process that began with the original Tzimtzum be brought to its intended completion, i.e. a physical world in which His Light would be almost completely undetectable. It is this step-down devolution that the Midrash describes as God creating and destroying universes.

> In review: God, the Infinite One, was everywhere. To create the world, He constricted and withdrew His Light, as it were, and formed a Vacated Space. The "necessity" of God's "withdrawal" from this Space was to facilitate the creation of Free Will, whereby man can find God even though He isn't apparently there. God then introduced the Kav, a thin Ray or Thread of Measured Light, into the Vacated Space, in order to create the supernal universes. Still, there was too much light. He therefore "destroyed" these universes and created "lower" worlds, i.e. gradually decreased the intensity of His Light through additional tzimtzumim, until He created the material world.

But other questions remain. Where was this Light headed and what happened to it? In addition, how can anybody experience this awesome Light? And why wasn't man created to be able to withstand this Light? Will he eventually be able to exist in its radiance? These questions are at the root of the entire purpose of Creation and, as such, they will provide the groundwork for understanding the purpose of the Mashiach.

* * *

18

The Sefirot

The downward filtering of God's awesome Light is to bring into existence a human being who, by his own efforts, will be able to earn the good that God wishes to give him. As mentioned, this filtering takes place through four general *Olamot*, universes or stages, called Atzilut, Beriyah, Yetzirah and Asiyah. There is a fifth universe, as well, higher than these four, called *Adam Kadmon*. The four lower universes are said to correspond to the four letters of the Tetragrammaton, YHVH. The universe of Adam Kadmon corresponds to the apex of the Yod.

The Five Olamot (Universes) and the Tetragrammaton:

Olam	meaning	Letter of Name
Adam Kadmon	Primordial Man	apex of *Yod*
Atzilut	Emanation	Yod
Beriyah	Creation	Heh
Yetzirah	Formation	Vav
Asiyah	Completion	Heh

The word *Olamot* itself gives us a clue as to the function of these universes. The Olamot serve to reveal God's Light at lower and lower levels, but they perform this function by doing the exact opposite, namely, concealing the Light and diminishing its intensity. Only thus can each lower universe exist without being overwhelmed by the light of the universe above it. This extremely important function of "concealing in order to reveal" is implied in the fact that the word *OLaM* derives from the same root as *ALaM*, meaning "hidden," "concealed."

Now it is important to point out that each of these universes is made up of Ten Sefirot. The Ten Sefirot of Atzilut, for instance, represent the inner makeup of Atzilut as it unfolds from potential to actuality. The same can be said of the Ten Sefirot of Beriyah, Yetzirah and Asiyah. Thus, the sefirot, in the same way as the universes, represent a step-down process of devolution from potential to actual, from hidden unity to revealed multiplicity. The difference is that the Sefirot constitute the internal structure of each universe.

The Ten Sefirot are:

Sefirah	meaning	concept
Keter	Crown	Will, Purpose
Chokhmah	Wisdom	Intellect
Binah	Understanding	Logic
[Daat]	[Knowledge]	[Application]
Chesed	Lovingkindness	Giving
Gevurah	Strength	Judgment, Restraint
Tiferet	Beauty	Harmony, Truth
Netzach	Dominance	Victory
Hod	Splendor	Empathy
Yesod	Foundation	Covenant, Channel
Malkhut	Kingship	Reciprocity

(We have also mentioned one quasi-sefirah which is called Daat, Knowledge. Daat might be considered the eleventh Sefirah. However, the *Sefer Yetzirah* (1:4) warns us that we only count Ten Sefirot, not nine and not eleven. The truth is that Daat is the external manifestation of Keter. It is therefore only counted in the array of the Ten Sefirot when Keter is not (see *Innerspace*, Chapter 5; *Anatomy of the Soul*, Chapter 30). Still, Daat has very important implications for the Mashiach, for the ARI explains that most of our efforts in bringing this world to its ultimate goal are intended to "build" the sefirah of Daat, which is the long-awaited Holy Temple (see above, Chapter 6).

The Ten Sefirot are divided into two groups. The first three Sefirot, Keter, Chokhmah and Binah, are referred to as *Mochin* (Intellect powers). The Lower Seven, Chesed, Gevurah, Tiferet, Netzach, Hod, Yesod and Malkhut, are referred to as *Midot* (Attributes). The Lower Seven are where the most basic interaction between God and man takes place. For this reason, we find time and space divided into seven days, seven continents, seven visible planets in the universe, and so on.

The ARI teaches that the Sefirot were originally arrayed in a single column and this made it impossible for them to interact with each other (see Appendix B). This was done on purpose. It was the perfect way to diminish the Light of *Ein Sof*, i.e. to cause the greater part of the Light to remain above and only a small fraction of it to descend, and in a fragmented way at that. Thus, as each of these original Sefirot were about to receive the Light, they were unable to contain the Light, and shattered.

This is the same idea we saw above in terms of the creation and destruction of the universes. Now the ARI is telling us that this process really took place in the Sefirot of each individual universe — and more precisely, in the seven lower Sefirot (Chesed, Gevurah, Tiferet, Netzach, Hod, Yesod, and Malkhut) of each universe. When speaking of this shattering process in terms of the Sefirot, it is usually referred to as the Shattering of the Vessels. Since the Sefirot were to act as conduits for the Light, they are called Vessels.

We said that the original Vessels could not interact with each other. As a result, when the powerful Light of *Ein Sof* descended to enter into them, they shattered. (These same Vessels were shattered even further when Adam sinned.) At the moment of impact, the major part of the Light recoiled back and up, while sparks of that Light and the shards of the original Vessels descended to become the "material" from which the next lower universe would be made.

We thus learn again that God brought lower and lower universes into existence (in which His presence was more and more concealed) through a series of shatterings and diminishings of His own Light. These lower universes would then further occlude and filter the Light as it descended to man.

Before man entered the picture, however, God performed another crucial operation. Until now, the entire system consisted of lower and lower universes brought into existence by a process of breakdown of Light. The original Vessels had shattered and their broken shards had fallen into these universes. The shards were also accompanied by sparks of the original Light. It is these sparks, scattered throughout the entire world, which must be rectified and elevated to their proper level. This was the mission of Adam, and it is the purpose of every human being, especially of Mashiach. How Mashiach will accomplish it will be explained below.

In the meantime, the time came for a partial repair. God gathered back to Himself the very sparks and broken shards that man would eventually have to rectify and elevate. (This kind of action on God's part is called "preparing the medication before the illness.") He then proceeded to reconstitute the shards into new Vessels that could work together to receive His Light and transmit it to every level below — only this time, without shattering. What would make the difference? The original Vessels had been unable to interact with each other. The new Vessels would interact.

Instead of Chesed and Gevurah, or Netzach and Hod, being polar opposites with nothing in common, they became complementary parts of a greater whole. This greater whole is called a *Partzuf* (a gestalt, or a multiplicity of seemingly contradictory forces arrayed in a unified structure). The easiest way to remember what a Partzuf is would be to apply to it the formula of the "whole that is greater than the sum of its parts."

A Partzuf is thus said to be distinguished by the three-columned array of its constituent Sefirot. Three columns represent a unified or gestalted structure with a full complement of "right," "left" and "center" positions. In this way, the opposing forces (e.g. Chesed and Gevurah) can interact without obstructing each other. This is the format of rectification (see Appendix B).

The Five Partzufim:

Partzuf	*meaning*	*related Sefirot*
Arikh Anpin	Extended Face	Keter
Abba	Father	Chokhmah
Imma	Mother	Binah
Zer Anpin	Small Face	Chesed through Yesod
Malkhut	Kingship	Malkhut

The Partzufim are arrayed in a right-, left- and middle-column system because the concept of "right" refers to unconditional giving in the Kabbalah, while "left" refers to conditional giving or restraint. The two concepts are diametrically opposed to each other. A third, "center," column is therefore necessary, to strike the perfect balance between the two opposites. In layman's terms, this defines our entire life's mission. To rectify and perfect ourselves, we must always strive for the perfect balance — between conflicting emotions, passions and ideas — as well as between our families, friends and neighbors, in fact, in every aspect of life. Were only one column to exist — e.g. unconditional giving — then humanity could never function. Neither would reward or punishment be possible.

Again, why did God purposely cause the original Sefirot to shatter? Why, in other words, did God create a broken world in which His Light is totally eclipsed and darkness prevails? In which man could turn away from God and deny His very existence? The answer again is free will, in order to create a dimension in which man could choose whether or not to recognize and serve God despite His concealment.

To fulfill his task, man must recognize God in the midst of His concealment. He must elevate the Godly sparks of light that he finds everywhere in his life back to their Source in God's Light. In doing this, he causes an influx of Light into all the universes. The more Light he causes to flow in, the more he is able to recognize that all of Creation is filled with God's Presence, that even the broken shards of this world must be seen as vessels of Godliness, and that God never really withdrew His Light from the Vacated Space! The more man recognizes God's Indwelling Presence, the more He will reveal His Light to man in ever greater intensity, first in the events of his life, and then directly through prophetic revelation, the revelation of Daat, the building of God's Temple on earth.

> In review: God "had" to contract Himself, as it were, in order to create the Vacated Space. Within the Vacated Space, He created Vessels which shattered and were subsequently reformed into the Ten Sefirot, in an array of three columns to maintain a balance through which He would direct His world.

*

The Ten Sefirot and Man

The Olamot, Sefirot and Partzufim act as conduits: on the one hand, they serve to reveal and express God's greatness. On the other hand, they function as vessels to limit that light in order to bring it from the Infinite Light into the finite realms of time and space. That is, when they acquire the light from Above, they serve as vessels which receive. But when they transmit this light to lower levels, then they are acting as the "light" itself. Through the media of the Olamot, Sefirot and Partzufim, God interacts with His world — and His creation, man, is able to interact with Him.

Man is the primary reason for the entire Creation, which is why man was last to be created. Everything had to be prepared beforehand for his use. Man can be likened to a great reflecting mirror for the sun's light. The moment the mirror is hit by this light, its function is to reflect it back to its source. As such, God's light is focused upon man, and subsequently man must be able to reflect that light — i.e. to focus his sight upon God. In this context, man himself becomes a vessel to receive God's light, and then returns that energy to God.

God's "light" is explained in several ways (e.g. as intellect and as bounty). For example, God sends messages to people every single day to awaken them from their spiritual slumber and to open their minds to the beauty and wonders found in Creation (cf. Avot 6:2). He sends these messages through His vessels, the Sefirot, in gradually decreasing intensity, until they are found in every single item of Creation. One who searches for Godliness begins to see these "messages" virtually everywhere: in nature, in daily conversations, in his own deeds and in those of others, until he is able to grasp and understand the spiritual messages he is receiving. Then, when man responds positively to these stimuli, he begins to "see" God. His search for God leads him towards the upper worlds — a greater intellect and a deeper understanding of God.

In a similar way, God sends bounty down to this world, transmitted through the Sefirot. When everything is in its proper place, then the bounty descends in graduated amounts that are sufficient to sustain each person. Man in turn responds by taking his bounty and using it for spiritual growth (even if engaged in mundane matters) and thus "returns" the bounty to God in the form of good deeds. But if the individual is unworthy, or the sins of the generation upset the structure of the supernal worlds, then he may be overwhelmed by God's bounty, or, God forbid, may not receive any at all.

Rainfall is a good example of man receiving God's beneficence. When descending in normal amounts and at regular intervals, rain is beneficial, irrigating the land and filling reservoirs. If too much rain falls at one time, flooding occurs, ruining topsoil and inundating reservoirs, sometimes even contaminating the water supplies. Conversely, there may not be sufficient rain, causing a drought. The same is true of affluence. When everyone receives his necessary amount, then this affluence is beneficial. But sometimes it's "too little, too late." Or, conversely, several people attain great affluence but become a target of envy and hatred — even theft and murder. This is "bounty" which is a product of a world where spirituality is concealed.

This same principle operates in terms of the Sefirot and Partzufim. They must be properly aligned to enable us to receive our proper supply of spiritual bounty. This occurs when man performs mitzvot (good deeds), bringing bounty to everyone in amounts that are beneficial to all. Thus, when man is "connected" to God, the Sefirot and Partzufim all act in unison to transmit God's light and energy in a properly-aligned form for man's benefit. But, if a man's sins this causes the alignment of the Sefirot to be altered, resulting in a further "Shattering of the Vessels," and upsetting the flow of spiritual light.

> In review: God, the Infinite Light, "had" to contract Himself, as it were, in order to create the Vacated Space. Within the Vacated Space, He created Vessels, which were formed into the Ten Sefirot. These vessels were shattered, spreading sparks of Godliness throughout Creation, and were subsequently rebuilt. The Ten Sefirot act as vessels to receive bounty from God and transfer it to this world. By performing good deeds, Man "reflects" this bounty in his recognition of God — and his thanks to Him — as the Source. These thanks are the pleasure God receives from His creation. Man accomplishes this by

gathering and elevating the sparks of holiness tnat were shattered and spread out throughout the Creation, "returning" them to God.

*

Atik: the place of Mashiach

"A man came and he approached Atik Yomin *[the level of] the Ancient of Days..."*

Daniel 7:13

Our discussion until this point, centered on the ARI's teachings about the creation of the world (the Vacated Space, the Ten Sefirot, bounty, etc.), was in order to set the scene for Mashiach being able to rectify the world. At this point, we introduce Mashiach and his level. In the following chapters, we will explain man's fall and ascent and how Mashiach, from his position in the scheme of Creation, can bring humanity to its rectification.

We have seen above that the Keter (*Arikh Anpin*), is the loftiest Partzuf. But, the ARI writes, Keter actually has two levels, a lower level corresponding to Arikh Anpin and an upper level, the intellect of Arikh Anpin, which corresponds to Atik (see *Etz Chaim, Heichal HaKetarim*). Atik is referred to in the holy writings by several names: Atik ("The Ancient One"), Atik Yomin ("The Ancient of Days"), Atika Kadisha ("The Holy Ancient One"). Though they do have different connotations, these names all refer to that exalted level of Atik. Therefore, to simplify matters in our text, we will use the term Atik.

The connection between Mashiach and Atik is learned from Daniel's vision: "A man came and he approached [the level of] the Ancient of Days..." Rashi explains that this refers to Mashiach, who will minister justice to the entire world. Our Sages also speak about Atik (see *Pesachim* 119a), but as Atik refers to the "deep mysteries" of Torah (see above, Chapter 10), they only made veiled references to it.

The ARI teaches that Arikh Anpin is the Partzuf that was employed at the beginning of the rectification of the Sefirot. It was the first Partzuf to be defined in a three-column structure. Thus, it has a "right side" (of giving), a "left side" (of restraint) and a "center column" (a blend of both characteristics). Atik, however, is *above* that level — no characteristics can be defined within Atik. From the level of Atik, only goodness and kindness emanate.

Atik thus transcends anything that we can conceive — giving and receiving, right and left, reward and punishment, and so on. At this level, there is neither past nor future. Everything is in the present. And, as we have seen, every part of Creation, from the first constriction until the lowest level of the world of *Asiyah*, is contained within the Keter, Atik (see Appendix B).

Thus, Atik includes all time and space — yet transcends it all. The soul of Mashiach "resides" within Atik, and it is from this level that all his powers will be drawn. And, since he transcends time and space, Mashiach can transcend every transgression ever committed and rectify it — for since he can transcend everything ever done, he can bring each person to a state *prior* to his having sinned. This is because in Keter, God overrides the rules that He set up for all the Sefirot and their interaction between each other and man. With the power inherent in this exalted level, Mashiach will be able to bring the world to a state of perfection.

*

Having discussed the origin of Creation, the Ten Sefirot, the Shattering of the Vessels, how interaction between God and man can take place and so on, we have arrived at the point where Mashiach fits into Creation. Now that we find that Mashiach is rooted in Keter, the lofty level of Atik, we can begin to understand how he will rectify the world. This will be developed in the forthcoming chapters. There also remain several concepts that must be dealt with in order for us to fully appreciate the total concept of the Mashiach. What was the deeper reason that God, the Master Craftsman, brought about the "Shattering of the Vessels?" How can the sparks of holiness found here on earth be elevated? What part did Adam's transgression play in all this? And how, ultimately, will Mashiach rectify the world?

* * *

19

The Fall of Man

Adam, like the rest of Creation, was brought into being by the Will of God. Unlike his descendants, he was not born of woman — rather he was an exclusive hand-crafted masterpiece of God. It was thus up to him to see that the purpose for which he had been created was achieved. To this end he was placed in the Garden of Eden. He was clearly on a lofty spiritual level. What then went wrong? Even more so, *how* could Adam have gone wrong?

As we have mentioned (above, Chapter 10), the *Zohar* speaks of "an arousal from Above" and "an arousal from below." "Above" refers to God, in which everything comes from Him alone. "Below" refers to man, who performs deeds. Originally, when the Sefirot were constructed, they were bound together. The concept behind this is that God is One, therefore everything that has to do with Him is really one unity. Only as things "appear" to become distant from God do they assume separate identities. (We have used the word "appear" because one can never be distant from God for He is everywhere.) Following their "separation" into the various energies that each Sefirah represents, they became vessels to interact with each other, receiving and transmitting God's light between themselves, until that light reaches this world. Then the reverse takes place. Man, through his deeds, can reflect this light back to God.

It is man's good deeds which enable him to experience Godliness, because then the Sefirot are all properly aligned (see above, Chapter 18). And, since man's good deeds reflect God's light, this "reflecting" serves to create greater and more perfected vessels than those already formed. Thus man, as the primary reason for the Creation, must perfect his deeds to the greatest degree possible, to receive and reflect the awesome light of God. The devotions man performs constitute "the arousal from below" which reflects God's light — i.e. the power of the Infinite One. Let us now examine how these ideas of the arousals from Above and below translate into our everyday life and form the purpose of the Mashiach.

*

"In a Godly image"

> "God created mankind in His image, in the image of God He created him; male and female He created them."
>
> Genesis 1:27

God designed the world in such a way that we can classify everything under one of two labels: benefactor or beneficiary. God gives bounty, He is the Benefactor. Man receives it, he is the beneficiary. Then, when man performs good deeds, he becomes the benefactor while God, as it were, becomes the Beneficiary of man's righteousness.

In this vein, God created everything in the world — mankind, animal life, plants, subatomic particles, and even the various components of the spiritual dimension — in pairs of "male and female." In order to "procreate" and bring forth life, all of these pairs must interact with each other.

For example, man irrigates his fields. He is the benefactor while the earth is the beneficiary. Then the earth yields its crops and the earth is the benefactor while man is the beneficiary. Another example is a married couple. A male provides the seed, the female receives it — the male is the benefactor and the female the beneficiary. Afterwards, the female gives birth, giving back a perfected vessel — a human child. Then the female becomes the benefactor and the child the beneficiary, until the child grows up, and so on.

We can now take a deeper look into this concept of "a Godly image." Adam was created, placed in the Garden of Eden and expected to adhere to God's single commandment to him — not to eat from the Tree of Knowledge of Good and Evil. Talmudic sources explain that this single commandment contained several prohibitions: idolatry, immorality, larceny and so on (see Sanhedrin 56b). Brought to life on the Friday of the Six Days of Creation, Adam was to guard himself from sin for the remainder of the day, until Shabbat, which conceptually stands for the rewards of the World to Come. He was also expected, as a Godly creation, to recognize his Master and pray to Him. Had Adam waited patiently for just a short while, he would have brought all of Creation to the level of perfection. But how?

At this stage, interaction between God and man had not yet taken place. God had repaired and rectified the fallen sparks of holiness from the Shattered Vessels (see Chapter 18). The ARI writes that some of those sparks were resurrected by God. Others were not rectified, and were left for Adam, created in "a Godly image," to rectify. Adam was in the realm of holiness and was a vessel formed by God to receive His light and return it Above. As such, his "vessel" could reflect that light and create greater and more perfected vessels. This was Adam's mission.

However, our Sages teach that Adam "gazed beyond his level" (see *Tikkuney Zohar* #69, p.115b; *Likutey Halakhot, Pesach* 9:2). His desire for Godliness was such that he wanted to ascend above the level of spirituality he was on. We have seen that God's light was refracted on each level, to enable man to interact with God on that level. This allowed for Adam to interact with God — i.e. receive His light, reflect it and perfect the vessels. But Adam sought a higher level. The light was too intense and this is how he failed.

Thus, instead of elevating all the worlds and all the sparks of holiness contained in them, Adam caused a "Shattering of the Vessels" on his own level. Instead of remaining on an exalted spiritual level in the Garden of Eden, Adam was banished from Paradise and cursed to lead a material life. And worse, as the paradigm of all humanity, Adam's fall spelled disaster for all his descendants, for they, too, would now be unable to partake of that spiritual delight without tremendous effort. Adam caused the holy sparks to be scattered throughout the entire world. These untold numbers of sparks must now all be rectified and elevated so that they too can be formed into perfected vessels, returned into the realm of holiness whence they were formed, and become united once again in the Light of the One God (see Likutey Halakhot, Arvit 4:32).

*

The holy sparks

Until now, we have only spoken about holy sparks being scattered throughout the world, first as a result of God's Shattering of the Vessels and later as a result of Adam's transgression. We have still not defined what these sparks are. By using Adam as a prototype, however, we can understand on some level what these holy sparks are.

God breathed life into Adam. The *Zohar* teaches that, "He Who exhales, exhales from within Himself." This means that God placed His own spirit within Adam. It is this spirit, this *life*, that permeated the entire Creation, from the Light of the Infinite One down to this material world. In this sense, the sparks of holiness represent the spirit of God that is contained within us, that is, our souls, the souls of all mankind.

Therefore, Adam (i.e. mankind), by not elevating the sparks of holiness found within him, caused God's design for a perfect world to be delayed. Had he repaired the shattered vessels, everything would have become perfected, allowing man to live a spiritual existence in a physical environment. All of Creation would have reached a state of perfection. But Adam failed, causing the "sparks of holiness" to scatter yet further. Thus, the sparks represent life, a life of holiness and spirituality. But as long as the sparks remain unrectified, Creation can never be whole, i.e. perfect, as is God's design.

Where are these sparks now? Everywhere. All over the world. The ARI teaches that all the souls of mankind were included in the soul of Adam. Thus, his soul is representative of every single human that has ever lived or ever will live. This means that when he erred and "shattered the vessels," he blemished and soiled every single soul. Few are the righteous who complete their mission in one lifetime. Therefore, these sparks of holiness — the souls — are still seeking a rectification.

* * *

20

The Rectification

But how are these sparks to attain rectification if man, and the world he inhabits, plunges deeper into materialism, especially as it has these last generations? The answer is through reincarnation and exile.

Reincarnation

Reincarnation occurs when a soul that has already been on earth in a human body is returned to earth for further rectification. There are many, many concepts in reincarnation, involving various forms of transmigration — some with frightening ramifications. The ARI wrote an entire work on this subject alone, which is known as *Shaar HaGilgulim* ("The Gate of Reincarnations") and details many of the teachings about reincarnation. Following is a short introduction.

A Jew is commanded to obey the laws of the Torah. The Torah has 248 positive commandments and 365 prohibitory commandments, totalling 613. These 613 commandments correspond to the structure of the soul as well as to the 248 limbs and organs of the body and the 365 veins and sinews (see *Makot* 23b; *Shaar HaMitzvot*, Introduction; *Anatomy of the Soul*). A person who upholds the Torah perfects both his soul and his body. As a result, when he passes away, his body is laid to rest, while the soul, having attained perfection, enters the Garden of Eden. When the Resurrection takes place, body and soul will delight in a spiritual life. In a sense, man's death parallels the idea of the Shattering of the Vessels, when the sparks descended to the lower realms and were considered "dead," and were later "rectified and resurrected."

But one who hasn't performed the mitzvot required of him lacks perfection. He has not gathered the "lost and scattered" parts of his soul to rebuild his vessel. He must therefore return again until he completes what he is lacking. And what if a person trangresses further, and thereby blemishes and fragments his soul even more than the previous times he was alive? He must certainly return again — and again — to gather up his sparks, the fragmented parts of his soul.

The "punishment always fits the crime" and suffice it to say that the soul of man does not always return as a human being. Depending on the severity of the sin, the soul might return as an animal or fowl (sometimes a kosher one, other times not even that), sometimes as vegetation and still other times in rocks and other mineral forms. In these cases, the purification process for the soul takes much longer. But even in these extreme cases, this is where the sparks of holiness can be found.

Thus, certain sins or an absence of mitzvot call for reincarnation. Having suffered through life — with its allure of materialism and the dangers of sin; with the pains of growing up, teenage and adult problems, ill health and death — a person must start out in life again. Perhaps... perhaps... this time he will reach his goal. Incidentally, suffering can be beneficial, in that it cleanses one from the effects of one's sins. Therefore, even the righteous aren't exempt from suffering. But suffering only brings atonement if a person regrets his former mistakes and repents. Then he can be assured that his mission in this world is complete. Without repentance, suffering doesn't help much and the person must be reincarnated for another try.

The question is: how are these sparks to attain rectification if mankind plunges deeper into materialism, necessitating more incarnations? And, adding to this question, how can these souls be rectified if they are in animal, vegetative or inanimate form and cannot perform mitzvot? All this is part of the mystery of the Shattering of the Vessels and the purpose of the exile.

However, the ARI points out that whatever level a spark of Creation stands, that spark is *always* connected directly to God! Nothing can exist without a spark of Godliness. Thus, even the lowest forms of the universe — even the inanimate, even the deepest realms of the *kelipot* — are sustained by the spark of Godliness within them. And so, when a person performs mitzvot, he gathers together the sparks of holiness that belong to him. This is indicated in the word miTZVah which is related to the word TZeVet, meaning "to join." When people perform mitzvot, the gathering of the holy sparks that takes place elevates even others in their vicinity. This way, even souls reincarnated in the inanimate can eventually achieve a rectification. They will be elevated and reach a higher stage of creation, until they may eventually be reincarnated again as a human being. And, as we have seen (Part III, see Chapter 10), Mashiach will be able to guide all humanity in the service of God. Therefore, everyone will eventually attain a rectification.

*

Reincarnation and exile

Had Adam not sinned, the world would have attained a perfected state immediately. His transgression plunged mankind into a realm where good and evil coexist, and where the fallen sparks of holiness must be recovered. Recovery is based upon man's deeds — good deeds elevate the sparks while evil deeds disperse them further and deeper into concealment. Reb Noson bases his explanation of this on the meaning of the word *asur*, which is usually translated "forbidden." ASuR derives from the root ASiR (bound up or imprisoned). The sparks become imprisoned in the realm of impurity (*Likutey Halakhot, Noten Taam Lifgam* 2:1).

So it is with each person. Every human being is a reflection of Adam, the First Man. Each mitzvah adds to this person's perfection and to the rectification of whatever sparks of holiness he needs to perfect — from this or previous incarnations. Each Shabbat and festival observed, each honest business transaction, every gift to charity, every word of encouragement and kind deed, all contribute to perfecting the soul. But any wrongdoing further shatters one's individual vessel, fragmenting one's soul even more. Is there then any hope for a sinner?

As we have seen (Chapter 17), each tzimtzum (constriction) of God's Light involved an initial concealment in order to bring about a revelation at a lower level of creation. Constriction and concealment are the main means of enabling these lower levels to be able to bear God's Light. The further from the outermost reaches (Keter) one is, the less intense the light experienced. Since each and every person's soul contains Godliness, it is naturally drawn to God, on whatever level it is capable of experiencing Him. Thus, it is axiomatic that people are always searching for some deep, inner satisfaction, which is reflected in a person's general longing for his Source. We therefore find that Keter corresponds to "will" — the longing, yearning and desire of the soul for God.

However, though man seeks his Source, he is usually — and unfortunately — deflected by his material surroundings. The yearning which people experience that could propel them into spirituality, in itself becomes a vehicle which can turn them away from God. Understanding the concept of revelation and concealment, we can easily see why people become distanced from God. Still, the source of stimulus people feel is always the soul's longing for spiritual satisfaction.

In order for a person to experience the Divine, he must have the proper "vessel," in body and mind, to receive this light. In a sense, this is why spirituality isn't easy to come by, for a person must *want* it — i.e. his *want* for spirituality should be more powerful than his physical cravings so that he will overcome his material desires. The pure desire for spirituality creates the vessel within which to receive Godliness (see Likutey Halakhot, Rosh HaShanah 2:6). This was expected of Adam when he was created — to desire spirituality, to serve God as he was commanded, and thereby perfect all his vessels — so that he could ascend to even greater spiritual heights. This perfection allows for an open manifestation of Godliness, and everyone can experience God through a state of perfection.

But since the Light of God is quite intense, if a person hasn't prepared himself as a proper "vessel" for a spiritual existence, the light (or longing) becomes too much for the person to bear. As with Adam, instead of attaining Godliness, a person may fall victim to materialism — his vessel shattered due to an intense revelation without a properly-developed desire for God.

But from this comes salvation — and the ability to return to God. On his previous level, the person was unable to receive the Light of Godliness. Now that he has sinned, he has shattered his soul, his sparks of holiness, into smaller fragments, and he himself has descended to a lower level. Still, it is precisely on this level, where the intensity of God's Light is greatly diminished, that a person can begin to experience God.

This is the deeper mystery behind why God fashioned the world by Shattering the Vessels. It was in this way that He created a system in which His Light would be reduced to minute proportions — all so that man would always be able to find Him. Man, who might sin and perform the most evil deeds, will eventually find himself on a level where — no matter how distant he is from God — his inner longing for spirituality will manifest itself in a desire for God, and he will return to God in repentance.

This turning to God is the first step in rectifying the spark of one's soul and one's holiness at that level. Then, as a person turns to God more and more, he begins to ascend the spiritual ladder, gathering in the other fragments of his soul that were shattered from earlier sins and previous lives. He learns to use all his strength, building all the while a more perfected vessel to receive and maintain spirituality. These efforts gradually cause the remaining fragments of his soul to be gathered and assembled and finally rectified.

This is an aspect of reward and punishment that will prevail in the future. Those tzaddikim who have never sinned can experience God on the highest of levels (although there will always be ever higher levels to be revealed because God is Infinite). Since their will was always directed towards spirituality, their level is that of Keter, which transcends any conception (as above, Chapter 18). The "shattered vessels" of those who have sinned *can* be rectified and perfected. The perfection they attain parallels that of the rectified Vessels after the initial shattering.

This is also the reason for reincarnation and exile. Each reincarnation is determined by a person's lack of perfection. He must descend again to this world to compensate for the sparks lost by sin or folly. He must perform mitzvot and turn to God, thereby gathering the fragments of his soul.

Exile too is a form of reincarnation. A soul is forced to leave the spiritual existence of the heavenly Garden of Eden and wander in a world where God is hidden. But this is because he must search for and retrieve those fragments of his own soul that have been scattered to distant shores. Gathering those fragments, he gathers himself. (In the next section, Part VI, we will discuss the concept of exile in greater detail.)

It is through this process of reincarnation and exile that God brings about the final rectification of Creation, as the verse hints (Psalms 147:2), "God is the Builder of Jerusalem. [He does this by] gathering in the outcasts of Israel." For all the individual sparks of each and every soul will be gathered and rectified, and everyone will return to join in unity with God (Likutey Moharan I, 80). This means that people will live together in peace — no broken homes, fragmented communities or embattled countries. And all people will actually join together to serve the One God!

*

The power of repentance

Now we can begin to understand how to repent and completely rectify our sins. As we have seen, there are three upper Sefirot, corresponding to the intellect, while the seven lower Sefirot correspond to the attributes. Time is divided into seven days, corresponding to the seven lower Sefirot. The *Zohar* teaches (III, 122a) that repentance is rooted in a higher sefirah, in Binah, which is above the concept of time. Therefore on the level of Binah repentance can take place, for God can forgive even the worst transgressions by transcending the time (and place) of the sin.

The more a person turns to God, the greater his ascent into the realm of holiness. The Talmud teaches (Yoma 86b):

> "Great is repentance, for it draws the redemption closer. Great is repentance, for it transforms an intentional sin into an accidental sin. Great is repentance, for it transforms sin into merits! But isn't this a contradiction?

The explanation is that repentance from fear of God or from punishment transforms an intentional sin into an accidental sin. But when one repents out of love for God, then an intentional sin is credited to a person as if he had performed a good deed!"

This is quite difficult to understand. Let us say that a man is brought into court on charges of having committed a serious crime. He is tried and found guilty of acting in a premeditated manner. Now, if he pleads for the court's mercy, and swears that he sincerely regrets what he did, at most he might succeed in having his sentence reduced. He could never, by any stretch of the imagination, expect the court to consider his crime a mitzvah!

God's judgment differs in this respect. In the Heavenly Tribunal, sincere repentance can change everything. Though a person's evil may have caused a shattering of vessels and a greater concealment of Godliness in the world, when he repents, he shows that he is ready to begin to collect and elevate those shards and rebuild them anew. He shows that he wants to take the same energy of holiness he misused and reclaim it for the service of God. When this is done out of love for God — to the point of giving up his life if necessary — it has the power to transform even the greatest sin into a mitzvah.

This is the meaning of the saying, "Great is repentance, for it draws the redemption closer." Each temptation is an obstacle to experiencing God. Each sin is an obstacle to returning to God. But when one does return to God, he tranforms his evil into good. For obstacles are *MeNIOT*, which, when transformed, become *NeIMOT*, pleasantness, a spiritual delight (see *Likutey Halakhot, Nizkei Shekheinim* 3:8).

*

Daat

For the world will be filled with the knowledge of God..."
Isaiah 11:9

The Talmud equates sin with foolishness (*Sotah* 3a). Man's foolishness has caused his descent into the depths of depravity and sin. Mashiach is on the level of Keter, which transcends even Binah. As we have seen (Part III) Mashiach has awesome powers to bring people to recognize and serve God. Truth, fear and awe of God, prayer and the wondrous advice which stems from the Torah of Atik, are but some of the weapons which he will employ.

But one of the most powerful weapons in Mashiach's armory is intellect, the great Daat that he will reveal. This intellect, the Knowledge of Godliness, will spread all over the earth as people begin to search for God. As foolishness is rejected and the search for the Word of God spreads, the sparks of holiness are gathered, revealing ever greater levels of knowledge (see above, Chapter 6). This is the Ingathering of the Exiles, the ingathering of the shards of foolishness and their transformation into great intellect. Interestingly, this intellect will not be revealed at once. Rather, it will come to a person as a revelation of *faith* in God. The more a person seeks God, the greater is one's faith in Him. The greater one's faith, the more one begins to see the Hand of God guiding one through life. The dawning of the great Daat (which has already begun; see above, Chapter 6) is actually the negation of idolatries and foolishness through faith. Thus, great Daat is actually faith. Strengthening one's faith in God is therefore the first step in repentance, in ingathering the exiles and in the ultimate rectification of one's sins (see also *Likutey Halakhot*, Pesach 7:21).

*

Descent for the sake of ascent

We have seen how Mashiach will rectify the world. His abilities will transcend everything that we know and, for this very reason, he will be able to bring revelations of Godliness to every human being, to every level of humanity. By illuminating even the lowest of levels, Mashiach will bring hope to everyone and unify all people, bringing peace among them and unifying them with the One God.

While attempting to understand how we will all be rectified, the question arises, "Why do things always get worse before they get better?" Why must mankind plunge to such depths in order to finally experience such a complete salvation? Why doesn't God begin the process of redemption earlier, and save us from descending to unfathomable depths?

But as we have seen, God gave everyone free will to do as he or she chooses. The effort each of us expends in finding spirituality determines to what extent we will succeed in rectifying our souls and the sparks of holiness that are connected to our souls. Less effort or no effort at all causes a descent which breaks the sparks down into even smaller pieces. If we wake up and realize what is going on at that point, fine. If not, the sparks are broken down into even smaller units — with the foolishness surrounding us becoming more and more obvious — so that eventually our own free will must bring us to search for God.

And, in a certain sense, when someone who has plummeted to the lowest of levels recognizes God, this causes a greater revelation of the Glory of God than the service of one who never fell. This is alluded to in our Sages discussion of who is greater — a righteous man who never sinned or one who has transgressed and completely repented (see Berakhot 34b). This is because those in higher realms know of God — each at his own level — and find it easier to submit themselves to Him. When a person who has fallen to the lowest of levels learns of God and submits to His authority, then the Light of the Infinite One illumines even those depths, causing the concealment of Godliness on those lowest of levels to be reduced and even done away with altogether (see Likutey Moharan I, 10:2; ibid. 14:2). That is, the Light of the Infinite One illumines from the Highest of Levels down through all the universes even into the lowest realms! This idea is also known in the holy writings as "the descent before the ascent."

This means that in order to come to a greater revelation or understanding of Godliness, one must suffer some kind of a descent before ascending to the next level. (This does not always mean one must suffer setbacks, though this occurs too. It does mean that one's ascent on the spiritual ladder is always accompanied by challenges — either in trying to understand the newer ideas or in facing difficulties previously not encountered; see Likutey Moharan I, 25:3, end.) The greater one's ascent is to be, the more difficulties one encounters — for then one will be causing a much greater revelation of God, the Light of the Infinite One, than has ever been experienced previously.

The concept is a little difficult to understand at first and therefore we will illustrate it with the following examples (also see above, Part IV):

*

The Generation of the Exodus

The Jews were exiled in Egypt. There, they descended to the forty-ninth level of impurity, and into idolatry. Their descent was so deep that only God Himself could redeem them from their impurities. Even so, Moshe was sent as a redeemer, for he had to reveal to them that God was with them. In doing so, he aroused the Jews to repentance and to turn to God for salvation. But just as their descent was so steep, their ascent was even more spectacular. Fifty days after the Exodus, God revealed Himself upon Mount Sinai, where the Jews received the Torah, bringing great spiritual light to the world. Thus, the Jews' descent to the lowest level "caused" a revelation of God that had to penetrate from the very highest of levels to the very lowest. This illumination of Godliness brought with it the greatest revelation of spirituality in history, the Revelation of the Torah.

However, Israel sinned and thereby forfeited their right to receive the Torah. When Moshe descended the mountain, he saw the Jews dancing around the golden calf. All of a sudden the Tablets that had been miraculously light felt unbearably heavy. As the letters that God had engraved on them flew heavenwards, Moshe understood what he had to do. With all his strength, he cast the Tablets down, replicating the shattering of the vessels. At the sound of their shattering, the people who had been worshiping the calf looked up. A dread silence fell upon the entire camp.

Why did Moshe cast the Tablets from his hand? The Torah demands the death penalty for idolatry. If they were to receive the Torah, they would be punished with death! So Moshe couldn't bring himself to reveal the contents of the Torah to the worshipers of the calf and chose instead to destroy the Tablets (see Rashi, Exodus 32:19). Now, as idolators, the Jews again descended to the level they had occupied in Egypt. But since now they could not experience Torah, how could they ever ascend again, or even survive? The judgment against them was so severe that it demanded the destruction of the entire fledgling Jewish Nation (Exodus 32-33).

But Moshe prayed on their behalf, imploring God for mercy. God then revealed to Moshe a level of compassion and love which extends beyond the constrictions of Torah — the Thirteen Attributes of Mercy (Exodus 34:6-7). There was a very great lesson to be learned from this, that, even if a person commits the worst crimes, there is still hope. A price must be paid, according to Divine Judgment. But God has ways of mitigating His own decrees, as He did when the golden calf was worshiped, and He can lighten and even remove the blemish, in order to effect the rectification.

When did God reveal the Attributes of Mercy? Only *after* the Jews had descended to a new low! Having risen to a level where they received the Torah, they plummeted immediately into a debasing predicament, into idolatry. But through Moshe's prayers, God revealed an even greater level of compassion — the Thirteen Attributes. The reason for this is as we have stated: When the Jews descended to the lowest depths, they concealed the light of Godliness in the world. But on that abysmal level, their repentance caused God to reveal Himself and His compassion on an even loftier level than they had experienced previously.

The Torah and mitzvot signify "constriction," something that is "contained" within certain boundaries (see above, Chapter 7). Thus, should a person sin, the Torah demands justice, itself a constriction. However, repentance is rooted in a higher level, that of Binah. The Torah demanded justice for the Jews' sin, but Moshe invoked a higher level, that of the Thirteen Attributes, and was able to effect forgiveness. The Jews again ascended to a higher level and this time were even more sharply aware of God's greatness, for a higher degree of God was revealed to them. Their repentance thus led to the rectification of their vessel and enabled them to experience spirituality — in the form of their building the Sanctuary, an open manifestation of God among them! (see *Likutey Moharan* I, 22:10, n.116; ibid. 22:11, n.144).

The same principle holds true today. Even though — or perhaps specifically because — we have strayed even further from God than did the Generation of the Exodus, we maintain the ability to reveal even greater levels of Godliness. The Jews repented then and were rewarded with the building of a Sanctuary to reveal Godliness, although that Sanctuary was founded as a temporary dwelling for God's Divine Presence. Today, we await the building of the Third Temple, a permanent structure, to reveal Godliness. Therefore, if our descent is appalling, it is because our ultimate ascent must reveal God on such an expansive scale that it requires — even demands — of us to cause Godliness to be manifest even on the lowest levels of Creation.

This most certainly does not mean that if we did not sin we would not attain those higher levels. As explained earlier, had Adam (i.e. mankind) not sinned, the revelation of spirituality would have been on the level of Keter and man would have begun from there to seek the ever greater revelations of the *Ein Sof*, the Infinite One. It does mean that, even if a person commits the worst sins and feels beyond hope, he should know that there are ever higher levels of Godliness than can be revealed to him through which he can effect salvation. For the salvation comes to the individual — and to the entire nation — according to the degree to which his vessel is rectified (see *Likutey Halakhot*, Pesach 5:2).

*

Mordekhai, Haman and Purim

When the First Temple was destroyed the Jews were told by Jeremiah that their sojourn in exile would last for seventy years. Afterwards, they would be able to return to the Holy Land and rebuild the Temple (Jeremiah 29:10; *Megilah* 11b). We have seen that the exile is itself part of the rectification process and elevates the sparks of holiness scattered throughout the world. Adam, who was mainly formed from the dust of the area known as

Babylon (today Iraq) (see Sanhedrin 38b), left behind many sparks of holiness waiting to be elevated. So it was there that the Jews went into exile.

Had they withstood the ravages of their non-Jewish neighbors, the Jews would have returned to the Holy Land without additional suffering. But they succumbed to the lures of the Babylonian and Persian cultures which were so alien to them. Instead of remaining pure, they feasted with Achashveirosh, worshiped idols and intermarried with non-Jews (cf. Megilah 12a). The Attribute of Judgment rose against them, as it did in the time of Moshe, and demanded their destruction. This is why Haman, a pedigreed Amalek who longed for the "honor" of wiping out the Jews, appeared just at that time. And he came very, very close to succeeding.

But God always provides the Jews with the opportunity for redemption and a redeemer. The Jews were in a terrible state, facing total destruction. But Mordekhai, the ARI writes, was rooted in Chokhmah, a level that transcends even Binah, which Moshe used to arouse compassion for his generation (see Appendix B; see Pri Etz Chaim, Shaar HaPurim 5). Thus, the light and power of Mordekhai were able to penetrate even to the lowest levels that his generation reached, arousing the entire nation to pray to God in repentance and to seek salvation.

The reason the Jews fell so deeply into transgression then was due to the corresponding ascent they were to experience. They were scheduled to leave the exile and enter the Holy Land, and to rebuild the Holy Temple. Accordingly, they were set upon by the forces of evil and led deep into temptation, nearly bringing about their destruction.

Correspondingly, the ascent following their salvation from Haman was also great. Previously, they had begun the work of rebuilding the Temple, but were forced to stop. The downfall of Haman and the miracle of Purim reversed their fortune, and the Jews renewed their acceptance of Torah (see Shabbat 88a). Then, they were finally able to rebuild the Holy Temple and reestablish themselves in the Holy Land (Likutey Halakhot, Eiruvei Techumin 4:9).

*

We can now better understand the idea of "descent for the sake of ascent" and why Keter (Atik) corresponds to will (see above, Chapter 18). **Rebbe Nachman once remarked:**

> "If you have some conception of God's greatness, you will not understand how one can claim to serve Him. The highest angel cannot say that he truly serves God. The main thing is *desire*. Always *yearn* to draw near to God" (*Rabbi Nachman's Wisdom* #51).

Atik represents Keter, will — the will to serve God Who *is* the Highest Level. Atik is also the level of Mashiach, who will draw upon the power of his source in order to direct people to serve God. A person's mission in life is to use his will for this purpose. However, people do err and sin and distance themselves from God. The further a person is from God, the further he is from Keter, will. But will (the desire and longing of the soul) never ceases. Eventually, a person's will, rooted in the level of Keter — "the will of wills" — awakens from its dormant state and motivates him to return to God. Thus, the descent a person experiences is actually *the vehicle which arouses him to strengthen his will to serve God. This then propels him to greater spiritual heights!* (*Likutey Halakhot, Arev* 3:4).

*

And so it is in our times, in the era of the "Footsteps of the Mashiach." We face "scorpions" and depravities (see Chapter 1), and find ourselves in a world filled with foolishness and idolatries as never before. As the twentieth century draws to a close, we have witnessed a bestiality of man the likes of which have never been seen before in the annals of mankind (e.g. the Holocaust). But then again, what awaits us at the other end, when Mashiach finally does come, is a height never imagined or conceived of by man. For Mashiach transcends the levels of Binah and Chokhmah; his source is Keter itself. The salvation brought through the Mashiach will truly rectify the entire world. He will build the Third Temple and reestablish the Davidic Dynasty with the Jews in the Holy Land. He will spread the awe of Godliness and bring all humanity to the level they were originally designed for — the level "Adam-Man!" And then the prophecy — concerning the Jewish Nation and the Mashiach — will be fulfilled:

My servant shall prosper, he shall be exalted and extolled... Who would have believed us...? He had no form or splendor that we should look at him... He was despised and rejected... But the Lord's purpose was that he should prosper... He will be given a portion with the great... for he bore the sin of many and interceded for the transgressor... (Isaiah 52:13-53:12).

May he come speedily, in our days, Amen!

* * *

Part VI

Mashiach:

Where?

In this part of the book we shall discuss several ideas relating to the messianic era such as: the ingathering of the exiles to the Holy Land, the difference between Jew and non-Jew, the joy of the Days of Mashiach, and so on. In addition, the messianic ideals already discussed will now begin to merge into a most beautiful mosaic, as all the pieces start falling into place.

21

The search is on!

We have discussed *who* Mashiach can be, *what* his mission is, *why* a Mashiach is necessary and *how* he will be able to rectify the world. The next question is, "*Where* will all this take place?"

The Prophets clearly depict the messianic era as one of grandeur for the Jewish Nation, in their own land. Torah literature defines this land as the Holy Land, the Land of Israel, with modern political maps depicting much the same area, albeit with different borders.

Yet, something seems to be not quite right. Mashiach is to rectify the entire world and elevate all the sparks of holiness. Will everybody and everything come *en masse* to the Holy Land? But what will happen then to the rest of the planet? Will it go to waste? That certainly doesn't make sense. God didn't create anything in vain.

Furthermore, if the messianic prophecies are specifically for the Jewish Nation, what will happen to the gentile nations? And why is there a difference between Jew and non-Jew? When the rectification takes place, won't all those rectified be able to experience Godliness — each according to the spiritual level attained? Then why will the Jews be singled out for extra reward? And what about the punishment and revenge God is to exact from the enemies of the Jews when Mashiach comes? If rectification takes place, isn't punishment unnecessary? But if evildoers go unpunished then justice will not have been done. And God is a just yet avenging God (cf. Deuteronomy 4:24).

*

Some of these topics were touched upon earlier. In this section of the book, we will discuss in detail the concept of the exile and the role of the nations vis-à-vis the Jewish people during their exile and after the Redemption. We will also discuss the Holy Land as it will be in the Days of Mashiach.

In addition, we will expand our discussion about the great wealth to be attained, as it ties in to Daat, the Great Knowledge to be revealed, and to the Torah of Atik. Also to be discussed are converts, Judgment Day, the Prophets' predictions of the final, decisive war between the forces of good and evil, or "The war of Gog and Magog." We will also tie together many of the aspects of Mashiach's mission (detailed in Part III), such as purity, faith and truth, etc. Then the picture of the Days of Mashiach should be fairly complete.

This is not to say there isn't more, for the information about the messianic era is vast indeed. But as the Rambam writes (Yad HaChazakah, Melakhim 12:1; see above, Part I), "We will only understand the entire picture when Mashiach actually arrives."

Speedily in our days, Amen.

* * *

22

The Exile

One of Mashiach's obligations is to gather the Jewish exiles from the four corners of the earth to the Holy Land. Earlier we saw that he will accomplish this by "building Jerusalem" — i.e. by instilling fear of God into mankind (see above, Chapter 7). As a person attains a heightened awareness of God, he will automatically begin to develop his search for spirituality. This will lead him to the Holy Land and the Holy Temple — i.e. the building of Daat — where God's Glory, the Divine Presence, is waiting to be revealed (see above, Chapter 6). This is ultimately how the exile will terminate.

*

A state of mind

> *God will disperse you among the nations... you will be serving man-made gods of wood and stone, that neither see nor hear... But from **there** you will seek God, and you will find Him...*
> Deuteronomy 4:27-29

The exile is quite clearly defined in the Bible. God speaks to Israel and says: You shall be dispersed among the nations where you will find yourselves serving idols that cannot help you at all... As we have seen (Part IV), these are the foolish pursuits that we deify, surrendering the better part of our lives, strength and resources for questionable — or even negative — returns. But the time will come when Israel and mankind as a whole will realize the futility of this pursuit and begin to seek God. "From there you will seek God and you will find Him..." "From *there*," from that point to which you have descended — be it even the lowest point possible —

from *there* you will begin to feel the lack in your life and start moving forward towards Godliness.

This is because we must build our own vessel within which we can retain Godliness. Building the vessel comes through the desire to serve God, prayer and performing the mitzvot (see *Likutey Moharan* I, 185; ibid. 73; *Likutey Halakhot, Sukkah* 6:11). By sinning, on the other hand, not only has he not made a vessel, he has destroyed one. He must therefore descend to a lower level. Perhaps *there* he will find spirituality, albeit a smaller dose, and begin to build a vessel there. If that fails, he descends still further... until he eventually realizes the error of purely material pursuit, and begins to search for God (see above, Chapter 20).

To better understand the idea of the exile and how it relates to each individual, we will now review what we learned about the power of truth, as well as the idea that exile is a state of mind (see above, Chapter 6).

*

> **The breath of a liar gives rise to the evil inclination. When Mashiach comes, falsehood will no longer exist. There will therefore be no evil inclination in the world.**
>
> The Aleph-Bet Book, Truth A:8

This teaching is based upon the verse (Zekhariah 13:2; see *Targum* and Rashi), "On that day, I will destroy the idols... and remove false prophets and impurity from the land." When truth prevails, idolatry and falsehood have no meaning and simply disappear.

There can be many lies but there is only one truth (*Likutey Moharan* I, 51; see also *Mayim*). The person who honestly seeks the truth will find it. Because truth is singular and all inclusive, this itself will then lead him to seek even more refined levels of truth, ad infinitum. Falsehood, on the other hand, has many faces. There are outright lies, misconceptions, little "white lies" to save face, etc. Why are all of these so much a part of our daily lives? Because every "little falsehood" a person utters gives rise to an evil inclination that is stronger than its predecessor. This in turn strengthens falsehood, which in turn strengthens the evil inclination, and so on. Thus, if a person slackens his spiritual pursuit and allows a misconception to take root, this tiny misconception can lead to greater misconceptions, until he is danger of completely severing his connection to God.

This is also the meaning of exile being a state of mind. "The whole world is filled with His glory!" (Isaiah 6:3). If a person is fully aware of God at all times and in all places, he is not in exile. He has not been removed from the place of holiness, from the palace of holiness, from God's Presence. But despite this great potential that we have, we allow ourselves to indulge in materialism for the sake of materialism. A snippet here, a snippet there, and before long we are totally involved in our man-made and self-serving pursuits; in effect we are worshiping idols. Instead of elevating and rectifying all our little "half" and "quarter" truths with the unifying power of God's *absolute* truth, we opt for a fragmented world of multiple falsehoods. If we accept falsehood as a viable way of life, we automatically create a system in which our minds "travel" (the essence of exile) from one compartmentalized thought to the next. This is the essence of spiritual exile.

Thus, because the Jews said (Exodus 32:4), "*Eileh* — these are your gods, Israel" — that is, these idols that man creates for himself in place of God— the result is (Numbers 33:1), "*Eileh* — these are the journeys of the children of Israel..." Exile is the punishment for idolatry (see Likutey Moharan II, 62).

The dictionary translates exile as a forced or voluntary absence from one's home, by one's self or by an authority. Isn't falsehood an exile? An exile in which we remove ourselves from truth and enter a world of fantasy? Truth endures precisely because it is not a fantasy but a reality. Falsehood does not endure, which is why it changes from moment to moment. We are thus constantly moving from thought to thought, emotion to emotion, without stability in our lives.

Adam and Eve accepted the Serpent's advice, outright lies about God and the Tree of Knowledge, and so were banished from the Garden of Eden. In front of the Garden, to bar their reentry, God placed (Genesis 3:24), "The revolving sword." Since their transgression was a result of bad advice, mankind's exile is maintained through the "revolving sword" — the never-ending stream of thoughts that change constantly, according to our feelings, environment, etc. Were we to focus our thoughts on seeking out the purpose in our lives, we would not be deflected from a spiritual lifestyle. But materialism and falsehood are always followed by a whole slue of second thoughts and altering moods, such that we have great difficulty rediscovering the correct path back to God (*Likutey Halakhot, Sukkah* 7:3).

This is exile as a state of mind. One's state of mind cannot remove or negate the physical exile in which we find ourselves. Nevertheless, it does help us put things into proper perspective when we examine the effects of being exiled and the physical dispersion of the Jews to the four corners of the globe.

*

The physical exile

Like Adam and Eve's banishment from the Garden of Eden, Israel's exile from the Holy Land was not only God's way of punishing them, but of bringing about their ultimate rectification. Exile serves the purpose of purifying the soul and the nation. In the End of Days, when our sins will be wiped clean, all the Jews will return to the Land of Israel, on the level of Adam and Eve before the sin, and truly begin life anew.

There are several methods of cleansing a soul. One is reincarnation; another is Gehennom. Physical suffering, together with repentance, can also cleanse the soul (see above, Chapter 20). When God created the world, He set up these systems to help us cleanse ourselves of the blemish of our sins and thereby attain perfection through our own efforts. When God made the Covenant of the Halves with Abraham, He informed him that his descendants would suffer in exile for four generations, but eventually leave the land of their oppressors with great wealth, both material and spiritual. They would then be worthy of receiving the Torah on Sinai, enter the Land of Israel and eventually build the Holy Temple. Before long, however, they would sin and deserve some kind of punishment. He showed Abraham two kinds of punishment, and asked him to decide which one he preferred. The choice was between Gehennom and exile. As the

Midrash puts it, "As long as your descendants occupy themselves with two (the Torah and the Temple), they will be spared two (Gehennom and exile). If they do not uphold the first two, they will suffer the second two." God then gave Abraham the option of choosing between exile and Gehennom as *the* punishment, *the* means of cleansing, for his descendants. After a day's deliberation, Abraham, with God's encouragement, chose the lesser of the two evils — exile (*Bereishit Rabbah* 44:21). (This does not mean that one who sinned is exempt from Gehennom, rather, as the commentaries point out, the severity of the cleansing process in Gehennom is greatly diminished as a result of the suffering of the exile.)

Why did Abraham, the very man who initiated the search for spirituality, chose exile? Exile is a carefully planned system of rectification for the errors and transgressions of the Jewish people. Who better than Abraham, who endured several exiles himself, would understand the benefits of an exile? He understood that each person's ultimate rectification will take effect according to his own search for spirituality. Then the search for Godliness will continue — and climax — when everyone is rectified. And as we have seen (Chapter 20), this rectification takes place as the sparks of holiness are gathered in. Reb Noson addresses this issue in a most unique way.

> The Jews were told that if they sinned, they would be punished with exile to distant lands, serving man-made idols. In the diaspora, they would rectify their sins and repent, merit the coming of Mashiach, and return to the Holy Land. But this idea is very difficult to comprehend. How, in exile, is there hope for us to return? In our Holy Land, where Godliness was manifest, the evil inclination overpowered us, causing us to sin. How can there be hope that, when banished from holiness into exile, and surrounded by alien cultures that further encourage sin, specifically *there* we will repent and rectify our wrongdoings?
>
> If we look at exile in this way, then there is no hope. But that cannot be, because God desires our rectification. His intention is not for revenge, God forbid. God's whole reason for the exile is that "from *there*" we will seek Him. Still, if when in our own Land we did not seek God, is it really expected of us to seek Him in the Diaspora? (*Likutey Halakhot, Birkat HaReiach* 4:45).

Reb Noson then discusses in detail the rectification process (as above, Part V). He writes about how God allows (i.e. arranges for) even those who fell to the lowest depths — to return to Him. He explains that the ascents and descents that each individual Jew goes through in his life parallel those times that our people lived in the Land of Israel, on the one hand, and the various exiles we have endured, on the other hand. Particularly now, during the period of the "Footsteps of the Mashiach," when all of our souls have come to earth for their final rectification, it is not by chance that so many have fallen into the realm of the *kelipot*. It is part of God's plan to bring back all the sparks. Reb Noson explains how this works:

> Know that the further and lower a person falls from holiness, there must be something there, some service he must perform for God's sake, that the greatest tzaddik could not do. In this way, this person elevates all the sparks of holiness that fell into that unclean place.
>
> For many holy sparks have been lodged and imprisoned [in these places] since the beginning of time, very deeply buried in the kelipot. They are buried so deeply that no one [in his right mind] would enter those places to retrieve them. Therefore, when a person who has sinned "happens" to fall into one of these places, God forbid, the moment he reminds himself that there is a God, and arouses himself to serve His Blessed Name... these sparks attach themselves to him. He then elevates them from there, and in this way gives God untold pleasure.
>
> This involves every Jewish soul who finds himself living anywhere in the world, in any place, no matter how far from the Land of Israel. [He must know that] there are sparks in that place that may have been there for thousands of years. Their affliction cannot be expressed... But for this very reason, if any Jew would come anywhere near them, even the greatest sinner (for though he has sinned, he is still a Jew), these holy sparks would "smell" the fragrance of the Land of Israel, revive from their stupor, and attach themselves to him. And they would do this even if there was still no chance for them to become elevated through this person. On the contrary, in the majority of cases such a person initially falls even farther due to the fact that the kelipot continue to cling to these sparks (which attach themselves to this person). Nevertheless, as long as this person is still

Jewish, he is very precious in God's eyes. It is therefore certain that he will eventually pick himself up and depart that place, and take those sparks with him. This will then serve as a rectification of his own sins, since he was instrumental in redeeming these sparks.

We thus learn that, in the end, every soul will be rectified. Not one will be lost. For God never forgets and is always mindful of those who have fallen. He never forgets the sparks that are buried deeply everywhere throughout the universe waiting to be redeemed, and He is always mindful of those Jews who have gone astray. He will not allow any of them to be lost altogether. Even if the latter have hit rock bottom, and even lower than that, specifically *there* they will feel an arousal towards God. And in this way they will serve to bring God's ultimate plan to fruition. This is happening now.

This also explains why, when the Jewish People were in the Holy Land and God showed them His love openly, they ironically became insensitive to spirituality. How did this happen? Because they mistook God's closeness as a sign that they had already "made it," they became lax in their service. Instead of realizing that the revelation of Godliness they experienced was only a beginning, they slackened their efforts. This led them into sin, bringing about the exile.

Now, in exile, under the influence of alien cultures and governments, the situation is reversed. The Jewish soul begins to think of God and spiritual living. Being so far away from the holiness of the Land of Israel, every thought and movement *towards* Godliness — even if it wouldn't have been considered pure enough when in close proximity to holiness — is considered a very great feat. This is the meaning of "From *there*." Precisely because it is so distant from Godliness and holiness, every effort is that much more significant in God's eyes.

In fact, Rebbe Nachman writes, the very fact that a person is so far from God, yet begins to realize that he is distant, is in itself a manifestation of God drawing the person closer to Him! (Likutey Moharan II, 68). Thus, at that very lowest point is where a person can begin the upward swing of his "spiritual pendulum." The rest is up to his use of his free will. God will always provide the means in consonance with how much a person really wants to rectify himself. This in turn requires restraint and patience (which are also messianic attributes, as explained above, Part III).

During a person's spiritual search, since it is holiness that he is seeking, he automatically attracts the sparks of holiness that are waiting to be rectified, and elevates them to his level. As people begin their search, one person repents, a second is aroused, then a third, and so on.... This end to the exile is alluded to in the verse (Deuteronomy 30:3), "And God will return with your captivity..." Rashi (loc. cit.), offers two explanations to the verse. The first is that God Himself is in exile, hence the words, "God will return with." God is "in exile," because the sparks of holiness which are part of His Unity are in exile. The second explanation is that the Ingathering of the Exiles is a painstaking pursuit, as if God Himself has to hold each individual's hand and lead him, personally, out of the exile.

The two explanations are really one. When a person chooses spirituality, God begins to reveal Himself to him. As God reveals Himself, people turn to Him, attracting and elevating the sparks of holiness. Then, as each person's portion of holiness becomes rectified, he becomes joined to God's Unity. Therefore, God takes that individual and personally leads him out of exile! (see Likutey Halakhot, Birkat HaReiach 4:45).

*

Ayeh? Where is God?

The search for spirituality really begins with a question, "*Ayeh?* — Where?" "Where is God?" Kabbalistically, the level of (the term) *Ayeh?* is that of Keter, that ineffable level on which even angels cannot know where God is, for He is far beyond any conception. Therefore, when they praise God, they say, "*Ayeh?* (where) is the place of His glory?" (Kedushah of Shabbat Mussaf).

But *Ayeh?* is also a question asked by man. Man is the main purpose of the Creation, and it is actually his questioning and search that causes Godliness to be revealed. And it is precisely *this* question of *Ayeh?* that leads to the Redemption, to the rectification of each person and the scattered sparks of his soul.

Ayeh? Where is the lamb for the sacrifice?
Genesis 22:7

On Rosh HaShanah, we blow the shofar, a ram's horn, in commemoration of the *Akeidah*, the sacrifice of Isaac by Abraham upon the altar. As the Bible relates (Genesis 22), when Abraham and Isaac were ascending the mountain, Isaac asked, "We have fire and wood. *Ayeh* (where is) the lamb for the sacrifice?"

The *Akeidah* is unfathomable: how could God tell Abraham that He will bring a nation forth from him through Isaac, and then command that he sacrifice his only son Isaac? But there are other things in this world that are equally as unfathomable — e.g. the paradox of Divine Foreknowledge and human free will. When Mashiach comes, he will resolve these paradoxes. For the moment, though, Isaac asked, "*Ayeh?*" Realizing at that point that he was to be the sacrifice to God, he was seeking God. "*Ayeh?*" Isaac's search for the continuation of spirituality led to the sacrifice of the ram instead of himself.

And this salvation is relived each year on Rosh HaShanah. Every year, the we blow the ram's horn on Rosh HaShanah, the first day of the Ten Days of Repentance, symbolizing the beginning of our return to God. (The Ten Days also climax at the conclusion of Yom Kippur with a blast from the ram's horn.) For repentance (in whole or in part) is the path that one chooses when one begins to ask for Godliness. Eventually, the continual blasting of the shofar will awaken the nation sufficiently, so that all seek spirituality, even "from *there*," the places most distant from God (see *Likutey Halakhot, Rosh HaShanah* 6:1). And, as we have seen (above, Chapter 7), the shofar is the voice of rebuke, which are the teachings of the tzaddikim that arouse the "sweet fragrance" of a person's deeds.

Reb Noson explains why the search officially initiated on Rosh HaShanah culminates on Yom Kippur when all sins are forgiven, as in (Jeremiah 50:20), "For on that day the sins of Israel will be sought but they won't be found... for I shall forgive those whom I will keep alive." Through the search of *Ayeh?* one literally takes one's sins — the fragmented parts of his soul — and brings them back into holiness, transforming them into merits (as above, Chapter 20). The reason that the sins won't be found is because they have turned into Torah, into holiness! (*(Likutey Moharan* I, 22:11; see *Likutey Halakhot, Rosh HaShanah, Roshei Perakim,* 6:1).

The Midrash thus teaches (*Bereishit Rabbah* 56:9) that the ram being entangled in the thicket by its horns is an allusion to the Jews being ensnared in difficulties and sins during their exile. But, just as the ram was eventually released, so too will the Jews be redeemed.

Then, we will all merit to hear the shofar of the Mashiach, as in (Isaiah 27:13), "For on that day, a great shofar will be blown; those who were lost in Assyria and outcast in Egypt will then come; and they will bow down to God on His holy mountain in Jerusalem."

May it be speedily, in our days, Amen.

* * *

23

Jew and Non-Jew

We have seen that the purpose of the exile is to rectify the sparks of holiness that have been scattered throughout the world. As discussed above (Part V), there are two types of sparks: those left intentionally by God (when He formed the lower levels of Creation) to be rectified by Adam; and those that were scattered through Adam's transgression and the transgressions of all succeeding generations, as a result of mankind not repenting and rectifying their souls. In the above chapters, we explained how one's spiritual search illumines the sparks, attracting them towards a person seeking spirituality, and eventually elevating and rectifying them. We are now ready to discuss the question of why the Prophets foresaw so glorious a future for the Jews, more so than for the gentile nations. If everyone is destined for rectification, what determines the difference between Jew and non-Jew?

*

The sparks and the dross

It is a given fact that when any vessel is produced, the raw material will yield waste matter as well as residue. For example, a goldsmith fashions a gold ring. Gold dross is mined together with the gold, but as it is waste matter it cannot be used. On the contrary, it must be removed and discarded. In addition, there are many single grains of gold that are residue, i.e. they fall away during the process of the formation of the ring. These grains are still pure gold, but are units that are too small to be of much worth in their current state. Gathered together, they can be recast into a vessel of pure gold, and regain their former worth.

When God began to form the world, He created Vessels. However, He formed these vessels in such a fashion as to be incapable of containing His light, and so they shattered. The Shattering of the Vessels caused sparks of God's Light to be spread all over the world, awaiting rectification by Adam. When Adam transgressed, the sparks scattered yet further, and are awaiting rectification through man's repentance and good deeds (see above, Chapter 18).

But there were also *sigim* (dross), extraneous matter that God placed within His Creation. This dross became the *kelipot*, the forces of evil, made to deter man from his spiritual quest. We see then that the Shattering of the Vessels served a dual purpose. While it resulted in setting up a system of potential evil, at the same time, it set the stage for man to be able to interact with God and thereby rectify the sparks of holiness (see *Etz Chaim, Shaar Shevirat Keilim* 8; *Likutey Moharan* I, 64:2). The dross became the potential evil, the realm of the *kelipot* which stands opposite the realm of holiness. If man performs good deeds, he strengthens the kingdom of holiness. If, on the other hand, man does evil, he transfers power to the kingdom and forces of evil (*Likutey Halakhot, Pesach, Roshei Perakim* 1).

By performing good deeds, man creates defending angels; by performing wicked deeds, he creates avenging angels (cf. *Avot* 4:11). When the *kelipot* gain strength, they are authorized to do nearly anything in their power in order to exact punishment from the evildoer. This is manifest in the difficulties and confusions people face every day (see *Likutey Moharan* I, 115). Worse, certain sins actually create demons and spirits that do real harm to a person. This is especially true of sins involving sexual immorality, such as masturbation and homosexuality. We are told that, during the 130 years he was separated from Eve, Adam spilled seed and created innumerable spirits and demons (*Eruvin* 18b; see also Rashi, 2 Samuel 7:14). It follows that the person who suffers — illness, exile or any other type of suffering — suffers due to his own deeds, as is written, "Evil shall slay the wicked" (Psalms 34:22; see *Likutey Moharan* I, 4:5).

This then is the general outline of the exile. By sinning, the Jews weakened their own kingdom of holiness and spirituality, and strengthened the kingdom of wickedness. This caused them to go into exile, i.e. to enter the realm of impurity and be oppressed by idolators. The more they sinned, the more the power of evil was able to divert them from their spiritual aspirations. And this evil that so tormented them was a direct result of their own deeds.

This explains why certain eras during the exile were especially difficult, such as the Crusades, the Spanish Inquisition, the blood libels, pogroms, and the Holocaust — while others were milder, such as the Golden Age in Spain, the pre-Chmelnitzky era in Poland (early 1600s) and some (though not many) quiet moments in between. God keeps very straight books and knows the exact score between good and evil. There are times when punishment for one generation can be deferred several generations (cf. *Bereishit Rabbah* 25:3; see also *Zohar* III, 190a). This is fair, because souls can be reincarnated and will receive their due judgment at a later date. Sometimes, based on the ascent or descent of the soul and its sparks of holiness, previous judgments are combined with current ones to bring about a greater rectification.

We shall now discuss why certain nations will benefit along with the Jews in the future, while others will be eradicated.

*

Esav and Yishmael

Adam contained within himself all the souls of humanity. The Godliness found in Adam's world was made available to everyone. This changed during Abraham's lifetime (1948-2123 after Creation).

As Abraham began spreading the Word of God, people became attracted to spirituality. But (as is common today), even those who were attracted to Godliness did not have the stamina to maintain their spiritual level. Those people and nations are represented by Esav and Yishmael, i.e. who were exposed to the path of spirituality of Abraham but rejected it.

In all fairness, it must be pointed out that there was no Torah available then to learn from, so people had to strive to maintain a level of spirituality learned from Abraham, without having the tools to continue on their own. But the time came when Moshe was about to present the Torah to the entire world. When that moment arrived, God first offered the Torah to all the nations (through their ministering angels) but they rejected it. Only the Jews chose to accept the Torah (see *Avodah Zarah* 2b; *Zohar* III, 192b). And it is in this that the Jews differ from all other nations.

We mentioned earlier a teaching of the Chofetz Chaim (above, Chapter 15). "At the time of the Revelation, there were many non-Jews who wanted to receive the Torah, but their compatriots refused. Throughout the generations, these souls eventually converted to Judaism. On the other hand, there were Jews then who did not wish to accept the Torah. These are the Jews who became apostates."

The Jews as a nation, having accepted the Torah, attained a greater affinity for study, understanding and practice of a spiritual life. This also gave them a greater responsibility to spread the teachings of spirituality — they are to be a "Light unto the Nations." The nations as a whole, having rejected the Torah, opted for a material and idolatrous life which distanced them from spirituality. And if those nations that did choose a spiritual way of life would examine their spiritual traditions, they would discover that they are rooted in Torah teachings, methods and ideals. Thus, a Jew who seeks Godliness will find the path to spirituality readily available to him. Any new revelation of God strengthens his faith and leads him to further ascend the spiritual ladder. Those of the nations who are now distant from God must work that much more before being able to receive that greater light of Godliness which filters into the world (see *Likutey Halakhot, Eruvei Techumin* 5:6).

In the Kabbalah, the knowledge of God that a person has already attained is called *or penimi*, "immanent light or intellect." The knowledge a person has yet to attain is called *or makif*, "transcendental light or intellect." As a person ascends the spiritual ladder, that which was transcendental becomes immanent, and a new and higher level of *makif* becomes available for him to attain. No matter how high a person ascends, there are always infinite levels of Godliness yet to be attained, for God is Infinite. In the future, Godliness will be revealed to everyone. Those Jews who have practiced Torah and mitzvot in this world will ascend to a higher level and will concurrently attain higher levels of *makifim*. The non-Jews will begin at that time to attain their own knowledge of God through performing the mitzvot. Because a person's standing in the Next World depends on their achievements in this world, the difference between the knowledge of the Jew and the non-Jew will be that the non-Jew will attain the level of the immanent intellect of the Jews in this world, while the Jews will attain the transcendental intellect (Likutey Moharan I, 21:15).

*

Sparks of holiness, as well as dross, exist everywhere in the world. Some of these sparks originated at the time of Creation, others were scattered later due to mankind's sins. Jews and non-Jews are also spread throughout the world and daily come into contact with these sparks of holiness. Those who search for spirituality attract the sparks, for everything seeks to attach itself to its source. Thus, both the Jew and the non-Jew who seek to do good act as magnets attracting sparks of holiness. And the sparks of holiness have their positive effect too. The Jew who seeks spirituality will experience a greater revelation of Godliness, for he will have experienced an illumination from the sparks. The non-Jew also experiences this illumination, and can also come closer to God on his level. Let us see how this works.

When the Jews were exiled, they came under the dominion of the nations. There are seventy principal nations, represented by Esav and Yishmael. The ideologies of these nations correspond to the concept of Adam's eating from the Tree of Knowledge of Good and Evil, for they wish to follow their own knowledge and thoughts rather than submit to the Torah, the Tree of Life (Likutey Halakhot, Yom Kippur 2:4). This is because Adam was exposed to a high spiritual way of life — the Tree of Life. Instead, he chose to partake of the fruit of the Tree of Knowledge, which is attached to the power of evil, and can therefore direct a person away from God. Thus the Jews, who accepted the Torah (spiritual direction, the Tree of Life), have currently become subjugated to the whims of ideologies which contain both good and evil (the Tree of Knowledge). When the Jew nevertheless persists in doing good, he elevates the good found within the nations. If the nations assist in this good, or even merely consent to allow the Jews to realize their quest for spirituality, then they gain a portion in that revealed Godliness. If the nations themselves do good, they also have a significant portion in spirituality.

If, on the other hand, they hinder the Jews from performing mitzvot, then it is as if they have "captured" and detained that good from being performed. However, that potential good remains alive in the form of sparks of holiness. When, at a later date, the sparks of holiness are revived through someone's good deeds, they integrate with the person who revived them. But, having been entrenched so long in evil surroundings, each spark was ensnared by evil with numerous bonds. It is impossible for the good to return by itself, due to the tight bonds with which it was fastened to evil. When the good, the sparks of holiness, begin their return to the realm of good, of holiness, some of the evil that was bound so tightly together with it will be uprooted with it and thereby converted to pure goodness. A good example of this is when non-Jews convert to Judaism and then perform those mitzvot which their ancestors previously withheld the Jews from performing. It is also true that when any Jew performs good deeds, it is effective in helping to return Jews who have wandered far from a Torah way of life, (see *Likutey Moharan* I, 17:6-7).

Those decrees that forced Jews to desecrate the Shabbat and forbid circumcision (*Me'ilah* 17a) are one example of the nations hindering spiritual growth. Almost every European nation did its share to terrorize and impoverish Jewish communities at one time or another throughout our history, preventing Torah study and performance of mitzvot. The Holocaust and the oppression of the Jews in the Soviet Union would be classic modern-day examples. These nations are from the dross of the broken vessels — that is, their strength comes from the potential evil that was formed at the time of Creation and which subsequently became powerful through the sins of mankind. Still, if these nations allow or assist the furthering of spirituality, then the good within — when it ascends back to its original level — will elevate that evil into the realm of good. If not, the good will ascend regardless, but those nations will be left without a spirit, without that spark of Godliness that sustains life.

And there is yet more to this issue.

*

"He has swallowed..."

We have seen how man's mission is to rectify the sparks of holiness spread throughout Creation. This is the purpose of Adam's exile from the Garden of Eden and of the exile, collectively and specifically, of each individual that came after him. The main reason for the original exile from Eden was a lack of faith on Adam's part. He didn't fulfill God's commandment, which is tantamount to idolatry (see Sanhedrin 56b). So, too, all subsequent exiles are due to a lack of faith, or indulgence in idolatry or other foolish pursuits, especially the pursuit of wealth (Likutey Halakhot, Eiruvei Techumin 5:14; see above, Part IV).

We have several tasks relating to the sparks of holiness. One is to elevate the good that is present in everything. Another is to subjugate and even destroy the powers that hold the sparks of holiness captive. In short, every iota of holiness must be redeemed, and every iota of dross must be removed so that it can no longer taint holiness. The Jew, rooted in the Torah and spirituality by virtue of having accepted the Torah (see Zohar III, 73a), will eventually return to God. But what of all those sparks of holiness which scattered as a result of the sin of Adam and which represent the other nations of the world? These sparks too will be rectified. But what of those nations that have cruelly oppressed the Jews?

Those oppressing nations stem from the dross, the extraneous matter of Creation, from which God formed the potential for evil. They also are in possession of, and govern, holy sparks — which have fallen under their dominion through mankind's sins. We have seen how God is life, and is therefore the life-force of all these sparks. Thus, as the sparks of holiness are elevated out of their hands, the vitality of those nations — hitherto nourished by the lifeforce in those sparks — is diminished. Eventually, as the sparks are rectified, their entire life-force abandons them, leaving them lifeless. This explains the demise of several major civilizations as the world knew them, even though life as an existence continues in those lands. This is because the sparks of holiness that were "captured" by those nations were elevated, leaving their ideologies — and idolatries — extinct. Examples are the Egyptian, Babylonian, Persian and Greek civilizations which once ruled large areas of the world. We can compare their reign of power to Adam's eating from the Tree of Knowledge. Their strength came from their ideologies, which contained some sparks of holiness which fell from the good contained within the Tree. When this good was eventually freed from bondage, their entire ideology disintegrated and their rule ceased.

This is the basic picture of the battle between good and evil, in which evil tries to entirely swallow up good, leaving no trace behind. This has been the pattern of history of the Jewish Nation — time after time, massacre after massacre, explusion after expulsion, the Jews were on the brink of destruction. But there were always tzaddikim, of the likes of Moshe, Mordekhai, Matityahu (of Chanukah fame), etc., who succeeded in inspiring the Jews to repent before it was too late. That repentance went a long way in elevating the sparks of holiness, for it caused Godliness to be revealed even in the darkest moments, in the darkest places. Eventually, the Jews were saved and each empire which sought their destruction was itself destroyed. (You'd think that some of the nations would learn from the others' mistakes, but for some reason they keep on trying!)

This is what is meant by our Sages' statement (Pesachim 87ba), "The Jews were only exiled among the nations so that non-Jews may convert." That is, because the Jews went into exile, where they began to search for and reveal Godliness, the illumination of the sparks of holiness extends even to those who are distant from God and people of the nations also begin to search for God. This leads to an open acceptance of God's Torah and His teachings as the true Word of God. This in turn leads to further revelations of Godliness, which bring yet others under the "Wings of the *Shekhinah*."

*

"He has swallowed wealth and will vomit it forth; God will remove [his catch] from his stomach."

Job 20:15

And as for those who are totally wicked, the verse states, "He has swallowed wealth and will vomit it forth; God will remove [his catch] from his stomach." This refers to Satan and the *kelipot*. They have swallowed up many, many sparks of holiness throughout the generations. As we have seen (above, Chapter 3), the forces of evil await the arrival of a great soul, thinking that they will be able to overpower and further entrap that soul in their clutches. The forces of evil have swallowed up many souls, concealing Godliness to a great degree. But the time will come when they will swallow "too much."

A person who eats too much can find the food getting stuck in his throat until he must vomit what he has swallowed. There are times when one begins to regurgitate and cannot stop — everything that has been swallowed previously is also brought up. Then comes the bile. If the person cannot stop himself from vomiting, his life is endangered. So too, the Evil One has swallowed innumerable sparks of holiness. But they are gradually being rectified. Still, he continues trying to swallow more and more. However, the time will come when he will have swallowed too much. A spark of holiness will be jammed in his throat and he will have to vomit forth his catch. When this happens, he will begin returning *all* the sparks of holiness he swallowed to the realm of holiness. These sparks of holiness will be manifest in the number of Jews returning to their faith and in the converts to Judaism. And he will continue to vomit, until he spits up every spark of holiness he has ever swallowed, until he has nothing left in his stomach. For every spark will be gathered and will reenter the realm of holiness. Then Satan will spit forth his very insides. Every spark of holiness he ever swallowed will be completely removed from him. When the last spark leaves, then nothing of the forces of evil will remain! (*Likutey Moharan* II, 8:3).

*

The good, the bad and the ugly

The good people, those who performed mitzvot and righteous deeds, will be rewarded with the treasures of spirituality and prosperity when Mashiach comes. The bad will be completely destroyed. What is yet unclear is the fate of the "ugly" — those sinners of Israel who have rebelled against God. As members of the Jewish faith who received the Torah at Sinai, they had an affinity for spirituality, yet they deliberately rejected it. Are they to be considered totally evil, to be done away with, or, because of their spiritual affinity, are they to be rectified?

An example would be Karl Heinrich Marx (1818-1883), a Jew who became an apostate. Not only did he reject Judaism, but his ideology — his fabricated deity — eventually caused unbearable suffering to millions of his fellow Jews, as well as to hundreds of millions of others. Is he entitled a proper rectification? The same would apply to Korach (who led a rebellion against Moshe and Torah law) and to Yerobam ben Nevat (who, as king of the Ten Tribes, introduced them to idolatry). (Yerobam's case is especially difficult for, as a result of his sins, Mashiach ben Yosef is destined to die; cf. *Tikkuney Zohar* p.146b; above, Chapter 4). He caused the one who could rectify him to die! And this would even apply to the likes of Barukh (Benedict) Spinoza (1632-1677; who taught heresy) and Moses Mendelssohn (1729-1786; whose "new" approach to Torah study culminated in the alienation of his adherents from Judaism and ultimately to massive assimilation). What will happen to their souls? The Mishnah addresses this problem.

> *All Jewry has a portion in the World to Come, as it is written* (Isaiah 60:21), *"Your nation, they are all tzaddikim... they will inherit the Land forever." But there are those who do not have a portion in the World to Come. They are: a) those who renounce the Resurrection; b) those who renounce Torah from Heaven; c) the heretics.*
>
> Sanhedrin 90a

The Mishnah debates several other cases, then continues: "Three kings and four laymen have no portion in the World to Come. The kings are: Yerobam, Ahab and Menasheh. The four laymen are: Bilaam, Doeg, Achitofel and Geichazi."

So there are cases of certain souls who have rebelled against God, who will never attain rectification. Or are there? For the Talmud later brings a different opinion from that of the Mishnah (Sanhedrin 104b): "Everyone will reach the World to Come — everyone, that is, except Bilaam." Why does the Talmud eliminate Bilaam? This follows from the fact that "every drop of good will eventually be rectified [but what is totally evil will be destroyed]" (see Likutey Halakhot, Birkhat HaReiach 4:45; cf. Shaar HaPesukim 188). Since these souls were at one time in their lives affiliated with good, then the good within them demands rectification, and they will receive it. However, because of the damage they did to themselves — and to others — their rectification will be very difficult.

A significant part of their punishment, which is actually an integral part of the rectification process, will be administered when Mashiach comes. At that time, people will be rewarded on a level commensurate with their accomplishments. Those who searched and yearned for spirituality will be rewarded at the highest levels. Those who were lax or distant from God will receive lesser rewards. Those who rejected God altogether will find themselves at the very bottom of the scale. Their punishment will be in seeing their compatriots luxuriating in God's splendor, while they are so very distant — a result of their own free choice. At the same time, however, their sins will be rectified and they will eventually also be able to bask in God's Glory, and to partake of the eternal good that will be bestowed upon mankind then.

*

Before concluding this chapter, we must point out one more significant factor in the rectification process concerning the concept of converts. Our Sages teach (Bereishit Rabbah 84:4), "The Patriarchs converted people to serve God." We find that Moshe Rabeinu took a "Mixed Multitude" of nations with him when he brought Israel out of Egypt. In the days of Mordekhai and Esther as well we find that many converted to the Jewish faith. Yet we also find that Jewish law discourages proselytization. As we have seen, everyone in the world is entitled, actually obligated, to serve God. As non-Jews advance in their awareness of and closeness to

God, they may feel inclined towards Judaism as the most effective means of expressing their newfound sense of nearness to the God of Israel. If this is their sincere wish, they are certainly permitted to convert to Judaism.

Moshe, Mordekhai and other tzaddikim were trying to establish God's Kingdom on earth. As such, their efforts were directed towards revealing Godliness more than towards converting people to Judaism. Nevertheless, as a result of the elevation of the sparks of holiness, more Godliness was revealed and actual conversions occurred. But as we see in the case of Moshe, the sparks were not yet ready for such an elevation. Therefore, the converts among the Mixed Multitude built the golden calf and regressed, never attaining their full rectification. The *Zohar* points out that the souls of the Mixed Multitude are constantly being reincarnated. They sought leadership — a false leader, idolatry, a golden calf; thus, in the generations preceding Mashiach's arrival, these souls will return in the form of "Jewish leaders" who are distant from God, and continue to distance people from God. Faith will become the main battle prior to Mashiach's arrival, for these "leaders" will cause much suffering to the Jewish People, testing their faith daily. Still, in the End of Days, evil will cease to exist and everyone — even they — will be rectified (see *Tikkuney Zohar* p.144a; *Zohar* III, 124b, 232b; see also *Likutey Halakhot, Geirim* 3:25).

*

And on that day (Isaiah 25:8), "He will destroy death (Satan and the forces of evil) permanently; and the Lord God will wipe away the tears from all faces; He will remove the insult of His people from the earth; for God has spoken it."

Speedily, in our days, Amen.

* * *

24

The Ingathering of the Exiles

Kibutz Galiyot, "The Ingathering of the Exiles": a most longed-for objective. For nearly two thousand years, Jews have prayed thrice daily to witness and participate in this supreme event. Today it is happening before our very eyes. If any of the signs of the messianic era are openly taking place, it is that of the Ingathering of the Exiles. Beginning in the late nineteenth century, people began flocking to the Holy Land, mostly from Eastern Europe. After the Holocaust, most of the survivors reached it shores and shortly afterwards, the Jews from the Arab countries made their way to the Land of Israel. Since the 1960s there has been a steady flow of Jews to the Holy Land from all parts of the globe.

In this chapter, we will discuss the idea of the Ingathering of the Exiles. To accommodate this discussion, we will review the idea of the gathering of the sparks of holiness from the perspective of judgment, humility and morality, which will make clearer the practical applications of the concepts (see Part III). We will deal with the ideas of the Torah of Atik and the necessity of wealth in revealing this Torah, as we will expand upon the idea of converts, and briefly discuss the unity of God — why He is known as the One God.

*

The rectification of Judgment

"*Shma Yisrael!* Hear Israel! The Lord our God, is [the] One God!" (Deuteronomy 6:4). This must be the most oft-quoted statement in Jewish history. It is recited (at least) twice daily. It is recited at the culmination of all prayers of repentance (e.g. Yom Kippur and Erev Rosh Chodesh). It is one of the first verses taught a Jewish child as he begins to speak, and it is recited at the bedside of one who is passing away. It has been on the lips of Jewish martyrs throughout the generations. For the Shma is our reaffirmation of faith; and at every point in our lives, faith must be reaffirmed and strengthened; for only with faith can we survive as a nation.

This faith is the faith in God: that He is the One God; that He created the world as a "something from an absolute nothing"; that He guides the world with Divine Providence; and that He is just and righteous, even when meting out punishment. This last idea is very crucial to our understanding of the eradication of evil from the earth, as well as the concept of the Ingathering of the Exiles. In the longest discourse presented in his works, Rebbe Nachman discusses these subjects as they apply to each person individually, as well as to the messianic era. We present here a freely translated synopsis of his lesson (*Likutey Moharan* II, 5).

> The most important thing in life is faith. Everyone must search himself constantly to judge whether his faith is intact, and to strengthen his faith continually. For if an individual falls from his faith, his prayers weaken and eventually become useless [because the person no longer believes that his prayers are potent]. He reaches a point of despair, where he feels nothing can help him.
>
> If a person has descended to the point of despair, then all that can save him are deep sincere cries from the heart, as in (Psalms 130:1), "*From the depths* I call out to God!" — from the "depths" of the heart. Then, with this deep cry, wondrous advice begins to flow from the heart, illuminating a person's path so that he realizes the proper course to take. This advice is in effect a strengthening of one's faith. When a person is in darkness he cannot see where to go. He requires faith to help him through the dark periods, until the light of day shines upon him. The same is true with advice. A person who doesn't know how to proceed in life is in "darkness." When he receives good advice, his life is lit up.

Rebbe Nachman continues his lesson:

> A weakening in one's faith causes a strengthening of false faiths, whereas rectifying one's faith weakens false faiths. Thus, when faith in God is

strengthened, even the gentile nations seek the One God. This attracts converts — of two categories. One category comprises non-Jews who recognize the One God and believe in Him, even if they do not actually convert. The other category comprises those who actually convert to Judaism. These converts — as they leave their previous faith and embrace Judaism — may bring arrogance and haughtiness into the Jewish Nation.

Rebbe Nachman explains this in the following manner: The verse states (Jeremiah 13:17), "My soul will weep in secret for Your pride." Our Sages teach (see Chagigah 5b), "What is this pride? This is the glory and royalty of God that is taken from the Jews and given over to the nations." [As we have seen, when the Jews sin, their spirituality comes under the dominion of the other nations. This is the transfer of God's Glory, His spiritual revelation, to the nations, where it becomes concealed.] Thus, the pride of God, His spiritual revelation, comes under the dominion of the nations. When non-Jews convert to Judaism, they bring with them what was "captive" under their sovereignty. Since this was God's Glory which they have corrupted, they bring with them this "glory" in the form of arrogance and haughtiness, which must then be subjugated to the Malkhut (Kingdom) of holiness.

> If the pride is converted into humility (a messianic trait; as above, Part III), then all is well. But if not, God forbid, then the "sword of arrogance" turns into a power play for domination of the Jews by unworthy leaders who seek to mete out judgment. But these "leaders" are not capable of meting out justice, because their natures are destructive. If, God forbid, these "leaders" retain control, they increase immorality in the Jewish Nation, especially the sin of masturbation. The only way to protect oneself from this immorality is through [accepting and following the advice of] the tzaddikim.

Rebbe Nachman goes on to describe the results of people attaining sexual morality, one of which is purified speech which can reach out to those very distant from God and revive their souls.

*

When reviewing this lesson, we can see the importance of strengthening faith, as it leads to the revelation of Godliness, even by those who might be very distant from God. But strengthening faith can also bring with it problems of its own. If faith is not channeled properly, a person comes to believe in any number of causes — worthy and unworthy — many of which lead to misplaced struggles for power "for the sake of saving mankind." This misdirected faith leads to arrogance, improper judgment and sexual immorality, eventually to masturbation, which further scatters the sparks of holiness into even deeper places throughout Creation.

Herein lies the focus of Mashiach's incredible powers — of humility, high morality, judgment and faith. He must strengthen faith and reveal it further; and he must do this while controlling immorality (eventually defeating it), because his job is to gather in the sparks of holiness rather than let them scatter further away. He must bring a true sense of justice to the world, thereby containing — and ultimately removing — false leaders who destroy their own people. For false leaders corrupt judgment, causing a dispersal of the sparks of holiness, rather than gathering them in. The rectification of justice is therefore of paramount importance because it leads to the ingathering of the sparks of holiness — the Ingathering of the Exiles. As pointed out in Rebbe Nachman's lesson, when people attain sexual morality and with it purified speech, they can reach out to those who are very distant from God and revive their souls. This engenders friendship and leads to peace — the peace that will reign in the Days of Mashiach.

*

The Godly image

Another aspect of the Ingathering of the Exiles is the unity and peace that will reign in the future. As with all messianic concepts, this will be miraculous, for when or where has mankind lived together in peace and perfect harmony, even for just a few moments... let alone an entire planet with such a diversification of races, cultures and ideologies? But this is the concept of the unification of the One God.

God is *Ein Sof*, the Infinite, as we have seen above (Part V). He began to create the world by diminishing His light in a series of tzimtzumim (contractions) until He completed this material universe. Since God created everything through a series of diminishing revelations of Himself, then every part of Creation contains a spark of Godliness within it. Without that minute spark of Godliness, nothing could exist.

Thus, every part of Creation destined for rectification — containing even only the tiniest iota of Godliness — is an integral part of God and therefore *must* eventually be returned to Him. This idea lies behind the very first mitzvah of the Torah (Genesis 1:28), "Be fruitful and multiply." It is also why this mitzvah bears the brunt of a most powerful evil inclination, the very cause of the spread of immorality prior to Mashiach's arrival. (This will be explained shortly.)

The ARI writes that the dispersal of the sparks of holiness caused a diminishing of the manifestation of Godliness in the world. Now that these sparks have spread out so far and wide, they cannot be rectified all at once. This is because all souls were included in Adam, the First Man. All these souls must now participate in the purification process. The process must therefore be an ongoing one, from generation to generation, until the sparks are sufficiently rectified to be restored to their originally intended place within the scheme of Creation. When Mashiach arrives, he will complete the rectification process (Shaar Maamarei Rashbi pp.168-169). This is the meaning of (Ecclesiastes 1:4), "A generation passes away and a generation comes." Our Sages consider the 600,000 Jews who left Egypt an entire generation, and they comment (Kohelet Rabbah 1:5), "Each day 600,000 die and 600,000 are born." That is, each day it is as if a whole new generation has been born, indicating that *each* day an entirely new rectification is to be made. Thus, each day has its unique *individualized* rectification, totally unlike those before or after it. This is also why repentance helps at *all* times. By accepting that each moment is completely *new*, a person can renew his individual sparks of holiness and rectify them at any time. Further, if the rectification applies daily to each person, then it certainly applies to each generation. This is why one must try to bring succeeding generations into being, to carry on the rectification of the sparks of holiness (Likutey Halakhot, Shechitah 4:3). And this is why the evil inclination exerts such a powerful counterforce to corrupt those succeeding generations.

> **The small one shall be a thousand; and the young one a powerful nation; I, God, will hasten it [the Redemption] in its time.**
>
> Isaiah 60:22

This is also the reason for the mitzvah of having children. Our Sages teach (Yevamot 64b), "Whoever refrains from procreation is regarded as if he had commited murder and diminished the Godly image." Imagine: Not having children is tantamount to murder! The simple explanation of this passage is that by not procreating, one diminishes the number of souls that should be in the world at any particular time. This is effectively equivalent to murder, which diminishes life on the planet. Furthermore, as we have seen, each person is, as it were, an extension of God, created in the image of God. One who procreates is bringing forth a soul through which a rectification can be made. One who refrains from having children is diminishing the Godly image, for he is restricting that portion of Godliness that would otherwise be revealed in the world. Thus, every soul born is another fraction of holiness added to the Godly image that will be manifest in the world when Mashiach arrives (see *Likutey Moharan* II, 37). Only when this image is complete will we be able to actually see the Godly image — i.e. the revelation of Godliness. And this is one of the main reasons behind the Torah's commandment to have children. Since Adam spread the sparks throughout Creation, the rectification of these sparks is an ongoing process and cannot be completed in one generation. Having children allows the continuation of the rectification process (see *Likutey Halakhot, Shvuot* 2:26).

This is why, today, in the generations preceding Mashiach, there is much ado about having children, contraception, abortions, and so on. This is also why sexual immorality has grown to astronomical proportions. As the time for the final rectification looms over the horizon, the evil inclination realizes that its time is running out. Considering it was man's sins — mostly sexually related, especially that of spilling seed — which caused the *dissemination* of the sparks of holiness deeper into the realm of impurity to begin with, the *kelipot* are now seeking to entrap these sparks further. This explains today's obsession with "family planning," abortions and perverted sexual acts, each in its own way tantamount to murder. Through these sins, the sparks of holiness are either detained from reaching the world in human form — the Godly image — for rectification, or they are further dispersed throughout the world by sin.

Conversely, moral purity is a powerful messianic trait. Those who attempt to procreate in a family structure, through marriage and with respect towards their spouses, are actively engaged in bringing the Mashiach, and in furthering their own rectification, as well as that of the world. They rectify and elevate the sparks of holiness, revealing the Unity of God. This is a paradox in that the greater number of people that exist there is a greater disparity of thought and ideologies. Yet, this itself reveals the greatness of God, for all those vast numbers of people, will *all* recognize the One God and join together to serve Him in unison. Thus, the more people there are who ultimately recognize Him, the greater will be His glory. This is the meaning of, "The small one shall be a thousand; and the young one a powerful nation..." For the larger the number of people who recognize God, each from his own, unique perspective, the greater the revelation of God's glory. As the world's population grows, the glory of God is revealed more (Likutey Halakhot, Prikah U'Te'inah 4).

*

Torah and the Godly image

Furthermore, the Torah is called "Man," as in (Numbers 19:14), "This is the Torah, Man..." The 613 mitzvot of the Torah, with its 248 positive commandments and its 365 prohibitory commandments, parallel the human body, which has 248 limbs and 365 sinews and ligaments (Makot 23b; see Anatomy of the Soul, Part 8). Each person has a portion in Torah. Thus, an increase in population automatically results in additional Torah revelations, that is, the Oral Law is expanded further complementing the Written Law (as above, Chapter 10), and our knowledge about God is thereby increased. The more Torah knowledge that is disclosed, the more the

Torah of Atik, the Daat of the Future, is revealed in the present (see *Likutey Halakhot, Sukkah* 7:10).

This also explains the difficulty one currently has while studying Talmud in order to ascertain the law. The *Talmud Babli* (Babylonian Talmud) is called thus because rulings on numerous (seemingly unrelated) matters are mixed (*belulah* throughout its pages (Sanhedrin 24a). Laws of ritual impurity can be found in the middle of the laws of Shabbat and those of blessings can be discussed where the Talmud debates the law of tithes. To be able to locate a clear, practicable set of laws is virtually impossible without the broadest possible knowledge of all aspects of Torah law. One of the basic reasons for the irregular structure of the Talmud was to prevent those unfamiliar with the entire Talmud from issuing rulings. This is similar to the judicial systems of most countries which insist upon a comprehensive and systematic study of their laws before permitting a legal advisor or counselor to practice.

But there is another reason for the seemingly random arrangement of the Talmud. As we have mentioned, the Torah is compared to man. While man is in exile, his sparks of holiness are spread out throughout Creation. So, too, the laws of Torah are very widespread. As the rectification of the sparks of holiness proceeds, the Torah itself begins to "be gathered together." This is why the *Rishonim* (early codifiers) began collecting the laws and arranging them according to topics, as we see for example in Maimonides' *Mishneh Torah* and Rabbi Yoseph Karo's *Shulchan Arukh*. In today's Torah world, many works are being published which clarify Torah law and lore even to the layman, and this leads to the "gathering together" of the Torah itself.

*

Rebbe Nachman once remarked (*Aveneha Barzel* p.21, #4), "A person should have as many children as possible — no matter how they turn out. For when Mashiach comes, he will rectify everyone and all their antecedents, every single one, all the way back to Adam!" Reb Noson adds (*Likutey Halakhot, Shabbat* 6:23), "Who knows? Maybe the person will have offspring who are so righteous that they themselves can rectify their own ancestors."

And as for ourselves, who knows? Any of us might, just might, be the parent of the Mashiach! (see above, Chapter 3).

*

Amalek

There is yet another aspect of the Ingathering of the Exiles relating to the sparks of holiness. We mentioned that when the sparks fell, they descended into every level of Creation. By performing mitzvot, man can elevate those sparks associated with himself. But how are the sparks in other levels of Creation elevated? How does the rectification actually work, causing all the sparks, everywhere, to be gathered in?

The ARI explains that there are four general levels of life on our planet. In ascending order, they are: mineral, plant, animal, and human. Each of these levels contains sparks of holiness which must be elevated back to their highest source.

The mineral element of earth, or those sparks contained in the mineral domain, are elevated by aiding the growth of vegetation. As the vegetation draws its nourishment from the minerals (in the soil), the sparks buried within the mineral are elevated to the level of plants. When animals now eat these plants, the sparks contained within them are elevated to the next highest level. When the animal is consumed by man, the sparks of holiness that give it life are elevated to the level of man. In all these cases, God, Who oversees everything with Divine Providence, will direct each spark into a channel where it can receive rectification. Thus, a forlorn spark lying somewhere in the mineral domain can be elevated by stages until a man is ready to consume it. But will each man see that the food was prepared in a kosher manner? Will he recite the proper blessing? The ultimate rectification of the elevated spark depends upon man's deeds.

And what about nonkosher animals that cannot be eaten? What about mineral substances that cannot be transformed into food? Are the sparks found there to be condemned forever? This cannot be, for everything will ultimately receive its rectification. But, as explained above, all sparks of holiness are parts of the human soul. Just as with the Ingathering of the Exiles, when all Jews will be drawn together to the Holy Land, the soul of each individual will be perfected when Mashiach comes. All its "parts" will be drawn together. But how?

The answer is through business and trading, buying and selling. This is another messianic concept that has been perverted today into the pursuit of wealth. Rebbe Nachman taught:

> There is a great beauty in coins — gold, silver, copper... — for these minerals contain a supernal beauty. Their supernal beauty lies in their being composed of holy sparks which radiate continually [according to the Sefirah to which each corresponds]. Those who are wise will look "inside the money" and will see therein the beauty of God and the revelation of the Malkhut of holiness. But this beauty can be misleading and can direct a person towards avarice. This strengthens the kingdom of impurity.
>
> The verse states (Ecclesiastes 2:26), "Surely He gives to a man that which is good in His sight, wisdom, knowledge and joy; but to the sinner He gave the task of gathering and amassing..." The Talmud comments (Megilah 10b), "'Surely He gives to a man' — this refers to Mordekhai. 'Good' — this refers to Torah. 'To the sinner' — this refers to Haman." This teaches us that Haman, a descendant of Amalek, corresponds to the evil attribute of avarice, gathering and amassing wealth. Thus the sinner, Amalek, will seek to gather the sparks of holiness that are located within the money, in order to swallow them up. However, the Malkhut of holiness will gather the sparks of holiness through Chokhmah and Daat and will elevate them. Not only will these sparks attain rectification, but they will even be transformed into Torah! (Likutey Moharan I, 56:5).

As we have seen, the concepts of "Man" and "Torah" are synonymous on certain levels. Thus, when the sparks of holiness found in every bit of matter in the world are elevated, they are unified with their source, their soul, and can even be transformed into Torah. This is why we see continual trade between people, countries and continents. People bring goods from one part of the globe to another, carrying with them the sparks of holiness that must now be elevated by a person in another place.

For this reason, many items continually change hands. This explains why certain items, such as family heirlooms, can remain in one family's possession for centuries, and are then given away or sold to another person, group or organization; all because the moment for the elevation of those sparks has come and it is time for them to move onward to a new rectification. Eventually a good deed is performed with the money received or perhaps even with the goods themselves (such as the mitzvah of hospitality where inanimate items — beds, linens and dishes, etc. — are used while honoring a guest).

But rectification occurs only when people conduct themselves honorably and honestly in business. If not, they are further dispersing the sparks, as we have seen in the case of sexual sins, for the result is the same (as can be seen in the Generation of the Flood, which was steeped in idolatry, immorality and theft; see Rashi, Genesis 6:11). Amalek, symbolizing avarice, has always been an unprincipled enemy of holiness. He tried to "gather" whatever holiness he could, by lying, cheating, stealing and so on. Those of other nations who break their lust for wealth will merit the revelation of the Malkhut of holiness. This will be at the time of the Ingathering of the Exiles, for the sparks of holiness will all be gathered and rectified, opening the way for Mashiach to come. Amalek, on the other hand, is completely evil. The only good he might possibly contain is that infinitesimal spark of Godliness that sustains him. When Mashiach comes, that spark will depart, and nothing will be left of Amalek. This is the meaning of the Torah's injunction (Deuteronomy 25:17-19) to leave no remembrance of Amalek. When Mashiach comes, every iota of good must be elevated, and then nothing will remain of Amalek.

We can understand this point better if we recall that the Torah calls Amalek (Numbers 24:20), "*Reishit Goyim*, the first or foremost of the nations." The word *reishit* also translates as "head," indicating that Amalek's goal is honor and the wealth that accompanies it, to be first and at the head of whatever is taking place. That is, the evil forces represented by Amalek correspond to haughtiness and false leadership which, as we have seen (above, Chapters 14-15), are a major impediment to Mashiach and messianic ideals (see *Likutey Halakhot, Orlah* 5:16).

In addition, we find that (Exodus 17:16), "God's battle with Amalek lasts from generation to generation." As seen above, "generation to generation" indicates the rectifications possible each and every day. This is because these rectifications cannot be completed in one day. Since Amalek represents the evil that delays the rectification, God's battle with him is in each generation. And this is yet another reason that having offspring is so important — because the more children born, the greater the power of the generation to battle Amalek's evil (cf. *Likutey Halakhot, Shechitah* 4:7).

*

This is also why great wealth will be made available to everyone in the future. "Just as a basic livelihood is necessary for a basic level of Torah study, great wealth is necessary for the study of the Torah of Atik" (*Likutey Moharan* I, 60:1; see above, Chapter 14). This wealth will be the outcome of the gathering of the sparks of holiness. As we have just seen, when the sparks contained within money are gathered together, they are transformed into Torah teachings. Thus, the great wealth of the future will be the catalyst for the revelation of the Torah of Atik (see *Likutey Halakhot, Rosh Chodesh* 3:11).

The sparks were scattered even among inanimate objects, and must be rectified through business, manufacturing and trading, because Adam ate from the Tree of Knowledge. Adam was required to fulfill God's commandment not to eat from the Tree. This is an aspect of Torah. He should also have prayed... (see Rashi, Genesis 2:5). Adam was banished from the Garden of Eden because he blemished his obligation of Torah and prayer. Thus, Adam's sin was a blemish of Torah and prayer. Therefore, instead of benefiting from the Garden of Eden, i.e. living a spiritual life without work, Adam was cursed with the need for material pursuits (Genesis 3:17-19), "You shall eat with sadness, by the sweat of your brow..." Therefore, the sparks of holiness must now be elevated through business. But, even in the here-and-now, one who seeks a life of spirituality removes from himself the curse of the need for material pursuits. He can benefit

The Ingathering of the Exiles / 267

from Torah and prayer, and feel a taste of the spiritual life that will materialize when Mashiach comes (see *Likutey Halakhot, Rosh Chodesh* 5:33).

Reb Noson adds that this is why the verse states (Zekhariah 13:9), "And I will refine them as silver is refined; and I will purify them as gold is purified…" The main test of a person is how he relates to money and wealth. One who breaks his lust for wealth merits to see Divine Providence clearly operating in his life. Then he can elevate the sparks of holiness found within money to the level of the Torah of Atik for, when that Torah is revealed, Divine Providence will be made clear to all (*Likutey Halakhot, Shavuot* 1:5).

Speedily, in our days, Amen.

* * *

25

The Holy Land

The end of the exile is fast approaching. The entire Jewish people are destined to return to the Land of Israel. The Holy Land itself is more productive today than it has been for centuries, and Jerusalem, its capital city, is experiencing growth and development as never before. We are fortunate to witness the beginnings of the messianic era with our own eyes — as the Biblical prophecies are being fulfilled.

But we are faced with several questions that require clarification. As is apparent from the Prophets, the focal point of the world in the messianic era will be the Holy Land, the focal point of the Holy Land will be Jerusalem and the focal point of Jerusalem will be the Holy Temple. Does that mean that everyone will come to live in the Holy Land? If so, what will happen to the rest of the earth? Will people live elsewhere? It is taught (*Likutey Moharan* II, 56), "when a person has a heart, his location is of no consequence." This is because Godliness is experienced in one's heart so that, no matter where one is, one can always find God. So what is the necessity of a "Holy Land"? Yet who would not want to live in the Holy Land, since that seems to be where the "action" will be taking place? Therefore, we shall first define the borders of the Holy Land according to Biblical description.

> Author's note: For clarity's sake, the author is citing political borders as they exist at the time of this writing in 1995 — with or without "ineffective peace treaties." However, the author is also taking the liberty of *not* becoming involved in political borders. We reiterate that Mashiach will conquer the world without waging war (see above, Chapter

5). Therefore, the borders imposed by Divine decree will be agreed upon by all parties involved, and will become effective when true peace reigns.]

*

The Biblical borders

> *On that day, God made a covenant with Abram saying, "To your descendants I have given this land, from the River of Egypt* (Wadi el Arish or the Nile) *to the great river, the Euphrates. [This land includes that occupied by] the Keini, the Kenizi and the Kadmoni* [Edom, Moab and Amon]. *The Chiti, the Prizi, the Refaim, the Emori, the Canaani, the Girgashi and the Yevusi.*
>
> Genesis 15:18-21

When God revealed the future exiles to Abraham at the Covenant of the Halves, He also promised him that the period of exile would come to an end. The land of the ten nations (mentioned in the above quote), which the Jews will inherit after their sojourn in exile, refers to the lands known today as Israel, Jordan, Lebanon and Syria northeast to the Euphrates River (probably including a small area of modern day Iraq). This is God's promise and, as Rashi comments (*loc. cit.*), "God's saying it is as if it is already done."

One might then have expected that the area described should have belonged to the People of Israel since they entered the Land. This would have been about three times what they actually received. But it wasn't. The land described belonged to ten nations and the Jews were given land that belonged only to seven nations: the area which is found mostly in the Israel of today. The northern part of Jordan was part of the Holy Land of biblical times; however the lands of Edom, Moab and Amon (southern Jordan) were never inhabited by the Israelites, and that land will become part of the Holy Land only in the future, when Mashiach comes (see Rashi, Genesis 15:19).

The reason for this is based on Kabbalistic teachings that time and space are based on a system of "seven," corresponding to the seven lower Sefirot (see above, Chapters 17-18). When Mashiach comes, Godliness will be revealed on a much higher level and will extend up to Keter, thus comprising a full revelation of all Ten Sefirot. Thus, the Jews' portion of holiness in this world corresponds to the seven Sefirot while the future portion of holiness corresponds to all ten levels. Furthermore, everything in this world is currently operating through Divine Providence in a concealed manner, through nature. In the Days of Mashiach, Divine Providence will be revealed and a miracle-filled lifestyle will be introduced. This is reflected through the higher sefirot, which are above the concepts of time and space. Hence, the Land of Israel, which is where Divine Providence will first be revealed, will correspond to the lands of the ten nations, enumerated in the verse cited from Genesis (see Likutey Moharan II, 8:10).

The biblical borders place Jerusalem in the center of the Holy Land. It was therefore the focal point of the Jewish Nation and the location of the Holy Temple. The Jerusalem of the future will also have a Temple which will be the focal point — as the House of Prayer — not only for the Jews, but for all the nations (as above, Chapter 5). Thus, everyone will agree on the centrality of Jerusalem as regards worshiping God, and they will also agree to the Jews' right to the Holy Land, whatever its borders may be. The acceptance will be unanimous, with neither a United Nations Security Council vote nor General Assembly opposition (or abstention), for evil will be destroyed and spirituality will reign. Total peace will reign. This brings us to some very interesting Talmudic teachings, which are the basis for a discussion of the Holy Land vis-à-vis the remainder of the world.

*

Future borders

In the future, Jerusalem will extend to the full area of the Holy Land. The Holy Land will extend and fill the entire world!
Yalkut Shimoni #503

When considering borders, we have also to bear in mind their significance regarding the nations. Are there to be no individual nations in the days of Mashiach? Is everyone to be one "homogeneous family?" Will there be no division of peoples according to ancestry? The answers are difficult to come by, living as we do without access to a crystal ball.

But there are sufficient teachings that can help us imagine what will take place.

> There was a stone in the Temple, in the Holy of Holies, that was called the *Even SheTiyah*. It was so called because from it the entire world *huShTat* — was founded (Yoma 54b).

When God created the material world, He first formed the *Even Shetiyah*. From this stone, he drew forth the land and everything in it. The entire world, in all its diversity, is rooted in the *Even Shetiyah* and connected to it through a system of "veins and arteries" that extend from the *Even Shetiyah*. Taking agriculture as an example, we find lands suitable for growing wheat, others better suited for corn, still others for beans, potatoes and so on. The various types of land are all rooted in the *Even Shetiyah* (Kohelet Rabbah 2:7; see also Rashi, Ecclesiastes 2:5). The same applies to natural resources, such as gold and silver, gas and oil.

The reason for these "veins and arteries" is that everything in this world is made with a *tzimtzum* (constriction) in order to receive God's light (above, Chapters 17-18). Thus, everything was defined according to its purpose, to provide for the needs of mankind. And everything in this world also contains sparks of holiness that require rectification. But as the sparks are elevated, the constrictions begin to ease, and greater revelations of Godliness take place. Instead of a certain plot of earth being suitable for only wheat, it can now be planted with several grains. Instead of just gold and silver, these "veins" can carry diamonds and emeralds too. The constrictions of nature are being nullified, for great Daat and Divine Providence — which are above the forces of nature — are becoming revealed.

The same applies to borders that currently exist between countries. Borders are a result of humanity being at odds with each other (even if not at war). Every nation is different, with a distinct culture. But this is all due to the constrictions and restrictions within which *they* have chosen to live. We have seen that the mitzvot, the culture of the Jewish people, are also constrictions (see Chapter 7). Now, as mankind is being elevated to higher levels through its spiritual search and are exposed more to God, they will put an end to the restrictions of their distinctive cultures. The same will apply to their distinctive borders, which will become unnecessary.

We see evidence of this in the relatively new phenomenon of open borders between countries. Some of these borders have been closed and heavily guarded for many decades. This is a messianic sign. The European Community now has few restrictions of travel between member nations. North America has long had several open borders, while those of the Eastern European countries are rapidly changing and opening as never before. And all this relates to the teaching that the Holy Land will extend to the entire world.

As more people seek higher levels of spirituality, the constrictions of materialism are removed. The sparks of holiness are elevated, causing a revelation of Godliness throughout the world. The Holy Land is distinct in that it was allocated ten levels of holiness (Keilim 1:6-9). There are seventy primary nations, and each was allocated its own territory. But as the nations are extricated from their material constrictions, their recognition of Godliness is heightened. This helps remove all constrictions — all borders. Everything and everyone becomes united under the banner of God and holiness. There is no need for borders (see Likutey Halakhot, Pikadon 5:19).

The tearing down of borders represents peace. People "confined" to certain limitations in travel or relationships are lacking total peace. Thus, materialism and strife are synonymous, while spirituality and peace are likewise similar. For spirituality is above the limitations of time and space. The greater the level of spirituality, the greater the degree of peace. Eventually, Universal Peace will be attained in Mashiach's Day (see Likutey Halakhot, Sefer Torah 3:11).

Each person has his own Daat, his own "mental border" within which he can assess his understanding of Godliness. This is reflected in each and every Jew who has a portion in the Holy Land, within the borders of holiness. Acquiring one's future portion in the Holy Land depends on how he is presently building his Daat (Likutey Halakhot, Shutafim b'karka 5:15-16).

This is also the reason why the Holy Land will expand to encompass the entire world. Since everyone will be seeking Godliness and spirituality will be revealed to all, every place will become holy. We have seen that every person will attain spiritual revelations according to his level. The same is true about the the entire world as opposed to the Holy Land. Since the Holy Land was always holy, it will continue to have a greater level of holiness and spirituality than the rest of the world.

Concerning the Holy Land, it is written (Deuteronomy 11:12), "The Land which God observes; the eyes of God are *always* upon it." This verse refers to the Divine Providence which is manifest in the Holy Land, since God *observes* the land (i.e. He "looks over it" with Divine Providence). Wisdom is compared to sight (i.e. one's "eyes are opened"). Since God is constantly observing the Holy Land, He is drawing His sight — His wisdom — into that land. This is what makes the Holy Land holy! This is why our Sages teach (Bava Batra 158b), "The air of the Holy Land makes one wise," for it contains Godly wisdom (Likutey Moharan II, 40). The same will apply to all lands in the future, when Godliness is revealed to all.

As for the present, lest a person think that spirituality is beyond him unless he lives in the Holy Land, Rebbe Nachman taught (Likutey Moharan I, 61:2), "Wherever people become aware of God and perform mitzvot, no matter where it is, that place assumes an aspect of the Holy Land!"

*

It remains to be explained what the "borders" of the Holy Land will be in the future, since Godliness will be revealed all over the world and the Holy Land will extend to encompass the entire earth. We can clarify this with our Sages' teaching (Keilim 1:6-9), "The Land of Israel was allocated ten levels of holiness." These ten levels of holiness relate mostly to the laws of specific items permitted in the Temple, as well as to the laws of purity. Only the first two levels apply outside the city of Jerusalem, the remainder apply to Jerusalem and more specifically to the Temple Mount and the Temple itself. Since the Torah is eternal, the same laws that apply today to the Land of Israel will most probably apply to the extended borders of the Holy Land given to Abraham, "From the River of Egypt to the

Euphrates." It thus appears that these boundaries will define the Land of Israel, where the Jews will reside.

However, the Prophet Ezekiel defines a Holy Land with smaller boundaries than the land of the ten nations (Ezekiel 47:13-20). The boundaries he delineates encompass the area from the Mediterranean Sea to the Damascus area as the northern border, the Jordan River to the Dead Sea as the eastern border (Jordan will not be part of the Holy Land at all) and from the southern tip of the Dead Sea to the Mediterranean Sea as the southern border. These borders are somewhat similar to those of the Holy Land that Moshe describes (Numbers 34:1-12). Ezekiel's vision also sees the Holy Land divided into twelve strips — west to east — one for each tribe, with Jerusalem in the center (Ezekiel 48).

As quoted earlier from the Rambam (Chapter 2), none of the prophecies will be clear until Mashiach himself comes and clarifies them for us. Thus, we are again left in the dark as to the verified positions of the boundaries of the Holy Land. The author suggests that the smaller boundaries will be the borders when Mashiach is revealed. As he conquers the world, through his extraordinary power of prayer, the borders of the Holy Land will automatically expand to include the land of the ten nations and subsequently, the entire planet.

Still, given their position of leadership in a spiritual world, the Jews will be in the "center of the action" where Godliness will be revealed, so that they can fulfill their obligation of being "a light unto the nations." Being "central" means being near the Holy Temple, to which people will be attracted in order to attain greater revelations of Daat. Thus, whatever the boundaries of the Holy Land may be in the future, that is where the Jews will be gathered.

*

Why a Holy Land?

Realizing the significance of the Holy Land, especially as it relates to the messianic concepts, will help us understand why so much emphasis is placed upon it.

In the Kabbalah, Heaven corresponds to the higher sefirot while the earth corresponds to Malkhut. It is the "heavens" (i.e. the upper levels) which give forth the bounty, while the earth receives it. The earth, as the manifestation of Malkhut, is in turn able to nourish its inhabitants, who can then return this "bounty" to God, through worshiping Him. (This is explained above, Part V).

As we have seen, Malkhut is the Sefirah which is the point of man's interaction with God. As such, there has to be a place within the Sefirah of Malkhut where Godliness can be perceived, in order for man to realize that he is interacting with God. This place is the Land of Israel with its various levels of holiness, and more specifically the Temple, for that is where God's *Shekhinah* (Divine Presence) was, and is to be, openly revealed. Simply put, from the time of the Creation, the Holy Land was chosen as the place where Godliness was to be manifest. Thus, the earth as a whole corresponds to Malkhut, for it is man, who dwells on the earth, who has to recognize God's Kingdom and serve Him. More specifically, the Holy Land is the focus of Malkhut, for that is where the Malkhut of God is evident.

The Torah thus begins with (Genesis 1:1), "In the beginning, God created the heavens and the earth." Rashi comments that the Torah, as the body of our laws, should have begun with the first mitzvah. The reason the Torah begins with the account of Creation is to demonstrate clearly to all that God created the earth and it is in His hands to partition it as He sees fit. It was the Land of Israel which He apportioned for holiness and for the property of the Jewish Nation. We see then that the Holy Land was already assigned its status from the time of Creation, much the same as Mashiach was chosen for his mission before life on earth even began. The mission of the Holy Land is to be *the* place where Godliness can best be manifest.

> *I will establish My covenant between Me and you and your seed... to be your God... And I will give you and your seed this land that you dwell upon... and I will be their God.*
> Genesis 17:7-8

The earliest mention of the Holy Land begins with Abraham, when God commands him (Genesis 12:1), "Go to the Land..." In the Holy Land, the first commandment God gave Abraham was the Covenant of Circumcision, which was to make the Jews a nation bound to God forever. In the account of the commandment of the covenant with Abraham, we find that the Holy Land was promised to his descendants at that time. We see then that circumcision is inextricably bound with the Holy Land. In the holy writings, reference to the mitzvah of circumcision generally indicates morality and purity of sexual conduct. Thus, the Holy Land is bound together with purity of deed, which is as much a messianic concept as the return to the Holy Land itself.

Another aspect of the Holy Land is prayer, specifically prayer with concentration and a clear mind. In one of his discourses, Rebbe Nachman teaches that the *maBuL* (the Flood), is similar to *bilBuL* (confusion). That is, when a person attempts to pray, he is inundated with various thoughts that overwhelm him and disturb his prayers. The Talmud tells us (Zevachim 113a) that "The Holy Land was not touched by the Flood." This teaches us that by entering the "Holy Land" — i.e. by attaining purity of mind — a person has rectified his mind and can avoid the "floodwaters" that try to overwhelm him (Likutey Moharan I, 44). When we remember that prayer is Mashiach's main weapon — and that every person's prayer becomes an integral part of Mashiach's mission (above, Chapter 5) — we can better appreciate the concept of a Holy Land.

In addition, to guarantee that there will never be another Flood in the world, God made the *keshet*, the rainbow, which is also referred to as a Covenant (Genesis 9:13; see above, Chapter 7). This also connects the concept of the Covenant with that of prayer and the Holy Land, for guarding one's covenant (i.e. sexual purity) is a sign that one will not be overwhelmed by a "flood of confusing thoughts." This person can pray properly. Likewise, the covenant is bound with the Holy Land. And the list continues. Rebbe Nachman taught:

> The main reason for the exile is a lack of faith. Faith is synonymous with prayer as in (Exodus 17:12, see Rashi) "His hands were faith..." — "spread out

in prayer." We also find that faith and the Holy Land are connected as in (Psalms 37:3) "Dwell in the Land and cultivate faith." It is also associated with miracles. The reason for this is that one who prays is one who knows that a more Powerful Force than nature exists. This person prays to God to transcend nature and reveal Divine Providence, i.e. miracles (*Likutey Moharan* I, 7:1).

We see then that prayer, faith, miracles and the Holy Land are all interconnected. Conversely, the continued exile results from and indicates a lack of faith and of prayer, a deficiency in the regard one has for the Holy Land. Therefore, the depths that one has sunk to in relationship to one's prayers, faith and the Holy Land determines how deep one's exile will be (*Likutey Moharan* I, 9:6).

*

Returning to the Land

We have seen that sparks of holiness are found in inanimate objects, and that this is why trading plays an important part in our lives (above, Chapter 24). For this same reason the Holy Land was once called the "Land of Canaan." Canaan can also mean "merchant" as in (Hoshea 12:8) "Canaan, the balances of deceit are in his hands." Many, many sparks of holiness were dispersed due to "Canaan's" deceitful business practices. It wasn't until the Jews entered the Holy Land that they were able to elevate those sparks. But their subsequent sins also caused a descent of the sparks. We find therefore that the holiness of the Land of Israel is not readily apparent nowadays because of the descent and concealment of the sparks of holiness. But whenever honesty (i.e. the attribute of truth) in business is observed sparks are elevated. Thus, eventually there will be no need for business or trading, for "Canaan" (merchant) will be transformed into the "Holy Land," where Divine Providence is revealed, and everything is miraculous (*Likutey Moharan* I, 14:12).

It is interesting to note that, in every generation since the beginning of the current exile, Jews made brief visits to the Holy Land. Many never intended staying and ended up returning to the Diaspora, but a minority did remain. All of this was part of the ongoing process of rectifying the sparks of holiness (by bringing them from outside the Land of Israel) and elevating them to their rightful stature of holiness in the Holy Land. But since this rectification is an ongoing process, most of those who ascended to the Holy Land in previous generations had to return to the Diaspora. Only when Mashiach comes will everyone be able to remain in the Land (Likutey Halakhot, Arvit 4:33). Thus, today, as we see more and more Jews coming to live in the Land of Israel, their intention with regard to their responsibility to bring Mashiach should be to "gather their sparks" — children and possessions — and bring them to the Holy Land. If this is not feasible, they visit the Holy Land as often as possible, for this in itself is an aspect of gathering the sparks and elevating them, thus hastening the arrival of the Mashiach.

Rebbe Nachman also taught that the revelation of the holiness of the Holy Land will manifest itself in the great peace that will spread throughout the world in the Days of Mashiach. Today, poverty is widespread due mainly to strife for "One argument can delay one hundred incomes!" Our Sages teach (cf. Pesachim 50a), "Canaan connotes, CaN ANi — here is an impoverished one." The Holy Land is referred to both as "the Land" and as "the Land of Canaan." It is thus written (Genesis 13:7), "There was an argument between the shepherds of Abraham and Lot, and the Canaanites then dwelt in the Land." This means that since there was an argument, i.e. strife, between the shepherds, that "the Canaanites dwelt in the Land..." there was poverty. But when Mashiach comes, peace will reign and strife will be forgotten. Then, the land will be "the Land," as in (Psalms 67:7), "The *Land* gives forth its fruits" — which connotes wealth and good health (Likutey Moharan I, 277).

> **Yearn for God and keep His way; He will then elevate you to inherit the Land; and you will behold the destruction of the wicked.**
>
> Psalms 37:34

We have already seen how prayer and the Covenant are bound together (above; see also Chapter 7). The covenant corresponds to purity, as well as to the rainbow. The rainbow comprises the three primary colors, which correspond to Chesed, Gevurah and Tiferet, as well as to Abraham, Isaac and Jacob. We know that where the Patriarchs are, there the Divine Presence is found (see *Zohar* III, 215a). Therefore, when the rainbow appears, it is a revelation of the three aforementioned Sefirot, i.e. the blending of opposing forces into a harmonious unity, and the spreading of peace. Further, the three Patriarchs were all promised the Holy Land, for themselves as well as for their future progeny. For when peace reigns it will be because the wicked have been destroyed and Godliness revealed to all. With this we reach an understanding of the verse: "Yearn for God..." relating to the concepts of faith, prayer and the necessity of guarding the Covenant in order to attain prayer. Then, "He will elevate you to inherit the Land," because the Covenant, prayer, the Holy Land and peace, are all interconnected. Then, "you will behold the destruction of the wicked," because with the promulgation of the concepts of the Holy Land and its related ideas, the wicked are destroyed, and the age of Divine Providence and miracles, is revealed (see *Likutey Moharan* I, 55:8).

May it be His will, speedily in our day, Amen.

* * *

26

Jerusalem and the Holy Temple

Jerusalem was, is and always will be the capital of the Jewish Nation. For several millennia, from the four corners of the earth, thrice daily, Jews have directed their prayers to the Holy Land beseeching God to rebuild Jerusalem and to restore His Presence to the Holy Temple. The *Birkat HaMazon* (Grace after Meals) has a separate blessing for Jerusalem and the Temple. Every wedding includes a ceremonial reminder of the "as-yet-to-be-rebuilt" Jerusalem just as in every condolence call we take our leave of the mourners by saying, "May you be consoled among the mourners of Zion and Jerusalem." The centrality of Jerusalem to Judaism is an indisputable fact. Some may disagree — it may not jibe with their ideologies. Regardless, the facts cannot be denied.

As we have seen (Chapter 7), *YeRuSHaLayiM* (Jerusalem) comprises two words, *YiRah SHaLeM*, which translate either as "complete fear" or "perfected fear." The rebuilding of Jerusalem is actually a dual objective: to rebuild the city physically and to build our fear and awe of God until it is perfected — until we become aware of God's presence at all times. In reality, these two functions are synonymous. Those who think of Jerusalem as a mere physical city might rebuild a city of stone and wood — but in doing so they will only raise the level of materialism found within the city, while simultaneously concealing its Godliness. On the other hand, those who view Jerusalem as a holy city will strive not only to build physically beautiful buildings to enhance the city's attractiveness, but will continually seek to intensify its spiritual character. This effort invariably leads to a greater respect for God, which in turn arouses a greater revelation of God, which in turn reveals yet a higher level of awe of God. This positive, upward cycle continues indefinitely. Thus, the rebuilding of Jerusalem must also constitute its spiritual rebuilding, and vice-versa. Spiritual rebuilding leads to an Ingathering of the Exiles which is effectively the gathering of the sparks of holiness, which further builds man's awe of God.... By the same token, the spiritual rebuilding of one's awe of God heralds the messianic era when fear of God will be commonplace. Then the great Knowledge of the Days of Mashiach, which is synonymous with the Holy Temple, will be revealed. (see above Chapters 6-7).

*

Jerusalem

> "The land shall convert to that of the Arava (i.e. flat)... but Jerusalem shall be lifted up, yet remain in her place..."
> Zekhariah 14:10

We have seen that in the future Jerusalem will extend to the boundaries of the Holy Land (Chapter 25). There are other Midrashim which state that Jerusalem will extend as far as Damascus (Sifri, Devarim 1; Shir HaShirim Rabbah 7:10). These Midrashim coincide with the borders of the Holy Land as envisioned by Ezekiel, with Damascus being the northern boundary. Thus, Jerusalem will first be rebuilt on its original site and will later begin to expand.

The Prophets depict fierce battles in the Holy Land and single out Jerusalem for terrible siege (Ezekiel 37-38; Zekhariah 12, etc.). In all likelihood, there will be several battles for possession of the city, culminating with Mashiach ben Yosef being killed at the city's gate (see above, Chapter 4). Whether the battles will be physical or spiritual is unclear from the words of the Prophets. As we have seen, Jerusalem stands for fear of God, and Mashiach ben Yosef for the tzaddikim who attempt to plant this awe in the nation. Quite possibly, the battle will be a spiritual one, and our Sages clearly allude to this (Esther Rabbah 7:23). But eventually, when Mashiach comes, Jerusalem will fully assume its name of YeruShaLayiM, "The city of *SHaLoM*." Shalom means peace; it also connotes perfection *SHaLeM*, — which one attains when one develops awe of God.

There are many prophecies about the Jerusalem of the future, but we will focus on those that pertain to its topography and boundaries. The Talmud states (Bava Batra 75a,b) "In the future, Jerusalem will have tall buildings, some thirty stories high and thousands of towers. Furthermore, Jerusalem will be physically elevated by three parasangs" (about twelve miles, higher than many jets fly today). Still, despite its height, there will be no difficulty in ascending to Jerusalem!

Zekhariah envisioned the land surrounding Jerusalem becoming flat, while elevated Jerusalem will stand out upon its mountain and be visible to all. "Yet," he adds, it will "remain in its place." This topography defies description, for how can a mountain be elevated higher yet remain in its place? Reb Noson writes that, in this sense, Jerusalem alludes to the humility of the people in Mashiach's time. As people become closer to God, they will ascend to great spiritual heights. Yet, Jerusalem, fear of God, brings humility. Therefore, instead of the pursuit of honor, people will "remain in their place." The higher they ascend the spiritual ladder, the greater their humility (Likutey Halakhot, Orlah 5:3).

This also explains our Sages' statement (Avot 5:5), "No-one ever said that Jerusalem was too crowded...." Since Divine Providence will be manifest, material constraints no longer exist. The opposite will be true. The greater the number of people seeking spirituality, the easier it will be for them to find a place for themselves in Jerusalem. Since they will be humble, they will not take up space for they will assume a spiritual nature (see Likutey Halakhot, Nizkei Shekheinim 4:14).

*

"'I will be for her,' says God, 'a surrounding wall of fire, and I will be her glory within her'."

Zekhariah 2:9

The Prophet Zekhariah also predicted the expansion of Jerusalem.

"I lifted my eyes and saw 'a man' holding a measuring rope. I asked, 'Where are you going?' He answered, 'To measure the length and breadth of

Jerusalem.' That angel left and another appeared... He said, 'Quickly, tell him that Jerusalem will be without walls...'" (Zekhariah 2:5-8).

The Talmud *(Bava Batra* 75b) explains the above passage as follows: God's original intention was to keep Jerusalem's area contained within a wall. He sent an angel to "measure the city" and set its boundaries. The angels protested, "God! Many cities of the nations have no boundaries; yet Your city — with Your Name upon it, with Your Temple, and Your tzaddikim in it — should be contained?" Immediately, another angel was dispatched out to inform the Jews that Jerusalem will not be walled in and confined to set boundaries. Jerusalem is destined to expand without a wall.

The commentaries *(Maharsha, s.v. Yerushalayim)* explain that this prophecy explains why Jerusalem will expand until it reaches the outer boundaries of the Holy Land. It also indicates that since Jerusalem will expand, the Holy Temple itself will also expand — to the size of the former city of Jerusalem! But God's original intention of placing a wall around the city must still be realized. Therefore, the passage concludes, "I will be for her," says God, "a surrounding wall of fire, and I will be her glory within her" i.e. the revelation of Godliness. Amen, may it be His will.

*

The Holy Temple

The Holy Temple was discussed above as being intimately related to Daat (Chapter 5). It is the place where sacrifices are brought to elevate people's animalistic desires to a higher level, to the level of man. This is why Daat is so much a part of the human being. In contrast, an animal is guided by impulse rather than by intellect. As we progress in our dicussions of the messianic era, we can understand a deeper significance to the concept of Daat and how it relates to the Days of Mashiach.

The Temple was not only the place for offering sacrifices, it was also the seat of the *Sanhedrin,* the highest court of law in the Land *(Rambam, Hilkhot Sanhedrin* 1:3). It also had a designated place for the kings of the Davidic dynasty *(Yoma* 25a). Further, it was positioned within the city of Jerusalem, also a location of judgment (Psalms 122:5). The Holy Temple is therefore parallel to judgment. When Mashiach comes, he will be the advocate of true justice. He will be the king of the Davidic dynasty, whose seat of justice will be in the Temple.

To understand the connection between Mashiach, Judgment and the Holy Temple, we must remember that Mashiach will judge with compassion; he will exonerate those who rectify themselves and will destroy the totally wicked. How will he do this? Kabbalistically, the attribute of Malkhut represents *Mishpat*, harsh judgment. However, the Malkhut of holiness, represented by Mashiach, is one of compassion. Mashiach receives his lifeforce from Keter, which transcends all judgments. With the power of Malkhut, he will punish and destroy the wicked. Likewise, as the administrator of true Justice, he will reward those who performed good deeds. But how can Malkhut, harsh judgment, be compassionate?

Malkhut is Judgment, but all judgments must be tempered with compassion, as in (Psalms 99:4), "You brought justice and righteousness to perfection in Jacob." Compassion is very closely related to intellect since, without intellect, one's compassion may be grossly misplaced. One might have compassion on murderers yet dismiss threats to innocent people. Such attitudes are not compassion, but rather cruelty. One might pity a whining child and give him a sweet when he should not have it, since it would be detrimental to his health. To give him the sweet is cruelty, not compassion. Disciplining a child might seem harsh, but it is true compassion, because the child thereby learns to discern right from wrong.

The building of the Holy Temple, of Daat, is the building of Judgment. Mashiach will bring this great Daat into the world, an intellect that projects true compassion. Every person's ability to decide upon the necessary steps to take in life will be cultivated through this Daat.

To understand this better, we need simply look at Atik, the Sefirah of Keter, the source of Mashiach. The other Sefirot all have defined "sides"; right (Lovingkindness), left (Judgment) or center (Beauty, the blend between them). But there are no "sides," in Atik, all is compassion. Thus, the great Daat to be revealed is a high degree of intellect which guides one on the proper way to life — with compassion towards others. This is why the revelation of Daat leads to greater understanding between people, as can be plainly seen. Because Daat *is* compassion!

*

Charity

> *"Zion will be redeemed with judgment; and its penitents with tzedakah (righteousness/compassion)."*
>
> Isaiah 1:27

On a personal level, the way we can build the Holy Temple and Daat today, prior to Mashiach's arrival, is through the mitzvah of charity. Charity is similar to judgment. The verse tells us, (Psalms 75:8) "God judges; He puts one down and sets the other up." Charity is similar to judgment in that when giving charity one is making a judgment as to whether or not to take one's own money and give it to the poor. That is, one who gives charity is putting himself down and setting another up. This can be seen in the word *shekel*, used in the Torah to describe the charity coin. The word *SHeKeL* comes from the same root as *miSHKaL*, a balance, for the person's free will must be carefully balanced in order to use proper judgment in choosing right from wrong (*Likutey Halakhot, Halva'ah* 3:8).

Furthermore, the decision to give must involve a judgment on the validity of the recipient or the cause, how much to give, etc. Thus, the concept of charity is synonymous with judgment. But charity also requires a great deal of compassion. One must try to feel the pain of the recipient and relate to him accordingly. Therefore, one who performs the mitzvah of charity is rectifying judgment — and through this he rectifies his Daat, his mind (*Likutey Moharan* I, 2:4).

In addition, we have seen that it is man who, by causing "an arousal from below," sets the Sefirot in orderly alignment to bring forth bounty to mankind (above, Chapter 19). The act of charity itself is a most powerful "arousal from below," because charity is called (Isaiah 32:17), *maaseh hatzedakah* ("the *act* of charity"). *MaASeH* corresponds to *ASiYaH*, the lowest of the Four Worlds, hence it is a most effective "arousal from below" (see *Likutey Halakhot, Rosh HaShanah* 6:10). Thus, "Zion will be redeemed with judgment; and its penitents with *tzedakah*." Because charity is the rectification for judgment, it is a major force in elevating judgment to its true level. This leads to repentance, the arousal from below, and causes God to give bounty and bring the redemption.

*

> **"Torah will come forth from Zion, and the Word of God from Jerusalem."**
>
> Isaiah 2:3

We have seen how sin causes the sparks of holiness to be dispersed throughout Creation, and that they must subsequently be gathered together and reestablished in holiness. This is true of wasted semen, dishonest business transactions, and all other sins. We know that strife causes poverty (above, Chapter 24); therefore, all these sins cause poverty — because by committing sins, man is creating a "conflict" between body and soul, one seeking materialism and the other spirituality.

We have seen how, when man sins, he diverts the bounty due him and that potential bounty is lost from the realm of holiness. Worse, it is given over to the *kelipot*, which then have greater power to cause man to sin, further dragging the bounty down to the depths. This is the main reason that there is such widespread poverty today, despite the fact that there is plenty of food for everyone. Through his sins, man has restricted bounty, and as a result much wealth has descended into the possession of the wicked. Thus, even though we find righteous people who do have some wealth, the aggregate total is a far cry from that which the wicked possess (*Rabbi Nachman's Wisdom* #4, p.107*ff*).

Rectifying judgment is a major reason for the mitzvah of charity. One must use judgment well, choosing a worthy cause. Some examples of worthy causes are: widows and orphans, the physically and mentally ill, the elderly, the poor, institutions that reveal Godliness. Any cause that can elevate human beings to their rightful level as man, is worthy. Any cause that reveals spirituality is worthy. Giving to unworthy causes is akin to wasting semen, because bounty (one's wealth) is taken away from the holy realm and placed into the realm of the *kelipot*, the unworthy —

directly by the person who has judged and chosen unwisely (as explained earlier; see Likutey Moharan I, 264). In making wrong decisions, one's sense of judgment becomes perverted.

What constitutes worthy causes can be decided by the reader, but they certainly do not include saving the whales, the dolphins, the minks and the skunks; and they don't include other causes solicited by anyone with a bright mind and a smooth tongue who might capture your heart. This is because compassion upon human beings will lead to peace, hence to Mashiach (when all animals will be safe). Therefore, humanity must be the priority when considering a gift to charity. One who gives to unworthy causes does not receive a mitzvah for giving charity (see Bava Kama 16b). He might get a tax write-off, but he will not receive any eternal reward for wasting his money. Men must make mankind their priority.

[Author's note: Following is an illustration of misplaced compassion and unworthy causes. It was reported in the summer of 1994 that a lioness mauled a young mother in California, killing her. The mother died and the lioness was subsequently put to death — both leaving offspring. An appeal for funds was made to support the children, and a separate appeal was made to nurse the lion cubs. The appeal for the children yielded about $10,000. The appeal for the cubs brought in about $100,000!]

Giving charity to worthy causes reverses the process of the dispersal of the sparks of holiness. By exercising proper judgment, one brings bounty back into the realm of holiness. The word mitzvah comes from the root word *TZeVet*, "to bind." By performing any mitzvah, one gathers the sparks spread out among the *kelipot* and elevates them. This is so much more true in the case of charity, which corresponds to rectified Judgment, for this mitzvah gathers many sparks and elevates them (remember that properly employed judgment makes converts, elevating many sparks of holiness; Chapter 24). Instead of one mitzvah elevating one spark, charity influences many. Therefore, charity is considered a primary rectification for sexual sins, through which one gives bounty to the Other Side. Charity brings those sparks back into the realm of holiness (Likutey Moharan I, 264; see also Likutey Halakhot, Purim 3:11).

The verse states (Proverbs 19:4), "Wealth adds many friends." Giving charity creates a friendly and tranquil atmosphere, wherein people can relate to each other. When a person uses his wealth wisely, by giving charity, he "adds many friends," for he takes those fallen sparks and draws them into the realm of holiness (Likutey Moharan I, 17:5). Furthermore, our Sages teach (Avot 2:7), "Whoever increases charity, increases peace." Charity is a catalyst which can bring hearts and minds together in a positive, bridge-building manner, drawing people closer to one another. This is reflected in the peace that will be attained in the messianic era. And this peace will be made possible because we will then attain Daat, that great knowledge, which is comprised of both Judgment and true Compassion (Likutey Halakhot, Purim 1:7).

Charity also helps reveal Divine Providence. We have seen how the desire for riches is rooted in the messianic reality of great wealth. At present, however, that desire is idolatrous in nature. By giving charity, one breaks one's idolatrous tendencies, and God, i.e. Divine Providence, is revealed (Likutey Moharan I, 13:1).

All this is alluded to in the commandment of the thanksgiving sacrifice that will be offered in the Holy Temple when Mashiach comes (see above, Chapter 5). The focus of that sacrifice is the prayer thanking God for the good that He has bestowed upon us. Thanking God entails recognizing Him as Master of the World. That sacrifice is not obligatory — it is a *donation* to God and to the Temple, stemming from one's inner desire to do what one feels is right. It is "charity," which is a rectification of judgment. It is a revelation of one's warmth and compassion. It elevates the sparks of holiness and reveals Godliness, Divine Providence and an age of miracles. It brings peace and spreads goodwill (Likutey Halakhot, Chailev v'Dam 3:1).

In addition, we have seen how money can be transformed into Torah (above, Chapter 24). This can be accomplished through charity, by supporting Torah scholars, Torah study and Torah publications. All these spread the knowledge of Godliness and help reveal the Torah of Atik, that Great Knowledge that will fill the entire world when Mashiach comes (Likutey Halakhot, Chanukah 3:6). This applies even more when one gives charity to the Holy Land, for in doing so, one is literally gathering the sparks and elevating them into holiness, the Holy Land, effecting a microcosmic Ingathering of the Exiles. This dynamic brings about the spread of Godliness throughout the world because (Isaiah 2:3), "Torah will come forth from Zion and the Word of God from Jerusalem."

Speedily, in our days, Amen.

* * *

27

Getting it together

> *Our Sages and Prophets did not long for the Days of Mashiach in order to rule over the world, or to lord over the nations, or that the nations venerate the Jews. Nor did they look forward to the Days of Mashiach to "eat, drink and make merry." They longed for the Days of Mashiach so that they could be free from material constraint in order to spend their lives in the pursuit of Torah and wisdom... For at that time there will be no famine, or war, or jealousy or rivalry. There will be plentiful bounty, and everyone will seek God...*
>
> Rambam, Hilkhot Melakhim 12:4-5

Our hope for a utopian life has sustained generations even during the most difficult and depressing times. The Rambam quoted above is summing up the idea of what the Days of Mashiach will be like. And he concludes his thought with the desire that accompanies us throughout our entire lifetimes though, for the most part, it has been misunderstood and overlooked.

The soul has a natural longing for satisfaction. Our souls constantly long for inner fulfillment, which is why most people — though they surely have many enjoyable moments — have difficulty feeling satisfied with life. The body may be sated, the material requirements provided, yet one continues to long for more. Mind, soul, and the very spirit of life, remains with that hollow feeling. The Rambam thus states that when Mashiach comes, the entire world will take to spiritual pursuits, to the pursuit of knowledge, the Daat of God. This is the "grand finale" of the six thousand years of Creation whose end is approaching.

The reason for this is that the mind is the *neshamah*, the upper soul of a person (Bereishit Rabbah 14:9). The word NeShaMaH is like NeShiMaH (breathing), life itself. It is the intellect that truly gives a person life, as in (Ecclesiastes 7:12) "Wisdom gives life to its possessor." On a simple level, we can see that those who have common sense make it through the day. Those who have studied know what to do in difficult circumstances. Thus, "Wisdom gives life...."

The soul is "a Godly portion," intimately connected to God. It is therefore the soul's longing for Daat of God, for a higher level and greater perception of Godliness, that causes us to yearn for more and the unceasing craving for fulfillment. Even those who study and attain knowledge of the material realm feel satisfaction when attaining their goals. However, the material pursuit usually fills the mind with "too much" knowledge which leads to "a headache," as in (Ecclesiastes 1:18) "Increased knowledge increases pain." Eventually it leads to suffering and depression. But spiritual pursuit does not — and cannot — fill the mind to capacity, for spirituality is above time and space. The more one studies, the greater his capacity for life, and the more one's *neshamah* grows and achieves greater fulfillment. Furthermore, the verse states (Genesis 2:7), "He breathed into his nostrils the breath of life." That is, man's life-source is God Himself. Thus, *neshimah* indicates an intimate breath, like someone breathing lightly on another's neck. This denotes that using one's intellect to search for spirituality can bring an intimate connection with God.

This is a fundamental idea behind the Torah of Atik to be revealed in the future, because this Torah is rooted in Keter, the level of *Ayeh?* (Where?). This Torah is so exalted that it cannot be disclosed as long as the question, "Where?" is not asked. On the other hand, as more and more people begin asking "Where?" then more and higher levels of the Torah of Atik will become revealed. Finally, we will all know *where* the action is taking place. We will know where the Holy Land, the revelation of Godliness, is happening. Our souls, *neshamot*, will breathe the fear of God, and we will become more aware of Him, as we attain that Great Knowledge of the future.

It is therefore fitting that we add to our discussion of "Where?" a review of the Torah of Atik and how it ties in with the other messianic concepts.

*

The Torah of Atik

Though the ARI writes of several very exalted spiritual levels, for the purpose of this book we will call this group of exalted levels Atik and Keter (because we have no way of defining these in human terms, let alone the levels above them). Since the higher the level, the more it can illumine below, Keter can extend down to the lowest of levels to attract and elevate those sparks of holiness. Sometimes, a person who is very distant from God calls out to Him seeking Godliness. In such a case, by asking "Where?" he draws upon himself the power of *Ayeh?*, that power of the Keter itself! This causes a great revelation of Godliness.

Reb Noson points out that KeTeR is the same letters as *KaReT*, which means "to be cut off." This is a punishment which the Torah stipulates against those who commit terrible sins (e.g. adultery, desecrating Shabbat, eating on Yom Kippur, etc.). The person who invokes *karet* eventually finds himself "cut off" from his family, friends and, most importantly, from God. He is banished to live a material existence. But when that same person invokes the power of *Ayeh?*, of the Keter, by asking for and seeking God, then he is rectifying the *karet* he is enduring and can find his rectification by returning to God (Likutey Halakhot, Milah 4:8).

The man who embodied such a revelation was Moshe's father-in-law, Jethro. Jethro was a grand idolator, a high priest for every idolatry that existed in his time. Having served every single one and having found them all useless, he turned to God. Our Sages teach (Exodus 18:11; Zohar II, 69a), "When Jethro said, 'I know that God is greater than all gods...' the greatness of God was revealed Above and below." The master idolator recognized God and this drew the light of Godliness down to the lowest levels and revealed it on those levels. It is this power of the Keter which reveals Godliness to all. And this is the level of the Torah of Atik.

The Torah of Atik is that great knowledge, Daat, which will be revealed in the future so that all may recognize God, for the Torah is the vehicle through which Godliness can be perceived. As more Daat, Godliness, becomes revealed, more people are attracted to spirituality. As Daat becomes a reality, peace becomes a reality. This is because as God's Unity is realized everyone is included and therefore joined together as one — i.e. in peace.

When peace reigns, as it will in Mashiach's time, everything becomes rectified and perfected. The Hebrew word for peace is *ShaLoM*, much like the word *ShaLeM*, meaning complete or perfected (see above, Chapter 6). As we have seen, Daat is knowledge based upon compassion, indicating that it is without restrictions (as above, Chapter 26). Angry and cruel people are lacking in knowledge as in (Ecclesiastes 7:9) "Anger rests with fools," which points to constrictions leading to strife and hostility. But, as Daat increases, anger is abolished and peace is attained. The greater the knowledge attained, the greater level of peace which is achieved.

Peace has been sought for millennia, to no avail. History records many peace treaties — most of which never amounted to much in the end. But the Daat that will be revealed in the future is Godliness itself. This Daat will lead to peace, and peace means not only the elimination of physical conflict between people or nations. Even in our times, the human body harbors conflict within, as when a person is sick. Then the body must "fight" the illness. But when *spiritual* peace descends upon earth, it will bring peace to *all* parts of Creation — even to the illnesses that afflict a person (see Likutey Moharan I, 56:8). Thus, the revelation of the Torah of Atik, of Daat, brings healing as well as peace. Let us see how.

The ARI teaches that the sin of masturbation is devastating, as it causes the sparks of holiness to spread throughout the world. Why is masturbation so terrible? Because it originates in the mind, but then goes totally to waste. It is a waste of mind, of intellect, of Daat. Therefore, the original sin of Adam, wasted semen, caused a blemish in the manifestation of Daat in our world (see above, Chapter 23). Consequently, our efforts should now be concentrated on rectifying, rebuilding and elevating Daat, through the elevation of the holy sparks. We have also seen how the Torah of Atik is able to descend to the lowest levels, to reach out to and illumine those unfortunate sparks. As the sparks begin their rectification by our calling out *Ayeh?* (i.e. Where?, the level of Keter), they are gathered together and elevated. These "collected sparks" are actually the wasted and forlorn sparks of Daat that were blemished by sin. Gathered together, they are rebuilding the edifice of Daat and the "fragmented passages" of the Torah (see above, Chapter 24). Thus, the rebuilding of Daat comes about through the revelation of the Torah of Atik, because they are one and the same. When the "rebuilding" of Daat is complete, every aspect of Creation will be at peace with every other. There will be no "fragmented sparks," nothing will be out of place. Rather, everything will be in perfect harmony and so peace will reign. Good will and good health will be available for all.

It is for this reason also that the exile is considered "a state of mind." The mind refers to Daat which, when complete, has no lack. But if a person feels a lack, it is because he feels a deficiency in the sparks of holiness, in his portion of Daat. The verse thus states (Isaiah 5:13), "My people are in exile because of an absence of Daat..." However, when an individual rectifies his Daat, when he repents and turns to God, he redeems his Daat from exile. He attains redemption! (see *Likutey Moharan* I, 21:11).

In discussing the concept of the gathering of the sparks and the Torah of Atik we begin to see how much this is a part of Mashiach's job. Reb Noson adds that, in the main, Mashiach's efforts will be concentrated on rectifying this sin. We find in the Torah that Judah's sons, Er and Onan, spilled seed. After they died, Judah came together with Tamar and begat Peretz, King David's antecedent (Genesis 38). As we have seen, the forces of evil work very hard to trap great souls in their realm. The sins of Er and Onan strengthened those forces, setting the scene for the entrapment of Mashiach's soul (see above, Chapter 3). Therefore, Judah was faced with a formidable test in order to draw down the antecedent of Mashiach and to rectify this sin, the spilling of seed and the waste of the sparks of holiness. But by Torah study (especially striving to earn an understanding of the Torah of Atik), we rectify the sin of masturbation. The sparks of holiness which are spread throughout creation, without any "body" to rest within, begin to gather and "take shape" in the form of one's Torah study and teachings. This rectifies one's Daat and gives form to the lost sparks (Likutey Halakhot, Piryah v'Rivyah 1:9-10; see also above, Chapter 24).

The ARI thus writes that Moshe corresponds to Daat (Etz Chaim 32:1). We find that when Moshe initiated the redemption from Egypt, his first task was to gather the people together. Having gathered them, he was able to lead them to Sinai. There, he ascended the mountain and received the Torah. Since Moshe is the Mashiach (above, Chapter 4), Mashiach's task now is similar. He must first gather in the sparks of holiness, the souls of the Jews, and bring about unity. The more sparks that are gathered, the greater Mashiach's ability will be to reveal the Torah of Atik. This gathering of the sparks takes place in every generation. As the sparks of holiness are gathered and rectified, more of the Torah of Atik becomes revealed, even now, before Mashiach comes! This in turn rectifies Daat, bringing about the end of the exile and the rebuilding of the Holy Temple (Likutey Moharan I, 13:1-2).

Speedily, in our days, Amen!

* * *

28

Joy: the World of Freedom

"You shall draw water with joy from the wellsprings of salvation."
Isaiah 12:3

Isaiah begins his chapter reflecting on the suffering of exile and the realization that the suffering was for our own good — to enable us to return to God by mitigating His judgments through our repentance. When we return to Him, His anger is withdrawn and salvation is made available for all. "You will say on that day, 'God, I praise You; You were angry with me and You withdrew that anger...You were my salvation...' With joy, you shall draw water from the wells of salvation. You will say on that day, 'Praise God....'"

The *Targum Yonatan* explains the "drawing of the water" on the day of the salvation, as "you will receive new teachings from the choicest of tzaddikim." This means that when Mashiach — the choicest of tzaddikim — comes, we will be able to draw entirely new Torah teachings from the wellsprings of salvation, the choicest advice available in order to serve God. This refers to the Torah of Atik. We will draw upon the Torah of Atik with unrestrained happiness and gladness, for when these teachings are revealed, Daat is revealed, the Temple is in place and mankind is at peace (*Likutey Halakhot, Halvaah* 5:3). What better reason can there be for joy?

*

MaShIaCh comprises the same letters as the word *SiMChIy* (rejoice!) and no book about the Mashiach would be complete without a discussion of the tremendous joy that will fill the world in the future. The Prophets describe days of intense joy and happiness, a gaiety that will fill the minds and hearts of all mankind, especially the Jews, who will no longer be subjected to suffering by their oppressors. Try to imagine a world without boredom and without depression, with only joy and happiness, and even greater joy and happiness waiting just around the corner. But is this the type of joy and merrymaking that lasts until the hangover sets in? The Rambam states emphatically that it is not (see above, Chapter 27). It must be a true joy, a deep-felt joy, one that is lasting and fulfilling. What then is this joy? Rebbe Nachman taught:

> The reason people are distant from God is that they do not have *yishuv hadaat* ("tranquility of mind"). The most important thing in life is to think things through clearly — "What is my goal? Where am I headed?" By thinking things through to their logical end, one will inevitably return to God (*Likutey Moharan* II, 10).

Tranquility of mind does not imply obliviousness to one's mental faculties. On the contrary, it includes several facets of the thought process: a) careful consideration; b) sober judgment; c) considered opinion. These combine to present the picture of a person who is at peace with himself, one who does not abandon his goals too easily. Rebbe Nachman continues his lesson.

> But know! One who is melancholy cannot have tranquility of mind. Only when one is joyous can one control one's mind. The reason is that joy and freedom are synonymous, as in (Isaiah 55:12) "You shall depart [the exile] with joy...." That is, through joy, a person becomes free and independent and can control his mind. In this way, he leaves the exile, for he becomes a free man.... To achieve joy, one must look for all the good points he has [i.e. feel good about oneself] (*Likutey Moharan* II, 10).

We see that joy is "The World of Freedom." A joyous person is not dependent upon "substances" for his highs, he is not a "needy person" dependent upon others for honor and fulfillment (see above, Chapter 8); he is not controlled by others (such as the media) who do his thinking for him, and so on. He is joyous and content with what he has in life — and feels good about himself. This person can think *clearly* for himself, and reach the proper conclusions about life and its goals.

*

Patience

We can illustrate this idea through examining the Exodus. Our Sages teach that the Egyptian exile was the prototype of all the exiles (Bereishit Rabbah 16:4). As such, the Exodus should be a model for the current, long-awaited end of our exile. The Jews left Egypt with great wealth, as will occur in the future. They then received the Torah, as will take place when the Torah of Atik is revealed. They had a redeemer, Moshe, who will also be their redeemer now, Mashiach (as discussed earlier, Part II). Their exodus from Egypt was replete with miracles, as we know it will be when we depart this exile. Many parallels exist, barring two major points, which are interconnected. The first is that not everyone left Egypt. Some four-fifths of the nation died, because they refused to believe in Moshe and the Exodus. The second is that the Jews were in a rush to get out of Egypt, having descended so low that leaving even one minute later might have been too late. There was no time to allow everyone to rectify himself, to attain that modicum of faith required to realize that salvation was nigh. Since everything at the time of the Exodus was "Rush! Rush! Rush!" — many Jews lost out.

In the scheme of God's Master Plan, had all the Jews at the time of the Exodus repented and turned to Him, they could all have left Egypt. Perhaps then the world would have reached a rectified state, as occurred temporarily when the Jews received the Torah at Sinai (cf. *Shabbat* 146a). Although complete rectification was lacking then, it remains crucial to God's Master Plan, which calls for the rectification of all humanity. Since the world was created to last for six thousand years, and the End of Days is fast approaching, everyone *must* now receive rectification. It is taking time — and it is taking its toll; but all is not lost.

> *For you shall not go out in flight, nor shall you leave in haste; for God will go before you, and the Lord Who gathers you will protect you..."*
>
> Isaiah 52:12

The implication here is twofold: first everyone will be gathered in, with none left behind, because nearly all will be rectified. But there is another deeper point, one that is meshed very tightly together with the concept of joy: This is the virtue of patience which is deeply rooted in the concept of Mashiach (see Chapter 14). A person with patience is a person who has the intellect to think matters through clearly, employing Daat to arrive at a satisfactory conclusion. It translates into an expanded consciousness. Anger is symptomatic of a manic type of behavior, a constricted consciousness, a small-minded person (i.e. lacking that Daat that will be revealed in the messianic age).

When Isaiah tells us that we will not leave the exile in flight, he means that everyone will have the chance to think seriously about himself — where he's been and where he's headed. In this way, he can begin to look at the *real* goal in order to rectify himself, and not be left behind, as many were in Egypt. This is because "The Lord *gathers you...* — God gathers everyone — through the gathering of the sparks of holiness. But even more, Isaiah is advising us to be patient (and patience is a mate to humility; see above, Chapters 14-15) because this is *the* means by which to leave the exile. Realizing that tranquility of mind is of the essence in attaining Godliness, we can understand the importance of patience and *yishuv hadaat* as harbingers of the Days of Mashiach.

*

Azamra!

We all accept the important role that joy plays in life, for it is an integral part of life's fulfillment. Without joy, or at least the hope for joy in the future, what reason does a person have to continue living? The importance of joy represents the World of Freedom, which is the basis for tranquility of mind. It releases us from the constrictions of an impulsive mind, from the mania that pushes us to act hastily, which we too often regret — very soon after we act.

Thus, true joy, a joy that leads to tranquility of mind, is a major prerequisite to leaving the exile, and one which is attainable in the here-and-now, simply by feeling good about oneself. This does not mean accepting one's faults and being proud of them — as we see today in terrorists who take "credit" for their deeds. The definition of "feeling good" implies a person taking stock of the good deeds he has performed or appreciating the good things he has in life, even if they may appear minimal.

For example, someone who has given some charity might afterwards reflect, "I should have given more," or someone who has striven to honor Shabbat or build a beautiful sukkah might afterwards think, "I didn't do enough." True, it is always possible to do more or better — everyone has room for improvement. But this should not detract from one's ability to rejoice: "I *did* perform the mitzvah! Perhaps it wasn't perfect. Perhaps it was far from perfect. But I did it! No-one can take that good away from me."

The same applies to the common, "little things in life" that most people take for granted. One might be facing troubles: at home, at work, physically, spiritually, emotionally and so on. Depression may set in, making a person feel "down and out." But when he begins to add up all the "little things," he'll see that there are many, many reasons to be happy with what he has — rather than suffer the extreme emotions or overwhelming depression that people often feel when confronted with the difficulties of life.

In short, the idea of "getting one's life together" can only work through *finding* means of being happy. And herein lies another important lesson regarding the observance of the mitzvot, which further clarifies for us the focus of the messianic era. We have seen that miTZVah is from the root word *TZeVet*, "to bind" (see above, Chapter 20). Performing mitzvot is therefore akin to "getting one's act together," for through mitzvot each person begins to gather in his sparks of holiness and bind himself to the Single Unity of God. Furthermore, the verse states (Psalms 19:9), "The statutes of God are virtuous, they bring joy to the heart." Thus, there is a joy that is found in each and every mitzvah. The opposite is also true, for sins disperse one's sparks and fragment one's soul. Immersed in sin, the person cannot "pull his act together." This state leads to depression and many other illnesses, as a person is beset with many "wandering thoughts" in his self-inflicted exile.

It is taught that there are 613 mitzvot, which correspond to the limbs and sinews of the body (Makot 23b; see above, Chapter 20; see also *Anatomy of the Soul*). Since the mitzvot are bound to joy, it stands to reason that joy itself is a construct of the "613 limbs and sinews." A person who is lacking the joy of a certain mitzvah cannot feel joy in the corresponding limb of his body. Rather, he feels a "heaviness," a lack of elation. Conversely, someone who actively seeks the joy of the mitzvot by strengthening himself in the performance of a particular mitzvah or through the knowledge that he *has* done a certain mitzvah (even if it was less than perfect), literally draws joy into himself, physically as well as spiritually and emotionally. Then, having finally attained joy, he can sing and praise God (the messianic ideal of prayer), as the Prophet says (Isaiah 51:3), "Joy and gladness will be found there, thanksgiving and the voice of melody" (see *Likutey Moharan* I, 178).

*

Joy and Thanksgiving

Rebbe Nachman taught:

> There is a Light which is above all other lights. This is the Light of the *Ein Sof*, the Infinite One. The soul yearns to attain this Light, but it is not possible to reach it other than by performing the mitzvot with great joy. The *Shekhinah* (Divine Presence) is attached to the mitzvot (see *Zohar* II, 93a). Thus, by performing mitzvot, one binds oneself to God. Just as the Jews are in exile, the Divine Presence is also in exile. As the Jews are gathered into the Holy Land, the Divine Presence is extricated from Its exile. The verse states (Isaiah 55:12), "You shall depart [the exile] with joy." Thus, performing the mitzvot with joy is *the* means by which to extricate the Divine Presence from exile, from Its concealment and, when this is achieved, Godliness will be revealed to all (*Likutey Moharan* I, 24:1-2).

Reb Noson comments that, since the end of the exile is bound up with the idea of joy, the exile itself is the place of depression, not only on a national level, but for each individual as well. Thus, the person who falls into "exile" — suffering, illness, strenuous travel, financial strain and the like — is often steeped in depression. This is the reason our Sages introduced a thanksgiving sacrifice and blessing to be recited when one is redeemed from suffering (i.e. "exile") (Orach Chaim 219:1). Thus, the end of the exile and the thanksgiving prayer are related. In the (near) future, all mankind will turn to God and praise Him in thanksgiving of redemption.

For a short introduction to the next few paragraphs, please turn to the Appendix, Chart of the Sefirot, where we can see that the Ten Sefirot correspond to four levels, with the fifth level, the ineffable Keter, being beyond all description. When anthropomorphically depicting the body, these four levels divide as follows: Chokhmah, Binah and Daat are the *mochin* (head). Chesed, Gevurah and Tiferet are the upper torso. Netzach, Hod and Yesod are the legs; and Malkhut is the feet or the lowest point. These also correspond to the Four Worlds. Reb Noson's full discourse on the topic is found in *Likutey Halakhot, Hodaah* 6:1-4. Reb Noson details his commentary to each concept, but we present here only a brief review, with inserted explanations as they apply to our text.

Sefirot	*anthropomorphic parallel*
Keter	beyond description
Chokhmah, Binah, Daat	head
Chesed, Gevurah, Tiferet	torso
Netzach, Hod, Yesod	legs
Malkhut	feet

The thanksgiving blessing was initially introduced to be recited over redemption from four types of dangerous suffering: illness, imprisonment, seafaring and desert traveling. These four categories conceptually represent the four elevations of the Divine Presence that occur when a person performs mitzvot with joy.

At present, the *Shekhinah* and humanity are in exile. This exile takes place in this world — a world where everything is "mixed up," as when a hurricane and storm wind come and turn the whole world upside down (see above, Chapter 13). This world is therefore known as the *Heichalei HaTemurot* ("The Chambers of Exchanges"), where evil is called good and good is called evil; [for them] light is darkness and darkness is light, [they make] bitter sweet and sweet bitter... (cf. Isaiah 5:20). In material surroundings people lose the ability to define their mission in life clearly.

The mission of the *kelipot*, the forces of evil, was to turn the world "upside down," causing the lost sparks, to go into exile.

Man's mission is to gather the dispersed sparks and elevate them from their exile. The elevation of the Divine Presence (the sparks of holiness) from exile begins with Malkhut, for it is at that point that the Kingdom of God is revealed. But we have seen that the goal of man is to be bound together with the Unity of God. Therefore, through the Divine Presence — and, by extension, man — they begin their ascent at Malkhut, and must rise all the way to the top of the spiritual ladder. Thus, performing mitzvot with joy extricates the Divine Presence from the realm of the *kelipot*, the Chamber of Exchanges, gathering the sparks of holiness and elevating them. This elevation goes through "four stages": from Malkhut, the very bottom, up through "the legs" and then to "the torso" until it reaches "the head." At this point, it becomes unified with the Keter, the ineffable point, i.e. the Unity of God.

This all takes place on a microcosmic level for each person according to his deeds, at every moment. It will take place on a much broader level for the nation as a whole when Mashiach comes. At that time Godliness will be revealed to all. This is the great benefit that will result from performing the mitzvot with joy. Simply put, performing the mitzvot with joy is the key to the ultimate Redemption.

We may add here that the four-level ascension of the sparks is predicated upon the idea that the Tetragrammaton, God's Holy Name, comprises four letters (see Appendix B). Furthermore, the joy of performing mitzvot extends throughout the Ten Sefirot. This corresponds to the Ten Types of Song which will be revealed in the Days of Mashiach (see above, Chapter 7). Thus, the greater the effort one exerts on performing the mitzvot with joy, the greater one feels the obligation to pray and offer thanksgiving to God, both for the "little things" (and small salvations) in life, as well as for one's general extrication from suffering and overall salvation.

Rebbe Nachman teaches elsewhere (*Likutey Moharan* I, 250), "This world was set up with a 'natural' system which conceals Divine Providence. As such, everything seems to be controlled by the "forces of nature." In the future, everything will be obviously miraculous, for all will function directly under God's Divine Providence. But miracles have occurred — the Ten Plagues, the Splitting of the Sea, manna, the clouds of glory, Purim, Chanukah, etc. — even when the world was under "nature's" rule. How could miracles occur then? The answer is that when God wants to perform miracles in the present, He draws upon the miraculous system of the world of the future, and allows it to be manifest even in the present.

The manifestation of joy nowadays functions in the same way. We are in exile, the place of depression, of suffering. Joy is an integral part of the World of the Future — the World of Freedom. By emphasizing our performance of mitzvot with joy, we are tapping the source of the joy of the future (Likutey Halakhot, Hodaah 6:10).

This now ties together with all the other messianic concepts. The Talmud teaches (Shabbat 88a) that when the Jews accepted the Torah they were adorned with crowns. Though these crowns were lost when the golden calf was made, God will return them to us. Crown in Hebrew is Keter which refers to Mashiach and the level of the Torah of Atik. Furthermore, the text upon which the Talmud bases the return of the crowns is (Isaiah 35:10), "Everlasting joy upon their heads." Thus, these crowns, Keter, are joy! Keter corresponds to will — which refers to everyone exercising their will to voluntarily serve God. Since everyone's will becomes directed to the One God, this indicates a common goal, unity and peace. As God's unity is revealed, so Divine Providence is revealed, introducing the era of miracles with the total negation of all forms of idolatry. All this is an outcome of exercising proper Judgment, using one's free will to seek truth and to choose wisely. And this is all attained through charity, which directs one's judgment to the correct choice, as explained earlier. Thus, Keter, joy, the Torah of Atik, Judgment, truth, Divine Providence, peace and charity are all interconnected. As these ideals become revealed, one is drawn nearer to God and will offer one's thanksgiving prayers to Him alone (see Likutey Halakhot, Arev 3:30, 40, 42-43).

May, we feel that joy, speedily, Amen.

* * *

29

In review

It would be very beneficial to sum up in a few words what we have discussed thus far, before proceeding to the next and final section of this book, "When is Mashiach coming?"

*

Mashiach is a personality that defies description. It is not possible even to try to conjecture who he might be. Any portrait one might think of is limited by the intellect and imagination of that person. Can anyone today imagine a leader the likes of Moshe or King David, with their tireless efforts and total self-sacrifice for the nation? We read about these figures of our past, but do we really understand them? Who, in the past millennia, could serve as such an example? We can only pray that God reveal the unfathomable character of the Mashiach as soon as possible (Part II).

*

Mashiach's mission is monumental, to say the least. He has to convince people of the folly of material pursuits and redirect their efforts towards spirituality. All material pursuits are basically rooted in the following characteristics: 1) pride and the pursuit of honor; 2) the urge to waste; 3) immorality; 4) eating; 5) making "merry" (e.g. drinking, drugs...); 6) the pursuit of wealth; 7) the pursuit of materialistic wisdom; 8) dishonorable speech. Mashiach's main strengths are his countertactics: purity and morality, honesty, faith, dialogue, patience and humility. His "weapons" are: prayer (the main weapon), faith and wondrous advice — i.e. the Torah of Atik. His objective is to reveal the awesomeness of God and, by extension, the Knowledge of Him — that He exists, that He created the world and that He is its eternal Master. When he accomplishes his objectives, Mashiach will introduce an era of miracles, for everyone will see that the world is completely ruled by Divine Providence. Great wealth and good health will be every person's blessing as well as a long life to enjoy it, as in (Isaiah 65:20) "For the youngest shall die at one hundred years of age" (Parts III and IV).

Mashiach's ability to rectify the world comes from the system with which God created the world. Introducing His light in various stages and in descending intensity, God formed the world in such a way that even if a person sins terribly and shatters his life, he can literally "pick up the pieces" and begin all over. All that is needed is faith that he *can* begin again. (If he doesn't, he'll be reincarnated and start over anyway! Might as well finish the job now [Part V]).

By gathering the sparks of holiness that have been dispersed throughout Creation, one merits to see the revelation of Godliness. As one ascends the spiritual ladder, one is exposed to ever greater revelations. As this Godliness is revealed, it attracts additional sparks of holiness, which further illumine the world with God's Glory. Eventually, God's Glory will be revealed openly in the Holy Temple in Jerusalem — in the Holy Land, which will eventually spread out to encompass the entire world, because everyone will then recognize God and worship Him. At that time, great knowledge will be revealed. Peace will reign, good health, immense wealth and every luxury will be made available to all mankind, to further the service of God in the world. Miracles will be the norm and joy will be everywhere! (Part VI).

And then:

> "The wolf will live with the lamb and the leopard will lie down with the goat; the calf and the lion will dwell together... the cow will graze with the bear and their young will forage side by side; and the lion, like cattle, will eat straw. The child will play with the cobra... for the world will be filled with the knowledge of God, as waters cover the earth" (Isaiah 11:6-9).

Speedily, in our days, Amen.

* * *

Part VII

Mashiach:

When?

In this part of the book we focus in on the birthpangs of Mashiach and those who predict Mashiach's coming; Elijah the Prophet, who must precede Mashiach's arrival; and the essential belief that Mashiach will indeed come to rectify the world.

30

When is Mashiach coming?

> *The world was created to last for six thousand years — afterwards will be a Sabbatical millennium.*
>
> Sanhedrin 97a

The Six Days of Creation parallel the six millennia that the world as we know it will exist. They are weekdays, when work is permitted — obligatory actually, because of Adam's sin. But the Seventh Day is Shabbat, the Day of Rest, which corresponds to the Seventh Millennium, when all will be peaceful and good. We are now in the sixth millennium, which denotes *Erev Shabbat*, the Eve of Shabbat.

The verse states (Genesis 7:11), "In the six hundredth year of the life of Noah... on that day, the fountains of the depths burst forth and the floodgates of the heavens were opened." Our Sages comment (Zohar I, 117a), "In the six hundredth year of the sixth millennium (corresponding to 5600 or 1840 c.e.), a life of *noach* (comfort in Hebrew) shall begin. The depths of [scientific] knowledge and the floodgates of [spiritual] wisdom will open up for people to enter into the Seventh Millennium in comfort — just as people prepare to enter the Shabbat."

In itself, this prophecy is a harbinger of all the messianic revelations. Our Sages made this prophecy in the first century of the common era. History records that the industrial revolution started at the beginning of the 19th century. But it was in the 1840s when electricity, steam engines and communications came of age!

There are six days in which to prepare for Shabbat. Some people begin on Sunday: "Where will we spend Shabbat?" Others plan their shopping and cooking schedules around Shabbat. Some think that Sunday is too early and begin on Monday or even Tuesday. By Wednesday, most people are thinking of Shabbat, buying their groceries, taking care of their laundry and so on. By Thursday, serious arrangements start. There are some who relax until Friday afternoon: With store-bought products, all they need is to bathe and light the stove before getting dressed for the Day of Rest. But for most people, the frenzy of preparations are in full swing — especially those last few hours before Shabbat begins...

We too are now involved in the "Friday afternoon" preparations for the Shabbat of the Mashiach. As of this writing (the year 5755 [1995]), we have less than "a few hours" (250 years) before Shabbat begins. We know that Shabbat always begins as the sun sets. Does that mean that Mashiach *cannot* come before that time? If that were the case, why are we always praying for him to come?

> *"I, God, will hasten it [the Redemption] in its due time."*
> Isaiah 60:22

The Talmud points out that the above verse is self-contradictory. If the Redemption comes "in its due time," it is not hastened — i.e. before its due date. If it comes "hastened," before its originally set date, then it is not in its due time?! The Talmud explains that if the Jews are unworthy of Mashiach, the redemption will take place "in its rightful time." Since God created the world with Mashiach as its intended redeemer, then Mashiach must come, ready or not, by a certain date. However, if the Jews repent and are meritorious, then the redemption will be "hastened!" — before its set date (Sanhedrin 98a).

Though Shabbat begins at sundown, the custom is to light the candles a few minutes earlier (40 minutes before sundown in Jerusalem, 18 minutes before sundown in most places), inaugurating Shabbat before its actual time. There are some who begin Shabbat a full half-hour prior to sunset while others begin even earlier. Thus, the time for Shabbat is set. If we're ready earlier, we *can* begin earlier. If we turn to God and repent now, then *now* is when Mashiach will come. Shabbat will begin early!

*

The birth pangs of Mashiach

As a woman with child who draws near to the time of her delivery, suffers and cries out in pain; so have we been before You, God.
Isaiah 26:17

Pregnancy is necessary for the development of a new life. An embryo must experience a period of growth before it is ready to come into the world as a human being. Similarly, wisdom must also "gestate" until it is revealed in a person's conscious mind. When wisdom is attained, the person has knowledge. The same is true of the messianic era. It is a whole new way of life, something much sought, but never before experienced. The messianic idea must "gestate" until it is ready to come forth and be revealed.

As the date of Mashiach's arrival draws near, we are becoming very impatient. Isaiah compares this anxiety to that of a pregnant woman who enters her ninth month and can't wait to give birth. This is especially true of a woman who has previously given birth, because she knows exactly what to expect. There are contractions. There is pain: a numbing pain, a pain that builds to an unbearable crescendo. The only thing that can justify this suffering is the end goal, the birth of a child.

But just as a child comes only through birthpangs, so too comes redemption. These are the sufferings that the Jews must endure prior to each of their salvations. This was so in Egypt, in Babylon, in Persia and under the rule of the Greek empire. Prior to each salvation, the Jews experienced unbearable suffering. But they waited, and each exile brought "its own child," its own salvation — the Exodus, Purim and Chanukah and so on. This applies even more today, as we remain in the exile of the rule of Edom. The "birth" we await now is that of the messianic era, the end to all the suffering of mankind.

The "contractions" we are experiencing are unbearable. As we have seen, contractions — i.e. constrictions, judgments — are the suffering one experiences. These are the decrees that the Jews have suffered during the past two centuries. As the Industrial Revolution began making life easier, the Cantonist decrees (forced conscription of pre-adolescent Jews into the Czar's army for a period of 25 years!), the pogroms, the world wars, the Holocaust, the Arab-Israeli wars, terrorism, and so on, have brutally shattered more lives than we are capable of conceiving — and this is a period unparalleled in world history. These are clearly the birth pangs of Mashiach. The world is being prepared to inaugurate Shabbat. But as we draw nearer to our "birth," the contractions increase. They are stronger, and they come closer together. They become more difficult to bear.

Still, with each contraction, we are that much nearer to giving birth. Each pain, each suffering, draws the time of Mashiach's "birth" closer. The time will come when all that is needed is "one more push," and then Mashiach will be here! As King David said (Psalms 90:15), "Make us happy, according to the days You made us suffer." For all those "pangs of birth" will have earned us a "healthy child" — an era of joy and good health, of Daat and peace. The suffering *itself* is what makes the aftermath all the more joyous (Bnei Yissaschar, Tishrei 6:1-4).

*

I believe...

> "I took faithful witnesses; Uriyah the priest and Zekhariah ben Yivarekhyah..."
>
> Isaiah 8:2

The Talmud asks: "Why are Uriyah and Zekhariah considered two reliable witnesses for the same fact? First of all, their prophecies are contradictory in nature. Secondly, they lived in different periods. Uriyah lived during the First Temple and spoke of the destruction of the Holy Temple. Zekhariah lived during the Second Temple and prophesied the rebuilding of Jerusalem and the glory of the Jews in the messianic era!" Rabbi Akiva explained this in the following manner:

> The two prophecies are very closely interrelated. Until Uriyah's prophecy of the destruction was fulfilled, I was afraid that Zekhariah's prophecy would never materialize. Now that I have witnessed the fulfillment of Uriyah's prophecy, I *know* that Zekhariah's prophecy will also come true! (Makot 24b).

Reb Noson writes that everyone experiences a personal destruction of the Temple and the subsequent salvation. As we have seen (Chapter 5) the Temple corresponds to one's intellect which is built — or destroyed — by each person on his own level, according to his mitzvot and sins. Just as Daniel cried (Daniel 12:6), "How much longer until Mashiach is revealed?" regarding the long-awaited salvation for the Jewish Nation, so too, each individual must cry out and seek God to bring him his personal salvation from the material exile in which he finds himself. We must believe in that salvation and reaffirm this faith by seeking God daily.

Just as the "prophecy" of the "destruction" of spiritual pursuit is obvious to each person, so must we be reassured that our spiritual salvation — his very own Mashiach — is ready and waiting for us, for the two are intertwined. And, "just as *I* destroyed my own 'temple,' *I* can rebuild it. I must pray to God and seek Him and my salvation is there for me. I must wait and be patient and long and yearn for God. And then I *will* see my very own Mashiach (*Likutey Halakhot, Eidut* 5:11).

*

"Wait for him..."

Belief in the coming of the Mashiach is a fundamental principle of faith of the Jewish religion, and it is required of every Jew to reaffirm this faith each day. Our Sages state (Shabbat 31a) that one of the first questions asked of a Jew when he faces the Heavenly Tribunal is whether he yearned for and anticipated the coming of Mashiach. The ARI writes that during the *Amidah* (Shmonah Esreh, the 18 Benedictions), when one recites the blessing of *Et Tzemach David*, one should bear in mind one's wish for the imminent salvation of Mashiach. By doing so, that person has fulfilled his obligation of reiterating this faith daily (*Pri Etz Chaim, Shaar HaAmidah* 19). This comprises one's obligation of praying for one's personal salvation, as well as for the general salvation of Israel.

*

Thus, no matter how difficult the circumstances, we must exercise patience and wait. We must wait for our individual salvation, we must wait for our universal salvation, we must wait for Mashiach. And (cf. Habakkuk 2:3), "Though he tarries, wait for him, for he will surely come..."

Speedily, in our day, Amen.

* * *

31

Elijah the Prophet

> *Remember the Torah of My servant Moshe... Behold! I will send you Elijah the Prophet before the advent of the Great and Awesome Day of God* [Judgment Day]. *And he will draw near the hearts of fathers to their children and the hearts of children to their fathers, lest I come and smite the land with a curse.*
>
> Malakhi 3:22-24

The Talmud teaches that Eliyahu *HaNavi* (Elijah the Prophet) was a disciple of Achiyah HaShiloni, who was among those who left Egypt during the Exodus (*Bava Batra* 121b). Others opine that he is actually Pinchas (*Yalkut Shimoni* #771). Thus, Eliyahu received the Torah at Sinai, either as a direct disciple of Moshe, or from a disciple of Moshe (Achiyah). Since he never died (2 Kings, 2:11; see *Kohelet Rabbah* 3:15), Eliyahu is a living testimony to the truth of the Torah of Moshe.

Legend has it that Eliyahu *HaNavi* will come a full "day" before the Mashiach comes, to announce his arrival (see *Eiruvin* 43b; *Raavad* on *Eduyot* 8:9). Having received the Torah from Moshe, he is cognizant of every single law — and each piece of advice — of Torah, and can direct each person to properly repent according to his deeds. Hence, he will come "a day before," to awaken the people to repent, lest they face the Judgment Day before they have rectified their sparks of holiness.

Interestingly, Eliyahu was chosen for this mission because of his zealousness. His prophecies were given in a period of widespread idolatry during which, due to his holiness, Eliyahu could not restrain himself from criticizing the Jews. God took exception to this because He always wants His tzaddikim to seek the good in mankind, despite His knowledge of their sins (*Likutey Halakhot, Hashkamat HaBoker* 4:11). Eliyahu must now seek the good in all mankind and bring the people together in peace.

Furthermore, Aaron was one who sought peace. As Aaron's descendant (Pinchas), Eliyahu is therefore chosen to be the initiator of the Messianic Era and the Resurrection of the Dead (see *Sotah* 49b). He must arouse and resurrect the good in everyone (*Likutey Halakhot, Prikah U'teinah* 4:9; cf. ibid., *Tefilin* 6:10).

Eliyahu figures prominently in our Sages' teachings as a source of law, wisdom and advice. And interestingly enough, just like the Master of Prayer in our story, he seems to change his appearance as he meets with different people. To some he appears as a wise man, to others as an important government official and to others as a harlot! (see *Avodah Zarah* 17b-18a). Thus, we might be staring Eliyahu in the face as he extends his hand to us, and yet be none the wiser for it (much as in the case with Mashiach; see above, Chapter 4).

Eliyahu will bring the hearts of parents and children together — so that the children will influence their parents to repent (and vice-versa) (see Rashi, Malachi, 3:24). As is evident in our generation, he is succeeding, for the pendulum has begun to swing away from atheism and nonsensical ideologies and to turn to the search for spirituality, for God.

This is because Eliyahu's strength lies in his ability to fight atheism, as he fought against the false prophets and idolators of his time (1 Kings 18). Scripture relates that Eliyahu waited an entire day, until Minchah time, the late afternoon, before he was able to totally defeat the idolators. The reason is that late afternoon symbolizes the end of that which we know, and the beginning of something new — a new day (*Likutey Halakhot, Minchah* 3:2). Thus, much as it is now "Friday afternoon," it is time for Eliyahu to make his appearance, to herald the messianic age.

Furthermore, Eliyahu (אליהו) has the same numerical value as *ana* (אנא), meaning "Please!" (an expression denoting prayer), for Eliyahu's strength to defeat idolatry was revealed through his prayers and supplications to God. This is why it is Eliyahu who will announce Mashiach's arrival, for he will aid those who seek to engage in prayer (see *Likutey Halakhot, Sukkah*

5:4). The more a person engages in prayer, Mashiach's main weapon, the more attuned he will be to recognize the signs that Eliyahu is here, and the more ready he will be to face and welcome the Messianic Era.

And there is more. Eliyahu is called the *Malakh HaBrit*, the "Angel of the Covenant." This is because he avenged the decree against circumcision (Malachi 3:1, Metzudat David, loc. cit.). Eliyahu therefore makes an appearance at each circumcision ceremony of every single Jew who enters the Covenant of Abraham. As we have seen (above, Chapter 7), sexual morality is a major messianic characteristic. During a circumcision, the foreskin is removed and the tip of the male organ is revealed. The foreskin represents the forces of evil — the obstacles to attempting to adhere to a spiritual life — which must be done away with. This was Eliyahu's mission, to break the forces of idolatry and reveal God's Unity. Thus, it is Eliyahu who must come prior to Mashiach, for he is the tzaddik who can show us how to overcome the obstacles we face and renew our covenant with God (see *Likutey Halakhot, Hekhsher Keilim* 4:31).

*

To make peace...

> Rabbi Yehoshua said, "Eliyahu will push away those that are close and draw close those that are far." Rabbi Shimon said, "Eliyahu will negotiate an agreement between the different opinions of the rabbinical authorities." The Sages say, "Eliyahu will not come to distance [some] or to draw [others] close. His mission is to make peace between people. It is thus written (Malachi 3:24), 'He shall turn the hearts of fathers to their children and the hearts of children to their fathers...'"
>
> Eduyot 8:7

We have seen that there are several contributing factors to why Mashiach has not yet come (above, Chapter 15). Among the obstacles are the pursuit of honor, anger, false beliefs and blemished speech. These major evil characteristics lead to strife, the opposite of the peace that will reign in Mashiach's era. More specifically, it is blemished speech — slander, falsehood, finding fault with others and so on — which leads to rifts between friends and family members, in entire communities, and on a national and global level. Since each person has his own view, each perceives himself as "being in the right" — i.e. the possessor of the truth — people find it almost impossible to draw close together and live in peace with each other. This obviously applies to those who are distant from spirituality and do not take heed to guard themselves from evil speech. But, it also has grave implications to those who consider themselves Torah scholars as well.

Eliyahu *HaNavi* has a "mission impossible." He must bring people together, so that they can accept Mashiach, who will then teach all of humanity how to live in perfect harmony. It is this "meeting of the minds" that Eliyahu is charged with, so that the truth will be revealed and all will accept it (see Likutey Halakhot, Ribit 5:8).

However, there are many who study Torah not for its own sake, but rather for their own honor and position. This improper Torah study leads a person astray to the point where strife becomes commonplace and disagreements in *halakhic* rulings abound. This invariably leads to further strife and the widening of the breaches in communities, for it becomes a formidable (though inexcusable) excuse to distance oneself from Torah ideals. Torah ideals require peace, as in (Proverbs 3:17), "All her pathways are peace." This means that, whenever there are opposing views, every effort must be made to negotiate an agreement which provides a clear ruling and which will bring the Jewish Nation closer to God. When people study Torah for its own sake, they invoke the truth of Torah and (see above, Chapter 8), "Words of truth are recognized."

Though versed in the laws of Torah as received from Moshe, Eliyahu cannot impose a ruling upon our generation. The "Torah is not in Heaven" (Deuteronomy 30:12), and "a Prophet may not issue new laws (Shabbat 104a). All rulings must be in accordance with the guidelines *we* received from Moshe at Sinai. Then how will we get to know the true law when so many views exist?

This is what is meant by, "Eliyahu will push away those that are close and draw close those that are far." The Hebrew for falsehood is *SheKeR* (שקר), three letters which are adjacent to one another in the alphabet. Truth,

ÆMeT (אמת), is spelled by the first, middle and last letters of the alphabet. Eliyahu will push away those that are close (falsehood) and draw close those that are far (truth)" (see *Likutey Moharan* I, 117).

This is Eliyahu's misson. To bring peace. To reveal truth, absolute truth. When people study Torah for its own sake, the truth within Torah will automatically bring them to seek the correct rulings. All strife will end. Everybody will engage in dialogue to interpret the passages correctly — without any desire to impose one's view or point. The truth will shine forth and everyone will agree (*Likutey Halakhot, Reishit HaGez* 5:12). Then, peace will come and Mashiach will reign.

*

Never on a Friday...

Eliyahu cannot come on Shabbat or on the Eve of Shabbat.
Eiruvin 43b

The Talmud explains that Eliyahu cannot travel on Shabbat and therefore will not appear then. But why not on Friday, the Eve of Shabbat? Since the Jews are getting ready for the holy day, he does not want to interrupt their preparations for Shabbat! But does this mean that we are to despair of salvation on Fridays and Saturdays? How, if we are never to despair? How, if it is required of us to expect Mashiach at any given moment?

Rebbe Nachman teaches that, since Eliyahu cannot come on Friday and Shabbat, then the aura of his imminent arrival becomes that much more powerful after Shabbat. Eliyahu will reject falsehood and reveal truth (*Eduyot* 8:7), that is, to reveal Daat (*Likutey Moharan* I, 117). As we have seen (above, Part III), truth, intellect and Divine Providence are synonymous and, in effect, Eliyahu is the catalyst for the revelation of Daat. As such, Eliyahu is actually above the constrictions of time and space.

As we have also seen (Chapter 28), Daat represents freedom from the exiles, both the physical and the spiritual. Eliyahu's mission is to instill the awareness of God, allowing people to repent before God and return to their spiritual roots. This brings people to a greater awareness of God, a higher level of faith and understanding of Divine Providence — which transcends time and space.

We do not know the day of Eliyahu's arrival, as we cannot know the day of Mashiach's coming. If Eliyahu transcends time and space, we still cannot expect him to violate Shabbat, the seventh day, though this seems to be within the constraints of time. Still, we are never to despair of salvation, even on a Friday, Shabbat or festival. If we cannot understand this Talmudic statement about Mashiach's days, it is simply another aspect of the messianic era to which we are not privy (see above the Rambam's teaching about the messianic prophecies; Chapter 2). But we can suggest that if the Jews *are* preparing for Shabbat and *are* observing the Shabbat, then, in a sense, Eliyahu is already with them! — because they have attained a level of awareness of God and are busily engaged in trying to serve Him.

May we merit to receive Eliyahu *HaNavi* and the redemption, speedily, in our days, Amen.

* * *

32

Mashiach, a windfall and a scorpion

Our full in-depth examination of Mashiach's nature, abilities, source of strength, influence and the social and world changes of his age, still leaves us with the unanswered burning question: "When is Mashiach supposed to come?" Anxiety is building, intensified by the severe crises we face daily as a nation. Despite the many signs of Mashiach's imminent arrival that we see clearly, we still don't see *him*. What's happening out there? This question has become especially disturbing due to the fact that there are certain "predicted" dates of Mashiach's arrival that have already come and gone. If they aren't genuine, then what is one to believe?

Our Sages address this issue with a dire warning (Sanhedrin 97b), "May those who calculate the time of Mashiach's arrival lose their breath [of life]." The reason given is that if one sets a certain time for Mashiach's arrival and he doesn't appear, then this weakens the faith of all those who believed in Mashiach. Rather, our Sages say, "Never despair. If he delays, wait for him, for he *will* come and will not be late."

The reason is that our notion of time does not limit Mashiach. He is from the level of Keter, which transcends time and space. Therefore, whenever he comes, Mashiach will be right on time. We, who function within the confines of time and space, feel this great urgency for his arrival. When Mashiach comes, he will elevate the world from its current status under the restrictions of nature (time and space) to one of obvious Divine Providence. Then all will see the *Chidush HaOlam*, the revival and renewal of the world (see Likutey Moharan II, 62).

*

Still, throughout the generations, there have been those who predicted dates of Mashiach's arrival. One of those dates, based on the teachings of the Zohar, was 5600 (1840 c.e.) which, as discussed above (Chapter 30), was a pivotal year for the Industrial Revolution. But the year was also a pivotal one for the "enlightenment," which led to mass alienation from Jewish observance.

Another predicted year was 5408 (1648) (see Zohar I, 139b). But the year 5408 turned out to be the beginning of the end of Polish Jewry. That was the year when Bogdan Chmelnitzky rose up against his Polish masters. Instead of it remaining a peasant rebellion, he turned it into a witch hunt against the Jews. In the course of a few years, more than half a million Jews were brutally massacred while nearly a million others were forced to flee to western and southern Europe. This led to the rise of Shabbetai Zvi, the famous false messiah, who further fragmented the already reeling Jews. Reb Noson reviews the Chmelnitzky massacres of 5408-5409, in the following manner (Likutey Halakhot, HaChovel b'Chaveiro 3:7):

> It is frightening to think that what was due to be such a great sanctification and elevation of God's Glory, culminated in such a devastating moment in Jewish history. Not only did Mashiach not come, but hundreds of thousands were brutally murdered. God's Glory was meant to be revealed as many people would gather together under the banner of spirituality (and the main time for this will be when Mashiach comes). God's Glory and Honor are the source of all souls (see above, Chapter 20, i.e. they are part of God's Unity). When God's Glory is revealed, it draws the souls to it, as in (Isaiah 58:8) "The Glory of God will gather you." Hence, the great glory of God will be openly revealed when Mashiach comes.
>
> But when, God forbid, the Jews are not ready for God's Honor to be revealed — because of their strife and a lack of peace among themselves, etc. (see above, Chapter 15; the Ten Groups) — the set time for the revealed Glory is still in effect. God's Glory descends and the souls are attracted to it. However, instead of increasing the Glory of God by having others draw closer to Godliness, the Glory of God which has been revealed, recedes. Since souls are part of God's Unity, the souls that were bound to Him then

recede with Him. This accounts for the deaths and the great loss of souls in the recent massacres.

The same can apply to the Holocaust and other instances of horrendous carnage throughout Jewish history. This is known as a *Kiddush HaShem*, a Sanctification of God's Name, which comes about through those martyrs who sacrifice their lives for God's sake. This explains why God's Glory can be effectively revealed through the living who strive for Godliness, as well as through those who are "gathered in" under adverse circumstances. To willingly sanctify oneself for God's Name is one of the 613 mitzvot of the Torah. But, as Reb Noson explains in his discourse, it is of far greater importance to sanctify God's Name by *living* a life of Godliness, than to have to die for it.

There is an inherent danger in predicting the date of Mashiach's arrival — it can lead to a loss of faith, as explained earlier. But there are many dates alluded to, so why shouldn't someone who sees these dates pass them on? Well, first of all, he might calculate incorrectly. Secondly, unless we are *all* ready to leave behind our own glory and seek only God's Glory, then it matters not whether the date is right or not. If we're ready, the date will materialize as one of salvation for the Jews; but if we don't set aside our infighting and desire for personal honor... the alternative is too frightening to contemplate.

The solution Reb Noson offers in the above-quoted discourse is to honor and respect other people. Those who do so are actively engaged in spreading God's glory honoring those created in the Godly image (i.e. all of humanity). Hence, when the question is asked "When is Mashiach coming?" we can at least understand the parameters of the question.

*

Mashiach, a windfall and a scorpion

> "Three things come unexpectedly to a person: Mashiach, a windfall and a scorpion."
>
> Sanhedrin 97a

In one of his classic discourses, Reb Noson applies our Sages' statement to our daily life, bringing the concept of Mashiach closer to home. This discourse was written in the year 5600 (1840 c.e.), a time when many people had predicted the coming of Mashiach, as mentioned above. Reb Noson strongly opposed such predictions, saying that they only hurt, and never helped, the situation. (The excerpts quoted here are from *Likutey Halakhot, Matanah* 5:32-34, with added commentary where it was felt necessary.)

> Our Sages' statement, "Three things come unexpectedly to a person...," contains effective pointers on how to live — in the here and now. A person should not calculate from one day to the next, for each new moment is different. Whoever is willing to give serious thought to this can see the wonders of God every moment of his life. And, more importantly, he will realize that he *does not know* anything about what is really happening to him or around him. The verse states (Proverbs 19:21), "Many thoughts are in the heart of man; but the counsel of God will stand fast."
>
> All this is alluded to in our Sages' statement, which teaches a person who is lost in thought that all worry or musing [about the future] is for naught. For just as a person begins daydreaming of some bright future, a "scorpion" suddenly appears and casts him into a maelstrom of confusion and chaos. At other times, just as things appear to be bad and getting worse, a "windfall" manages to brighten his life. If we examine carefully the incidents happening to us, we will notice that everything happens — "suddenly"!

Reb Noson then ties this to the messianic concepts of judgment and compassion, which are God's unfathomable ways. When a person truly seeks God, He will guide him on the best path to achieve his goal. God loves justice; yet He always tempers that justice with compassion (cf. Psalms 33:5). One must always be made aware of judgment, the "scorpion;" but one will always be able to see the compassion, the "windfall." No-one is immune to the ravages of time — except through prayer (*the* messianic weapon): prayer both before trouble comes and even after it has passed. Prayer always helps, for just as trouble comes suddenly, salvation can be just as near — God's judgment is always tempered with compassion.

Prayer ascends to the highest of levels (see above, Chapter 11), that of

Keter, Compassion. Therefore, engaging in prayer arouses the Attributes of Mercy and draws compassion into the Judgment, even as the Judgment is being issued. Judgment is a constriction, a "scorpion." Compassion is thus drawn into the constriction, "expanding" it and sweetening the decrees, the constrictions, the judgments. This is the mission of all the tzaddikim, and especially of the Mashiach, who will rectify all judgments by revealing the ultimate compassion (see also Likutey Halakhot, Shiluach HaKen 4:17).

This is the explanation of the psalm which refers to the Mashiach (Psalms 72:1-2, 15; see Targum): "Give judgment to Your king, and Your compassion.... He should judge Your nation with compassion... always pray..." For Mashiach, a windfall and a scorpion — three seemingly unconnected concepts — were grouped together by our Sages to teach us that they are as closely intertwined as judgment, compassion and prayer. They come suddenly, for they are God's unfathomable ways.

Reb Noson's discourse continues with the central idea that Mashiach is the connecting factor between these three sudden events.

> Our Sages were discussing the date of the coming of Mashiach (Sanhedrin 97a). Rabbi Zeira said, "Please! I beg of you! Do not delay Mashiach (by calculating his due date)." Others said, "Mashiach will not come until people despair of the Redemption," "Mashiach will come in the right time..." May those who calculate Mashiach's arrival lose their breath [of life]..." But these statements appear to be contradictory. Who can despair of the Redemption? Is it not our obligation to reflect on it and pray for it constantly?! Yet Mashiach will only come unexpectedly! Our obligation is to know and believe that God's Master Plan will be fulfilled. He guides each and every one of us, on the path suited for our individual rectification, as only God can assess through His righteous Judgment. And Mashiach will come, as does each person's individual "windfall," unexpectedly.
>
> Our Sages differ as to how the redemption will come. Rabbi Eliezer says, "only with repentance." Rabbi Yehoshua says, "even without repentance." As we have seen (Chapter 20), there must be repentance in order for the rectification to take place. Then what is the essence of their argument? Rabbi Eliezer brings proof from the verse (Isaiah 59:20), "A

redeemer will come to Zion, and to those who repent from sin..." — i.e. a redeemer will come when the sinners repent. What then is Rabbi Yehoshua's claim? Rabbi Yehoshua emphasizes the idea that judgment must be tempered with compassion. Considering the enormity of the sins, how can our meager repentance help? Alone, it is certainly insufficient to bring the redemption. But when coupled with God's compassion, aroused through prayer, this leads the penitent to his complete rectification, whether he is worthy or not, whether he is ready or not. Then we will see the glorious fulfillment of the verse (Isaiah 1:27), "Zion will be redeemed with judgment; and its penitents with righteousness (compassion)."

Whether we are ready or not, Mashiach will come. He will come as soon as we are willing to turn to God, whether we are worthy or not. This is when Mashiach will come. As we have seen, the tempering of judgment with compassion leads to Daat, the building of the Holy Temple and the ultimate revelation of Godliness (see Likutey Moharan I, 13:5). This is what is meant by (Psalms 18:51), "He does kindness to His Mashiach...." For every act of kindness and compassion leads to the revelation of Mashiach. If we will but inject kindness and compassion into our every act, then "Today!" becomes the day that we have injected Mashiach into our lives. When these achievements of kindness add up, Mashiach will come.

And as the Prophet said (Habakkuk 2:3), "There is yet another vision of the expected time; a testimony of the end [of days] which does not lie. If it tarries, wait for it, for it will surely come and it will not be late."

Speedily, in our day, Amen.

* * *

33

Today!

The Rambam enumerates thirteen principles as being fundamental to the Jewish faith. One of these essential articles of faith is:

> I believe with complete faith in the coming of the Mashiach. And though he may tarry, I will await his coming *every day*.

When we ask, "When is Mashiach coming?" we know the answer: Today! for he *can* come today.

*

The Talmud relates (Sanhedrin 98a):

Rabbi Yehoshua ben Levi asked Eliyahu *HaNavi*, "When will Mashiach come?" Eliyahu told him to go and ask Mashiach himself and told him where to find him. Rabbi Yehoshua went and asked the Mashiach:

"When are you coming?"

"Today!" the Mashiach replied.

Rabbi Yehoshua waited the entire day with great anticipation. But evening came and Mashiach had not arrived.

Disappointed, he again sought out Eliyahu *HaNavi* and told him about his meeting and his ensuing frustration. He told Eliyahu that Mashiach had lied to him because he had said that he was coming "Today!"

Eliyahu explained that *Today!* means (Psalms 95:7), "Today! If you hearken to His voice!" Mashiach can certainly come today. But we must first turn to God.

*

> **Repentance is great. For the sake of the one individual who repents, God forgives him and the entire world!**
>
> Yoma 86b

A follower of Rebbe Nachman once complained to him that he wanted to serve God, but that every devotion he attempted was too difficult. As a result, the follower was lax in several of his devotions. Rebbe Nachman asked him if he *really* wanted to serve God and the follower replied, "Yes!" Rebbe Nachman said to him, "Do you really want to *want* to serve God?!"

This is what is meant by "Today!" The matter is much more within our control than we may think. Each one of us counts. Every mitzvah performed, every thought, word or deed, brings Mashiach closer.

"**Today!** If we hearken to His voice!"

*

May it be His will — and may it be our will — that we merit to see the coming of the Mashiach, the Ingathering of the Exiles and the Building of Jerusalem and the Holy Temple, speedily, in our days. Amen!

* * *

APPENDIX A

The Master of Prayer

The Master of Prayer

The story, "The Master of Prayer," was told by Rebbe Nachman of Breslov in the fall of 1809. It is one of his classic tales found in *Sippurey Ma'asiot* ("Rabbi Nachman's Stories"). The following is a translation from the original text and we have divided the story into subheadings for the reader's convenience.

Once there was a Master of Prayer. He was constantly engaged in prayer, and in singing songs and praises to God.

He lived away from civilization, however, he would visit inhabited areas on a regular basis. When he came, he would spend time with the people, usually those of low status, such as the poor. He would have heart to heart discussions with them, speaking about life's goal. He would explain that the only true goal was to serve God all the days of one's life, spending one's days praying to God and singing His praise....

He would speak to an individual at great length, motivating him, so that his words entered the other's heart and the individual would join him. As soon as an individual came to agree with the Master's ideals, he would bring him to his place away from civilization.

For this purpose, the Master of Prayer had chosen for himself a place far from civilization. There was a river flowing there, as well as fruit trees, from which he and his followers would eat. He was not at all concerned about clothing.

It was the custom of the Master of Prayer to visit inhabited areas, and spread his ideas, influencing people to emulate him, serving God and constantly praying. Whenever people wanted to join him, he would take them to his place away from civilization, where their only activities would be praying, singing praise to God, confession, fasting, self-mortification, repentance, and similar occupations. He would give them his books of prayers, songs, praises and confessions, and they would occupy themselves with them at all times.

Among the people he brought there, he would find individuals who had the ability to lead others to serve God. He would allow such individuals to visit inhabited places, and to also bring people to serve God.

In this manner the Master of Prayer spread his teachings. He would constantly attract people and bring them away from civilization.

Eventually, his teachings began to make an impression, and his activities became well known. People would suddenly vanish without a trace; no one knew where they were. A person might lose a son or a son-in-law, and not have any idea of his whereabouts. But finally people began to realize that all this was due to the Master of Prayer, who was attracting people to serve God.

People tried to capture him, but it was impossible to recognize him. The Master of Prayer devised clever plans, and he would constantly disguise himself in different ways. Every time he visited a person, he would be disguised differently. With one person he would be a pauper; with another a merchant; while with others he would have different disguises.

On many occasions when he spoke to people, he saw that he could not make any impression on them, and could not draw them to his goal. He would then engage in subterfuge, so that they would not be aware of his intention. It would appear that his intent was not at all to bring people to God; it was totally impossible to recognize that this was his purpose. Although his main intent was only to draw people close to God, and this was his entire motivation, whenever he saw that he was not making any impression, he would use roundabout ways so that the person would not recognize his true intent.

The Master of Prayer kept this up until he began to make a major impression on the world. He also became quite famous. People tried to capture him, but it was not possible.

The Master of Prayer and his men lived far away from civilization. They would spend their time engaged only in prayer, song, praise to God, confession, fasting, self-mortification and repentance.

The system of the Master of Prayer was to provide each of his followers with what he needed. If he realized that one of his followers, according to that person's mentality, needed to wear golden robes in order to serve God, then he would provide them for him. On the other hand, occasionally he would attract a wealthy person and bring him away from civilization. If he understood that he needed to wear torn, humble clothing, he would instruct him to do so.

This was his general custom. He would provide each one with what he understood to be necessary for him.

For the people he attracted to God, fasting and self-mortification were better and more precious than all wordly enjoyment. They would derive greater pleasure from fasting or self-mortification than from all worldly pleasures.

*

The Land of Wealth

Meanwhile, there was a land that had great wealth. Everyone there was wealthy.

This land, however, had very strange and unusual customs, since everything was made dependent upon wealth. Thus, a person's status and worth were determined solely on the basis of his wealth. One who had thousands or tens of thousands in cash had a certain rank, while others who had different amounts had a different rank. The entire order of social rank was thus determined by the amount of money that each one had. According to their constitution, the one with the most money was king.

The people there had banners. Each banner denoted a certain amount of money, and a certain rank was associated with that banner. For a different sum of money there would be a different banner, with a different rank associated with it. Thus, a person with one degree of wealth would have a banner conferring one rank, and one with a different degree of wealth would have a different banner, conferring a different rank. Each person's rank and status was thus determined by the amount of wealth he had.

Rank was determined in the following manner: If a person had a certain amount of money, he was considered an ordinary human being. If he had less than this, then he would be considered a bird or a beast. Some people even had the status of harmful animals and birds. If a person had only a small amount of wealth, he might be considered a human lion or the like. Thus, the poorest among them were considered no better than birds or beasts, since money was the most important thing to them, and status was decided solely on the basis of wealth.

News of this land began to spread. The Master of Prayer sighed because of this and said, "Who knows how far they will go because of this and what great errors they will make!"

Some of the followers of the Master of Prayer visited the land without even seeking his advice. They wanted to bring the people back to the good way, since they had great pity on them for having fallen into such great error through their desire for wealth. They were all the more concerned since the Master of Prayer had said that the people of that land could fall into even greater error. These men therefore went to the land, hoping to be able to influence them to improve their ways.

When they came to that land, they approached an individual. Most probably they approached a "wild beast," that is, a person who had so little wealth and such low rank that he was considered a wild animal. They began to speak to him in their way, telling him that wealth is no goal at all, and the only true goal is to serve God.

The individual, however, would not listen to them at all. The belief that money was the main purpose in life was too deeply rooted in the people there. They approached another individual and he too would not listen.

Finally, one of the Master of Prayer's followers engaged a man in conversation, speaking to him at great length. The man eventually said, "I don't have any more time to speak to you."

"Why?" asked the other.

The man replied, "Because we are all preparing to move away from this land. We are migrating to another area. Since we realize that the main goal in life is only wealth, we have decided to move to a land where we can amass greater wealth. It is a place where gold and silver can be taken from the ground. We are all prepared to migrate to that land."

Around this time, the people of the land agreed that they wanted to establish the ranks of "stars" and "constellations." If a person had a certain agreed-upon amount of wealth, he would be a star.

The logic was that one who had such wealth had the power of a star, since they believed a star can increase the amount of gold in the world. Wherever gold ore exists, it is because the star made gold dust grow in that area. Therefore, gold is derived from the stars; hence, one who had a certain amount of wealth was considered to have the power of a star, and he himself was also a "star."

They also conferred the rank of "constellation." A person who had a certain determined amount of wealth, would be a "constellation."

Eventually, they also established the rank of "angel." This too depended on a person's wealth.

Finally, they also agreed to confer the rank of "gods." If a person had a huge amount of wealth as set up in their rules, then he would be a "god." Since God had granted him such great wealth, that person would also be a "god."

Once this had been established, they agreed that it was not fitting for them to remain in the atmosphere of this world. Moreover, it was not considered fitting for them to mix with other people in the world, since this would defile them. They considered all other people in the world to be unclean.

They therefore decided that they would search for the highest mountain in the world and live there. Then they would be higher than all the air in the world.

They sent out explorers to find the highest mountains. They explored and found very high mountains, and all the people of that land migrated to these mountains. On every mountain there was a group of people from that land.

Around each mountain they erected great fortifications. They also made deep trenches around the mountain, so that it would be utterly impossible for anyone to approach them. The only approach was through a hidden path to the mountain, so that no strangers would be able to come to them. Similar fortifications were also erected around all the other mountains.

Guards were stationed far from the mountains so that no strangers would be allowed to approach them. They lived there in the mountains and abided by their customs.

These people worshiped many gods. Their gods were appointed on the basis of wealth, since wealth was the main thing to these people and through a great amount of wealth, one could become a god.

This, however, brought about great concern about murder and robbery. People would be very ready to kill and steal, since they could become gods with the stolen money. They were afraid to, however, because the wealthy were themselves considered gods and they were thus considered to be able to protect themselves from robbery and assassination.

They set up a system of services and sacrifices to their "gods." They would also offer human sacrifices. Many people would also voluntarily offer themselves as sacrifices to their "gods," believing that in this way they would become incorporated into them, and later be reincarnated as wealthy men.

They thus institutionalized their belief in wealth. They had services, sacrifices and incense which were used to serve the extremely wealthy people who were their gods.

Nevertheless, there was much killing and robbery in the land. People who did not believe in their religion became murderers and thieves in order to amass wealth. Their main purpose in life was money. With money, one could buy anything, whether it be food or clothing. According to their belief system, human existence was based on money.

Wealth was therefore the focus of their belief. Every effort was made that there not be any lack of money since it was the main object of their faith and the focus of their gods. They made every effort to bring wealth from other places to their land. Merchants were therefore sent out to do business in other lands so as to earn money and bring it back to their homeland.

According to their religion charity was a very great sin. They believed that if a person gave charity, it would diminish the influx of wealth that God had given him. The main goal was to have as much wealth as possible, and if one gave charity, it would blemish and diminish one's wealth. It was therefore forbidden in the strongest terms to give charity.

They also had inspectors. These inspectors were in charge of determining whether or not each person had as much wealth as he claimed. Each individual would have to be able constantly to demonstrate his wealth in order to retain his wealth-status.

Sometimes an animal would become a human being, and at other times, a human would become an animal. If a person lost his wealth, then he would become an animal, who did not have to have so much money. Similarly, if an animal amassed wealth, he could become a human being. This was true of all ranks; rank could be gained or lost depending on one's wealth.

These people also had images and icons of the wealthy people who were their gods. They would embrace these images and kiss them. This was part of their religious service.

*

The Master of Prayer's virtuous followers who had visited the land returned home and told the Master of Prayer about the foolishness and great error of the land. They related how these people had become confused because of their lust for wealth, and how they wanted to move to another land and set up the rank of stars and constellations.

The Master of Prayer replied that he was afraid that these people would become involved in even greater error.

Later he heard that the people of the land had made themselves into gods. The Master of Prayer said that this had been his original concern. He had great pity on these people and decided that he himself would go there, since he might be able to make them abandon their error.

When the Master of Prayer arrived in that land, he approached the guards who stood around the mountain. These watchmen were probably insignificant individuals of low rank, since they were allowed to breathe the atmosphere of the world. Citizens who had higher rank as a result of their wealth would not breathe the atmosphere of the world and could not mingle with other people, since they believed that this would defile them. They could not even speak to foreigners, since they believed that they would become defiled by their breath. Therefore, the guards who stood outside the city must have been of very low rank.

Nevertheless, the guards had images which they would constantly embrace and kiss. Belief in wealth was also their religion.

The Master of Prayer approached one guard, and began to discuss the goal of life. He explained that the main goal is only to serve God through Torah, prayer and good deeds. Wealth is mere foolishness, and is not the goal at all....

The guard would not listen to him at all. All his life he had been imbued with the belief that the main goal is wealth.

When the Master of Prayer went to a second guard and spoke to him, this guard also would not listen to him. He went to all the guards in this manner, but none of them would pay any attention to him.

The Master of Prayer finally made up his mind that he would go into the city on the mountain. When he arrived, the people considered it a great wonder. "How did you get here?" they asked. "It is impossible for any outsider to come here."

"I have already got in," he replied. "It does not matter how I did it. Why bother asking me about it?"

The Master of Prayer began to speak to one of the people about the goal of life, but the other refused to listen. He went to a second, and the same thing happened. None of them would listen to him, since they were totally immersed in their false beliefs.

The citizens of the city found it very surprising that someone would speak to them in this manner, which was directly opposed to their faith. Soon, however, people began to realize that this stranger might be the Master of Prayer. They had already heard that such a Master of Prayer existed.

The existence of the Master of Prayer was already well known in the world. Throughout the world, he was called, "The religious Master of Prayer." However, it was known that it was impossible to recognize or capture him, since he would always appear in a different disguise. He would appear to one person as a merchant, and to another as a pauper.

When the Master of Prayer realized that his identity had been discovered, he immediately fled from the land.

*

The Mighty Warrior

Meanwhile, there was a Mighty Warrior. Many other warriors had joined him. The Mighty Warrior and his men were conquering one land after another.

The Mighty Warrior demanded only subjugation. If the citizens of a land subjugated themselves to him, he would spare them; but if not, he would destroy them. He went and conquered. He did not want any wealth, he only wanted the people to subjugate themselves to him.

It was the custom of the Mighty Warrior to send soldiers to a land when he was still far away, some fifty miles distant. The message was that the populace must subjugate themselves to him. In this manner, he conquered many lands.

When traders from the land of wealth returned home from doing business in other lands, they brought back reports of this Mighty Warrior. All the people were terrified.

Initially, they wanted to subjugate themselves to him. However, they then heard that he despised wealth, and did not want any wealth at all. This was diametrically opposed to their faith, and it was therefore impossible for them to subjugate themselves to him. To do so would be apostasy, since he believed not at all in their faith, which was wealth.

Because of their great fear of him, they began to worship and bring sacrifice to their "gods." They took people of lesser wealth whom they considered "animals" and sacrificed them to their gods. They also engaged in other similar acts of worship.

Meanwhile, the Mighty Warrior was coming steadily closer to them. He began to send soldiers asking if they were willing to submit to his way, and they became terrified. They did not know what to do.

Their traders came forth with advice. They told them of a land where all the people were gods who rode on angels. All the people of that land, great and small alike, were so wealthy that according to the standards of the land of wealth, they would all be gods. Even the lowliest among the people in that land was so wealthy that in the land of wealth he would be a god.

The people of that land used "angels" for transportation. Their horses were bedecked with so much gold and treasure, that their ornamentation alone would be enough to confer the status of "angel" upon a person in the land of wealth. They therefore used "angels" for transportation. They would harness three pairs of "angels" to their coaches, and this would be their means of transportation.

"Therefore," the trader said, "You must send messengers to this land. Since all the people in this land are gods, they will certainly be able to help you."

They believed that they would surely be helped by that land, since everyone there was a god.

*

Meanwhile, the Master of Prayer decided to return to the land of wealth, hoping to wean them away from their erroneous belief. When he arrived, he approached the guards and began to speak to them. He spoke to one guard in his normal manner, but the guard began to tell him about the Mighty Warrior, relating how terrified they were of him.

"What are you going to do?" asked the Master of Prayer.

The guard told him that they were planning to send a delegation to the land where all the people were gods.

The Master of Prayer laughed heartily at him. "What great foolishness!" he said. "The people in that land are human beings, just like us. The same is true of you. Your gods are just human beings, not deities. There is only one God in the world, and that is the Creator, may His name be blessed. He alone deserves our worship, and to Him alone must we pray. This is the main goal."

The Master of Prayer spoke to the guard in this manner at some length, but the guard would not listen to him, since he had been immersed in his erroneous beliefs for so long. Nevertheless, the Master of Prayer spoke to him for a long time, until the guard finally replied, "Besides, what can I do? I am only one and they are many!"

To some degree, these words were a consolation to the Master of Prayer. He understood that his words had begun to make an impression on the guard. The words that the Master of Prayer had spoken to this guard the previous time, combined with the words he spoke this time, had begun to make a bit of an impression on his heart. The guard now had begun to have doubts and to lean toward the Master of Prayer's teachings somewhat, as was evident from his reply.

The Master of Prayer went to the second guard, and spoke to him in the same manner. This one at first also would not listen. However, in the end, he finally said, "But I am only a single person opposing all the people in the land...." In the end, all the guards gave him a similar reply.

The Master of Prayer then entered the city and began to speak to the people in his way. He told them that they were in great error, and theirs was not the true goal at all, since the main goal was to engage in Torah and prayer. However, since all the people had been immersed in their beliefs for a very long time, they would not listen to him.

When they told him about the Mighty Warrior and their plan to send to the land where everyone was a god, he laughed at them. "This is foolishness," he said. "They are all mere human beings... and they will not be able to help you in the least. They are not gods at all. You are human beings and they are human beings and none of you are gods at all. There is only one God, may His name be blessed."

About the Mighty Warrior he said, "Can this be *the* Mighty Warrior?" From the tone of his voice, it seemed as if he knew the Warrior.

The people did not understand what he was getting at.

He also went to other people and spoke to them. Whenever the Warrior was mentioned, he would say, "Can this be *the* Mighty Warrior?" No one understood what his point was.

*

The Hand

There was a great commotion in the city, since there was someone there mocking their faith and preaching that there was only one God. He was also making strange remarks about the Mighty Warrior. They understood that this was the Master of Prayer, since he was quite well known by this time.

Orders were given that he be found and captured. Although he was constantly disguising himself, sometimes appearing as a merchant and at other times as a pauper, they were already aware of his disguises. They gave orders that he be found and taken prisoner.

They searched for him, and when they succeeded in capturing him, they brought him before the ministers of state. When they began to speak to him, he told them that all of them had very foolish beliefs and were in error. "Wealth is not the goal of life at all," he said. "The only goal is the Creator, may His name be blessed... You may think the people of that land are gods, but they will not be able to help you at all, since they are only human beings...."

He was considered mad. The people in that land were so immersed in their belief in wealth that anyone who spoke against it was considered a madman.

They then asked him, "Whenever the Mighty Warrior is mentioned, you ask, 'Can this be *the* Mighty Warrior?' What is the meaning of your words?"

"I was once with a king," he replied, "and he had a Mighty Warrior who was lost. If the warrior is this Mighty Warrior, then I know him. Furthermore, your faith in the land where you consider all the people gods, is mere foolishness. They will not be able to help you. In my opinion, if you trust in them, it will be your downfall."

"How do you know that?" they asked.

He replied:

"The king with whom I was had a Hand. That is, he had an image of a hand with five fingers. The lines on the Hand formed a map of the world.

"Everything that existed from the time heaven and earth were created until the end, and even what will exist after that, was inscribed on that Hand. The lines in the Hand provided a picture of the structure of every universe with all its details, just like a map. The lines also formed letters, like the inscriptions on a map, so that one can know what each thing represents.

"Thus, one can know that in one place there is a city, and elsewhere a river and the like. The lines in the Hand were like captions on a map, inscribed next to each detail on the Hand, so that one could know what it was. Inscribed with the lines on the Hand were the details of all the lands, cities, rivers, bridges, mountains and other details, in this world and in other worlds. Next to each detail there were letters describing it.

"Also on the Hand were inscribed the names of all the people traveling in each land, as well as everything that happened to them. It also had inscribed all the paths from one land to another, and from one place to another.

"This is how I knew how to get into the city, even though it would be impossible for anyone else to get in here. Also, if you wished to send me to any other city, I would know the way. Everything through this Hand.

"Also inscribed on this Hand is the path from one world to another. There is a road and a path upon which one can travel from earth to heaven. The only reason that it is impossible to go up to heaven is because people do not know the path; but on the Hand is inscribed the path to heaven.

"On it are written all the paths from one universe to another. Elijah went up to heaven on one path, and that path is inscribed on the Hand. Moses went up on a different path, and that path is also inscribed. Enoch went up to heaven on still another path, and that is also inscribed there. The paths from one world to another are also inscribed in the lines of the Hand.

"Also inscribed on the Hand is everything as it existed at the time of Creation, the way it exists now and the way it it will exist later. Thus, Sodom is inscribed as it was when it was inhabited, before it was destroyed. The destruction and upheaval of Sodom is then inscribed, as well as the way Sodom exists after it was destroyed. Thus, inscribed on the Hand is what was, what is, and what will be.

"On the Hand I also saw the land which you described, where you claim that the people are gods, as well as all the men who are going to seek help from them. All of them will be annihilated and destroyed."

(All the above was the answer that the Master of Prayer gave them.)

This was a great wonder to them. They realized that he was speaking the truth, since they were aware that everything could be drawn on maps. They also recognized his words as being true, because they saw that it was possible to bring together and connect two lines on the hand and form a letter. They realized that it would have been impossible for him to fabricate such an account. It was therefore a great wonder to them.

"Where is your king?" they asked. "Maybe he can tell us how to gain more wealth."

"You still want wealth!" he replied. "I don't want you to mention wealth at all!"

"Still," they insisted, "where is the king?"

"Actually, I don't know where the king is," he answered. "This is what happened."

*

The Holy Assembly

The Master of Prayer then related the following story:

"There was a King and Queen and they had an only Daughter. When she came of age, they sought advice from their counselors as to who would be fit to marry her. I was among their advisors, since the King was very fond of me.

"My advice was that she should marry the Mighty Warrior. The Mighty Warrior had captured many lands, and brought great benefits to the kingdom, and therefore it would be proper to have him marry the Queen's Daughter. My advice was well taken and everyone agreed to it. There was great joy in the kingdom, since a husband had been found for the Queen's Daughter. She married the Mighty Warrior.

"The Queen's Daughter gave birth to a Child, and the infant was extremely beautiful. His beauty was beyond all human bounds. His hair was gold with all colors in it, and his face was as bright as the sun. His eyes were like stars.

"The Child was born with a fully-developed intellect. As soon as he was born it was recognized that he was fully intelligent. When people said something humorous, he would laugh. They recognized that he had a great intellect, except that he did not yet have the coordination of an adult enough to speak, etc.

"The King had a Bard, an orator who was a master of rhetoric and poetry. He could speak and compose wonderful poems, as well as songs and praise to the King. Although the Bard was very skillful in his art in his own right, the King showed him a path through which he could ascend and receive poetic skills. As a result he became an extremely skilled bard.

"The King also had a Wise Man. The Wise Man was very intelligent in his own right, but the King showed him a path through which he could ascend and receive wisdom. Through this, he became an extraordinarily wise man.

"The Mighty Warrior was also a warrior in his own right. But the King showed him a path through which he could ascend and receive great strength. Through this he became an extraordinarily fearsome warrior.

"There is sword that is suspended in midair. This sword has three powers. When the sword is lifted, all the enemy's officers flee in panic, and the enemy is automatically defeated. Without any leadership, they cannot do battle.

"Still, it is possible for the survivors to join together and do battle. But the sword has two edges, and these have two additional powers. One edge makes the entire enemy army fall. The other edge causes them to become emaciated, with their flesh falling away. One need only stand still and swing the sword toward the enemy, and each edge has this effect. The King showed the Mighty Warrior the path to that sword. It is from there that he received his great strength in battle.

"The same was true of me. The King showed me the path to my occupation. From there I received what I needed.

"The King also had a Faithful Friend. The bond of friendship between him and the King was wonderful and awesome, so that it was impossible for them to go without seeing each other for any length of time. Nevertheless, there were times when they had to be separated to some extent. Therefore, they had portraits made of themselves together. Whenever they were separated from each other, they would derive great pleasure from these portraits.

"The portraits showed the great friendship between the King and his Friend, how they embraced and kissed each other with great affection. These images had the power that anyone looking at them would be imbued with feelings of extremely deep love. That is, the attribute of love would come to whoever gazed at these images. The Faithful Friend also received love from the place that the King showed him.

*

The Hurricane

"There came a time when each of the King's men went to the place where he would receive his power. The Bard, the Mighty Warrior, and all the other King's men went to their places to renew their powers.

"At that time, there was a powerful hurricane, which threw the whole world into confusion. It transformed sea into dry land, and dry land into sea; desert into inhabited land, and inhabited land into desert. The entire world was thus turned upside-down.

"When this hurricane struck the King's palace, it did not do any damage. However, when the storm struck, it carried away the Child of the Queen's Daughter. In the middle of the panic caused when the beautiful child was carried away, the Queen's Daughter ran after it. The King and Queen also pursued. They became scattered, and no one knows where they are.

"The rest of us were not there at the time, since each of us had gone up to his place to renew his power. When we returned, we could not find them. The Hand was also lost at that time. Since that time, we became scattered, and none of us can go to his place to renew his power. The whole world was turned upside-down and thrown into confusion, where all the places were exchanged, the sea becoming dry land and the like. It is certainly impossible now to go up on the original paths; now that places have been altered and exchanged, we need different paths.

"Therefore, we are no longer able to return to the places where we renew our powers. Nevertheless, the trace that remains with each of us is still very great.

"Now if this warrior is the King's Mighty Warrior, he is certainly a very great warrior."

All this was the Master of Prayer's reply to the men. When they heard what he was saying, they were very astounded. They kept the Master of Prayer with them and did not allow him to leave. They realized that the Mighty Warrior advancing on them might just be the warrior whom the Master of Prayer knew.

*

The Chronicles

Meanwhile, the Mighty Warrior was coming closer and closer, constantly sending messengers. Finally he arrived and camped right outside the city. When he sent his emissaries, the people were terrified.

They asked the Master of Prayer for some advice. He told them to investigate the ways and customs of this warrior, so as to determine whether or not he was indeed the Mighty Warrior of the King.

The Master of Prayer left and went out to the Mighty Warrior. When he came to the Mighty Warrior's camp, he began to speak to one of the Warrior's guards, to determine if his master was the King's Warrior. The Master of Prayer asked him, "What is your occupation? How did you join up with this Warrior?"

The soldier replied to the Master of Prayer, telling him this story:

It all happened in this manner:

In our chronicles it is written that there was a great hurricane in the world. This hurricane turned the whole world upside-down. Sea was transformed into dry land, and dry land into sea. Desolate areas became inhabited, while inhabited areas became desolate. It threw the whole world into confusion.

After this period of panic and confusion, wherein all the world was disoriented, the people of the world decided to elect a king. They then delved into the question of who would be most fit to be elected king. Upon deliberation, they finally said, "The most important consideration is the goal of life. Therefore the person who strives the most toward this goal is the most fit to be king."

But then they had to determine the goal of life. Regarding this question, there were many factions.

One faction said that the main goal is honor: In the world, the main consideration is honor. If a person is not given proper honor, or if people say something that impinges on his honor, he can even commit murder. He is mortally offended, because honor is most important among people.

Even after death the main consideration is honor. People are careful to honor one who is dead, burying him with honor. They even say to him, "Whatever is being done is being done for your sake, for your honor." The dead have nothing more to do with wealth or pleasure, but still, people are very careful to honor the dead. Therefore honor is the main goal of life. They also had other confused, foolish "logical" reasons.

(The same was true of all the other factions, which shall be discussed presently. They also had logical arguments for their confused, foolish opinions. Some of them are discussed, but the Rebbe, of blessed memory, did not want to present all the confused logic for these opinions. Some of the logic is so twisted that it would be possible for people to take it seriously and thus fall into error.)

They were thus led to agree that the main goal is honor. They also pursued honor. Such an "honored man" would be one who pursued honor and also gained honor. If he was an honored man who already had honor, then when he pursued honor, and desired it, his nature would help him attain it. Since the goal is honor, such a man would be striving for that goal and also attaining it. In their foolish and confused opinion, such a man would be most fitting as king.

They went out to find such a man. They finally discovered an old gypsy beggar who was being carried and followed by some five hundred gypsies. The beggar was blind, crippled and mute, and the people following him were all members of his clan. They were his brothers and sisters, as well as the children that he had sired. These were the people who followed him and carried him.

This beggar was very particular about his honor. He had a nasty temper and was always angry at them and scolding them. He constantly ordered different people to carry him, and then became angry with them.

Obviously, this old beggar was a highly honored person. He also pursued honor, since he was so particular about it. This faction therefore felt that it would be best to accept him as their king.

The land itself also had influence. Some lands had an influence that was particularly conducive to honor, while other lands were conducive to other traits. Therefore, the group which had determined that the main goal was honor sought a land conducive to honor. They found a land which was particularly good in this respect, and settled there.

Another faction decided that honor was not the main goal. Instead, they concluded that the main goal was murder.

It is obvious that all things come to an end and decay. Everything in the world, whether herbs, plants or people, deteriorates and decays. Therefore, the final goal of everything is decay and destruction.

Hence, a murderer who kills people and destroys lives is doing very much to bring the world to its goal. This group therefore concluded that the goal of life is murder. The man who would be most qualified to be king would be a murderer who was easily provoked and was fiercely jealous. According to their warped opinion such a person would be qualified to be king.

While seeking such a person, they heard an outcry. "What is this loud outcry?" they asked.

They were told, "The reason for this outcry is that a man just slit the throats of his father and mother!"

"Could there be a murderer with a harder heart or a fiercer temper than this?" they exclaimed. "Here is a man who killed his own father and mother!"

According to their opinion, this man had attained the goal of life, and it was good in their eyes. They accepted him to be their king.

They then chose a land that was conducive to murder. It was a hilly, mountainous land, where murderers lived. They settled there with their king.

Another faction maintained that the person best qualified to be king would be one who had a great abundance of food, but who did not eat the food of ordinary people, but highly refined food such as milk, which does not make the mind too physical. Such a person would be qualified to be king.

They could not, however, immediately find a person who was nourished in such a manner. They therefore chose as a temporary king a wealthy man who had a great abundance of food. He would rule until they could find the kind of person whom they desired, who did not eat like other men. Meanwhile, until they found a person with the full qualifications, this wealthy man would be king, after which he would resign.

They accepted this man as king and chose a land that was conducive to their goal, settling there.

Another faction maintained that a beautiful woman was most qualified to rule. They held that the main goal was that the land be populated, since it was for this reason that the world was created. Since a beautiful woman arouses the desire to populate the world, she brings about the goal, and such a beautiful woman is best qualified to rule.

They chose a beautiful woman and she became their queen. They then sought out a land conducive to this, and settled there.

Another group maintained that the main goal was speech. The primary advantage that man has over other animals is that he is able to speak. They accordingly sought an orator who was expert in language, who knew many languages, and spoke them all the time. Such a person would be closest to the goal.

They went and found a crazy Frenchman who was constantly talking to himself. They asked him if he knew languages, and he did.

According to their foolish, confused opinion he had reached the goal. He was a master of language and knew many languages. Moreover, he spoke very much, since he was constantly talking to himself. He was very good in their opinion, and they accepted him as king. They also chose for themselves a land that was conducive to their concept, and they settled there with their king. One can be sure that he led them in a straight path!

Another faction maintained that the main goal was joy. When a child is born, people are joyous. When there is a wedding, they are joyous. When they conquer a land, they are joyous. Therefore, the goal of everything is joy. They therefore sought a man who was always happy. He would be closest to the goal, and was best qualified to be king.

They went and found a heathen wearing a filthy shirt and carrying a bottle of whiskey. A number of heathens were following him. Since he was very drunk, this heathen was very happy. When they saw that this heathen was very happy and had no worries, he was very good in their opinion, since he had attained the goal of joy. They accepted him as their king. One can be sure that he led them in the straight path!

They also chose a land which was conducive to their concept. It was a place of vineyards and the like, which they could use to make wine. Out of the seeds they made brandy, so that nothing would go to waste. Their main goal was to become drunk and thus always be happy. Actually, of course, this had nothing to do with their concept of joy, since they had nothing for which to be happy. Still, they felt that they were attaining their goal by being happy even though they had no reason. They therefore chose a land conducive to this, and they went and settled there.

Another faction maintained that the most important thing was wisdom. They sought for themselves a very wise man and made him their king. They also sought a land which was conducive to wisdom and they settled there.

Another faction maintained that the main goal was to pamper oneself with food and drink, and thus develop large muscles. They therefore sought a man who had large muscles, and who exercised to enlarge them, since such a person would have large limbs, thus having a greater portion in the world, taking up more space in the world. The person with the largest limbs would therefore be closest to the goal, and should be king.

They went and found a very tall athlete, and he was good in their opinion. He was a person with large limbs, and close to the goal, so they accepted him as king. They also sought a land that was conducive to this, and they went and settled there.

There was another faction who maintained that none of these could be the goal of life. The main goal was to pray to God and to be humble and lowly.... They sought for themselves a prayer leader and made him their king.

(If one examines this, one will understand that each of these factions was greatly in error except for this last group. Their goal was a true one; happy are they.)

All this was what one of the soldiers told the Master of Prayer.

*

The Mighty Warrior

The soldier explained that those who had joined the Mighty Warrior belonged to the faction of body builders, who took as their king a man with a large body.

One day, a group of these men were following the main group with the supply wagons carrying food, drink and the like. In general, people were very much afraid of these body builders, since they were large, powerful men. Whoever encountered them would turn aside from the road to avoid them.

As this camp was traveling, they encountered a warrior. When he reached the camp, he did not turn aside from the road. Instead, he went right into the middle of the camp, and scattered the men in all directions. The men of the camp were very much afraid of him.

He then went into the wagons that were following the camp, and ate all their provisions. This was all a great wonder in their eyes. He was so strong that he was not afraid of the entire camp. He went right into the middle of them and ate all their provisions.

The men immediately fell before him and exclaimed, "Long live the king!" They knew that this Mighty Warrior was certainly qualified as king, since in their opinion, the main goal was to be a body builder. Therefore, the king would relinquish the kingdom, since they had found a Mighty Warrior who was such a great body-builder to rule them.

The Mighty Warrior whom they encountered was thus accepted as the king of the group who had concluded that the main goal was to be a body builder.

The soldier concluded, "He is the Mighty Warrior with whom we are now conquering the world. But he said that he had an ulterior motive for wanting to conquer the world. His intent is not that the world be subject to him. Rather he has a completely different motive."

"This Mighty Warrior who is your king," asked the Master of Prayer, "what sort of power does he have?"

He replied, "There was one land that did not want to surrender to him. The Mighty Warrior took his sword, and it has three powers. When he lifted it, all the enemy officers fled...." He then described the three powers of the Mighty Warrior's sword, as discussed earlier.

The Master of Prayer heard this, he realized that this was certainly the Mighty Warrior who had been with his king.

The Master of Prayer asked if it would be possible for him to meet with the Mighty Warrior who was their king. They replied that they would have to speak to the Mighty Warrior and ask if he would grant an audience. When they asked, he granted the audience.

When the Master of Prayer came to the Mighty Warrior, they immediately recognized each other. They were both very happy at being reunited. Their joy, however, was intermingled with tears; when they remembered the king and his men, they wept. Thus, the two of them both rejoiced and wept.

The Master of Prayer and the Mighty Warrior then discussed how they had come to be where they were.

The Mighty Warrior told the Master of Prayer that at the time of the great hurricane, they had all been scattered. When he came back from the place he had gone to renew his power, he did not find the King or any of his men. However, as he traveled, he passed by the King and all his men. Although he could not actually find them there, he understood that these were the places of each of the men.

Thus, when he passed by one place, he understood that the King was certainly there, but he could not search for him so as to find him. When he passed by another place, he understood that the Queen had been there, but he could not find her. Similarly, he passed by the places of all the King's men. "However," he concluded to the Master of Prayer, "I did not pass near your place."

The Master of Prayer replied to the Mighty Warrior, "I also passed by the places of all of them, as well as your place.

"I passed by one place and saw the King's crown there. I understood that the King was certainly there. However, I had no way of seeking him or finding him.

"I went further and passed a sea of blood. I understood that this was certainly made from the tears of the Queen, who had wept because of all that had happened. The Queen was certainly there, but it was not possible to seek and find her.

"Similarly, I passed a sea of milk. I understood that this was certainly made from the milk of the Queen's Daughter, whose son was lost. She was strained by her abundance of milk, and this produced the sea of milk. The Queen's Daughter was certainly there, but it was not possible to seek and find her.

"I went further and saw some of the infant's golden hairs lying on the ground. I did not take any of them. I knew for certain that the infant was there, but it was not possible to seek and find him.

"I traveled further and passed a sea of wine. I knew for certain that this was made from the words of the Bard, who consoled the King and Queen, and then consoled the Queen's Daughter. These words produced the sea of wine as it is written, 'The roof of your mouth is like the finest wine' (Song of Songs 7:10). However, I could not find him.

"I traveled further and saw, standing, a stone upon which was engraved an image of the King's Hand, with all its lines. I realized that the King's Wise Man was there, and that he had engraved an image of the Hand on a stone for himself. However, it was impossible to find him.

"I traveled still further, and saw, arranged on a mountain, golden tables and credenzas and other treasures of the King. I understood that the King's Treasurer was certainly there, but it was not possible to find him."

The Mighty Warrior replied, "I also passed by all these places. I took some of the child's golden hairs. I took seven hairs, each of a different color, and they are very precious to me. I remained in my place, and nourished myself with grass and the like as much as possible. Finally, when I did not have anything else to eat, I went on my way. However, when I left my place, I forgot my bow."

"I saw the bow," replied the Master of Prayer, "and I knew for certain that it was your bow. But I could not find you."

The Mighty Warrior told the Master of Prayer what happened after he left there. "I was traveling continuously until I came to the camp of the body builders. When I entered the camp, I was ravenously hungry, and I had to eat something. But as soon as I came in, they made me their king. I am now conquering the world. In doing so, I hope that I will be able to find the King and his men."

The Master of Prayer spoke to the Mighty Warrior about what could be done with the people of the land which had fallen into the desire for money to such an extent that they made the wealthiest citizens into gods. He told him about all their foolish beliefs.

The Mighty Warrior told the Master of Prayer that he had heard from the King that when a person becomes entrapped by any desire, it is possible to pull him out. However, if somebody becomes trapped by the lust for wealth, it is totally impossible to get him out of it. Therefore nothing can be done for these people. It is totally impossible to pull them away from their error.

However, he had also heard from the King that the one remedy is the path to the sword, from which he received his power. Through this path he could get a person out of the desire for wealth, even though he has fallen into it and is immersed in it.

The Mighty Warrior then sat together with the Master of Prayer for a while. Regarding the respite that the citizens had asked the Master of Prayer to gain for them, he got the Mighty Warrior to grant it, and to spare the citizens for a period of time. The Master of Prayer and the Mighty Warrior then established a code with which they could communicate with each other, and the Master of Prayer went on his way.

*

The Master of Prayer

Along the way, the Master of Prayer saw people walking and praying. They were carrying prayer books. He was afraid of them, and they were afraid of him.

He stood up and prayed. They also prayed. Then he asked them, "Who are you?"

They replied, "At the time of the great hurricane, all the people of the world were divided into different factions, each with its own ideology. (These were the various groups mentioned earlier.) We chose for ourselves to pray constantly to God. We found ourselves a prayer leader and made him king."

When the Master of Prayer heard this, it was very good in his eyes, since this was also what he desired. He began to speak to them, and revealed to them the way he prayed, as well as his works and ideas. When they heard his words, their eyes were opened, and they realized the greatness of the Master of Prayer. Their king abdicated, and they immediately made the Master of Prayer their king, since they realized that he was a very great person.

The Master of Prayer taught them and enlightened them, making them into very great saints. They were righteous people before, since they engaged only in prayer, but the Master of Prayer enlightened them so that they became awesome saints.

The Master of Prayer sent a note to the Mighty Warrior informing him of how he had discovered this group and had become their king.

*

The Treasurer

Meanwhile, the people of the Land of Wealth became even more devout in their practices and modes of worship. The deadline that the Mighty Warrior had set was coming closer and closer, and they were extremely frightened. They performed their services, offered sacrifices, incense and prayers, worshiping their gods.

They agreed among themselves that they had no other choice but to carry out their original plan and send to the land of extraordinary wealth, where they considered all the people gods. Since all these people were gods, they would certainly be able to help them. They sent emissaries to that land.

On the way, the emissaries got lost. As they traveled, they encountered a stranger, walking with a staff. The staff was worth more than all of their gods' wealth. It contained precious stones that were worth more than the wealth of all of their gods both in their homeland, and the gods to whom they were going. This staff was more precious than the wealth of all of them.

The stranger was also wearing a hat set with precious stones that was also worth an enormous amount.

The emissaries immediately fell before him, bowing and prostrating themselves. This stranger had such extraordinary wealth that in their opinion he could be the god over all their gods.

Actually, the stranger that they met was the Treasurer of the Master of Prayer's King.

"Do you find this surprising?" remarked the stranger. "Come with me. I will show you real wealth!"

He took them to the mountain where he had set out the King's treasures, and he showed them to the emissaries. They immediately fell down, bowing and prostrating themselves. According to their beliefs, this was the god over all gods. This was their false belief in money and wealth, discussed earlier.

Nevertheless, they did not offer sacrifice to him there. Although they considered him the god of gods, and would have sacrificed themselves to him, these emissaries had been warned before leaving that they should not offer sacrifice. There was concern that if they offered sacrifice on their journey, none of them would survive. Perhaps they will find some treasure on the way. One of them might go to relieve himself, and find a treasure there, and he would be considered a god. If they began to sacrifice themselves to it, not one of them would survive. Therefore the people of the land warned the emissaries that they should not offer any sacrifice at all along the way. This is why the emissaries did not offer sacrifice to the Treasurer.

Nevertheless, because of his tremendous wealth, it seemed obvious to them that he was the god of all gods. The emissaries therefore decided that it would be unnecessary for them to go to the "gods," that is, to the land of extraordinary wealth where they considered everyone to be gods. This stranger could certainly help them, since he was the greatest god of them all according to their twisted belief. After all, he had more wealth than all of them. They therefore asked him to accompany them back to their land. He agreed and went with them.

When they arrived home, the citizens were very happy to have found such a god. They were certain that he would bring them great salvation, since with such tremendous wealth he was obviously a most powerful god.

The King's Treasurer, whom the people took for a god, issued orders that prior to the carrying out of certain reforms in the land, they should not offer sacrifices at all. Actually, the Treasurer was an extremely righteous person, since he was one of the King's men, who were all great saints. He detested all the evil and foolish customs of this land, but was not able to make them change their evil ways. But the least he could do at the time was to stop them from bringing sacrifices.

The citizens began to ask him about the Mighty Warrior who was threatening them. The Treasurer also answered, "It is possible that this is the Mighty Warrior whom I know."

The Treasurer went out to the Mighty Warrior. He asked the Warrior's men if it would be possible to meet with him.

They said that they would inform him, and when they asked him, the Mighty Warrior gave permission. When the Treasurer came to the Mighty Warrior, they recognized each other, and there was great joy and weeping. The Mighty Warrior told the Treasurer, "I have also seen our saintly Master of Prayer, and he has become a king."

The Treasurer told the Mighty warrior that he had passed by the places of the King and all his people, but he had not passed by the places of the Master of Prayer or the Mighty Warrior. He had not passed near either of these two places.

The Treasurer and the Mighty Warrior discussed the Land of Wealth and spoke about how they had become so confused until they believed in utter nonsense.

The Mighty Warrior gave the Treasurer the same reply that he had given the Master of Prayer, telling him that the King had said that if a person is so immersed in a lust for wealth, it is impossible to bring him out except through the path to the sword where he got his power for battle. This was the only way to get people out of it.

The Mighty Warrior again extended the deadline. The Treasurer spoke to the Mighty Warrior asking him to extend the deadline and the Mighty Warrior did so.

The Treasurer and the Mighty Warrior then set up a code between them. The Treasurer then left the Mighty Warrior and returned to the Land of Wealth.

The Treasurer admonished the people of the Land for their evil ways, telling them that they were in error and totally confused in their lust for wealth, but it did not help at all. They were already too deeply immersed in it. However, since both the Master of Prayer and the Treasurer had admonished them so much, they became perplexed. Even though they maintained their beliefs very strongly and did not want to turn away from their error, they would say, "If this is true, please get us out of our mistaken beliefs." Whenever they were admonished, they would reply, "If it is as you say, and we are in such great error, do something to change our beliefs."

The Treasurer was able to give them advice, telling them that he knew the source of the Mighty Warrior's power, and the place from which he received his power to wage war. He told them about the sword from which the Mighty Warrior had the power to be victorious, concluding, "Therefore, let us all go — all of you and myself — to the place of the sword. We will then be able to gain power against him."

The Treasurer's intent was that if he could bring them there, he would be able to release them from their erroneous beliefs. He knew that the path to the sword was the only remedy for the lust for wealth.

The citizens accepted his advice and agreed to go with him to the place of the sword. The Treasurer thus set off, along with the greatest people of the land, who were considered gods. These "gods" were bedecked with gold and silver jewelry as they traveled together.

*

The Search

The Treasurer informed the Mighty Warrior that he was taking the people to the place of the sword, and that his intent was that along the way they might be successful in finding the King and his men.

"I will go with you," declared the Mighty Warrior.

The Mighty Warrior disguised himself so that the people accompanying the Treasurer would not recognize that he was the Warrior. He disguised himself and accompanied the Treasurer.

They then decided that they would inform the Master of Prayer. When they informed him, he said that he would also go with them. The Master of Prayer went to them, instructing his men to pray to God to make their mission successful so that they would be worthy of finding the King and his men. This had always been the supplication of the Master of Prayer, and he had instructed his men to pray for this and had composed appropriate prayers. But now that he was setting out with the Treasurer and the Mighty Warrior, he told them that they must pray even more at all times that he should be worthy of finding the King.

When the Master of Prayer came to the Treasurer and the Warrior there was great joy and weeping. The three of them, the Treasurer, the Mighty Warrior, and the Master of Prayer, set off along with the wealthiest people of the Land, who were considered gods.

They continued traveling until they came to a land surrounded by guards. They asked the guards about the affairs of the land as well as the identity of their king.

The guards replied that when there was the great hurricane that divided the human race into different factions, the people of their land concluded that the main thing in life was wisdom. They had originally accepted upon themselves a great sage as king. However, recently, they had discovered a great Wise Man, who had extraordinary intelligence. Their king had abdicated his throne, and they had accepted this Wise Man as their king. For them the main goal in life was wisdom, and therefore, since they had discovered such an extraordinary Wise Man, they accepted him as their king.

The three of them, the Treasurer, the Mighty Warrior and the Master of Prayer observed, "It seems that this is our Wise Man." It seemed that this was the Wise Man of their King. They asked if it would be possible to meet with him.

The guards replied that they would inform him and seek his permission. They went, and when they asked, the Wise Man granted an audience.

The three went to the Wise Man who was king of that land, and they immediately recognized each other. This sage was indeed the Wise Man of their King. There was obviously great joy and weeping. They wept since they did not know how they would be able to find the King and his other men.

They asked the Wise Man if he knew where the King's Hand was.

He answered that he had the Hand with him. However, since the time that they had been scattered by the great hurricane and the King had been concealed from them,.... he no longer looked at the Hand, since it was only meant to be used by the King. But he had engraved an image of the Hand on a stone, so that to some degree he would be able to use it for his own purposes. He would not gaze at the Hand itself at all.

They spoke to the Wise Man and asked him how he had come to this land. He told them that at the time of the great hurricane, he traveled on his way. As he traveled, he passed by the entire group, except for the places of those three, the Master of Prayer, the Mighty Warrior, and the Treasurer, whom he did not pass. Finally, the people of this land found him and took him as their king. Now he must lead them according to their way, which is the way of wisdom, until after a long time he would be able to bring them back to the truth.

They spoke to the Wise Man about the people of the land which had erred and had become confused by the worship of wealth. They said, "If all of us had been isolated and scattered only to be able to make that land good again, it would be enough for us, since they have become so foolish and imbued with their error."

Actually, all the factions were in error and confused, and needed to be brought back to the true goal. This was true even of the group that had chosen wisdom as a goal. Even this group had not attained the true goal and still needed rectification and repentance, since they had chosen for themselves secular wisdom and heresy. Nevertheless, all the other groups were relatively easy to bring back from their errors. The group of money-worshipers, however, were so immersed in it that it would be virtually impossible to get them out of it.

The Wise Man also told them that he had heard from the King that it was possible to draw a person out of any desire except for the desire for wealth. If one has fallen into that desire, one can be brought out only through the path to the sword.

The Wise Man also wanted to go with them, so all four set out together. The foolish "gods" also went with them.

They traveled on until they came to another land. There they also asked about the land and the identity of its king. The people replied, "Ever since the great hurricane, the people of this land concluded that the main thing in life is speech, and therefore they sought a master of language as king. Finally, they found a master of language and poetry who was an extraordinary speaker, and appointed him as king. Since this man was such a great speaker, the previous king abdicated his throne for him."

The four observed, "This is our Bard." They realized that this was their King's Bard, and they asked if it would be possible for them to meet with this king. The people said that they would inform him and seek permission; when they asked, the Bard granted an audience.

The four went to the king of this land, and they saw that he was indeed their King's Bard. They recognized one another, and there was great joy and weeping among them.

The Bard joined them, and they traveled on, hoping to find the rest of the King's men. They saw that God had granted them success, and that they had already been successful in finding some of their companions. They realized that this was due to the merit of their saintly Master of Prayer, who was always praying for this; through his prayers they had been worthy of finding their companions. They thus traveled on, hoping that they would also be worthy of finding the others.

Eventually they came to a land, and they inquired about the land and the identity of its king. They were answered that this was the group that had chosen for themselves joy and drink as their goal. Their king therefore had been a drunkard who was always happy. They had then found a man sitting in a sea of wine. This was very good in their opinion, since this man must be an extraordinary drunkard, so they accepted him as their king.

They asked to meet with him, and were granted an audience. The five companions went to this king, and discovered that he was their King's Faithful Friend. He was sitting in the sea of wine made from the words of consolation spoken by the Bard. The people of that land had seen him in the sea of wine, and had thought him to be an unusual drunkard; therefore they appointed him king.

They recognized one another and there was great joy and weeping.

The Faithful Friend joined the others and they continued their journey, and came to another land. They asked the guards, "Who is your king?"

The guards replied that their ruler was a beautiful woman. She brought people closer to the goal, since the goal was to populate the world. At first they had chosen a beautiful woman as queen, but they had later found a very extraordinarily beautiful woman to be queen. The companions understood that this must be the Queen's Daughter, so they asked to meet with her and were granted an audience.

When they came to the queen, they recognized that she was indeed the Queen's Daughter. Their great joy was beyond estimation. "How did you get here?" they asked her.

She answered that when the hurricane came that snatched away her precious infant from his crib, she had gone out after the infant in the panic, but she could not find him. Her breasts were engorged with milk, and this created the sea of milk. Then the people of this land found her, and accepted her as their ruler.

There was great joy at the reunion, but they also wept very much because the precious infant was lost, and because she did not know the whereabouts of her father and mother.

The Mighty Warrior, who was this queen's husband, had now arrived, and the land now had a king.

The Queen's Daughter, who was queen of this land, asked the Master of Prayer to cleanse this land of its lasciviousness. Since their main goal involved beautiful women, they were very much immersed in sexual desire. She therefore asked the Master of Prayer to cleanse them at least temporarily, so that they not become engrossed in lust; it was a matter of faith to them that this was the goal of existence.

Each of the factions had chosen a bad trait as their goal, and each one treated their trait as a matter of faith. Therefore, they were very much immersed in it. The queen therefore asked the Master of Prayer to cleanse them of their trait to some degree at this time.

After this, they all set out to seek the King and the other ones.

They traveled and finally came to a land, asking, "Who is your king?"

The people answered that their king was a "yearling." This was the faction that had chosen for themselves as king a person who had an abundance of food, and who did not eat the food of other people. They had temporarily accepted a wealthy man as king, but later they had discovered a person sitting in a sea of milk, and this was very good in their eyes. All his life, this person had been nourished by the milk, and therefore, he was not sustained by the food of the rest of the world. The people therefore accepted him as king. They called him "the yearling," since he was nourished by milk like a one year old child.

They understood that this was the lost Child, and they asked to meet with him. He was asked, and they were granted an audience. When they went in, they recognized one another. The infant who had become king recognized them even though he had been a tiny infant when he was separated from them. Still, he had possessed a high intelligence from the time of his birth, having been born with a fully-developed intellect. He therefore was able to recognize them. They certainly recognized him and there was awesome joy. But they still wept, since they still did not know anything about the King and Queen.

"How did you get here?" they asked him.

He replied that the great hurricane had snatched him up and carried him someplace. He sustained himself with whatever he could find, in any way possible. Finally, he came to a sea of milk, and he understood that this milk was certainly from his mother. She had become engorged with this milk, and it had produced this sea. He had sat in that sea of milk, and had sustained himself with it until the people of this land had come and taken him as their king.

He joined them, and they continued traveling until they came to another land. When they asked, "Who is your king," the people answered that they had chosen murder as their goal, and had set a murderer as their king. Then, they had found a woman sitting in a sea of blood, and had accepted her as their ruler. Since she was sitting in a sea of blood, she must have been a very fierce murderess.

They also asked to meet her, and were granted an audience. When they went to her, they saw that she was the Queen. She was constantly weeping, and out of her tears the sea of blood was formed. When they recognized one another there was very great joy, but they still wept, since they did not know anything about the King.

They went further, and came to another land. They asked, "Who is your king?" and the people replied that they had chosen for themselves an honored man as king, since for them, the main goal was honor. Then they had found in a field an old man sitting with a crown on his head. Such a man appeared very honored, and he was good in their eyes, since he wore his crown even in a field, so they accepted him as king.

The companions realized that this was certainly their King. They asked if it would be possible to meet him, and they were granted an audience. When they went in, they recognized that it was indeed the King. The joy that they experienced is impossible to imagine.

The wealthy leaders of the Land of Wealth, who were gods in their land, who were accompanying them, did not have any idea of what was happening and the reason for this joy.

Now the entire holy gathering had come together. They sent the Master of Prayer to all lands which had chosen evil traits as their goals in life so that he would rectify and purify them, and get them to repent their foolishness. Each land had its own foolishness and error, but the Master of Prayer had the power to go to them and bring them to repent. He had power and permission from all the kings of these lands, since their kings were all members of the Holy Gathering of the King. The King had now been restored and had assembled his men, who were kings over all the factions.

The Master of Prayer left with their authority to cleanse their lands and bring them to repent.

*

The Mountain of Fire

The Mighty Warrior spoke to the King about the people in the land which had fallen into the worship of wealth. The Warrior said to the King, "I heard from you that the only way to release those who are immersed in the worship of the lust for wealth is through the path that I have to the sword."

"That is true," replied the King. The King then told the Mighty Warrior that on the road to the sword there is a path to the side. That path leads to a Mountain of Fire upon which crouches a lion.

When the lion wants to eat, he attacks the flocks, taking the sheep and cattle and eating them. The herdsmen know this, and watch their sheep very carefully because of him. The lion, however, does not pay any attention whatsoever to this. Whenever he wants to eat, he attacks the flocks, and even though the herdsmen strike him and shout at him, the lion does not pay any attention. He takes whatever sheep and cattle he wants, roars and eats them.

The Mountain of Fire is totally invisible.

There is another path off to the side leading to a Kitchen. There are all kinds of food in that Kitchen, but no fire. The food is cooked by the Mountain of Fire, and although the Mountain of Fire is very far away, there are channels and pipes from the Mountain of Fire to the Kitchen, and these cook the food.

The Kitchen is also invisible. However, there is a sign of where the Kitchen is; birds hover over it, and one can thus know the location of the Kitchen. By flapping their wings, the birds either make the fire burn more fiercely, or bank it so that it will not burn more fiercely than necessary. They thus make the fire burn as required by the food. One type of food may need one heat, while another needs a different heat, depending on the food. They make the fire burn accordingly.

All this was what the King told the Mighty Warrior. Speaking of the "gods" of the Land of Wealth who had accompanied the others, the King said, "You must bring them in this manner. First bring them downwind from the Kitchen so that the fragrance of the food will reach them. Then, when you give them the food, they will denounce the lust for wealth."

The Mighty Warrior did as he had been bidden. He took the leaders of the Land of Wealth, who were gods in their land. These "gods" were there because they had accompanied the Treasurer. When they had left their land with the Treasurer, the citizens had given them authority to do anything necessary, and the people of the land would abide by anything these emissaries did. These emissaries were the most important people in their land, as well as their gods, and no one would refute whatever they did.

The Mighty Warrior took these men who were considered gods in their land because of their wealth, and brought them along his path. When they came near the food Kitchen, he brought them downwind so that the fragrance of the food reached their nostrils. They began to beg that he give them some of these delicious foods.

Then he brought them away from the wind. They began to cry out that there is a horrible stench. He once again brought them in the path of the wind, and when they smelled the delicious fragrance of the food, they again asked that he give them some. He again took them away from the wind, and they cried out that there was a very awful stench.

"Don't you see that there is nothing here with a vile odor?" exclaimed the Mighty Warrior. "The vile odor is coming from you yourselves. There is nothing else here that has a foul odor."

He then gave them some of the food. As soon as they ate it, they began to throw away all their gold and silver. Each one dug himself a hole.

Each person then buried himself in the hole out of great shame. As a result of tasting the food, the money smelled as vile as excrement. They tore at their faces and buried themselves, and could not lift their faces at all.

Each one was ashamed of the other. In that place, wealth is the greatest shame. If someone wants to insult another, he says that the other has money. Money is so great a shame, that the more money a person has, the greater his shame. Because of their great shame, they buried themselves. They could not bear to face even their friends, and much more so, the Mighty Warrior.

Each one who had a *gulden* or a *grush* immediately got rid of it and threw it away as fast as he could.

The Mighty Warrior then came and took them out of their holes and graves. He said to them, "Come with me. Now you no longer have to be afraid of the Mighty Warrior. I myself am the Mighty Warrior."

They asked the Mighty Warrior to give them some of the food to bring back to their land. They themselves now totally rejected wealth, but they also wanted all the people of their land to abandon the lust for wealth.

He gave them the food, and they brought it back to their land. As soon as the people were given this food, they began to throw away their gold and silver. Out of great shame they hid themselves in dirt caves.

The wealthiest ones, who were their gods, were all the more ashamed. The inferior ones who were considered beasts were also ashamed for feeling inferior because of their lack of wealth. Now it was revealed that wealth is the main thing of which to be ashamed. This was because the foods had the special power, that anyone who ate them would become extremely repulsed by money, and to him it would have a stench like excrement and filth.

They then cast away their gods of silver and their gods of gold.

The Mighty Warrior then sent for the Master of Prayer, who gave them a means of repentance and rectification, and thus purified them.

The King ruled over the entire world. The whole world returned to God, and occupied itself only with Torah, prayer, repentance and good deeds.

Amen, may this be His will. Blessed be God forever, Amen and Amen.

*

The above story with a running commentary was translated and compiled by Rabbi Aryeh Kaplan and published by the Breslov Research Institute. It is found in *Rabbi Nachman's Stories*, #12, pp.278-353.

* * *

APPENDIX B

Charts and Diagrams

THE ORDER OF THE TEN SEFIROT

THE STRUCTURE OF THE SEFIROT

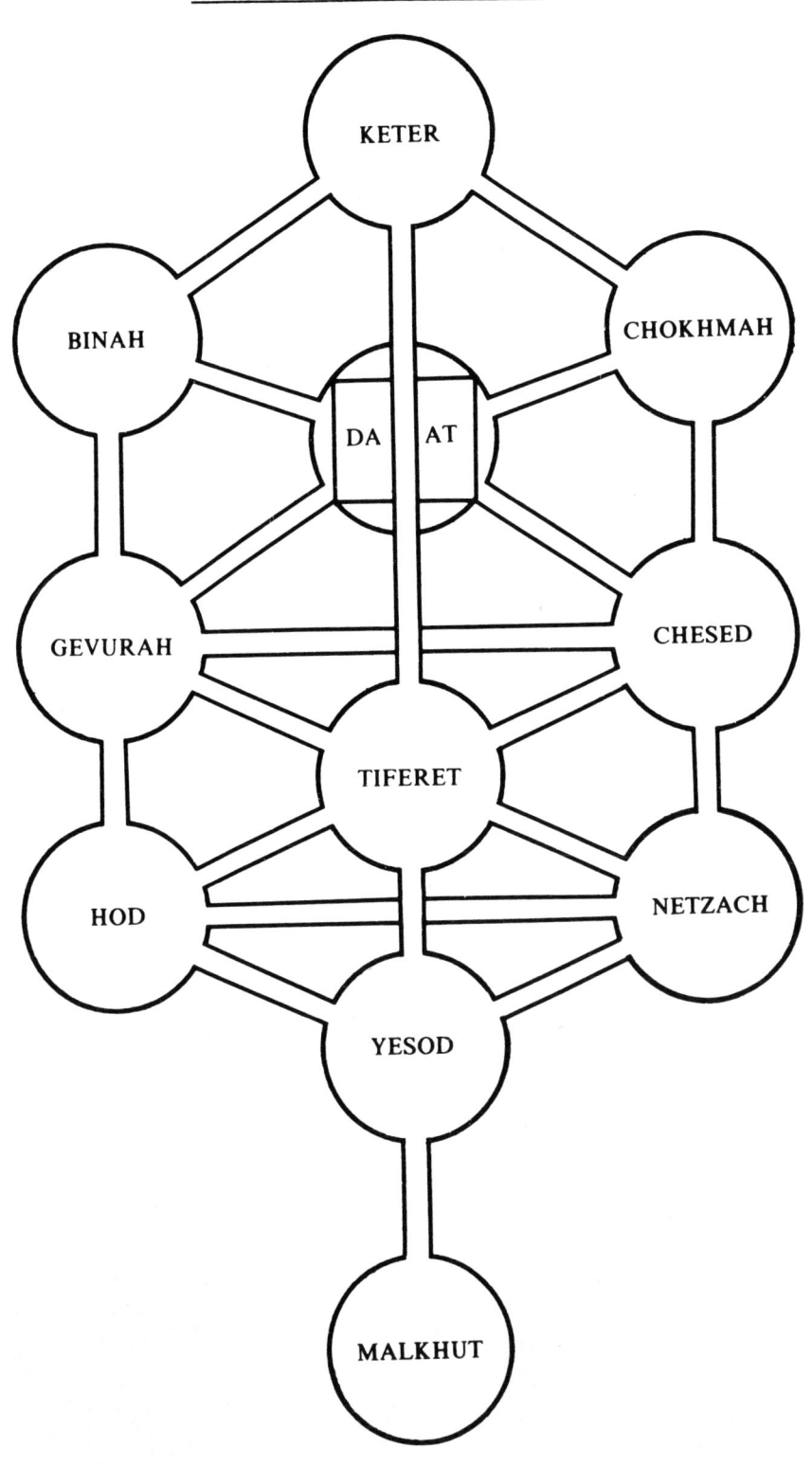

left   center   right

THE PARTZUFIM - THE DIVINE PERSONA

Sefirah		*Persona*
KETER		ATIK YOMIN
		ARIKH ANPIN
CHOKHMAH	⎫	ABBA
	⎬ Da'at	
BINAH	⎭	IMMA
TIFERET	⎧ Chesed Gevurah Tiferet Netzach Hod Yesod ⎫	Z'ER ANPIN
MALKHUT		NUKVA of Z'ER ANPIN

HEBREW LETTER NUMEROLOGY — GEMATRIA

א=1	י=10	ק=100
ב=2	כ=20	ר=200
ג=3	ל=30	ש=300
ד=4	מ=40	ת=400
ה=5	נ=50	
ו=6	ס=60	
ז=7	ע=70	
ח=8	פ=80	
ט=9	צ=90	

EXPANSIONS OF THE HOLY NAMES OF GOD

YHVH — Expansions of the Tetragrammaton — יהוה

Expansion		Partzuf	Value		Expansion
YOD HY VYV HY	AB	Chokhmah	72	עב	יוד הי ויו הי
YOD HY VAV HY	SaG	Binah	63	סג	יוד הי ואו הי
YOD HA VAV HY	MaH	Z'er Anpin	45	מה	יוד הא ואו הא
YOD HH VV HH	BaN	Malkhut	52	בן	יוד הה וו הה

The Sefirot and Man

Keter-Crown	Skull
Chokhmah-Wisdom	Right Brain
Binah-Understanding	Left Brain
(Da'at-Knowledge)	Middle Brain
Chesed-Lovingkindness	Right Arm
Gevurah-Strength	Left Arm
Tiferet-Beauty	Torso
Netzach-Victory	Right Leg
Hod-Splendor	Left Leg
Yesod-Foundation	Sexual Organ
Malkhut-Kingship	Mate

LEVELS OF EXISTENCE

World	Manifestation	Sefirah	Soul	Letter
Adam Kadmon		Keter	*Yechidah*	Apex of *Yod*
Atzilut	Nothingness	Chokhmah	*Chayah*	*Yod*
Beriyah	Thought	Binah	*Neshamah*	*Heh*
Yetzirah	Speech	Tiferet [six sefirot]	*Ruach*	*Vav*
Asiyah	Action	Malkhut	*Nefesh*	*Heh*

הספר הזה הוקדש לעילוי נשמות

ר' **יהושע** ב"ר **ליפא** היעג ז"ל

האי **פרומא** בת ר' **חיים חנינא** היעג ע"ה

ר' **לייב אברהם** ב"ר **יהושע** היעג ז"ל

ר' **ברוך ליפא** ב"ר **יהושע** היעג ז"ל

ר' **שלמה** ב"ר **אליהו** בערגער ז"ל

ת.נ.צ.ב.ה.

This book is dedicated
in memory of

Julius Haag

Fannie Haag

Leo Abraham Haag

Phillip Benjamin Haag

Samuel Berger